CHURCHES ENGAGE
ASIAN TRADITIONS

GLOBAL MENNONITE HISTORY SERIES: ASIA

Authors

I. P. Asheervadam, Adhi Dharma, Alle Hoekema, Kyong-Jung Kim, Luke Martin, Regina Lyn Mondez, Chiou-Lang Pan, Nguyen Thanh Tam, Nguyen Thi Tam, Takanobu Tojo, Nguyen Quang Trung, Masakazu Yamade and Earl Zimmerman

General Editors
John A. Lapp, C. Arnold Snyder

Good Books
Intercourse, PA 17534
800/762-7171
www.GoodBooks.com

co-published with

Pandora Press
Kitchener, ON N2G 3R2
519/578-2381
www.PandoraPress.com

Photography and Illustration Credits

Cover photograph, John F. Lapp, Mennonite Mission Network; Cover photo scroll (left to right), Jonathan Bartel; Hiroshi Kaneko; EMM archives; Unattributed; Center for Mennonite Brethren Studies; Chiou-Lang (Paulus) Pan. Back cover photograph, EMM archives.

Courtesy KITLV/Royal Netherlands Institute of Southeast Asian and Caribbean Studies, Leiden, Netherlands, 24 top and bottom; courtesy Archives Raad voor de Zending NHK, Netherlands, 31; courtesy Netherlands Bible Society, 35; courtesy GITJ Amsterdam Archives, 43; courtesy Archives of the Dutch Mennonite Mission SAA, 44, 45, 47, 48 top and bottom, 49, 50, 51, 59, 76 top, 118; courtesy Alle G. Hoekema, 58, 63, 65, 66, 70 top and bottom, 72, 103, 114, 120; courtesy Sinode GKMI, 76 bottom, 78, 80, 82, 83, 84, 87, 88, 91, 94, 95, 96 top, 98, 104, 123; Lawrence M. Yoder, The Muria Story, (Kitchener, ON: Pandora Press, 2006), 93; Johann Thiessen, Pakantan,een belangrijk gedelte can Sumatra (Apeldoorn, Netherlands, 1911), 117, 118; courtesy Lawrence M. Yoder, 119; courtesy Centre for Mennonite Brethren Studies, Winnipeg, Manitoba, 137; courtesy I. P. Asheervadam, 141, 157, 188, 191, 196, 204 all, 211; courtesy Center for Mennonite Brethren Studies, Fresno, California, 142, 143, 144 all, 145, 146, 147, 148 all, 149 all, 151, 152, 155; courtesy Werner Kroeker, 150 all, 161 bottom; courtesy John F. Lapp, Mennonite Mission Network, 158, 160, 161 top, 162, 165, 166 all, 167 top, 168, 171 all, 172, 174, 175, 179 top, 182, 217; courtesy Mennonite Church Archives, USA, Goshen, Indiana, 167 bottom, 169 all, 179 bottom, 187; courtesy UBS Contact, 173; courtesy MWC, Strasbourg, 189; courtesy Merle Good, 210; courtesy Conrad Grebel University Archives, 215; courtesy Hette Hoekema, 221; courtesy Johnathan Bartel, 224, 225 all, 226 top, 228, 239; courtesy Bethel College Archives, 226 bottom; courtesy Paulus Pan, 227, 237 bottom, 241, 245 bottom, 247, 252, 253; courtesy Roland P. Brown, 229, 230 all, 231, 233, 236 all, 237 top, 238 all, 243 all, 244 top; "The Mennonite Church in Taiwan: 1954-1964" Faith and Life Press, Newton, Kansas, 244 middle, 245 top; Commemorative publication of the 40thanniversary of the Mennonite Churches in Taiwan, FOMCIT, 1994, 248, 249; C. J. Dyck, ed. An Introduction to Mennonite History (Scottdale, PA: Herald Press), 261, 263; courtesy Eladio Mondez, 262; courtesy Timothy John Taburico, 264; courtesy Regina Lyn Mondez, 265, 266, 267 bottom, 268, 270 all; courtesy Dann Pantoja, 267 top and middle, 269; courtesy Hamie Bansan, 272 middle and bottom; courtesy Rio Rana, 273; courtesy Masakazu Yamade, 287, 293 bottom, 295, 300 all, 302; courtesy Teiko Arita, 288; courtesy Nobue Nishimura, 293 top, courtesy Kazuko Kanaya, 296 all; courtesy Takanobu Tojo, 299; courtesy Takashi Manabe, 303, 304 top; courtesy Hiroshi Kaneko, 304 bottom; courtesy Chizuko Katakabe, 305; courtesy Tadayuki Ishiya, 307; courtesy Kyong-Jung Kim, 312, 315 all; courtesy EMM archives, 317, 318 all, 319 all, 320, 321, 323 all, 324, 329, 331, 333, 335; courtesy Gerry Keener, EMM, 330. Unattributed, 32, 56, 96 bottom, 244 bottom, 272 top.

Book Design and Layout: C. Arnold Snyder
Map Design: Cliff Snyder

CHURCHES ENGAGE ASIAN TRADITIONS
Copyright © 2011 by Good Books, Intercourse, Pennsylvania 17534
ISBN: 978-1-56148-749-3
Library of Congress Control Number: 2011939373

Publisher's Cataloging-in-Publication Data

Asheervadam, I.P.
Churches engage Asian traditions : global Mennonite history series : Asia / I.P. Asheervadam ... [et al.] ; general editors, John A. Lapp, C. Arnold Snyder.
p. cm.
ISBN 978-1-56148-749-3
Includes bibliographical references and index.
1. Mennonites --Asia --History. 2. Brethren in Christ Church --Missions --Asia. 3. Asia --Church history. 4. Missions --Asia. 5. Christianity and culture --Asia. I. Lapp, John A. II. Snyder, C. Arnold. III. Series. IV. Title
BV2185 .A84 2011
266/.25 --dd22   2011939373

Table of Contents

List of Maps

Foreword

The five volume Global Mennonite History celebrates the geographical spread of the world-wide Mennonite and Brethren in Christ movement. These volumes are written by individuals from the major continental regions. In the case of Asia, this includes writers from Indonesia, India, China (Taiwan), Japan, the Philippines, and Vietnam. This Asia volume is the fourth of the series to be published. One more volume on North America will appear in 2012.

We are grateful to the writers of this volume for telling the story of their churches from their own points of view. They have interpreted oral and written records and have collected written and visual sources. These dedicated writers are deeply immersed in the life of their churches as pastors, teachers, conference leaders and theological educators.

Asia is a very large region both spatially and in population. There are hundreds of languages with ancient histories in China and India as old as the cultures of the Middle East. All the major world religions have large populations in Asia. Christianity, as noted in the introductory chapters, was present in Western and South Asia before it appeared in northern Europe or the Americas. Indeed the Mennonite and Brethren in Christ churches have also "engaged" the richness of Asian traditions.

Dutch and German Mennonite merchants were in Asian waters beginning in the seventeenth century. The first Mennonite church from the Netherlands was established in Java in the mid-nineteenth century. Russian Mennonite missionaries arrived in India in 1889, and other missions arrived throughout the twentieth century. Today the Mennonite and Brethren in Christ churches are well established in thirteen countries, organized into thirty-one conferences with a membership of more than 265,000.

While the goal of this history was to have a comprehensive vision, the dynamic quality of the Christian movement means the story is always in process. The church in Asia is no exception. Hence this volume is not able to tell the stories of much contemporary Mennonite and Brethren in Christ work. In countries like China and India there are groups at work that are not included in this story. We have been able only to mention Mennonites in Australia, Cambodia, Laos, Myanmar and Nepal. We wish there could have been a chapter on the Asia Mennonite Conference. We have not been able to describe Mennonite churches in central Asian countries or Asiatic Russia.

In addition to these writers, a number of other individuals made significant contributions to this volume. Alle Hoekema not only wrote two introductory chapters but along with Wilbert Shenk read the entire manuscript. Kenneth Hoke, Werner Kroeker and John F. Lapp were readers of the India chapter. Janet Reedy translated the Indonesia chapter, and Ken Shenk translated the Japan chapter and the concluding essay. Luke Martin interrupted his personal writing to assist the Vietnamese authors. Within each country there was additional support staff in typing, research assistance and writing, and we are grateful to each one and all.

We thank churches in each country for opening their hearts, minds and records so that these writers could gain an understanding of their churches experience. This requires trust, confidence, and faith in the integrity of these writers. We believe the churches of Asia have been well served.

We are mindful that this is a pioneering history. No one has tried in recent years to tell the complete story of all the churches in any one of the Asian countries, let alone all of Asia. In many ways this is a first draft which future historians will enlarge and revise, based on new source discoveries and explorations, deepening the insights expressed here. Nonetheless we believe this present volume faithfully bears witness to God's work.

This project would not have happened without the sponsorship and strong support of Mennonite World Conference particularly that of the general secretary Larry Miller. His wisdom appears in this volume as well as in earlier ones.

The Global Mennonite History project has enjoyed the strong financial support of United Service Foundation, Mennonite Central Committee, Goodville Mutual Casualty Company, Oosterbaan Foundation through the Algemene Doopsgezinde Societeit, Good Books, Mennonite Mutual Aid (now Everence) and Mennonite Foundation Canada. Mennonite historical societies in Canada, the United States and Paraguay contributed to this volume as did individuals in North America and Europe.

As editors we have lived with this volume for a number of years. We feel privileged to work with these deeply committed authors. We offer this volume to the churches of Asia and the rest of the world as a testimony to the continuing work of God "reconciling the world to himself." (II Cor. 5:18)

John A. Lapp, Akron, PA.
C. Arnold Snyder, Waterloo, ON.

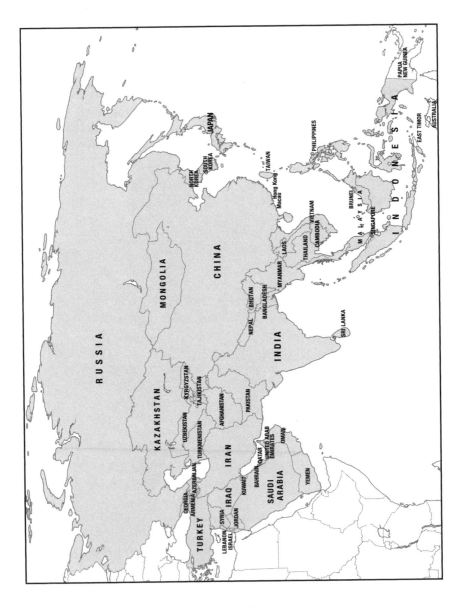

Asia

Asia: A Brief Introduction

by Alle Hoekema

The first issue we encounter when speaking about Asia is the matter of its borders. The Asian part of Turkey (Anatolia) forms its western border and its historical and cultural link with Western Europe. South of Turkey, the Arab peninsula and the Middle Eastern countries (including Israel-Palestine, Lebanon and Jordan) as well as Iraq and Armenia, all belong to West Asia (or Southwest Asia), according to the United Nations sub-division. The main countries belonging to South Asia are Pakistan, India, Sri Lanka, Bangladesh and Nepal. Iran, located between Iraq and Afghanistan and Pakistan, is sometimes said to be a part of West Asia, and sometimes a part of Central Asia, which includes countries such as Kazakhstan, Tajikistan and Uzbekistan. For the most part, Afghanistan and sometimes Mongolia are reckoned among the Central Asian countries as well. Southeast Asia comprises the mainland countries of Burma, Thailand, Malaysia, Laos, Cambodia and Vietnam, and the archipelagoes of Indonesia and the Philippines. And finally, East Asia consists of the People's Republic of China (eventually also Mongolia), Japan, North and South Korea and Taiwan. To the north, Russian Siberia forms an inhospitable part of Asia as well. The great island of New Guinea is not reckoned as a part of Asia but of Australasia; however, its western part, Papua Barat or West Papua, during many centuries was a part of the colonial Dutch East Indies and became a province of Indonesia when the Dutch were forced to turn it over in 1962. Papua New Guinea and East Timor are neighboring Australia, which is related to Asia in many respects.

All in all, the total area of Asia, thus described, comprises almost 45 million square kilometers; Europe, by comparison, covers an area of only 10 million square kilometers. The mainland of Asia has the highest mountains in the world (the Himalayas) and vast deserts like the Gobi in China and the Thar desert in the northwestern part of the Indian subcontinent. It also contains some of the largest rivers in the world, such as the Euphrates, which has its source in Eastern Turkey and flows through Syria and Iraq to the Persian Gulf; the Indus and Ganges rivers in India; the Yangtse and the Huang He (or Yellow) rivers in China. The deltas of some of these rivers can experience devastating floods, such as have been experienced on the Ganges delta in eastern India and Bangladesh, where over 125 million people live. The threat of earthquakes (Turkey, Iran, Pakistan, China) and dangerous volcanic eruptions, such as the historic events at the Tambora (1815) and the Krakatau (1883) in Indonesia, can make life insecure for people living in those areas. There is also the threat of typhoons and – as several Asian countries experienced on December 26, 2004 – tsunamis. Parts of the archipelagoes of Japan, the Philippines and Indonesia are located on the so-called Pacific Ring of Fire which continues to experience very intense seismic and volcanic activities.

On the other hand, Asia also has large areas of fertile land. Nevertheless, a clear shift has taken place from rural areas to urban centers. Istanbul, Karachi, Delhi, Mumbai, Jakarta, Seoul and Shanghai each have over ten million inhabitants and some twenty other Asian cities count between four and ten million inhabitants. The percentage of urbanization in Asia is slightly lower than that of Latin America and Africa; nevertheless the absolute number of people living in Asian metropolitan areas is much higher than in other continents, an estimated two billion people.

The Silk Route and Civilization

Asia is the cradle of several ancient civilizations and religions that developed agriculture, astronomy, alphabets and Arabic numerals long before any western civilization had come into being. During the Bronze Age, 3000 years BCE, the Indus valley civilization was functioning with well-built urban centers like Harappa (in present-day Pakistan). In the same period Mesopotamia in the west developed an important advanced culture as well; in the east the coastal regions of China and Vietnam had centers of sophisticated metallurgy. It was often thought that Central Asia was simply home to "barbarian" nomads, but in the second millennium before Christ it was an area where horses, camels and sheep were domesticated, important for overland transportation, military technology, warm clothing etc. Bronze and stone art objects, including religious artifacts, from that period have been found in Bactria (now Balkh, a center of the cotton industry in northern Afghanistan). These ancient civilizations were not isolated from each other, but were connected by overland trading routes.

The most important trade route was the so-called silk road. Actually there were several routes, from China to the Mediterranean sea with a total length of 6,500 kilometers. Some routes went overland, through Persia and Central Asia as early as the second millennium before Christ. Especially during the Han dynasty in China (100 years before Christ), which had its center in the western city of Chang'an (now Xi'an, famous for its Terracotta Army, dating from 210 BC), a large extension of this intercontinental trade took place. During this same period maritime trade routes were developed. Silk was a product from China, exported to the west, but many other goods were transported from east to west or from the west to the east, such as jewels, spices, glassware and medicine. Unfortunately, slaves also were sold and traded utilizing these same trade routes. These contacts clearly contributed largely to the exchange of ideas, cultures and religions over the period of many centuries.

The Role of Religions

It has long been believed that the northern parts of the Indian subcontinent were invaded by Aryan groups from the Caucasus around 1500 before Christ – although this theory has recently been debated and even rejected by some scholars. The Aryan groups were said to have brought along the Veda texts, the basis of the manifold holy scriptures of Hinduism which became the main religion in India. The later development of Hinduism also led to a strict caste system in society. In the latter part of the twentieth century many Dalits, the "untouchables" at the bottom of this caste system, began to protest and demand liberation in theological terms. Large numbers of Dalits converted to Buddhism, Islam or Christianity. These protests also found a voice in novels by contemporary Indian novelists.

In the northeastern part of the Indian subcontinent (present-day Nepal), Gautama Buddha was born, around 560 years before Christ. The enlightenment or awakening he experienced as to the causes of suffering and the ways to eliminate suffering (the four noble truths) brought a community into existence which in later times experienced both prosperity and decay in India itself. Centuries before Christ's birth, Buddhism's various forms and schools succeeded in becoming very influential outside India, particularly in Sri Lanka, Tibet, China, Korea and Japan. Buddhist teaching and thought was represented by several quite different schools. The Pure Land (Shin) Buddhist tradition in Japan shows remarkable similarities with Protestantism. Both Hinduism and Buddhism even reached the Indonesian archipelago; Javanese culture carries the marks of Indian religion, as the famous Borodudur (Buddhist) and Prambanan (Hindu) temples near Yogyakarta (Central Java) demonstrate. Balinese culture is purely Hindu, although without a caste system.

In China three interconnected philosophical systems have stamped the culture: Buddhism, Confucianism, and Taoism. Confucius or K'ung fu-tzu, lived between 551-479 before Christ and left his well-known aphoristic Analecta, which have been developed into a systematic philosophy in which virtue ethics play a major role. Once Confucianism had been established, especially in the imperial courts, its relationship with Buddhism and Taoism sometimes became problematic. Buddhism was suspect because it came from outside China, whereas Taoism, especially Zhuang Zi's fascinating Inner Chapters with its allegories, satire and many layers of understanding, was criticized by classical Confucian scholars during the Han dynasty (from 200 before Christ till 200 CE) because of its non-conformism. Nevertheless, in the end Confucianism incorporated many aspects of Buddhism and Taoism. All three philosophies of life also entered Korea, where shamanism was integrated with them.

The arrival of Buddhism in Japan (around 550 CE) was a consequence of the earlier arrival of Buddhism in China, brought by traders along the silk route. Both the Pure Land school of Buddhism and Zen Buddhism have developed into complex systems of philosophical thought and practice. Most often they have not collided with the indigenous and inclusive Japanese spirituality called Shintoism. Shintoism has nationalist traits, especially where the spirits or gods (*kami*) are associated with shrines where also the spirits of the dead (such as war heroes) are revered.

Finally, according to one recent scholarly source, beginning in the early seventh century Islam spread "like wildfire" through much of

Central Asia. It succeeded in becoming the major religion there, whereas Manichaeism and Nestorian Christianity, also arriving from the Middle East, had failed to become dominant. Islam was welcomed both by some of the old rulers for their own convenience and by the population anxious to get rid of the old regimes; many merchants supported it, and conversion also guaranteed protection from enslavement. Soon Islam was able to penetrate into other areas of Asia, mostly by making use of trading channels like the silk route. Parts of the Indian subcontinent (mainly the present Pakistan and Bangladesh), and coastal areas such as Malaysia, the Indonesian islands and the southern parts of the Philippines became Islamized in the next centuries.

In general Asian people feel a deep connectedness and unity with the cosmos around them. Whereas in the west a duality between human beings and nature became the principal mindset, in Asia people experience a unity between these entities. This leads to different modes of appreciating life, death and eternity. Many Asian people, including Christians, are aware of the fact that they are basically dependent on the ungraspable cosmic reality around them, which is full of spirits, deities and secrets. It is perhaps not surprising that a feeling of "sacred resignation" can be evident even in times of great disaster.

The Nineteenth and early Twentieth Centuries

It is, of course, impossible to describe within the brief scope of this introduction, the whole history of Asia. Since this volume deals predominantly with the nineteenth and twentieth centuries, we must pay attention, however briefly, to the age of colonization by western powers. Beginning in the early sixteenth century the Portuguese, followed by the Spanish, were the ruling colonial nations. Small pockets in Asia still have reminders of their presence (such as Goa, East Timor [Timor Leste]). The Philippines in particular had a long colonial history because in 1521 the Portuguese explorer in Spanish service, Ferdinand Magellan, arrived there. At the end of the nineteenth century an independence war took place in this country. However, the USA did not recognize the independent nation and occupied the Philippines, until the Japanese took their chance in 1942.

The British and the Dutch overcame the Portuguese and the Spaniards from the seventeenth century onward. After the Napoleonic era the British ruled the Indian subcontinent, Burma and Nepal as well as present-day Malaysia; the Dutch were masters of the Indonesian peninsula. In the 1860s and 1870s the French occupied Vietnam, Laos and Cambodia. Christianity arrived (or returned) in the wake of these colonizing western powers, a story we will outline in the following chapter. The colonial situation remained mainly unchanged in these areas until the end of the nineteenth century.

Japan and China tried to preserve their independence, sometimes at the cost of the total rejection of foreign influences, until the middle of that century. In China the confrontation with western powers started in 1840 with two opium wars (1839-1842 and 1856-1860) against illegal opium trafficking from British India into China. In the end the Chinese government had to sign unfavorable treaties, allowing unrestricted foreign trade and the ceding of Hong Kong to the British. This humiliation also contributed to the Boxer rebellion of 1898-1901 and finally led to the end of the Qing dynasty in 1912.

Modernization and cultural and economic openness started in Japan around 1860. A conflict concerning Korea led to the first Japanese-Chinese war (1894-1895), which actually was won by Japan. Japan's influence in Korea expanded and in 1905 Korea was declared a Japanese protectorate; five years later Korea was completely annexed, a situation that lasted until 1945. During these decades more than two million Koreans migrated or were forced to migrate to Japan. Some 600,000 Koreans still form an ethnic minority there. A second Japanese-Chinese war took place when the nationalistic and expansionist Japanese army occupied Manchuria in 1937. Only a few years before, hundreds of Mennonite and Lutheran refugees from Russia had taken refuge in the Manchurian city of Harbin until they were finally allowed to go to Paraguay and Brazil.

In the British, Dutch and French colonies nationalistic movements began after indigenous people saw that Japan was able to defeat Russia in 1905, in the dispute between these two countries over Korea and parts of Manchuria. However, these movements did not lead to independence until the end of the Pacific War (1939-1945). After 1945, independence came to many of the former colonies, most often accompanied by armed struggle and temporarily disturbed relations with the former western colonizers.

The time of Independence and Globalization

Most of the history of the period after 1945 will be described in the separate chapters of this volume. We will make only a few general remarks here.

After the defeat of Japan with the atomic bombings of Hiroshima and Nagasaki (August 6 and 9, 1945), the flight of the Chinese nationalist leader Chiang Kai-shek to Taiwan in 1949 and the coming into being of the People's Republic of China, Asia became the theatre of fierce wars between western superpowers on the one hand and communist Russia and China on the other. The wars in Korea (1950-1953), leading to the still-existing division of this peninsula between North and South, and in Vietnam (from 1955 to the fall of Saigon, April 30, 1975) became Cold War conflicts which dominated the political, military and economic world for many decades. India, Indonesia and the Philippines suffered also from this worldwide conflict, and the process of democratization experienced a serious setback because of it. Later the Iraq war caused ripples as well in other parts of Asia, especially since the position of Islam was endangered and many Asians again sided against the western powers.

From the nineteenth century onwards, many peddlers, sojourners and migrants followed the tracks of trade and industrialization. Thousands of workers from South China and India were attracted by the plantations, tin and gold mines and other possibilities of employment in Malaysia. At present almost half of the Malaysian population belongs to these ethnic groups. Already many centuries earlier the Chinese had begun to disperse over all of southeast Asia, most often maintaining connections with their relatives on mainland China. Recent estimates count some 35 million Chinese in Asian countries outside China itself. Of course, given present nationalistic sentiments in several countries (such as Indonesia), these immigrants have sometimes faced difficulties. A modern phenomenon is also the growing number of female domestic workers from the Philippines, Indonesia, the Indian subcontinent and elsewhere who find employment in Hong Kong, Malaysia, and the Arab States. The insecure legal position and personal security of these women (over 1.5 million) often results in painful situations. Besides the minority position of Koreans in Japan, hundreds of thousands of Indians live and work in the East African diaspora, dating back to the mid-nineteenth century, when the British used them as coolies. As the result of the independence war in Indonesia (1945-1949) tens of thousands of Ambonese (Eastern Indonesian) soldiers of the colonial army were forced to seek refuge in the Netherlands and remained living there. Beginning in 1873 the British even sent laborers from India to Suriname, on the northeast coast of Latin America, and beginning in

1890, the Dutch sent Javanese farmers there. Together the Indian and Javanese groups now make up over forty percent of the population of that country. The global migration picture is even more complicated: many of these Surinam Javanese moved to the Netherlands in the 1970s. In a similar way and at the same time, many Pakistani, Indian and Chinese people came to Britain and settled there, or migrated to North America to find a future there.

Finally, the supposed moral and intellectual superiority of the western world is under serious attack in Asia at present. Earlier Asian leaders such as the Japanese intellectual Yukichi Fukuzawa (1835-1901) and the Turkish leader Mustafa Kemal Atatürk (1881-1938) would point to western civilization as a model to be followed by Asia. That sentiment has definitely passed, partly because of a restored feeling of self-confidence in Asia itself, and partly because of resistance to the western wars in Iraq and Afghanistan. Furthermore, globalization makes it less necessary to look up to the West. Chinese, Japanese and Indian companies are strong economic competitors all over the world, Asians study at many western universities and some stay in the West as scholars, artists, musicians or writers. So far, more than 45 Asians have received Nobel prizes, many of them in Physics and Chemistry, but also in Medicine, Economics, Literature and nine in Peace. As an indicator of a resurging Asian confidence, we only need to point to Asian writers and novelists like Rabindranath Tagore, Salman Rushdie and V. S. Naipaul (India), Kenzaburo Oë and Haruki Murakami (Japan), Pramoedya Ananta Toer (Indonesia) and the Chinese writer Wei Hui whose novel *Shanghai Baby*, though banned by the Chinese government, became an international bestseller as have the novels of several other Asian authors.

All in all, this vast and fascinating area, with its many centuries-old cultures and languages, its huge problems mastering the elements of nature, its immense population (problematic but also an asset), and its serious globalization efforts, is home to many competing, clashing or more often harmoniously cooperating religions. In the next chapters we will see how and why Christians, and particularly Mennonites, arrived on the scene and how they have accommodated to the specific contexts of the Asian countries where they are at home.

Christianity in Asia

by Alle Hoekema

Soon after the time of the apostles Peter and Paul, small Christian communities came into being in the eastern regions of the Roman empire. Christianity had arrived in Persia, via Edessa (Syria) already early in the second century. At that time a normative trinitarian understanding or Christology had yet to be defined. Differing Christologies became divisive issues, particularly for eastern Christians in the fourth and fifth centuries. Many Christians in Persia became followers of Nestorius (ca 380-ca 451), bishop in Constantinople (now: Istanbul). Nestorius interpreted the unity of the divinity and the humanity of Christ as an ethical bond between two persons, one human and one divine. Further North, Armenia became a monophysite Christian country around the year 300. The Monophysites emphasized the divine nature of Christ at the expense of his being human; they had been influenced by ideas which were generally accepted in Alexandria, Egypt. The Copts, the Ethiopian Church and the so-called Jacobites belong to this stream.

The Council of Chalcedon (451 CE) formulated a Christological position that over time would become the "orthodox" view. The Council condemned both Nestorianism and Monophysitism, declaring that Christ's nature was both fully human and fully divine, in one person. The Nestorian and Monophysite churches thus did not comply with Chalcedonian ecclesial orthodoxy. In Persia, Christians generally lived in peace but at times suffered hardship; the Sassanide rulers (ruled 225-600 CE) saw them as the fifth column of the Romans and later as allies of Constantine the Great. The Nestorian church in Persia sent Christian tradesmen as pioneers to other parts of Asia, extending Christianity well beyond the borders of the Roman empire.

The "Hidden" History of Christianity in Asia – to 1500

As early as the third century there was a Christian church in India. The historical tradition contained in the apocryphal *Acta Thomae* (Edessa, ca. 200) even traces the origin of the church back to the apostle Thomas. Either by a northern route through the mountains, or by sea (or both ways), Christianity arrived in India. These Syrian-descended Christian communities in Malabar and elsewhere remained isolated groups, however, and led an obscure existence until the Portugese missionaries and tradesmen arrived in the 16th century.

Long before the sixteenth century, however, the Nestorians from Persia managed to arrive in Malaysia, North Sumatra and especially China via the silk route. In the year 635, during the rule of the T'ang dynasty, Alopen (or Aloben) paid his respects to the Chinese Emperor in Chang'an (now Hsian or Xian). Records bearing witness to his visit and its results are the inscriptions made in 781, chiseled upon a pillar. Fragments of manuscripts from the 7th to the 11th centuries, recently found in Buddhist monasteries in Tun-huang and Turfan, confirm that there was a Christian church in China already in the seventh and eighth centuries. These churches prospered for a time because of a surprising tolerance; however, when the T'ang dynasty fell in 907, the continued existence of Christian churches became less secure.

Later contacts are also recorded. The Italian tradesman Marco Polo arrived in China bringing along papal letters to the Mongolian ruler Kublai Khan. He stayed in China fifteen years (1275-1291). Shortly after that, the Franciscans arrived from Europe. In a reciprocal visit, a Chinese Nestorian monk named Rabban Sauna met the Pope in Rome in 1287 and expressed his surprise at the claims of papal authority.

By the thirteenth century, however, Islam had already established a stronghold in Asia; the entire Mongolian world converted to Islam. The Mongolian dynasty in China was in decline and was to be succeeded by the Ming dynasty. This change of power had serious repercussions both for the Nestorian Christians in China and for European missionaries. Out of a fear of foreign influences, Christians and others (like Buddhists) were banned from China in the fourteenth century. Christianity in China disappeared – or at least became invisible – after 1368.

Two centuries later the political and military power of the Ming had crumbled, among others reasons because of internal rebellions and a war against the Japanese general Hideyoshi who was trying to expand his realm. In spite of, or maybe because of the politically unstable situation, intellectual life in China prospered and China opened again to outside views. In 1583 the Jesuit Matteo Ricci was able to enter China and once more initiate Christian missions.

The age of discovery

The 16th century has been called "the age of discovery" by Stephen Neill, missiologist and Anglican bishop of Tinnevelly, India. Spain and Portugal were the leading trading nations of that century. Japan did not have a strong central government at that time, but was ruled by some 250 *daimyos* or feudal lords. For that reason the Spanish Jesuit missionary Francis Xavier (1506-1552), who had been in India and Malacca between 1542-1547, was able to establish a church in Japan. He arrived in 1549 on the heels of Portuguese traders. At the turn of the century this church was estimated by some historians to have had as many as 300,000 members. The respective *daimyos* appreciated the missionaries as scholars who followed the ruling etiquette, albeit for strategic reasons; furthermore the economy blosomed as trading contacts were established with the west. Then the fate of this young church turned. A new, strong ruler, Iemitsu (1603-1651) became suspicious of Christians, partly because of competition from the side of Spanish Franciscans and Dominicans who were based in Manila and who tried to evangelize the masses in Japan instead of siding with the rulers. The fear was that this could lead to rebellion. Also, the Dutch "rednecks" opened a trading post in Hirado in 1609. Their fierce competition with the Spanish and the Portuguese was another reason for suspicion, because next to trade, religion was also involved.

In the ensuing persecution, many Christians, including missionaries, became martyrs; others renounced their faith by stepping upon the so-called *fumi'e*, a wooden board on which the face of Christ had been painted. This period of persecution has been described in a moving way by the Japanese novelist Shusaku Endo (1923-1996), both in his novels *Silence* and *The Samurai* and in several short stories. During the next centuries, almost nothing was left of this once-flourishing

Japanese church, except for groups of hidden Christians who survived in isolated areas.

A little later Roberto de Nobili (1577-1656) and other missionaries started churches in Goa, Cochin and other parts of India. These churches grew in number and became influential. From India these missionaries went eastward to Macao, Malacca and other places. The Philippines remained a solid base for the Roman Catholics and in the end it became an almost entirely Roman Catholic country, except for the southern part which is predominantly Muslim. The renewed Catholic presence in China lasted until the end of the 18th century, at which time the church in China once again virtually disappeared, as Catholic missions elsewhere also collapsed tragically. There were various reasons for this collapse: the power of the bishops was increasingly centralized, at the cost of the autonomy of the religious orders; the so-called "Rites controversy" among the Roman Catholics themselves, which contested some missionaries' accomodation to the Confucian rites and ancestor worship; the growing influence of the Enlightenment; and the colonial competition between Protestant and Catholic nations in Europe. All of these events dealt a serious blow to Catholic missions overseas.

Protestant Missions

From the early seventeenth century on, the Dutch, English and the Danes began to take over eastern trade from the Spanish and the Portuguese. The Dutch negotiated trading monopolies in several important harbours of India, Sri Lanka, the Malay coast and Taiwan (then called Formosa). The Dutch East Indies turned out to be an especially profitable area. Since Protestantism, and more specifically the Reformed tradition, had become the state religion of the Netherlands, the Dutch Reformed church took over several of the Catholic regions in the eastern part of the Dutch Indies (the Moluccas), even though economic motives, rather than religious ones, motivated the arrival of the Dutch Reformed. In the beginning the Protestant ministers, pastoral workers (*ziekentroosters*) and teachers only ministered to the Dutch expatriates in these areas. They were all civil servants on the pay roll of the *Verenigde Oostindische Compagnie* or V.O.C., the trading company which had been given the official monopoly in Asia by the Dutch government. A little later the native population was given some attention as well, though we cannot speak of intentional missionary activities in this early period. Both in Sri Lanka and in Taiwan tiny indigenous churches came into being, but they ceased to exist after the Dutch left.

During the eighteenth century the trade competition between the Dutch and the English resulted in a victory for the English in India, Sri Lanka and Malaysia; Taiwan, which was part of China, closed its doors again to Western influence. The eighteenth century, labelled "the age of Enlightenment" in Europe, also saw the rise of Pietism with a corresponding rise of interest in missions. In 1698 the *Society for Promoting Christian Knowledge* (SPCK) came into being, followed four years later by the establishment of the *Society for the Propagation of the Gospel in Foreign Parts* (SPG). Under the auspices of the Danish king, the German missionaries Bartholomaeus Ziegenbalg and Heinrich Plütschau started missionary work in Tranquebar, India, in 1706. They were good organizers and also scholars of language and culture. With their work and that of the Moravians (followers of the pietist Count von Zinzendorf), the modern missionary movement in Asia began. Therefore the eighteenth century is also the age of missionary societies, especially in England and in Germany.

First in India and later elsewhere in Asia, these missionary efforts led to the founding of various kinds of Protestant communities next to the older existing churches. A famous name is that of William Carey who was sent from England to Bengal in 1793 by the newly founded *Baptist Missionary Society* (BMS, 1792); the English and North American Baptists also deserve credit since they were instrumental in awakening missionary zeal among Dutch and Ukrainan Mennonites in the nineteenth century. Many other mission organizations were to follow in that century, in countries like the Netherlands and France.

Post-colonial times

One of the reasons for the spread of Protestant missions was the fact that European nations in the nineteenth century were striving for colonial power. In their wake, missionary efforts could spread into almost all Asian countries. The wish to educate and the longing to propagate the Gospel went together, and though colonial powers often opposed the work of missionaries and limited the fields and geographical areas where they were allowed to serve, on the other hand these powers needed the help of the Christian missions in the fields of education and health care. Often, the new Christian missionaries were granted more privileges than were the adherents of the older, dominant religions.

The Roman Catholic Church made a new start as well during the ninetheenth century. This meant that there was a struggle between Protestants and Catholics in Asia that lasted until the beginning of a more tolerant ecumenical era, following Vatican II in the 1960s. It is not necessary to enter into details here; let it suffice to say that many young Protestant churches in India, Sri Lanka, Malaysia, Indonesia, China and Japan originated in the 19th century. Often they became independent in the first four decades of the twentieth century. The political and religious situations differ strongly in the respective countries of Asia. Therefore we cannot speak about one specific period during which the independence of Protestant churches took place. It is also true that indigenous Christians often were not aware of what was happening in neighboring countries; the theological and ecclesiological effects of the great international missionary conferences in Jerusalem (1928) and Tambaram (1938) became visible only after World War II.

The churches of the Indian subcontinent, including India and Pakistan, were in the forefront of the movement to establish independent national churches. In India, indigenous forms of learned theology emerged in the nineteenth century. Christians in other colonized countries were slower in gaining independence. The situation in non-colonized, formerly closed countries like China and Japan was different again. After the Boxer Uprising in 1900, the position of Christians in China improved and soon they started to promote the implementation of the "three-self" principle. The origin of this idea can be ascribed to Henry Venn (1796-1873), Secretary of the Church Missionary Society. The Three Self movement in China included the elementary principles of self-support, self-government and self-extension. It appears that Yu Guozhen, who set up the Chinese Jesus Independent Church in Shanghai in 1906, was the first to promote this Three Self Movement. Other independent, all-Chinese churches followed. After 1949 the Christian Church of China used these principles to close the gap between the people and the church.

Of all Asian countries, Japan had the best contacts with Europe (especially with Germany), both politically and in terms of higher education. Theological reflection started in Japan at the end of the nineteenth century and Christianity attracted quite a few intellectuals in the first decades of the twentieth century. However, fierce patriotism and the strength of Japanese Shintoism, Buddhism and Confucianism impeded the growth of Christianity in Japan.

In most Asian countries Christians enjoyed certain privileges in the decades before the Pacific War. This privileged situation ended when Asian countries became independent nations after the Second World War. More and more indigenous Christians had to stand on their own feet. As minorities they did not emphasize their denominational differences, but looked for unity; sometimes governments enforced such unity. Hence in Japan the *Kyodan* came into being, in China, the *China Christian Council* (CCC), and in Indonesia the *Dewan Gereja-Gereja di Indonesia* (DGI, Council of Churches in Indonesia), later the *Persekutuan Gereja-Gereja di Indonesia* (PGI, Community of Churches in Indonesia). In Indonesia the Mennonite churches (GKMI and GITJ; see the chapter on Indonesia) joined the DGI/PGI; in China the remnants of Mennonite missionary work also became part of the CCC. In other countries, Mennonites stayed outside the ecumenical mainstream or joined evangelical organizations.

Early Mennonite Presence in Asia

Due to their position as dissenters with an inward-looking identity, Mennonites arrived late on the Asian missionary scene. In Europe, the Dutch Mennonites were the first to start a missionary organization. In 1820 two English Baptists (William H. Angas and William Ward, who was a co-worker with William Carey in Serampore, India), paid a fraternal visit to the Mennonites in the Netherlands. As a result of this visit, a group of influential Mennonite individuals established an auxiliary missionary society of the BMS in the Netherlands. For almost thirty years the society sent financial assistance to London. Later however, the Dutch Mennonites decided to establish their own, fully Mennonite mission organization. It was founded in 1847 and became known as *Doopsgezinde Zendings Vereniging* (DZV,

Mennonite Missionary Society). In 1851 the DZV's first missionary, Pieter Jansz, arrived in Batavia (now Jakarta), the colonial capital of the Dutch Indies.

Nevertheless, Pieter Jansz was by no means the first Mennonite in Asia! The very first one may have been Jeronimus Cornelisz, a shrewd merchant who must be called infamous rather than famous. He was the leader of a bloody mutiny aboard the commercial vessel *Batavia* which left for the Dutch Indies in 1629 but was wrecked near Australia's west coast. After an extensive interrogation by a maritime court, Jeronimus was hanged on Robben island, South Africa on October 2, 1629. Since several Dutch Mennonites were active in the trading and shipping business, there may have been other Mennonites present in Asia in the next centuries. When Pieter Jansz arrived in Batavia in 1851, one of the first persons he visited was the medical doctor and biologist P. Bleeker, a Mennonite who had worked in Batavia from 1842 on, as director of a medical school for indigenous nurses.

Around the same time Anske Hielke Kuipers (1833-1902) sailed over the Dutch Indies' seas as captain of a naval vessel. In 1859 he married the daughter of the German missionary J. H. Barnstein of the *Rheinische Mission* in Bandjermasin (Kalimantan). Back in Haarlem, Netherlands, he became the father-in-law of the South-Russian Mennonite missionary Gerhard Nikkel (1861-1932). Also, the most famous Dutch author of the nineteenth century, Eduard Douwes Dekker (1820-1887), who wrote sharp indictments against the Dutch colonial regime in the Indies, using as his pen name Multatuli, came from a solid Mennonite background; one of his brothers was a *doopsgezind* pastor in Friesland, though Multatuli himself later became a convinced atheist. He worked in the Dutch Indies between 1839 and 1857 as a government official. And just to mention one last name: Louis Frederik Dingemans (1874-1955) was resident of Yogyakarta around 1925 and would have become a member of the highest Advisory Council in the Dutch Indies (*Raad van Indië*) if only "a streak of madness" had not brought him into conflict with the influential Javanese Sultan of Yogyakarta.

Of course many others, mainly Dutch but probably also North-German Mennonites, worked in Asian countries in previous centuries. None of them, however, set out to establish a Mennonite church. So, after the Baptists had given the starting signal, the Dutch and North-German

Mennonites were the first of this denomination to do missionwork in Asia; they confined their activities to the Dutch Indies.

The great Indian famine of 1897-98 became the catalyst for three other Mennonite missions to begin working in India between 1899 and 1908. In India, too, the Baptists were instrumental in the arrival of the first Mennonite missionaries. The *American Baptist Missionary Union* in Hyderabad accepted Abraham Friesen (1859-1919) and his wife Mary from South-Russia as missionaries in 1890. The Friesens belonged to the Mennonite Brethren and had studied at the Baptist Seminary in Hamburg, Germany. At that time the Russian government prohibited the establisment of an independent MB mission board. At the urging of the Baptists, the North-American Mennonite Brethren started its own mission program in Hyderabad in 1899.

An example of a totally different kind of temporary Mennonite presence was the so-called "Great Trek" undertaken by Claas Epp and some six hundred followers, from the Am Trakt settlement in the province of Samara, Russia to Central Asia, during the years 1880-1884. Epp was influenced strongly by chiliastic ideas, convinced that the second coming of Jesus was at hand; he also was afraid that soon the privilege of exemption from military service would end in Russia. The Trek did not end well, and the remainder of the group which originally accompanied Epp finally settled in Ak Metchet (also spelled Okh Mejid), not far from Khiva (Xiva) in the present-day Central Asian Republic of Uzbekistan. In 1873 the khanate of Khiva had been conquered by the Russians. Though most of the Mennonites sooner or later left and returned to Russia and from there to North America, a small group remained there and contributed to modernization, agricultural prosperity and Muslim-Christian relationships. Then, however, they were deported by the communist regime to Tajikistan, nor far from the border with Afghanistan.

Finally, in China the first Mennonite missionaries in the 1890s also initially worked under non-Mennonite missionboards. Nineteenth-century North-American Mennonites at that time lacked the necessary international networks and were not yet ready to start their own missions. However, in the early days of the twentieth century this situation changed quickly. H. C. Bartel from Hillsboro, Kansas (but born in Gombin, Poland) arrived in China in 1901 and began independent work at Ts'ao-hsien, Shantung in 1905. Like most European missionary organizations, his *China Mennonite Mission Society* drew its support from individual friends.

Recent developments within Mennonite/Anabaptist communities

A new phase started in 1920, when a Indonesian Chinese business-man, Tee Siem Tat, founded an Anabaptist fellowship in the town of Kudus, Central Java, Indonesia. His church, now the GKMI, is in fact the oldest Mennonite church in Asia, which brought self-support, self-government and self-extension in practice.

Another new stage began with the activities of *Mennonite Central Committee* (MCC) in Asia and the activity of several North-American Mennonite mission boards immediately after the Second World War, which consequently led to the founding of young and small churches in the Philippines (1946), Japan (1950), Vietnam (1954), Taiwan (1954) and Hong Kong (1960s). The MCC policy of intentionally creating a Mennonite presence at many places where development assistance is needed, has had a great impact.

The fact that Mennonites arrived rather late in Asia proved to be a hindrance at first. Many of the more hospitable cultural, religious and climatic areas had been occupied already by other missions. Furthermore, the early Mennonite mission boards in Europe and North America did not consider theological education to be important, either for their missionaries or for indigenous believers, nor did the early mission boards and missionaries emphasize a strong Anabaptist identity. Therefore it took time before a strong and trustworthy indigenous leadership could arise, and many of the mission churches remained small.

Real growth and a stronger identity came after these churches became independent, sometimes as the result of intentional evangelism, sometimes because of political, social and religious circumstances. On the other hand, political factors also led to the virtual disappearance of some churches, such as the churches in China and Vietnam; and leadership problems could cause a temporary rupture in the Mennonite presence, such as occurred in the Philippines.

Useful networks, the training of local leadership, diaconial activi-ties and the strengthening of Anabaptist identity have grown as a result of the organization of the Asia Mennonite Conference – the first one held in 1971 in Dhamtari, India – and the assemblies of the Mennonite World Conference; and also, in some cases, thanks to Mennonite participation in the Asia Christian Council and global gatherings of evangelical bodies. Therefore, in several Asian countries Mennonites are well-known and respected in spite of their small number.

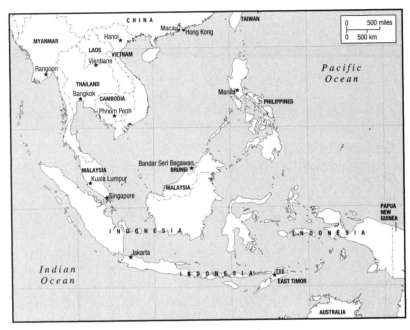

South-East Asia

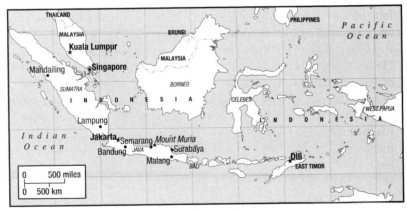

Indonesia

The Mennonite Churches of Indonesia

by Adhi Dharma

General Introduction

Geography and History

Indonesia is known as "the emerald of the equator," a tropical country with thousands of islands in an area of 1,900,000 square kilometers. The islands of Indonesia stretch for 5,000 kilometers from east to west and about 2,000 kilometers from north to south. Indonesia has about 13,000 islands, more than one hundred ethnic groups and more than 300 local languages. Among these thousands of islands there are five large ones. The first, the island of Borneo (*Kalimantan*) has an area of 736,000 square kilometers. (Only 540,000 square kilometers are within the boundaries of Indonesia. The remainder is a part of Malaysia). The second, Sumatra (*Sumatera*) contains 440,000 square kilometers and the third, West Papua has 442,000 square kilometers (part of an island with a total of 775,000 square kilometers). The fourth, Celebes (*Sulawesi*) has an area of 190,000 square kilometers, and the fifth, Java (*Jawa*) contains 132,000 square kilometers.

Denys Lombard, a historian specializing in Southeast Asia says: "Truly there is no other place in the world with the possible exception of central Asia, like Indonesia, where almost all the great cultures of the world are present, side by side or melted together into one."[1] Lombard's statement is based on the location of the Indonesian islands which are at the crossroads of the continents of Asia and Australia, between the Indian Ocean and the Pacific Ocean. This location has made possible the meeting of influences from Indo-China, India and Australia. The result is that Indonesia is a wonderful laboratory for studying history, tradition, acculturation, ethnicity, and religious life.

Multiple influences from the cultures of China, India, Melanesia and the modern West have shaped Indonesian religions and cultures. One theory in anthropology, archaeology and linguistics asserts that there is evidence that around 3,000 B.C.E., migrants belonging to the so-called Proto-Malayan group arrived from the plains of south Asia around Yunnan in southwestern China. Later streams of migrants in the period 300-200 B.C.E. arrived from Indo-China as well. Proof is found in several surviving bronze artifacts. A bronze drum found in South Sumatra measuring more than one meter high and weighing more than 100 kilograms shows a relationship between the Indonesian archipelago and China at the time of the Han dynasty.[2] At the time of the Emperor Wang Ming in the Han Dynasty, (1-6 C.E.) the archipelago was known as Huang-tse[3] which was portrayed as a rich and peaceful country. At the time of the Javanese kingdom of Airlangga (928-1049 C.E.) Chinese colonies developed in Java, such in Tuban, Gresik, Jepara, Lasem, and Banten. Most of the Chinese who came to Indonesia lived in the coastal areas, married indigenous women and adopted the local culture.

In addition to China, the culture of India also added color to the archipelago, especially in Sumatra, Java and Bali (5th to 15th centuries). The influence of the culture and religion of India can be seen in the use of the Sanskrit language, the Hindu kingdoms in Java, ancient temples in Java, and systems of irrigation and rice cultivation. Hinduism is still practiced in Bali, and Hindu epic stories dramatized by shadow puppets *(wayang)* are still very important in Javanese tradition.

Beginning in the 13th century the first signs of the presence of Islam can be traced by Islamic gravestones in North Sumatra. Significant influence of Islam in Indonesia begins in the fifteenth century in Sumatra and Java and also in the eastern parts of Indonesia such as Celebes and the Moluccas. Trade, the influence of Sufism and the impact of military expeditions are factors contributing to the rapid spread of Islam. The growing influence of Islam in Java can be summarized in three phases. First, direct Islamization came with trade through the ports on the northern coast. Second, Islamic entrepreneurs moved into the interior with a form of Islam that was more organized and modern. Third, the system of boarding schools for teaching the Koran *(pesantren)* and Sufi mysticism *(tarikat)* played an important role in creating an Islamic network in the villages.[4] By means of these three approaches, Islam was very successful in overcoming the domination of the Hindu kingdoms and replacing them with Islam in the three "hearts of the Javanese people," that is the village, the market and the government bureaucracy. That is why Javanese Islam can be divided into three groups: *abangan, santri,* and *priyayi.*

The *abangan* are village residents who practice Islam mixed with beliefs colored by animism and dynamism. The *santri* are traders who practice a pure and strict form of Islam. The *priyayi* are descendants of the traditional nobility who combine Islam with the Javanese Hindu traditions inherited from their ancestors. Islam's extraordinary ability to adapt to these three communities made it possible for Islam to develop without significant opposition. According to official government statistics, 90% of the population is Muslim, and Indonesia claims to be the country with the largest number of Muslims in the world.

In the sixteenth century the people in Indonesian territory began interacting with modern Western civilization in economic matters as well as in ethnology, technology and ideology. The Spanish, the Portuguese and later the Dutch arrived, bringing their cultures with them. Dutch influence was strong for three and a half centuries of colonization from the seventeenth to the nineteenth centuries. The Dutch came to Indonesia for two reasons: to obtain access to natural resources (natural gas, gold and various spices). The sea, which in some ways separated the nations, also provided a transportation link which united them. Economic and cultural relations often connected one coast with another rather than one region within the archipelago with other regions. In the early sixteenth century, the Portuguese led by d'Albuquerque resided at the port of Malacca (1511) and the Spanish led by Magellan arrived in the Philippines (1521) after opening a new route for traveling to the Pacific Ocean. Europeans became aware of Indonesia. The coastal areas of Indonesia began to appear on world maps.

The first Dutch armada arrived in the waters of the archipelago in 1596 under the command of Cornelis de Houtman. Because of their interest in the rich natural resources of the archipelago the Dutch established the East India Trading Company (*Vereenigde Oostindische Compagnie - VOC*), a strong organization that oversaw Dutch trade in the archipelago and also from Sri Lanka to Japan. Under Jan Pieterszoon Coen the port of Batavia (Jakarta) became the center of the network of VOC trade. The VOC network then spread to Ambon (1605), Banda (1621) and the Moluccas (1641), all along the coast of Sumatra (1663),

Macassar (1667) and throughout Java and Bali until the end of the seventeenth century.

Because the Dutch used force and violence to defend the trading company and to strengthen their position in the archipelago, the pattern of relationship changed from trade to colonization. At the end of the eighteenth century the VOC ceased its activities and its possessions became the property of the Dutch government, which was under French control from 1795 until 1811. In 1808 the French emperor Napoleon appointed Herman Willem Daendels as governor of the East Indies. Daendels instituted forced labor, requiring the Javanese to perform labor for the Indies government. Daendels also sold land rights to the Chinese creating a situation where the Chinese were the hands and feet of the Dutch as tax collectors and administrators of forced servitude.

Jan Pieterszoon Coen

Opposition and rebellion arose everywhere. Among the many wars, the most important ones were the Padri War in Minangkabao, Sumatra (1817-1837), the Diponegoro or Java war (1825-1830) and the war in Aceh, North Sumatra (1837-1906). This continued into the twentieth century with wars in Bali (1906) and Flores (1907). Then more united national efforts against Dutch colonialism began: *Budi Utomo*, an organization promoting the education of Javanese *priyayi* (1908), *Sarekat Islam*, an Islamic trade union (1911), the Communist Party of Indonesia (1920) and the Nationalist Party of Indonesia (1927). This culminated in the *Sumpah Pemuda* (1928), a pledge adopted at a youth congress in Batavia which promulgated three ideals: one fatherland, one nation and one language.

Dutch colonization in Indonesia lasted for 350 years and only ended after Japan invaded Indonesia on February 28, 1942 three months after Japan attacked Pearl Harbor. The Dutch were interned, use of the Dutch language was forbidden and the name of the city of Batavia was changed to Jakarta. Forced labor (known as *romusha*) was instituted again. In Java the People's Labor Center (*Pusat Tenaga Rakyat* or *Putera*) was established as the agent of Japanese control of security. In addition, a military organization called

H. W. Daendels

Peoples Resistance (*Perlawanan Rakyat* or *Peta*) was formed with the intention of opposing the Allied forces. Japan became visibly stronger, enlisting the manpower of the people through portraying the Dutch and their allies as enemies of Indonesia. Although at the beginning Japan had portrayed itself as the "older brother" who would help prepare for Indonesian independence, Japan also treated Indonesia as its colony. Before Japan could take further measures, however, the bombing of Nagasaki and Hiroshima forced Japan to surrender to the Allied forces. The people of Indonesia, under the leadership of Soekarno and Hatta as president and vice president of the unitary Republic of Indonesia, immediately benefited by taking this opportunity to proclaim Indonesian independence on August 17, 1945, exactly three days after Japan surrendered. Soekarno and Hatta became president and vice president of the unitary Republic of Indonesia. A new phase for Indonesia as a free nation began. After independence, Indonesia continued to struggle to build a unitary Republic of Indonesia.

Realizing independence was not as easy as had been imagined, especially after colonization and deception had been experienced for so long. The country with more than 13,000 islands was laden with potential for conflict and social disintegration. Soekarno and Hatta followed a shrewd political path whereby three large political parties, allied with nationalism, religion and Communism respectively, were all given equal weight and became the pillars of the nation of Indonesia. However, the development of the strength of the military and the religious sector overcame the power of the Communist Party which is remembered for the 1965 event known as *G30S PKI* (the Communist Party of Indonesia movement of September 30). After that the equilibrium of the Indonesian nation was maintained by an unchallenged centralized power under the government of President Suharto which was known as the New Order (*Orde Baru*, 1965-1998). The New Order kept its power by concentrating on the growth of the economy and national stability. Stability and loyalty were assured throughout the New Order by the use of repressive political measures when necessary. In 1997, with the political changes known as the "Reform Movement" (*gerakan reformasi*), the New Order could no longer be maintained. The economy was fundamentally fragile due to the self-interest of various groups. Indonesia is still experiencing serious economic and political effects up to the present time.

Javanese Culture

Most Indonesian Mennonites live on the island of Java so we will describe the religious- cultural background of Java in some detail. The island of Java is about 1,100 kilometers long and on average about 120 kilometers wide with 132,187 square kilometers (including Madura). Java contains seven percent of the land of Indonesia, but 64 percent of the 220 million inhabitants of Indonesia. Population density is on average 726 people per square kilometer. The largest part of Java remains agricultural, and the inhabitants still live in villages.

A large number of the Javanese people are of the Muslim group *abangan* or *Kejawen*. This means that they do not strictly observe the dictates of Islam. A large number of Javanese still believe in a variety of unseen spirits that cause accidents and illness if they are angered or if people are not careful to appease the spirits' anger. In order to prevent disaster people can protect themselves by making offerings consisting of rice, flowers and incense with the aid of an indigenous medical practitioner or shaman (*dukun*). Aside from that the Javanese believe that they must carefully maintain the stability of their emotions, deflecting shocks or surprises, always maintaining their inner spirits (*batin*) in a calm and acquiescent state. The basis of the Javanese view of life is that the arrangement of nature and society is pre-determined in all aspects. Each individual within this total structure plays only a small role. The main aspects of life and status have already been determined and one's fate has been settled beforehand. In this framework the individual must patiently bear the difficulties of life. This belief is closely connected with the belief in supernatural guidance and aid from the spirits of the ancestors or from God.

A religious rite important to the Javanese, especially to Javanese *kejawen*, is the *slametan,* a simple ceremonial meal. All the neighbors are invited and as they partake together, harmony with the universe will be restored among the neighbors. In the *slametan* the values that are felt most deeply by the Javanese are expressed, that is, the values of togetherness, neighborliness and harmony. No wonder that in a recent study by Aristarchus Sukarto striking similarities between *selamatan* and the Lord's Supper have been noted.

Unlike other Indonesian ethnic groups the Javanese do not use family names. Even though family relationships outside the nuclear family are not tightly regulated, relationships with the extended family are very important for the Javanese. This includes those who are related by blood, especially niece/nephew and aunt/uncle relationships, and sometimes also members of in-laws' families. Within the family they can expect various kinds of assistance. Social relationships within the village are mainly based on a system of mutual aid that takes various traditional forms. Mutual aid is not limited to family relationships but can also be understood as a broadening of the family system which influences all interpersonal relationships throughout the village.

The arrival and spread of Christianity

It can be said that the Christian church in Indonesia began in 1522. In that year the Portuguese built a fort on the north Moluccan island of Ternate. Probably not long after that, the first people were baptized. Especially in the eastern parts of the archipelago, the Portuguese Catholic church grew, though mainly among Portuguese and people of mixed blood. Nevertheless, through the missionary work of Francis Xavier, who worked in the Moluccas in 1546 and 1547, Malay-speaking congregations in came into being at Ambon and other places. Portuguese rule lasted until 1605. Then the Calvinist Dutch took over, which meant that many Catholic congregations became Protestant. During the next two centuries Catholicism played a minor role only.

Until about 1800 the government controlled matters of religion in general and the church in particular. Churches grew in eastern Indonesia. In western Indonesia, especially in Java, churches remained restricted to the city of Batavia (the capital since 1619, renamed Jakarta in 1942) and several trading centers such as Semarang and Surabaya on Java's north coast, Padang in Sumatra and Makassar in South Sulawesi. The VOC paid the Dutch pastors; they were state clergy who mainly served Dutch Christians, but some of the congregations consisted of soldiers of Portuguese descent and Malay-speaking indigenous people. The church's rules and by-laws were translations and partial adaptations of the Calvinist church in the Netherlands. During the second part of the eighteenth century, trade and also Christianity decreased in Indonesia.

During the French occupation of the Netherlands (1796-1814), the Dutch lost control of their colony. In 1795-96 the British already occupied Padang (Sumatra) and Ambon; from 1811-1816 they ruled over the whole archipelago. During these years Thomas Stamford Raffles, the lieutenant governor, allowed missionaries to enter the country. One of them was the British Baptist William Robinson (1784-1853) who worked in Batavia between 1813 and 1821. Best known was Joseph Kam who arrived in 1814 together with two colleagues. Kam, who died in 1833, became the "apostle" of the Moluccas, as a pastor in the service of the Protestant church. Another of his missionary colleagues in 1814 was the German-born Gottlob Bruckner (1783-1853) who during most of the time of his service worked in Semarang as an independent missionary. Soon after he arrived there, he joined the British Baptists. Hence the Baptist Missionary Society supported him. He was the first to translate the New Testament into the Javanese language, but never succeeded in baptizing a single convert. Unfortunately, the colonial government did not allow the spread of his translation, maybe as a result of the Diponegoro War (1825-1830). Nevertheless, parts of his translation reached independent Christians in East Java, and some of them were among the first to evangelize in the Muria area. When the first Dutch Mennonite missionary, Pieter Jansz, arrived in the Muria area east of Semarang, he had frequent respectful contact with the then old "Father" Bruckner, as he called him.

In line with the results of the French revolution in Europe, the new colonial government kept a greater distance from religious matters after 1816. The Roman Catholic Church was allowed to resume its ecclesiastical structure and mission and gradually, the colonial Protestant Church in Indonesia developed new structures as well. Besides this church, however, missionary organizations of other churches began sending their missionaries. The oldest of these organizations, the *Nederlandsche Zendeling Genootschap* (1797) was not confined to one denomination. Dutch Mennonites supported this NZG as well in its early years, until the *Doopsgezinde Zendings Vereniging* was established in 1847. In addition to several Dutch organizations, the *Rheinische Mission* also started its work in Borneo and in North Sumatra. Other organizations followed.

Through the work of non-denominational Protestant Churches, the activities of many missionary organizations and finally through the work of independent Christians, Christianity began spreading rapidly in many areas of the archipelago. Especially in the first decades of the twentieth century, Christianity was associated with education, medical assistance and modernity. In line with the national struggle against the colonial structures, during the 1920s and 30s many young churches began asking for, and receiving their independence. When World War II broke out in 1939 this process was well underway, though not yet completed.

The names of several people who were instrumental in the spread of the Gospel in East and Central Java during the first half of the nineteenth century have to be mentioned. The first is C. L. Coolen (1775-1873), the son of a Dutch father and a Javanese mother. At first Coolen worked as a plantation overseer. Then he cleared the jungle at Ngoro in East Java and turned it into an area of farming and villages. As a pioneer and village leader, Coolen became a very powerful landowner. He established the rules for the people who wanted to live there. Coolen invited the people who lived in his villages to gather in his home every day to study *ngelmu* (Javanese spiritual knowledge) which for Coolen was connected to the Gospel. For him the Gospel was *ngelmu* above all *ngelmu*. The lessons given by Coolen were a Confession of Faith with twelve tenets of faith, the Ten Commandments and the Lord's Prayer.[5]

Coolen used Javanese culture such as *tembang* (Javanese sung or recited poetry), *wayang* and *dzikir* (prayers and praise chanted together after an Islamic religious service). In his teaching Coolen rejected the idea of sacraments. He did not stress baptism, because for him that made the Javanese congregations followers of Dutch traditions; the confession of faith and a moral way of living were enough. As a Javanese Christian one must definitely remain Javanese. This attitude definitely was considered extreme and was a serious deviation from the "official teaching" which was brought by the missionaries in the future. In fact later on many congregations left Coolen to study baptism and the sacrament of Holy Communion with Jellesma, the NZG missionary who at that time was in Surabaya.

The second person who was instrumental in spreading the Gospel in East and Central Java was Johannes Emde (1774-1859), a pietistic watchmaker who married a Javanese woman. Through her he made contact with followers of Coolen, such as Dasimah. Emde's wife was amazed in a conversation with Pak Dasimah's son when she realized that this youth who was selling grass already knew about Christ. She called her husband and they learned that in the village of Wiyung there was a gathering of Christians. Emde wanted to get acquainted with Pak Dasimah and invited him to his home in Surabaya.

Pak Dasimah's visit aroused the desire of the Emdes to visit the congregation in Wiyung. Emde and his wife were very friendly and natural and this made the Wiyung congregation very happy. They began to compare the Emdes' friendliness with Coolen's harshness. For example, when people met Coolen they were not allowed to stand.

This was customary when Javanese spoke with Dutch people at the time. It was different with Emde. Everyone was treated the same; there was no differentiation of low or high position in accordance with the teaching of the Apostle Paul who said that in Christ there are no longer Jews and Greeks, or slave and free; all are equal.

The association with Emde not only brought about a spirit of solidarity, holy friendship and equality but also resulted in teaching about baptism. This truly amazed the Wiyung congregation because they had never received instruction about baptism from Coolen. Several people from Wiyung then went to Emde in Surabaya and asked to be baptized. Emde introduced them to a pastor from the Indonesian Protestant Church and 35 of them were baptized on December 12, 1843. Those who were baptized were allowed to take part in the sacrament of Holy Communion with the Surabaya congregation.

Coolen, who lived in Ngoro at that time, was angry to hear that his followers had received baptism. For him, water baptism was only for the Dutch. Javanese did not need baptism because it was a reminder of a foreign tradition and culture. Javanese were different from the Dutch. Coolen forced Pak Dasimah and his friends who had received baptism to leave the village of Ngoro. From that came the epithet "Dutch Christian." The tension between Coolen and Emde was similar to the tension between the indigenous Javanese mystical evangelist Ibrahim Tunggul Wulung and the Mennonite missionary Pieter Jansz.

A third person instrumental in spreading the Gospel in East and Central Java was the NZG missionary J. E. Jellesma (1817-1858), who worked in Surabaya and later in the Christian village of Mojowarno from 1848 onwards. Pieter Jansz had many contacts with him as well, and several early evangelists and teachers of the DZV in the Muria area came from East Java.

In Central Java we see similar developments. On the one hand independent Christians, such as Mrs. C. P. Philips-Stevens (1825-1876), wife of the administrator of a coffee plantation, spread the Gospel. She and her sister-in-law and also the lawyer F. L. Anthing worked closely together with the independent Javanese evangelist Sadrach (1840-1924) who tried to indigenize western church forms in his movement. Originally Sadrach may have been a follower of Tunggul Wulung, whom we will meet below. On the other hand, in Semarang we find the western NZG missionary W. Hoezoo, who cooperated with Pieter Jansz for several decades insofar as practices of baptism and church order did not divide them. Only after his death in 1890 was it possible to bring the congregation in Kayuapu (near Kudus) under the aegis of the Mennonite mission.

From Dutch Mennonite Mission to Independent Churches (ca. 1850-1945)

J. E. Jellesma

In 1847 the Dutch Mennonites founded the *Doopsgezinde Zending Vereniging* (*DZV*) as a sign of their self-confidence among other churches in the Netherlands. Their intention was to proclaim the Gospel in the Netherlands overseas possessions. In 1851 the DZV sent its first missionary to Java, Pieter Jansz (1820-1904), a teacher by profession and a pietistic evangelical believer. Education was viewed as a safe field of endeavor for the mission without risking conflict between the government of the Dutch Indies and the Indonesians, the majority of whom were Muslim. Jansz prepared at the *Koninklijke Akademie* in Delft, studying Bible, theology, language, ethnology and geography under the guidance of professor Jan Van Gilse from the Mennonite Seminary in Amsterdam.

Pieter Jansz: a Western Missionary Pioneer

Jansz and his wife, Wilhelmina Frederica Schmilau, arrived in Batavia (Jakarta) in November 1851. Because the DZV didn't support Jansz as a full time evangelist, he had to find other work to support himself so he began to look for work as a teacher. He visited several areas such as Banyumas, Tegal, Pasuruhan and Demak. While in Demak, Jansz had the opportunity to work as a private tutor for the children of the *Bupati* (the government official who was head of a regency) of Demak. However within a short time he moved to Jepara, a harbor city in the western part of the area around Mount Muria, an extinct volcano about 1600 meters high. Here he worked as a private tutor for the children of a wealthy sugarcane plantation owner named Markar Soekias. Soekias was a Christian of Armenian heritage who hoped that Janzs's Christian teaching could help him pacify the 700 plantation laborers. Jansz definitely did not support this idea and he quarreled with Soekias.

Jansz left Soekias and moved to Sumbring near the village of Mlonggo. Here he began to direct his attention to evangelism free from the dictates of others. His background as a teacher made it easy for Jansz to begin his mission of evangelism by offering education to Javanese children. He was given permission to teach Javanese children because his work in education was viewed positively by the government of the Dutch Indies. At that time only the children of the wealthy and those who had a high position such as a *bupati* were able to go to school.

Jansz received permission from the governor general of the Dutch Indies to open a school and even to carry on evangelism in the *kecamatans* (sub-district jurisdictions) in the Jepara area (the northern part

of Central Java). This was truly amazing considering that the government of the Dutch Indies was usually very careful to prevent conflict, thereby protecting its economic interests, by forbidding evangelism in areas where Islam was strong. The activities and locations of missionaries were tightly regulated by the Dutch Indies government.

At the beginning, the school that Jansz established had only three students. Eventually the school flourished. Also, he succeeded in preparing several adults for baptism. At the Easter celebration, April 16, 1854, Jansz baptized five people, one man and four women. The following year two believers were baptized, and the year after that, there were

A page from Pieter Jansz' diary

a total of seven.

Of course if compared with the missionary service of his contemporary Jellesma in Mojowarno, the growth of Jansz's following could be said to be slow. This was because there were at least three big challenges that Pieter Jansz had to confront. First, the location around Mount Muria[6] was not a fertile area for evangelism because it included the three important cities, Demak, Kudus and Jepara, where the influence of Islam can be said to be the strongest in Central Java. In this area there were three *sunan* (Javanese Muslim holy men) out of nine *sunan* who were very influential in the development of Islam in Java. They were Sunan Muria, Sunan Kudus and Sunan Kalijaga. Historically the city of Jepara itself was a strong Islamic area within the Demak sultanate.

Second, conflict developed with the Dutch Indies government. At the end of 1859 Jansz wrote and distributed a tract with the title "The Time has Come." It was feared that this tract could trigger social disturbance, especially religious conflict. Governor General C. F. Pahud forbade Jansz distributing the tract, because of its religious overtones. From this it can be understood that for the Indies government a stable security situation was of utmost importance to promote economic interests. Therefore in the midst of a population, the majority of whom were Muslim, the Indies government exercised care in guarding against social conflict caused by efforts to spread religion.

Third, anti-colonial struggles were increasing in strength, especially after the Diponegoro War (1825-1830). The Diponegoro War was an explosive expression of nationalism against the Dutch oppressor. This Diponegoro War is known as the Javanese War because there was a convergence of interests between upholding Islam and the mystical hope of the Javanese people for the presence of the Just King (*Ratu Adil*). By marrying the struggle to uphold Islam to the hope of the presence of *Ratu Adil,* the Diponegoro War had a broad impact. With strong nationalism opposing the colonizing nation, the Christian religion had to be opposed because it was seen as the religion of the colonizers. Because of that, the work of evangelism by the European missionaries on the island of Java did not flourish.

Pieter Jansz and government authority

On March 17, 1860 Jansz's permission to preach the Gospel in Jepara was rescinded by the Dutch Indies government. The police watched his church so that only Christians could enter. At the same time, Christians were ridiculed and harassed by the people and often called to the police station. The Minister of Colonial Affairs J. J. Rohussen told the leaders of the DZV that Jansz could receive permission again, provided he showed signs of change. This really offended Jansz and he refused on the principle that he was more afraid of God than of the government. So beginning in 1860, Jansz again worked as a teacher and at the same time led his little congregation. Ten years later he gave this defense: "I definitely cannot accept conditions that require me to request permission from worldly leaders, because if I request permission from them it means that I am quietly saying that the Gospel is only valid if they give permission."

Working within this cultural and political dilemma was not easy, and Jansz finally realized that mission work could not depend on foreigners, especially not Europeans. Evangelism and the work of the church must be from and by indigenous people. Jansz contacted his Reformed colleague Jellesma in Mojowarno, East Java, to request a Javanese assistant and Jellesma sent Sem Sampir to help Jansz. With

Sem Sampir's assistance Jansz developed a new plan: to form a nucleus of trained personnel and appoint local assistants such as Pasrah Karso, Tresno, Petroes and Filemon. The role of the mission began to change from focusing only on conversion, to training and enlisting the indigenous people to become evangelists to their own people. Jansz began this work in his school in Jepara and he also opened a Bible school to prepare local evangelists.

One of Pieter Jansz's assistants, whom it is appropriate to mention here, is Pasrah Karso (which means "fully surrendered to the will of God"). Pasrah learned about Christianity under the leadership of Filemon, a student of Hoezoo who lived in Kayuapu, but he was baptized by Jansz on February 24, 1859. He then became Jansz's assistant in spreading the Gospel from Pulojati where he lived to Blingoh (Kelet), Karanggondang, and Kedungpenjalin.

The results that Jansz's assistants achieved in building a community of believers gave Jansz the idea to establish a community in a Christian village in the area around Jepara. He was inspired by the results obtained by C. L. Coolen who had cleared the jungle and established a Christian village in Ngoro, East Java, and also by Tunggul Wulung who had cleared the jungle at Bondo and established a Christian village. Jansz wanted to try to do evangelism with this structural approach to the Javanese community. He thought about having capable and trustworthy Javanese Christians work one or two plots of land near

The first baptismal ceremony, 1854

During an evening service at Easter Sunday, April 16, 1854, Pieter Jansz baptized the first five converts in the open verandah (*pendopo*) in front of his house. This is what he reports in his diary:

"At six thirty p.m. everything in the front gallery had been arranged festively with lamps and Chinese lanterns. The five baptismal candidates were sitting separately on a bench, in front of my place. Before them five simple cushions, with green coverings, and also an empty bench, to kneel. Things had been arranged in a similar way for me, as this is the custom in our Amsterdam congregation. Further back on the left, some twenty Javanese men were sitting on mats; they belonged to the confirmation classes or were interested people and outsiders. On the right were about twenty women, and behind the baptismal candidates (in order not to make those shy when looked at) some twenty Europeans were sitting as spectators; the [baptismal] witnesses sat in front, likewise the family of the landlord Soekias. Sem [Sem Sampir, Jansz' assistant from East Java] read the first sermon of Peter to the heathen, and the baptism of Cornelius and his house. After a hymn and a prayer, I took some words from this story as the introduction to my sermon, which was based upon Luke 18:13, 14a. After a prayer, each candidate listened, standing, to six questions from the Christian confession and answered each question with "Yes." Then the baptismal candidates and I kneeled and prayed for the enlightenment and strength of the Holy Spirit. The ceremony itself took place as is done in our native [Dutch] congregations."

the village of Senenan to the south of Jepara. In this village the laws of the government would be applied as well as rules based on Christian moral principles, such as forbidding the sale of opium or *ledek* dancers, most of whom were also prostitutes.

Jansz was assisted by several other Dutch Mennonite missionaries. The first was Hillebrandus Cornelis Klinkert (1829-1913) who arrived on the mission field in 1856. Unfortunately he and

Pieter Jansz and his assistant, Rd. Mg. Djojo Soepono, translating the Bible

Jansz didn't get along very well and in 1859 he left Jepara and went to live in Semarang. Klinkert was to become a noted linguist, translator of the Bible into the Malay language and the first editor/publisher of the "Malay Trumpet," one of the first Malay-language newspapers in the country. However, his direct role in the development of the Mennonite churches in Indonesia was limited. The second one was Nicolaas Dirk Schuurmans (1838-1908) who worked together with Jansz from 1863-1878. Unlike Jansz, he was a moderate follower of modernism. Since during these years Jansz was working hard to compose a Javanese grammar and Javanese dictionary on behalf of his Javanese translation of the Bible (which was to serve the Indonesian churches until 1940!). Schuurmans was mainly responsible for the education of indigenous evangelists and teachers. Also, the colonial government trusted him and Jansz fully in their medical work among the local population at a time when no doctors were available at all. Finally, from 1877 on, Jansz was assisted by one of his sons, Pieter Anthonie Jansz (1853-1943). He will be mentioned again below. But first we turn our attention to Kyai Ibrahim Tunggul Wulung (ca. 1800-1885), Jansz's main antagonist on the mission field.

Tunggul Wulung: an Indigenous Evangelist
and Seeker of Javanese Wisdom

Many people consider the name Tunggul Wulung to be a symbol of Javanese opposition to Dutch colonialism, especially the Diponegoro War. The Diponegoro War is also known as the Javanese war against the Dutch. Although the Diponegoro War was won by the Dutch colonizers, it did not end the struggle against colonialism. According to a story that circulated among the people, Tunggul Wulung was formerly named Raden Mas Tondo.[7] According to other sources he was a *guru ngelmu* (teacher of wisdom) who was named Kyai Ngabdoolah (which means "servant of God"). After the defeat in the Diponegoro War he fled, moving from one place to another. Finally he hid on Mount Kelud (Kediri in East Java) to meditate, and he changed his name to Tunggul Wulung (meaning "black banner"or "one who has defeated an eagle").

The choice of the name Tunggul Wulung at the time he was meditating on Mount Kelud can be said to be a proclamation that he was continuing the Diponegoro struggle. Meditating at Mount Kelud was connected to Tunggul Wulung's mystical vision. Mount Kelud was seen by the indigenous population as a place to receive inner strength after a defeat. The name Tunggul Wulung was taken from the name of King Jayabaya, a mystical figure of the twelfth century, who was famous among the Javanese people. For the Javanese, Jayabaya was not just a king, but also a prophet whose prophecies are still believed. According to these eschatological expectations, King Jayabaya had a chancellor and a general. Both died together with the king, but their ghosts were supposed to protect the area of Jayabaya's kingdom from the top of two mountains in East Java, Mount Wilis and Mount Kelud. The general, whose name was Tunggul Wulung, resided on Mount Kelud.

The mystical strength of Mount Kelud and Tunggul Wulung, its protector, made it seem to be an appropriate place for Kyai Ngabdoollah to meditate and absorb mystical power. Belief in the vision of King Jayabaya's nation and the loyalty of the service of Tunggul Wulung who awaited the Just King in the twelfth century, caused Kyai Ngabdoollah to change his name to Tunggul Wulung.

There are many interesting stories about the way Tunggul Wulung became a Christian. A story that circulated among the people of the villages was that one day when Tunggul Wulung woke up he saw a piece of cloth covered with the words of the Ten Commandments underneath the floor mat on which he slept. As a Javanese, Tunggul

Wulung believed that finding this scrap of cloth was a divine revelation from God to him. So he began to try to find out the meaning of the Ten Commandments. When he heard that there was a faith that taught the Ten Commandments, Tunggul Wulung quietly tried to find out about and study this teaching. And truly this teaching was very much in agreement with his vision for building a free people. When he met the group of Christians at Ngoro (about 40 kilometer from Mount Kelud), Tunggul Wulung was very attracted to the communal life of this group that Coolen had started. The mystical power that people talked about in this community increased his interest. For example in 1848, at the time Mount Kelud erupted, the village of Ngoro was not hit by lava. And in 1852 when there was a famine throughout East Java, there was still rice in Ngoro. A strong Christianity attracted Tunggul Wulung, because it was not just another religious teaching, but power for change, rich with Messianic hope. Christianity exceeded Javanese mystical wisdom or the teachings of Islam that were embraced by the *santris*.

Christianity for Tunggul Wulung was new wisdom that was laden with mystical power. This became clearer when Tunggul Wulung met Endang Sampurnawati, another seeker after wisdom, who became his wife. This wisdom could be captured in riddles, as in the Old Testament. One such riddle taught by Tunggul Wulung says: "The Just King arrives as a guest, but it is this guest who serves the house owner. He comes without any provisions." The answer to such a riddle could clearly point to Jesus Christ.

This Christological wisdom created a new consciousness on the spiritual path of Tunggul Wulung and Endang Sampurnawati. Their belief in messianic Christology fit with the Javanese mysticism that was based on the hope in the coming of the Just King, the Savior. "Christian wisdom" was not just higher than other Javanese wisdom, but also made the guarantee of salvation clearly understandable. Christianity was deeper than Javanese wisdom because it provided an answer to the meaning of life in the teaching about the personal form of God's mercy, Jesus Christ. Jesus Christ, the Son of God, descended and was absorbed into this world. Jesus Christ is not a visionary image of the Just King who will come, but is already here and guarantees salvation for people who lived long before Jesus Christ came. And Tunggul Wulung was attracted by the purpose of the coming of the Just King, Jesus Christ, who came, not in order to be served, but to serve. This was truly extraordinary.

Pushed to deepen his knowledge of this Christianity which inspired him, Tunggul Wulung went to Mojowarno, in East Java to meet with Jellesma and ask for guidance. It is estimated that the total number of Christians in East Java in 1850 had already reached 530 people.

There are several oral traditions about the meeting between Tunggul Wulung and Jellesma. According to one version, Tunggul Wulung went to the place where Jellesma was teaching the congregation. Tunggul Wulung applied *ngelmu panglimunan* which can make one invisible. He sat at the window while listening to Jellesma teach. But Tunggul Wulung was startled when the members of the congregation had left the room, and Jellesma addressed him. Tunggul Wulung realized that his wisdom was defeated by Jellesma who was able to see him even when he was protected by his *ngelmu* which, according to his understanding, made it impossible for anyone to see that he was present.

In 1854 Tunggul Wulung visited Pieter Jansz at Sumbring near Jepara accompanied by Sem Sampir, the student of Jellesma who had been assigned to assist Jansz. Unfortunately the styles of these two men didn't fit in a way that would have made it possible for them to work cooperatively. Tunggul Wulung thought Jansz was too much a stereotypical missionary figure, stuck in a stiff and proud western model of leadership. At the same time Jansz viewed Tunggul Wulung, who never wanted to kneel to the Dutch, as being too strong in his mystical belief. His teaching was suspected of being a syncretistic mixture of the teachings of Islam, Buddhism, Javanese mysticism and Christianity. Jansz considered Tunggul Wulung's knowledge of Christianity to be superficial: he had only memorized the Lord's Prayer, the Ten Commandments and the Apostles Creed which had become like a mantra. Because of this Jansz refused to baptize him.[8]

In the end Tunggul Wulung went back to Jellesma and after studying for two months, he and his wife were baptized by Jellesma in 1855. He chose the name Ibrahim as his Christian name. After he was baptized, Ibrahim Tunggul Wulung returned to the area around Mount Muria in Central Java. He became a member of Jansz' church but later he left to build his own community. Tunggul Wulung put the news of the Gospel in a format of *ngelmu* teachings. He even had the courage to oppose teachings of Javanese *ngelmu* in debates whereby whoever lost the debate had to give up his own knowledge and beliefs in order to follow the winner. *Ngelmu* debates such as these were already common in Javanese circles. Tunggul Wulung's dream was to build a free utopian Christian community where the return of the Just King provided motivation for the way of life. Tunggul Wulung saw a parallel between the messianic hope in Christian knowledge and the hope of the Javanese in the coming of the Just King as was prophesied by Jayabaya.

In his wandering ministry of evangelism, Tunggul Wulung finally chose to begin his work by clearing the jungle at Bondo (Jepara) to build his Christian village. Tunggul Wulung thought that Christians should be separated from the rest of the population so that they could form a new type of community. In his diary on January 17, 1854 Pieter Jansz wrote that Tunggul Wulung said, "If a new Christian congregation is formed but doesn't gather and live in the jungle in order to develop, but stays in the midst of Muslims, then that group will not amount to anything." This statement implies that Christians must live in community and develop a large family away from the influence of Islam.

There are many stories of torture of Christians within the fanatic Muslim community. For example, according to oral history sources, in Tegalombo, a representative of Tunggul Wulung named Benyamin Djojotruno was tortured and killed by crushing his vital parts while he slept. And though Jansz, at that time, did not follow Tunggul Wulung's example, he was inclined to agree with him on this point.

Aside from avoiding Islamic influence and pressure, the establishment of the Christian village Bondo was also an attempt by the Christians to evade the Dutch government's labor obligation. Resistance to the labor requirement was one way of affirming to themselves that "Christians were free." This was a concrete way to build a Javanese Christian community that was not under the shadow of Dutch political power. A Christian people must have its own leadership, according to Tunggul Wulung, who reflected a political attitude that was clearly the legacy of Prince Diponegoro's political attitude. The vision of the Just King influenced the messianic Christianity of Tunggul Wulung.

The establishment of the settlement at Bondo by Tunggul Wulung was influenced by the prophecy of Jayabaya, and this was evident in the reasons he chose this particular place.[9] First, it was believed that the political utopia of the kingdom of the Just King would develop in the jungle where it was quiet and eerie. Tunggul Wulung found these characteristics in the village of Bondo, which was indeed quiet and eerie. Formerly, it had been a place where native people had been slaughtered by the Dutch military. Second, according to a Javanese calculation, the sum of the numerical value of the letters of the words Bondo and Tulung Wulung is the same as the numerical value of *ratu* (king), which is the highest number possible. Third, geographically the Bondo jungle was a fertile area that was very suitable for farming. And fourth, the Bondo jungle fulfilled the requirements for constructing a mystical defense based on the Javanese philosophy of *mancapat* or *mancalima* and belief in *bahureksa* (the spirit that guards the jungle or an eerie place.)[10]

Tunggul Wulung did not only establish the village of Bondo but also the areas around it such as Dukuhseti, Banyutowo and Tegalombo. He also sent some of the young people for spiritual instruction under the tutelage of Jellesma in Mojowarno, Coolen in Ngoro and Anthing in Batavia. After they were finished with their studies they would be sent to the areas that had previously been evangelized by Tunggul Wulung.

Tunggul Wulung himself traveled throughout Java becoming a vital link for evangelism from East Java, through Central Java to West Java. More than any other person in the decades between 1853 and 1875 he traveled all around as an evangelist into almost every corner of Java. Jellesma even dubbed him the "Javanese apostle." Throughout his travels to various places he met with other independent evangelists, such as Mrs. C. P. Philips-Stevens in Banyumas and Judge F. L. Anthing near Batavia (Jakarta). Aside from this he was one of the teachers and models for Sadrach Suropranoto, who at the end of the nineteenth century became the famous leader of several independent Christian congregations in Karangyasa in the Bagelen area in Central Java. According to the oral tradition, Sadrach received a spiritual call to leave Bondo and build a community of his own.

In February 1885 Tunggul Wulung died, leaving the fruits of his service, the congregations in Bondo, Dukuhseti, Tegalombo and Banyutowo where it is reported that the number of his followers had reached 1,058 people. These congregations were then served by his grandson, Rustiman. The time for charismatic leaders such as Tunggul Wulung and Sadrach seemed to be over by then. People were looking into an age of modernity, of which the missionary work was an example. Therefore it is not surprising that Rustiman sought contact with the missionaries. And because the people who adopted Tunggul Wulung's Christianity had never been baptized, Rustiman requested Jansz's son, Pieter Anthonie, to teach them the catechism and baptize them. In 1886 Rustiman and seven others were baptized. One year later, the congregations in Bondo, Dukuhseti, Tegalombo and Banyu-

The power of prayer

One of the harshest criticisms directed against Tunggul Wulung was the allegation that he continued to use *rapals*, the kind of magical formulas animistically-oriented Javanese use in dealing with adverse circumstances. [...] It was hardly unreasonable that Tunggul Wulung taught his followers prayers to pray when they found themselves in such situations. ... He even created a special prayer with a clearly Trinitarian focus...:

Father God, Son of God, Holy Spirit of God,
The three are one in essence.
Dangerous places, evil infested woods, all poisons become harmless.
May God grant us safety forever.

towo were turned over to the care of the DZV and Rustiman himself was appointed an evangelist. Nevertheless, the spiritual influence of Tunggul Wulung continued among many Christians in the Muria area well into the twentieth century. Even Reverend Soehadiweko Djojodihardjo, who led the Javanese church until 1983, acknowledged his spiritual dependence on Ibrahim Tunggul Wulung.

Expansion through Colonization

For the time being, Jansz's original vision to bring the Christians together in a separate village, as Coolen, Jellesma and Tunggul Wulung had done, could not be realized. Too much money, originally estimated at 100,000 Dutch guilders, was needed, and the Mission Board in Amsterdam hesitated. Spreading the Gospel was not the same as becoming a village chief! Nevertheless, against strong advice from Amsterdam, Jansz and his son Pieter Anthonie pushed their ideas through. At his own cost, Jansz even wrote and published a booklet, "Land Reclamation and Evangelization in Java" (1874) and he succeeded in winning wealthy private patrons for his plan. Finally the Board gave in. After all, so far Jansz's efforts had only produced 102 believers. One of his indigenous evangelists, Pasrah, already led a settlement, Kedungpenjalin. Unfortunately this settlement could not be enlarged. In 1881, the DZV received permission from the government to develop a 200-hectare piece of land to the north of Tayu near the coast. The land was not owned but made available as a long-term lease by the colonial government. P.A. Jansz moved there and was followed by Christians from Jepara. The educational administration was also moved there. On June 9, 1883 the land was cleared and given the name Margorejo. In 1884, 137 residents of the village of Margorejo worked 44 hectares. The younger Jansz acted as the manager and he levied taxes from the residents. He also made the rules for the residents. Those who lived in Margorejo were not forced to become Christians, but they were expected to follow the Christian regulations such as not working on Sunday. Children from the ages of 6-12 were required to go to school. Men were not allowed to have more than one wife, smoke opium, drink alcohol or follow pagan and superstitious traditional customs that could be stumbling blocks for Christians. Other colonies were to follow such as Margokerto. They were to become the founding congregations of the Javanese Mennonite church in Indonesia.

Decades of growth

Pieter Jansz, the father, did not follow his son to Margorejo but moved to the home of his daughter who had married the missionary De Boer in Salatiga, Central Java. In his old age, he worked to translate the Bible into Javanese at the request of the British and Foreign Bible Society. In 1904 he died at Kayuapu, at the home of his son-in-law Johann Fast. The translation work was continued by the younger Jansz.

In the meantime the mission work experienced much growth during the last decades of the nineteenth century. In 1871 a second mission field, Mandailing in Sumatra, was opened. We will come back to the developments there below. However, both there and on Java the work would have been impossible without a large amount of financial help from brothers and sisters in North Germany, Prussia and especially from those in Gnadenfeld, Ukraine. They assisted not only in financial matters, but also by sending missionaries. The first of them, Heinrich Dirks, worked in Mandailing from 1870 until 1881 and became a tireless promoter of the mission work in the congregations in the Ukraine as well as in Prussia. In 1888 Johann Fast, who was to become Jansz's son-in-law, arrived. Several more followed: Johann Huebert in 1893, Johann Klaassen in 1899, Nicolai Thiessen and Jacob Siemens as well as the nurses Helena Goossen and Susanna Richert during the first decade of the twentieth century. At the same time, the source of Dutch missionaries seemed to dry up. Therefore this reinforcement was most welcome. It meant that many mission posts could be staffed and also, that the educational work (the main responsibility of Pieter Anthonie Jansz) could be extended. This made possible the participation of a number of Javanese schoolteachers and evangelists.

Unfortunately our knowledge about the important role of the latter is very limited. Between 1883 and 1898, 215 persons in Margorejo alone were baptized. In 1897 (when the DZV had been in existence for 50 years), the Margorejo congregation counted 130 adult members. The total number of inhabitants of the "colony" was 360. As we noticed earlier, the members of

The Javanese church of Bondo, 1920s

the group around the late Tunggul Wulung could be added to this, as well as the people in the congregation of Kayuapu from 1897 onwards after it had been handed over by the NZG.

The development of a Christian village or colony was one model and a good way to make it possible for the Javanese to embrace the Christian faith. They no longer had to fear ostracism or being viewed as people without a social foundation. Here they had their own village, a Christian village. The Christian villages can be said to have been more advanced compared with other villages in education, health and economics. This added additional value to their work compared with the proselytizing of other religions at that time.

A negative aspect was the fact that the missionaries who worked in the "colonies" tended to play a double role, as missionary and as village chief. Also, the growth and prosperity of these "colonies" prevented the mission from looking seriously at cities like Pati and Kudus. Probably the rural background of the Ukrainian missionaries was an additional factor in this.

Modernization during the first decades of the twentieth century

At the turn of the twentieth century, the vision of the colonial government in the Dutch East Indies changed as the Dutch developed a concern for the welfare of the indigenous population. This was called the "ethical policy." Attention to medical care and education increased, and missionary organizations, too, were able to use government funds to establish hospitals and schools. As a result, the work of the Mennonite mission grew considerably.

The Christian hospital in Kelet

Already in 1894 a hospital had been opened in Margorejo and another one opened in Kedungpenjalin in 1902. After that, outpatient clinics were opened in Kelet, in Tayu and other places. At first the missionaries themselves, assisted by Javanese staff, served in these hospitals and clinics. Johann Klaassen was especially interested in this work, and in 1911 the above mentioned nurses, Helena Goossen and Susanna Richert, both from Nikolaifeld near Chortitza, arrived. Yet it became clear that academically trained doctors were needed, as in Mojowarno, East Java. In 1907 Dr. H. Bervoets, who was not a Mennonite, arrived. He opened a hospital in Kelet in 1915. He and his wife had an extensive social network outside the Mennonite world. On the occasion of the birth of Princess Juliana in 1909, this network collected funds for a leprosarium north of Kelet that was officially opened in November 1915. This place was given the name Donorodjo which means "gift from the queen." Many people from outside Jepara came to be cared for at the leprosarium at Donorodjo.

Already in 1902 a young woman named Justinah had been sent to Mojowarno for training as a midwife. Beginning in1906 she worked in the Muria area. Later the Kelet hospital trained nurses and midwives who received a government-recognized diploma. Faithful and capable nurses like Sukarjo and Soemartoadi and the midwives, Kasmirah, Artinah, Wasti, Waginah, Kani and Rasimah, dedicated their lives to the work in the Mennonite hospitals. All in all, twenty midwives were trained in Kelet by 1940.

In 1920 Dr. Bervoets left after a conflict with the missionaries who wanted to keep spiritual control over his work. He was succeeded by Dr. Karl Gramberg, who reorganized the leprosarium (it had 200 patients in 1936) and started an auxiliary hospital in the more densely populated town of Tayu with several out-patient clinics in surrounding villages. Other Dutch doctors and nurses worked here for a shorter or longer term as well.

The teacher training school that was established by the younger Jansz in Margorejo in 1903 developed well. This was the successful result of Pieter Anthonie Jansz's service and it should be noted that within a period of only three years, this school grew in an extraordinary way. In 1915 forty-three teachers graduated. This school used Javanese as the language of instruction and this drew many people because other teacher training schools still used Dutch as the language of instruction. Jansz also worked hard to translate textbooks into Javanese. Because government subsidies ceased at the end of 1924, the teacher training

Justinah

The midwife Justinah, who worked in the mission hospital of Kelet for many years, was a remarkable and intelligent woman. She was trained in the mission hospital of Mojowarno, East Java, and sent to Kelet at the request of the missionary doctors there. In one of the letters of R.A. Kartini (August 14, 1903) she is described as "a girl from the *desa* [village] ... she listened with much concern and had many interested questions.....The brave young woman has already assisted 48 women in giving birth. And yet, she is still so young, almost a child yet...". Justinah worked in Kelet for many years.

Teacher Bedjo, Teacher Training School, Margorejo (ca.1930)

school had to be closed down, much to Jansz's distress. It was briefly re-opened in 1930. By 1933 five secondary schools had been established, as well as fifteen elementary schools with a total of about 1264 students.[11] Nevertheless, here too, withdrawal of government subsidies caused many difficulties.

Beginning in the 1930's the Mennonite mission improved its organizational structure. The DZV divided the Javanese Christian congregations into four districts as follows:

Kedungpenjalin (Jepara) which included Margokerto and Pakis with a total of 627 adult members and 649 children.

Margorejo, which included the Bumiarjo district with a total of 1,203 adult members and 1,189 children.

Kayuapu, which included the districts of Kudus and Pakis with a total of 159 adult members and 91 children.

Kelet and Donorodjo, with 1,145 adult members and 94 children. Thus, the total membership of the Javanese (Mennonite) Christian congregations was 2,130 adults and 2,023 children. The Margorejo congregation was the first congregation to come to maturity with the ordination of the first pastor, Roebin Martoredjo in 1929.[12]

Problems of Autonomy

As seen through the eyes of the mission, the work of the mission, especially in the area around Mount Muria, was very productive. Their service has left a large legacy: pioneering efforts in the congregations, in education and also in health. However, if seen from the perspective of the time when the mission began in 1852 until the time the first congregation reached maturity in 1925, it is clear that there was a serious problem called autonomy. Of course there were many positive results, such as property owned by the churches, education and hospitals. However the issue of dependence in the matters of funding and leadership shadowed the Javanese congregations formed by the DZV mission and this has not been easy to resolve even until the present.

As already noted, nationalist movements gained momentum from the beginning of the twentieth century. This was felt within the Protestant churches as well. The Reformed congregation of Mojowarno in East Java was the first to have indigenous leadership. Other congregations followed. In general, the older generation of Dutch and Ukrainian Mennonite missionaries was slow to accept the changes. The German missionaries Hermann Schmitt (from 1927 on) and Otto Stauffer (from 1932) were much more open to the new developments, as was a modern medical doctor like Karl Gramberg. An instructive case is the maturation of the Margorejo congregation, the old congregation that had been started on the land where Pieter A. Jansz had established a community in 1883.

Margorejo was a risky venture, and it was uncertain whether the work of the DZV would bear fruit or not. Its development required a considerable amount of financial assistance. They had sought for at least thirty-four years since 1917 to place the congregation on a solid footing by forming a church council (*majelis*). The council was organized to

Hospital in Margorejo, built in 1906 by Nicolai Thiessen (photo 1922)

provide training for the congregation for the time in the future when it would become autonomous. In 1928, missionaries Schmitt and Thiessen advised that Margorejo (and also Kedungpenjalin and Kayuapu) be given a *pemomong* (one who serves the local congregation) to lead worship and serve the sacraments. On June 27, 1928 the congregation chose Roebin Martoredjo as their *pemomong*. But when this action was passed on to the mission board in the Netherlands they were surprised and deplored this decision. The tension that arose caused the ordination of Roebin Martoredjo as *pemomong* of the congregation to be postponed until August 12, 1929, and Margorejo was given a probationary period of five years. Financial matters were still in the hands of the mission and only in 1933 were they finally handed fully to the Margorejo church council.

The sequence of these events shows how difficult it was for one congregation to become autonomous. In addition to their feeling that they were not trusted by the mission, dependence in many aspects became a major obstacle to the congregations' achieving autonomy. The missionaries invited the well-known Dr. Hendrik Kraemer to visit the Muria area and give advice as he had done on other mission fields as well. According to the records of a meeting of Mennonite

Pharmacy at the Margorejo Hospital, ca. 1930

missionaries on March 26-31, 1931, in Kelet, he said the following:

Self-reliance is the only way out. Autonomy has been talked about for a long time, as long as eighty years...You don't want to promote something that makes you conspicuous. What should we do? Grant autonomy if they don't want it? That is the same as dropping them into a deep hole. Now the mission has the duty to show the congregations the way to achieve autonomy which they must reach by their own initiative. They must be guided in such a way that the feeling of standing on their own feet grows within them. They must be trained to use the autonomy that is given...[...] First, the missionaries will not pay salaries anymore.

Pastor Roebin Martoredjo and his wife

This is a change in the missionaries' position toward the congregations that is very important for the Javanese so all these matters have to be brought to the church council, no longer to the missionaries...[13]

In 1937 Kraemer also attended a meeting of the DZV Board to inform them about the many changes occurring in Indonesia. Autonomy for the GITJ was of course a dilemma. On the one hand the work of the mission had already borne fruit in the large number of congregations, the health service and hospitals, and the schools, all of which, if not supported with large amounts of money, certainly would experience a decline. But if continually helped, this would destroy the enthusiasm of the congregations for autonomy. This dilemma continued up to the final decades of the twentieth century.

As a result of the changing attitudes of the missionaries, it was finally decided that promising young men would be given the opportunity to get theological training. It took some time to find good candidates. In 1937, however, Soedjono Harsosoedirdjo and I. Siswojo (and somewhat later Soeratman) were sent to Malang where the Reformed Church of East Java had opened a theological school, *Bale Wijoto*. Also in 1934 a Higher Theological School had been opened in Batavia (Jakarta), and Soehadiweko Dojodihardjo was the first to study there. It provided him not only with the necessary theological foundation, but also with a very important network of young fellow theologians in other denominations all over the country.

History of the *Gereja Injili di Tanah Jawa* – GITJ (Javanese Evangelical Church)

Suffering and Preparation for Autonomy

A new phase for the autonomy of the GITJ congregations began on September 1, 1939, with the political crisis of World War II brought about by the German Nazi government. The mission was aware that they had to begin turning over the leadership of the church to local leaders. The most likely alternative at that time was to appoint a *pemulang* for the congregations (a kind of evangelist) from among the graduates of the Teacher Training School in Margorejo. Begining in 1941 Sardjoe Djojodihardjo was appointed as evangelist in Pati to replace Leonard Silalily, an Ambonese member of the mission staff who had already asked to retire. Wigeno Mororedjo was appointed to replace Gersom Filemon in Kayuapu. Sukar Arnan was designated to serve in Kedungpenjalin together with Samsoeri Radijo Nitihardjo who was appointed in Margokerto. Samuel

Samuel Hadi Wardojo and family, evangelist in Tayu from 1935

Hadi Wardojo was appointed as evangelist in Tayu. Arbi Kertosudirdjo, was appointed as the first assistant to Hermann Schmitt in Kudus. Lukas Herdjosuwitodi and Pariman Martosentono were appointed in Kelet, and Soedjono Harsosoedirdjo was chosen as *pemomong* or *pemulang* in Margorejo to replace Roebin Martoredjo.

As the political situation in Europe worsened, autonomy for the churches could not be postponed any longer. The time of preparation for autonomy came in Kelet on May 30, 1940 when there was a meeting to take over leadership of the churches from the hands

of the DZV mission. Four weeks earlier the relationship with the Netherlands had been cut when the German Army invaded Dutch territory. The result of this meeting was an agreement to form *"Patunggilan Pasamuwan Kristen Tata Injil ing Karesidenan Pati, Kudus lan Djepara."* They chose the word

Javanese pastors and their wives, ca. 1930

"patunggilan" to show their consciousness of being a fellowship of believers which was a unique characteristic of the Mennonite congregations. Dr. Karl Gramberg and Daniel Amstutz, a missionary from Switzerland since 1934, advised the use of this term. In view of the fact that autonomy requires a process, Amstutz was chosen as chairman and Gramberg was chosen as assistant chairman. Other leadership functions were held by local people. Sardjoe Djojodihardjo was chosen as secretary. Wigeno Mororedjo was the treasurer assisted by committee members Soedjono Harsosoedirdjo (committee I) and (committee II) Samuel Suritruno. The total membership of the congregations at that time had reached 5,000 adults.

At the time of Synod Session II in Kedungpenjalin in June 1941, Amstutz announced that he would step down from the leadership of the synod as a result of tension with the Indonesian leaders of the congregations and turn over leadership of the synod to them. Dr. Gramberg also stepped down so that the real leadership would be held by the leaders of the congregations themselves. Temporary leadership of the synod was given to Evangelist Sardjoe Djojodihardjo, a graduate of the Teacher Training School in Margorejo and since August 1940 the head of the Association of Christian Schools in the Mennonite mission area.

The churches were severely tested in the first years of autonomy. Japan's invasion of Indonesia in 1942 caused social and governmental turmoil. The Dutch colonial government began to collapse, and with no effective authority, there was looting and killing in many places. An organization of hard-line Muslim youth from the Nahdathul Ulama party known as Ansor used this opportunity to wage holy war, trying to force Christians to return to Islam. Christians were considered to be infidels and spies for the Dutch. This dislike for Christians flared into violence and torture. The hard-line Muslims moved from Bulumanis (in the Tayu area) to

Participants of the first Synod meeting of the Javanese church, 1940 in Kelet

Christian centers in the north such as Tegalombo, Margorejo, Kelet and Kedungpenjalin. These riots were referred to as "the time of plunder" (*jaman rayahan*). There was rioting and looting in the homes and shops owned by the Chinese who fled, looking for a safe place. Those who were captured met a sad fate. The men were marched to Bulumanis and circumcised *en masse,* and the women were raped. Many Javanese Christian congregations could not bear to see the anger that was unleashed on the Chinese due to the imbalance of their relative wealth compared to the rioters. The Javanese Christians reached out to protect the Chinese by hiding them in their homes or in the male nurses' dormitory at the Tayu Christian Hospital.

The Javanese Christians who offered protection to the Chinese did not escape the violence of the hard-line Muslims. On Sunday, March 8, 1942, the leaders of the congregation in Tayu, Samyanadi, Oesade, Yosep, Soeyono and Moenadji were seized by a group of Ansor youth. They were loaded into horse-drawn carts and driven at gun point to Bulumanis where they were tortured, accompanied all the way by the recitation of "*Allahu Akhbar*" (God is great).

The torture of the Christians on Sunday, March 8, continued with a plan to seize Dr. Gramberg, the head of the hospital in Tayu. He had been accused of poisoning people's wells. But Sunandar, an employee of the Pakis sugar factory, telephoned Dr. Gramberg from the *kecamatan* of Bulumanis to tell him about the plan of the Ansor youth. Hearing this news, Dr. Gramberg with his family slipped away to Kelet via Ngablak.

With the departure of Dr. Gramberg, Dr. Ong Yong Soen, who was on duty that morning, remained at the hospital with several nurses. Actually the hospital had been emptied and the patients sent home to prepare for all possibilities. There were only some babies and three other patients. One was from Kalitelo and the other two were Dutch-Australian soldiers who were being cared for there because they had been brought ashore at Banyutowo when their ship was torpedoed by Japan. Dr. Ong was advised by the nurses to run away. However he refused. Dr. Ong even said, "It's not necessary to be afraid. I'll be out in front." When the Ansor gang attacked the hospital about 4:00 in the afternoon, Dr. Ong quickly became the first target. When they did not find Dr. Gramberg, the crowd, as if possessed by an evil spirit, dragged Dr. Ong and cut him beneath his waist and near his head so that he fell flat on the ground smeared with blood. His glasses were taken off and thrown into the middle of the raging fire, set by the Ansor and others in the crowd that was burning the hospital buildings. Dr. Ong did not die. He was protected by God's love. Among those in the crowd who were overcome by an evil spirit, there was one person who dragged him out of the hospital and took him to safety in front of a nearby shop. The name of this person was not known but it is clear that many people believed that he was sent by God to save Dr Ong.

The church building, the Tayu hospital and the leprosarium at Donorodjo were all damaged. H. C. Heusdens, a Reformed pastor who had been serving at Donorodjo, was arrested and given the choice to deny his faith or be killed. He refused to deny his faith or change his conviction. He held firm in his faith and, as a result, he was tortured and finally

---

War, as experienced by S. Djojodihardjo

I had just finished seminary [in Jakarta] when the Japanese armies invaded Indonesia in 1941. They drove out the Dutch who had ruled our country for 350 years. There was terrible fighting. ... The train on which I was returning from school was bombed. I escaped unharmed, but the boxes with all my books were destroyed. ... But I had been carrying my Bible when the train was hit and so I had it, fortunately. [...]

At that time my father was the preacher in Pati, a larger town. One day, the crowds became angry with the Christians, and the Christians met together in the church. As my father prayed in his house behind the church, the people in the church saw a vision of a white-robed man with his arms stretched heavenward. They gained strength from the vision, and the angry crowd did not harm. [...]

We were asked to serve the church in Margorejo. ... One night we had a church council meeting in our house. Suddenly we were interrupted by a knock on the door. The house was surrounded by the police. They arrested me and took me to the police station. "What were you doing in that house?" they asked. "Were you planning a revolution?" "Only against the devil," I replied. They laughed and finally let me go.

killed in a despicable way. Pastor Heusdens was victorious in this painful struggle; he died as a martyr for his faith.

Many Javanese Christians were also seized, threatened and tortured. The leaders of the congregations were captured and forced to deny their faith and become Muslims. Harsosoedirdjo, Samuel, Soetjiptowardojo, Gondowardojo and Samuel Hadi Wardojo were leaders who were seized and taken to Ngagel to be tried. But through the help of God the torturers quarreled among themselves, and finally the leaders of the church were freed.

The arrival of Japan in the coastal areas in the north of Java prevented the hard-line Muslims from continuing this action because the Japanese military was known to be very hard and cruel. They did not tolerate rioting. The schools and the Christian hospital were taken over by the Japanese. The rioting began to abate, but with the presence of Japan, the Europeans also felt pressure. Daniel Amstutz and Dr. Gramberg quickly prepared to turn over all the mission property to the Javanese leadership, including the Christian land, buildings, schools, churches and homes.

The Javanese Mennonite Church during the Time of Independence

For four years after Indonesia declared its independence on August 17, 1945, the Dutch tried to maintain their influence in the archipelago by means of international political lobbying and military action in the country. For some time, the demarcation line between the area held by Sukarno's Republican forces and the Dutch armies went through the Muria area. In general, it was impossible for Dutch mission workers to work in the areas where fighting was going on or where the Indonesian armies were present. This prevented the Dutch mission from resuming its work in Central Java. However, the Swiss missionary, Daniel Amstutz, was able to work in the area beginning in 1946, and surprisingly, the Russian missionary nurse, Maria Klaassen (with her old father Johann Klaassen), was able to remain in Kelet during the years of Japanese occupation. Fortunately, the Mennonite Central Committee (MCC) decided to start a relief program in Indonesia. In early 1947 A. E. Kreider made a preliminary study visit. Others followed, and in June 1947 Orie O. Miller came to Java to plan for this relief work. Though they were unable to visit the Muria area itself, they had contacts and assembled information about the Mennonites.

In December 1949, Miller finally was able to visit the Mennonite churches themselves. These visits formed the beginnings of MCC's enduring presence in Indonesia.

In the meantime many Christians, especially the younger generation, were involved in the struggle for independence, and all Protestant churches in Indonesia, no longer under the tutelage of foreign missions, were looking for closer cooperation and ecumenical unity. Several conferences were devoted to this theme and in Central and East Java all the Javanese-speaking churches were working in unity. In 1950 the Council of Churches of Indonesia came into being. Regional councils of churches followed. It was a thrilling but also a difficult time for the churches, which had to stand on their own feet from 1942 on.

Responsibility for Church Leadership

In 1945, at the third session of the Synod (October 20, 1945), the Javanese Christian congregations changed their name to Association of Christian Congregations in the Muria Area (*Patoenggilan Pasamoewan Kristen Sekitar Muria-PPKSM*). This name change was a result of the need for closer organization and because there were influences from other Javanese churches in East Java and the southern part of Central Java. There was yet a third name change in May 1948, at the time of the Synod Session IV. At that time a new name was agreed on: Javanese Christian Church in the Muria Area (*Gereja Kristen Jawa di Sekitar Muria*). It is interesting to observe here that the new name used the word "*gereja*" (church) where it formerly had been the word "*pasamoewan*" (congregation). What was formerly "*patoenggilan*" (association), now became "*sinode*" (synod).

At the Synod Session V in Pati, in June 1949, the name Javanese Evangelical Church *(Geredja Indjili di Tanah Djawa - GITD)* appeared, and that name has been used since the 1956 Synod Session VII at Kudus. Adapting the name to the modern Indonesian spelling it became *GITJ – Gereja Injili di Tanah Jawa – GITJ)*. The use of the words "church" and "synod" clarified the purposes of the organization.

At the time of Synod Session V in Pati in 1949 the chairman of the GITJ Synod, Rev. S. Harsosoedirdjo (who had been appointed a year earlier to replace the deceased Sardjoe Djojodihardjo) was still in jail, and he was replaced as chairman by Rev. Soehadiweko Djojodihardjo. At that time a representative from the Central Java Christian Church (GKJ), Reverend S. P. Poerbawijoga, a noted Reformed theologian and church leader from Yogyakarta, was present. He asserted that GITJ could not stand by itself, in view of the suffering and the work that was not yet going smoothly. Because of this he proposed that GITJ join the GKJ. This offer was refused by the synod session. Even though the total membership had declined by more than half compared with the pre-war situation (there were only 2,000 members), the GITJ congregations still hoped to be revitalized. Two things were necessary for this to happen. First, they needed to develop immediately the human resources necessary to provide leadership for the churches. Second, they needed to structure matters such as a

> **A dream**
>
> After Indonesia declared its independence from Holland, the Javanese Mennonite Church was no longer supported and began to have a very difficult time. ... One night Pak Djojo [Soehadiweko Djojodihardjo] had a dream. He was standing on the shore at the edge of the ocean, looking out over the water. Suddenly he saw a man walking out in the water, coming toward him. He came out of the water and told Pak Djojo that help was on the way. A very short time later, Martin Schrag came to Java and to Pati to talk with Pak Djojo and offer assistance from MCC. Pak Djojo then recognized Martin as the man he had seen in his dream, the one who had come out of the water. To Pak Djojo, this was a sign from God.

church order and liturgy and organize the many assets needed for the work of the church, such as the hospitals and schools.

At Synod Session VIII in 1957, Poerbawijoga revised his assertion. He acknowledged that GITJ was developing well, with graduates of the theological school now ready to serve the congregations. Evidence of this was that the GITJ had grown to eleven congregations (Pati, Margorejo, Kelet, Bandungharjo, Margokerto, Bondo, Kedungpenjalin, Jepara, Ngeling, Kudus and Kayuapu) with 2,410 adult members and 2,850 children.

The role of Soehadiweko Djojodihardjo

The administration, identity (*jati diri*) and service of GITJ are linked to the role played by the indigenous leader Soehadiweko Djojodihardjo (1918-1988). His leadership reminded the Javanese Christian congregations of the Muria of the charismatic leadership of Tunggul Wulung. Soehadiweko's leadership brought new inspiration to the GITJ congregations in the midst of a difficult social situation between the years 1945 and 1970. It is very interesting that precisely in these difficult times, the GITJ Synod contributed much to the role of Christianity in Indonesia.

Soehadiweko Djojodihardjo was one of the generation of youth who were prepared by the mission to study theology in a formal way. In 1937 he was sent to the Jakarta Theological Seminary. He was

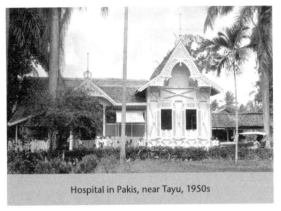

Hospital in Pakis, near Tayu, 1950s

very intelligent and had great leadership ability. He excelled at his studies at STT in Jakarta, a theological school with European standards. Founded in 1936, STT's purpose was to train high quality leaders for the Indonesian church in the future.

The leadership of Djojodihardjo, or Pak Djojo as he was often called, was tested and formed in difficult conditions, at a time when the connection with the Dutch Mennonite Mission Board was broken as a result of the defeat of the Dutch by Japan and the struggle for Indonesian independence was underway. During that time of political disturbance many church leaders were killed or jailed, and the congregations were in a very precarious condition. The GITJ congregations also experienced a sharp decline after the rioting and independence.

Soehadiweko was conscious that there were three things he must do quickly. First, he had to consolidate the congregations by making visits to strengthen and rebuild the communities that had been separated. Second, he must build an organization that could stand on its own. The change in the terminology of *"patoenggilan"* (association) suggests that the synod wanted to stress that the fellowship of the Javanese churches of the Muria needed to be equipped with a solid structure under the central leadership of the synod. In a time full of confusion and separation, changing the association to become a synod was a clear step in accordance with the style of Javanese leadership, whereby there is a partnership, but connected to a central symbol. For more efficient coordination and consolidation of the synod leadership, the synod was divided into districts. Three administrative districts were formed, the western district consisting of congregations in Jepara/Pecangaan, Kedungpenjalin, Bondo and Margokerto;

the northern district including Margorejo, Kelet and Bandunghardjo; and the southern district consisting of the congregations at Kudus, Kayuapu and Pati.[14] Clarifying the structure in this way made the church stronger in preparation for formalizing the system of church administration which had been prepared previously by Rev. Sardjoe Djojodihardjo and completed by Soehadiweko at the synod session in 1949.

It was clear that the national and international network had to be strengthened. Soehadiweko was aware that the GITJ Synod would not be strong enough to endure without the support of a national and international network. Pak Djojo was one of the key persons in shaping a cooperative relationship between the three synods of the Javanese church, the East Java Christian Church (GKJW), the Central Java Christian Church (GKJ) and the Muria Javanese Church (GITJ) to promote the development of Javanese-speaking churches, including the translation of the Bible and song books into Javanese. When the Council of Church in Indonesia (DGI) was formed in 1950, Soehadiweko Djojodihardjo was fully involved in its formation. When the relationship with the mission was broken by Japan's defeat of the Dutch and Indonesian independence, he formed a connection with the Mennonite Central Committee which came to Indonesia in 1948. In 1951 Soehadiweko led the GITJ to membership in the Mennonite World Conference. The addresses which he gave at the assemblies of the Mennonite World Conference (1952, 1957, 1962) graphically described the difficult struggle of the Mennonite churches in Indonesia in the midst of a strongly Islamic environment. He issued a call to give attention to evangelism in Indonesia.

Soehadiweko was a key player in the formation of two schools for theological education in Pati, one in the 1950s and one in the 1960s (see below). He also was involved in cooperative theological and other higher education initiatives in Malang (*Bale Wiyoto*), Yogyakarta (*Duta Wacana Christian University*) and Salatiga (*Satya Wacana Christian University*), serving as chair of the boards of both *Duta Wacana* and *Satya Wacana* for many years. In addition, he also helped neighboring churches, like the Muria Christian Church of Indonesia (GKMI) to train new young leaders, and also provided consultation as they faced difficult transitions. He willingly supported the proposal that one of the newly-trained pastors of the Javanese Synod (GITJ) become pastor for the GKMI congregation in Kudus.[15]

Under the thirty-five-year leadership of Soehadiweko (1948-1983) the GITJ Synod, which had only six active churches in 1950, had grown very quickly. Statistics gathered by Martati Ins. Kumaat from 1963 to 1972 show that by 1972 the number of GITJ churches had grown to twenty-three adult congregations, 119 worship groups ("branches") that had not yet organized as congregations, six congregations that were candidates for independence and four church districts. The total membership was about 40,000 (adults and children). Membership increased rapidly in those years.

Soehadiweko Djojodihardjo with a painting of Bima, a well-known Javanese mystical figure

Admittedly, another reason for the rapid growth of the Indonesia church, including the GITJ, was the tragic event which became known as "G-30-S," September 30, 1965. An attempted coup against the army led to a civil war for which the (atheistic) Communist Party was blamed. Hundreds of thousands of people were killed or imprisoned for many years. The new government of President Soeharto decided that all Indonesians should belong to one of five recognized religions: Islam, Hinduism, Buddhism, Protestantism or Roman Catholicism. Hence many people reported themselves as new Christians so they would not be suspected as Communists. Because the Javanese church in the Muria area was known as a church that devoted much attention to education and medical work, this made the GITJ especially attractive.

On the one hand, the strong leadership of Pak Djojo led the GITJ to play a large role nationally and internationally. On the other hand he left behind the significant problem of his succession: who was capable of replacing him to take the GITJ into the future? Dependence on Djojodihardjo's leadership as chairman of the synod until the 1970's resulted in a critical attitude on the part of many youth. This critical attitude and suspicion of the youth came to a head in September 1967 when some of the youth in the GITJ indicated their dissatisfaction with Djojodihardjo's leadership when he was not at home because he was on a trip abroad. But this youth movement was muffled when he returned. He called the people who opposed him to request an explanation. With his authority he was able to restore his leadership of the GITJ and continued to hold the confidence of the people; he led the GITJ Synod until 1983. At that time he stepped down and was replaced by Rev. Soesanto Harsosoedirdjo. However, various hidden issues flared up during the leadership of Soesanto Harsosoedirdjo and all the leaders who followed him. This raised questions as to whether this was the result of poor leadership by Pak Djojo or the shortcomings of those who followed him.

The life of the church

Beginning in the 1950s and 60s local congregations began to grow, and a number of local communities became mature congregations. This process has continued until the present, although the growth rate is much lower now than in the 1970s. One reason is that present Muslim communities are less open than they were earlier to permitting the construction of new church buildings and allowing conversions to Christianity.

Many congregations now choose educated pastors. In 1965 Esther Soesanto Harso-Andries became the first female pastor to be ordained. A strong personality, she became pastor of the Pati congregation and director of the teacher training college which prepared young people to become teachers of religious education at government and private schools. A second female pastor is scheduled to be ordained at the end of 2011.

In many respects the liturgy that the GITJ congregations follow resembles the liturgy of the Reformed churches in Java. Here we see the interdependence of the respective Protestant denominations. Normally a confession of sin and a proclamation of grace finds a place in the Sunday morning services. Also, the Apostolic Confession of Faith is read by an elder or deacon. The GITJ congregations use either the Javanese hymnal, which is used by many churches in Central and East Java (*Kidung Pasamuwan*), or an ecumenical, Indonesian language hymnal, prepared in 1985 by a committee of the Community of

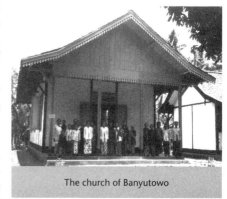

The church of Banyutowo

Churches. The latter hymnal also contains a number of original Indonesian hymns. One Mennonite pastor, Saptajaadi, composes hymns himself using authentic Javanese melodies. One of these can be found in the Mennonite World Conference hymnal. In most rural congregations, the Javanese language is used during the service; in urban communities the Indonesian language is dominant now, partly because an increasing number of members from other islands in Indonesia belong to these congregations.

A Hymn by Saptajaadi

Duh Pangeran ingkang maha suci
Kula sami marek tetunggilan
Salir bangsa salumahing bumi
Amemuji dateng asma Tuwan.

Oh Prince of peace, oh holy God and King,
To fellowship today with thee we come.
All nations of the earth rejoice and sing
To sanctify and glorify thy name.

Though the GITJ as a whole has experienced many internal conflicts, as will be recounted below, during the last twenty years many local congregations have prospered. A visible sign of this is the construction of new, modern church buildings or the reconstruction of existing buildings. Renewal also takes place in more openness towards charismatic forms of worship and modern musical instruments to attract young people.

In 1983 the GITJ accepted a new church order to replace older ones. It begins with a confessional preamble. After a quotation of John 3:16 (which has a prominent place in many church buildings) this preamble continues as follows:

> The Lord Jesus calls and gathers those who believe in Him and orders them to form a community of believers, that is, the church, which is His body whereas Christ is the head of that body. Therefore the church has been called to participate and play a role in the task and calling of Jesus Christ, in making visible signs of the presence of God's Kingdom in this world in daily life. In her presence in this world, the Church is both the local church and regional churches, which become a community in the Holy Universal Christian Church.

Theological education

A congregation must be managed well if it is to grow, and for that to happen it is necessary to establish schools as P. A. Jansz did in Margorejo. When Orie O. Miller visited at the end of 1949 for MCC, Soehadiweko Djojodihardjo took the opportunity to express the need for educating the leaders of GITJ. He related the problem of a shortage of personnel to serve in the congregations while at the same time the mission schools had been closed. Many of the old leaders had died, the hospitals were in bad condition and economic conditions were not stable. Considering how many members needed pastoral care, it was necessary to have an institution to co-ordinate theological education which, it was hoped, would help overcome the problem of leadership in the GITJ. At that time the Muria Christian Church of Indonesia (GKMI) was not yet ready to work together in this matter, in view of the fact that the scope of GKMI's service was still limited and lay leadership still dominated. Therefore, the Javanese synod (GITJ) established its own institution for theological education.

A program for theological education was opened on January 28, 1950, with fifteen students who had Javanese or North Sumatran backgrounds. This was a five-year program intended for students who had completed middle school. The curriculum included General History, History and Geography of the Bible, Church History, Mennonite History, Bible Knowledge, Mennonite Doctrine, Islam, Psychology, English, Indonesian Language, and Javanese. The first teachers were Rev. Soehadiweko Djojodihardjo and Daniel Amstutz (from Switzerland). In the middle of 1951 Jan Matthijssen, accompanied by his wife Mary Matthijssen-Berkman, arrived to help teach. Then in 1953, Roelf Kuitse joined the teaching staff.

After only five years there were discussions about the possibility of uniting the theological education program in Pati with *Bale Wijata*, the program of the East Java Christian Church (GKJW), a Reformed church. These two institutions, aside from having a historical connection (both in the service area of the NZG), also had a similar approach to serving the people of the villages, and both used Javanese as the language of instruction. The board of the DZV supported the union of the two schools and an additional group joined in, the GKI of West Java, which at that time had a theological school in Bandung (West Java). In 1955 these theological schools merged with the name Bale Wijata.

In 1961, Bale Wijata in Malang decided to join together with Duta Wacana, a theological seminary in Yogyakarta, that had a higher-level program of education. The union of Bale Wiyata with Duta Wacana became the Duta Wacana Higher Theological School (*Sekolah Tinggi Teologia Duta Wacana)* and had the effect of diminishing GITJ's role, especially when the Mennonite professors were no longer in Indonesia.

Joining with Duta Wacana didn't meet the needs of the GITJ congregations who had a lower level of education. Therefore, the GITJ leaders
thought about starting their own theological school like the one they
had had previously. Aside from that they wanted to stress Mennonite
values and teachings in order to protect their identity as a church.

In 1965 a Mennonite theological school was opened named Wiyata
Wacana Christian Academy (*Akademi Kristen Wiyata Wacana* or AKWW),
providing six years of education above middle school. It also offered a
two-year program for the training of evangelists. At that time the Muria
Christian Church of Indonesia (GKMI), which consisted predominantly
of ethnic Chinese members, joined with GITJ to manage AKWW. The
professors who taught there among others were: Eduard and Tiny van
Straten from the Netherlands; Adolf and Anna Ens, MCC personnel
from Canada; Albert Widjaja (GKMI) and Soehadiweko Djojodihardjo
(GITJ). The students came from GITJ and GKMI as well as from pioneer
congregations started by the Mennonite mission in Mandailing (South
Tapanuli, Sumatra). Several other teachers from Europe and North
America followed as colleagues of local seminary teachers from GITJ
and GKMI including Koembino, Hadinoertjito, Mrs. Martati Insuhardiq
Kumaat, Herutomo and Mesakh Krisetya.

The theological school, AKWW, flourished and trained many
church leaders whose influence continues to the present. There was
an offer to join together with a theological school in Ungaran in 1976,
but in the end that was abandoned. In 1981 GKMI withdrew from
the AKWW board. At that time there were no longer GKMI members
studying there, and also at that time Rev. Mesakh left to continue his
studies in India. There were several reasons why GKMI withdrew from
the AKWW board. First, the GKMI youth looked to the theological
schools in the big cities and believed that AKWW stressed the intellectual aspect too much over the spiritual. At the same time in GKMI
circles there was a spiritual reawakening among the youth as a result
of the KKR (*Kebaktian Kebangunan Rohani*, "Spiritual Revival Meeting")
carried out by evangelists from Hong Kong and China such as John
Sung, Dzao Tze Kwang and others. Finally, there was a lack of trust
between GITJ and GKMI in the management of AKWW.

Between 1980 and 1990 AKWW experienced many setbacks. Many
young people with potential preferred to continue their studies in other
places, the number of teaching staff declined, there were no expatriate
professors, especially guest professors. The most serious problem was

internal conflict within GITJ (beginning in 1986) because of a lawsuit over the control of the church-owned institutions, claims in civil court and the selling of church property. In 1997 AKWW was temporarily closed. After the internal conflict within GITJ was resolved in August 2003, the theological school was re-opened with financial and educational conditions that were far from optimal.

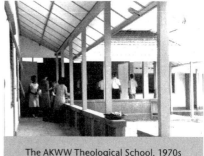

The AKWW Theological School, 1970s

The partners from the Netherlands and MCC were prepared to assist with the rebuilding of AKWW as a coordinating institution for Mennonite theological education for those being prepared as future leaders in the GITJ.

Restructuring the Educational Program

In addition to theological education, it was necessary to begin again organizing and establishing elementary and middle schools, which had been the basis of the work of the Mennonite mission. Attention was given again to redeveloping the educational and health work in the calmer social and political atmosphere.

In 1950, several members of the Pati congregation, R. Suryatna Marchasan, Samuel Hadi Wardojo, Pirenomoelja, Soehadiweko, Simanjuntak and Soedijiono Hardjosoemarto, who became known as the "group of six," felt a burden to build up education as the basis for the service of the GITJ. As a result, they pioneered in establishing the schools known as SMP BOPKRI (*Badan Oesaha Pendidikan Kristen* – Organization for Promoting Christian Education – Middle School).[16] These schools worked together with and got assistance from the BOPKRI Christian school in Yogyakarta. SMP BOPKRI was opened with very simple facilities, using the building that was formerly the Indies Protestant Church. Three years later the school succeeded in buying some land and building a school building with assistance from the Dutch Mennonite Mission and the proceeds from selling a piece of land belonging to the church in Tayu. The school developed well and was then given to the GITJ synod to manage under their Council for Evangelism.

During the years 1955-1957 the GITJ Synod together with the local congregations began opening elementary schools (SD BOPKRI) in Pati and Margorejo, middle schools (SMP BOPKRI) in Kudus, Kayuapu, Pati, Margorejo, Kelet, Kedungpenjalin and Jepara, and a high school (SMA BOPKRI) in Pati. These schools were managed at first by the local congregations and experienced many difficulties, including lack of funding, a shortage of dedicated teachers and inadequate facilities. The middle schools in Kudus and Jepara were finally closed, and the school in Jepara joined with the Jepara Masehi Middle School (another Christian school). The problems of the educational program were discussed repeatedly in the meetings of the GITJ executive board until there was finally an agreement to form a BOPKRI foundation. On November 11, 1959 the first officers were chosen for the BOPKRI board. Since then the responsibility for the educational program has been held by the Synod.

Providing for the needs of the work of the church and also the educational program has not been easy or inexpensive. It has forced the GITJ Synod to depend on financial assistance from foreign friends such as EMEK (European Mennonite Evangelism Committee), and MCC. Unfortunately, this assistance, which should have been temporary, has grown into dependence on foreign assistance. As a result the role of the congregations and the BOPKRI board has been weakened. Some tensions began to appear concerning the matter of foreign assistance and this later played a role in the conflict within the GITJ Synod. In the 1950s and 60s the BOPKRI schools often were the only schools in a community. Later both the government and other private organizations (both nationalist and Islamic) opened schools as well. The increasing government demand for laboratories, libraries and textbooks became a heavy burden for the non-

A hospital in sugar factory buildings, as recalled by Mrs. Armini Djojodihardjo

For years the sugar factory in Pakis/Tayu had been closed. The big houses occupied by the director and staff stood empty. About 1958, the Muria Christian Health Foundation made plans to erect a small emergency hospital for patients with critical needs. Two large houses, connected to each other, were rented. The renovated structure would make a suitable small hospital.

When the renovations were completed, many people, including important officials of the village, were invited to the opening ceremony. The usual speeches were given by the director of the hospital and the head doctor (Marthe Ropp). Because the wives of the village officials could not attend, I was asked to do the ribbon-cutting. Never before or since have I been asked to perform such a duty!

A second event was far more important than this first one: in that same old building I gave birth to our seventh and last child, on May 12, 1959, at exactly noon, assisted by Dr. Friesen and a midwife, Ramun Atmo.

subsidized Christian schools. Therefore several BOPKRI schools had to be closed in recent decades.

Medical Work after 1945

As has been touched on above, medical work also played an important role in the growth of the GITJ. Several hospitals and outpatient clinics which had been confiscated by the Japanese government and not cared for during the time of the war for independence and the "time of plunder," began to receive attention again. The clinics in Pati, Wedarijaksa, Tayu, Kelet and Donorodjo had been taken over by the government. At

The Christian hospital in Tayu, 1980s

the same time the hospitals in Kayuapu, Kedungpenjalin and Margorejo were closed.

MCC, which had already helped in the educational work, was also open to help in the health field. In 1950 MCC began to open clinics in Kayuapu and Margorejo. A year later, MCC sponsored Dr. Marthe Ropp and Sister Liesel Hege from the Mennonite churches in France and Germany. They were seconded to GITJ to assist in forming a Christian health organization in 1954. With support from EMEK and MCC, this organization began to reorganize the health work. The Synod requested without success that the hospital in Kelet, which the Indonesian government had confiscated from the Japanese, be returned. The hospital in Tayu remained closed as well in those early years. However, outpatient clinics were opened in Margorejo, Kayuapu and Kedungpenjalin. In 1958 a small hospital was opened in Pakis (near Tayu) which functioned until the old Tayu hospital was allowed to re-open in 1962. With the help of agencies in Europe and North America, a modern hospital building was built with over 100 beds. In the course of time, a number of Indonesian medical doctors and nurses worked here next to North American and European colleagues. For a long time Dr. Pudjihardjo served as its medical director. Unfortunately, the conflicts within the GITJ during the late 1980s and 90s also affected the hospital. In addition, an Islamic organization opened another hospital about five kilometers from Tayu. And finally, government regulations have become more stringent in recent decades. Therefore, the future of the Tayu hospital is rather insecure.

Development Work

In the 1960s MCC and EMEK began assisting the churches with the goal of achieving full independence by trying to increase their economic independence. In 1967 a Joint Economic Commission (KKEM) was formed as a cooperative effort between the GITJ Synod, GKMI Synod, EMEK and MCC. Willis Sommer, an MCC worker, and Subandi Kernowidjojo, from the GITJ Synod, were appointed as KKEM staff. KKEM's primary responsibility was to think about, study and research the economic situation in the Muria area, and to conduct surveys of projects that could improve the economic situation of the people in the area.[17] The basic reason for the formation of KKEM was to assist the Mennonite churches, GITJ and GKMI, in acquiring funds of their own so that in the future they would be strong enough to stand on their own.

KKEM helped to irrigate forty-four hectares of rice paddy in Jerukrejo by building a dam. For the people of Kalangsari and Margokerto who also experienced drought, KKEM helped by giving loans for water pumps. A rice huller project was carried out in Tlogowungu, Ngemplak Kidul and Gabus with the goal of increasing the number of capable entrepreneurs while serving the needs of the people for milling their rice. KKEM gave loans to the fishermen in Banyutowo, Ujungwatu, Bondo, Jepara, Margorejo, Tayu and Juwana for buying fishing boats. There was also a citrus orchard project in Tlogowungu and a vegetable project in Jollong. In the matter of land transportation, KKEM loaned capital for buying a pick-up, bus and truck in Bangsri and Kudus. In Margorejo Tayu and Margorejo Pati there was a tofu production project. In Welahan and Trangkil there was a sewing machine project that involved giving loans

The "Elim" dam

In the 1970s the Development Committee of the GKMI and GITJ, assisted by MCC and EMEK, was very active in initiating agricultural projects. One of them was building a dam near the village Jerukrejo (Jepara area). This dam, called Elim, facilitated the flow of sufficient water to irrigate an area of 75 acres, which now would have two crops a year. It was anticipated that the dam would hold for ten years. However, the dam is still functioning well today!

for sewing machines, to be repaid in installments, from the income received. A photography project in Kelet was intended, among other things, to provide for the needs of school children and the general public for documentation. There were also some animal husbandry projects, among others, raising cows in Gilimulyo-Jerukrejo, because there were many farmers who needed livestock for preparing the fields for planting. The goal of a goat project in Sambirejo was the same as an ox project in Gilimulyo. A chicken project in Jepara had the goal of training members of the congregation to become good entrepreneurs by loaning them capital in order to raise thoroughbred chickens. Another project was raising pigs in Kedungpenjalin with the goal of preparing superior stock, which would eventually be distributed widely to pig farmers around the Muria. In a project for fattening cows in Langse Pati, KKEM gave cows to be cared for until they were fat enough to resell them at the market. There were also projects for raising coconuts in Ujungwatu, bean seeds for farmers in Tanjungsari and many others.

Unfortunately, the hoped-for strong economic foundation that would contribute to the independence of the church could not be created as had been outlined on paper. The congregations' dependence on aid from the mission organizations had continued for so long and was so strong that it was very difficult to awaken a consciousness of independence in economic matters. This was especially true because people felt that the mission organizations were still very important for carrying on the life of the congregations and obtaining results from their service that they could take pride in. Of course there was an evaluation that said that the board of KKEM was more reactive than pro-active, or that KKEM only functioned in a coordinating role to collect and disperse capital and did not have the courage to control and evaluate. However it is clear that the basis of the relationship that was unequal from the beginning had created a mental attitude of givers and receivers that was difficult to change for everyone involved.

Efforts to collect funds from within the church, such as the "one rupiah" movement and the "ten percent" movement that were set by the twelfth session of the synod in Tayu in 1972 also met obstacles. Every member of the GITJ was expected to contribute one rupiah every month. If the GITJ membership at that time was, according to 1969 statistics, 18,438 baptized members, 6,944 attendees who were not yet baptized, and 18,640 children, then on the average the synod should have received at least 30,000 rupiah each month.[18] In order to encourage this, MCC even agreed to give twice as much, that is, they would contribute two rupiah to the synod for every one rupiah from the churches. Unfortunately this challenge or opportunity to increase the results of the offerings of the congregations did not have the hoped-for results.

The same thing happened when there was an appeal for an offering of ten percent. This was received with various unsympathetic attitudes: many churches and members objected to giving ten percent to the synod. Because many members understood that the synod received assistance from outside, they thought that those who were needy should not give to the synod, but the synod should give to them. Others objected to the church setting a standard for a specific amount for offerings. This was seen as levying a tax. For those who didn't have enough for their daily lives, why should the church levy a tax of ten percent?

In the late 1970s, the foreign partners EMEK and MCC decided to reduce their role in the churches in order to give them more freedom to handle things their own ways. They withdrew from several church-related boards, such as YAKEM. For several reasons, YAKEM had to be disbanded not long after that, though the GITJ continued its work for some years.

Seeds of Dissension

The GITJ congregations grew very quickly until the 1980s and it even seemed that they might pass the limits of the leaders' ability to control them. It can be said that since the missionaries and organizations of the Dutch mission had left Indonesia, the understanding of leadership in the church had become hazy. Soehadiweko Djojodihardjo's leadership of course muffled the fire and even gave direction to the movement toward building up the church nationally and internationally. But serious problems quickly arose when Soehadiweko was no longer the leader of the synod (1983) and when he died (1988). GITJ did not find a leader with charisma equal to his. At the same time the many assets that the mission had left behind blinded many eyes and obscured the values of community that had been built up with such hard work.

In its journey as a local church, several times GITJ experienced testing that culminated in the splitting of congregations. In their life together with other Javanese churches (Christian Church of North Java and Christian Church of South Java), GITJ experienced both a difference of interests and a pull to join together with these two Javanese churches. As mentioned before, in 1949 a representative of the (Reformed) Christian Church of Java had tried in vain to convince the Muria Church to unite with the other Protestant churches of Central Java. In 1952 the Kudus congregation experienced dissension because of differences in doctrine concerning baptizing children. The result of this disagreement was that one part of the Kudus congregation separated itself from the GITJ and joined with the Christian Church of North Central Java.

In addition to outside influences, the attitude of leaders from within could also trigger conflict in GITJ. This happened in Bondo in 1958. The dissension was triggered by the appointment of an evangelist named Barnawi as pastor in Bondo. He was ordained on May 26, 1958 by Rev. Djojodihardjo, as chairman of the GITJ Synod. But his appointment was opposed by several members of the congregation because he did not have formal theological education. As a result, a group of members split from the congregation and held their own worship services. In the end, reconciliation took place.

Conflict and dissension in the local churches such as took place in Bondo also occurred in several other congregations, including Bandungharjo and Blingoh. In the end the result was that the congregation was not reunited but one group separated to form a new GITJ congregation. One of the strongest reasons for this split was that the bonds of the community were weak under a leadership that was also weak. These conflicts were not always handled wisely and quickly by the synod. In fact, the synod body itself also experienced prolonged conflict and dissension.

Conflict and Dissension in the Synod

Conflict in the GITJ Synod rose to the surface in 1989 even though long before that the seeds of conflict had been visible here and there. At the time of the death of Soehadiweko Djojodihardjo in 1988, conflicts that had accumulated came flooding out for the synod leaders in the years 1989-1994. The problem of leadership of the synod and boards had a strong influence on the political tone and ability to mobilize members. The system of regulations, like the "Basic Order and Orders for Implementation," were a means to express truth, but in fact these instruments were not sufficiently complete to respond to the interests of the congregations. Because of that, tension arose between the Synod officers and the officers of the boards of the various institutions. In this

A meeting of the GITJ Synod Board, Pati, 1982

situation, with the systems of regulation incomplete or insufficient to address some problems, many measures were taken outside of the Orders (which of course were not possible to regulate). Subjective interpretations that violated the church order became points of debate that increasingly fertilized the bitter roots of dissension.

The Synod Session became an arena for debate and mutual accusation; within the church groups arose for and against the synod leadership. As a result the sessions came to a halt, and between 1990 and 1995 there were no meetings of the full synod leadership or of the greater synod body as mandated by the rules of basic Synod Order. The synod broke into two, and conflict broke out among the congregations. The number of congregations declined, assets were confiscated by the government and the synod executive committee sold assets. Friends from abroad stopped giving aid and the GITJ was

The GITJ church in
Semarang, 1970s

absent from the fellowship of churches at the national and international levels. The dissension of the GITJ Synod reached a peak in October 1996 in Pati when not all the congregations attended the general Session of the synod. In fact fifty-four churches out of seventy-three that did not attend formed a competing General Session with the agenda of forming an executive committee for a new synod. This larger group met in Margokerto.[19]

The new GITJ Synod (which they called Diponegoro) grew stronger not only because it was supported by fifty-four congregations, but also because of support from the government. As a result, there was no way for GITJ to follow a path of unity.

The effort to rebuild GITJ unity began in the middle of 1998, undergirded by the youth and the church leaders. There were meetings between congregational officials and the synod at Bandungan (Ungaran-Semarang) and as a result of these meetings a decision was made to have meetings between the two GITJ synods' executive committees on July 25, 1998 in Semarang. There was another meeting on July 30. From these meetings some decisions were made, as follows:

a. Agreement to re-unite GITJ.

b. Agreement to work together to resolve the remaining issues.

c. Agreement to form a joint team to carry out points a. and b. This team would consist of four representatives each from the old synod and the challenging synod. In the meantime, several buildings which were owned by the church had been sold by people who were not entitled to do so. That made mediation by a third party necessary.

In this matter Lawrence Yoder played a very meaningful role. Supported by the ADS board in the Netherlands and also by MCC, he repeatedly came to Indonesia to assist the process of unification of the GITJ. The joint team began to work and began to put together a draft of the "Basic Order and Order of Implementation." More important than the church order was the ordering of heart and vision that made possible the joining together of all sides to overcome the past and enable a new beginning. Lobbying, informal and formal meetings filled Lawrence Yoder's agenda when he was in Indonesia in 1999 and 2000.

Division of powers in order to unite the GITJ finally was agreed upon on November 22, 1999. During the transition the new synod would be led by four representatives from each synod. In August 2000 a large meeting was held in order to confirm the agreements and to prepare the agenda for a broad synod gathering in November of the same year. During that synod meeting the two sides were united again. The path toward uniting the GITJ had been long and tiring but finally it bore fruit and GITJ was once again one single body. Much remained to be done and many of the assets or wealth of the church had been sold. So with what resources would the board of the transitional synod and the new synod build the GITJ? With the power and leadership of God's spirit, they began to take steps.

At the time of this writing, the Javanese churches of the Muria are under the care of the united GITJ Synod which has ninety-six mature congregations, 112 branches and five districts (east, west, south,

The church at Kartaraharja, Lampung, South Sumatra, 1970s

north and Sumatra). In the Sumatra district itself there are already ten adult congregations and fifteen branches. These churches in Lampung are the result of proclamation of the Gospel and pastoral care among the thousands of Javanese migrants who went there, especially during the 1970s and 80s. A number of young GITJ pastors served these congregations, some of them for long periods of time. In the first period of this transmigration, the so-called Sumatra Committee, in which MCC played an important role, was very helpful. At the time of this writing, the total number of members is estimated to be about 63,000, including children, while the number of baptized members has reached 3,000. Is this not a proof that God still leads?

Conclusions and Perspectives

In the 1950s the European missionary committee EMEK was formed for the purpose of providing financial support to help the Mennonite congregations in Indonesia become autonomous. The assistance that was given was in the form of additional honoraria for the pastors, evangelists, employees of the GITJ Synod and various forms of assistance to improve the economic situation of the membership. At the same time MCC also gave much assistance for building BOPKRI schools, for AKWW, for funding the medical program and hospital, for buying vehicles and funds for meetings of the synod executive committee. This aid was given to strengthen the foundation of the life of the members so that in the future they would achieve financial independence and self-responsibility. However without real collegiality this assistance created a problematic dependence.

This dependence has been one of the underlying causes of the internal conflict which came to the surface in the 1980s. When the financial aid from abroad dried up, it became difficult to maintain old structures such as schools and a hospital. Another reason may have been that the GITJ has remained a rural church (except for small congregations in Semarang and the university city of Yogyakarta) without a strong international network, and consequently without strong intellectual and administrative leadership. Other rural (or ethnic) churches elsewhere in the Indonesian archipelago face similar problems. Nevertheless, the restored unity and the participation of a new generation of young church leaders are confident signs of a hopeful future.

History of the *Gereja Kristen Muria Indonesia* – GKMI (Muria Christian Church of Indonesia)

The initial contacts between the Chinese community and the Dutch Mennonite mission in Central Java took place indirectly through education and medical care. This is understandable because the goal of the mission in Central Java was evangelism among the Javanese people. In addition there were linguistic and social obstacles that separated Jansz and the Javanese community, which spoke Javanese, from the Chinese community, which spoke Malay. The Dutch evangelist H. C. Klinkert, who was mentioned above, solved the problem of language by marrying a Malay woman and translating the Bible into the Malay language.

Aside from language, there was a social gap that was not easy to bridge. Because the Chinese community was very close-knit, it was not easy for a Chinese person to change religion or culture, and becoming a Christian meant changing one's community and culture. As with the Javanese, it was difficult for Chinese to separate religion or belief from social identity. They understood religion as a part of culture that was passed down from their ancestors. For the Chinese, religion helped them reinforce their identity as Chinese, not the other way around. What we see here is definitely not a matter of doctrine, but of social identity. Toleration toward new teachings or beliefs could happen insofar as they did not threaten the unity and togetherness of the Chinese. Respect for the land of the ancestors and for blood relatives was very high.

The Dawn of Christianity for the Chinese in Kudus

In 1856 the *Genootschap voor In- en Uitwendige Zending* (Society for Evangelism and Mission) in Batavia, in which Mr. Anthing played a role, invited Gan Kwee from Amoy, China, to come to Java as an evangelist. He stayed till 1873 and traveled all over Java. One of his early converts was Khouw Tek San in Purbalingga, who from 1866 on became the initiator of mission among Chinese in Central Java. In 1870 Gan Kwee visited Jepara for one month, but without lasting results. During the first decade of the twentieth century the German-Russian missionary Johann Fast had been looking in vain for a Chinese evangelist to work in the Muria area. Finally in 1913, Yap Boen

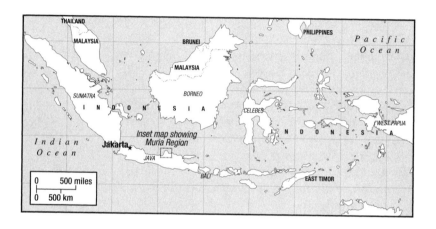

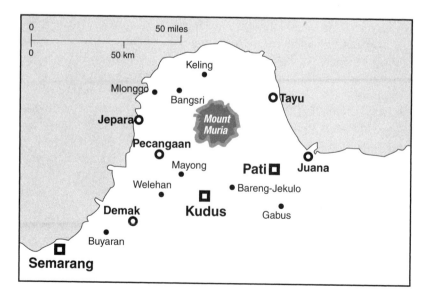

Pho, a *totok* (full-blooded) Chinese from Jepara who did not speak the Malay language, was appointed. He served the mission until 1925, but since most Chinese were *peranakan* (of mixed ethnic origins) his success was limited as well.

An entrepreneur named Tee Siem Tat began the work that led to the founding of the Muria Christian Church of Indonesia in the area served by the DZV mission. Before he became a Christian, Tee and his family were followers of the Confucian religion. Tee's wife, Sie Djoen Nio, was of a very gentle nature. They were blessed with three children, two boys (Tee Yan Poen, Tee Yan Siang) and one girl (Tee Pen Nio). The Tee family was well-known and respected and owned several businesses including an office supply store, an automotive supply store and a printing press.

The seeds of the Gospel began to enter this family when Sie Djoen Nio received a Bible in the Malay language from an aunt who lived in Yogyakarta. Djoen Nio was happy to read the Bible in her free time. At the same time the children were attending a Catholic elementary school. In 1908 the Tee children were baptized as Catholics, and four years later they received catechism instruction and were confirmed. As a tolerant and pragmatic follower of Confucius, Tee did not see this new faith in his family as something to upset his own convictions.

Tee's personal encounter with Jesus Christ happened when Tee and Djoen Nio visited their uncle, Oei Biauw An, in Rembang. Biauw An introduced them to Lieutenant Tanuhatu, a Salvation Army officer serving in Rembang. At that time Tee was suffering from an illness from which he was not recovering. This illness seemed to be caused by a deep restlessness in his soul. He had tried traditional medicines, treatment by traditional healers, the teachers at the temple, and also a doctor of western medicine, all without results. But upon hearing the Gospel and being prayed for, Tee experienced an extraordinary recovery in his soul and body.

There are two possibilities concerning the illness Tee suffered. The first is the bubonic plague (1911) which spread throughout Java causing many deaths.[20] This was followed by the influenza (1918) that attacked almost the entire world. The second possibility was spiritual turmoil caused by economic and political pressures at that time. The years 1900-1927 can be called years of national movements: the appearance of *Tiong Hoa Hwee Koan* (THHK, 1900), an organization with the goal of advancing education, *Boedi Oetomo* (1908), *Sarekat*

Dagang Islam (1909) which later became *Sarekat Islam* (1912), the Islamic organization *Muhammadijah* (1918), the Islamic organization *Nahdatul Ulama* (1920), with several world political flare-ups such as the Russian Revolution in 1905.

These social changes and political upheavals concerned the Dutch Indies government so they re-instituted their policies of playing one

side against another. The Chinese were the target of this policy. As an example, the *Sarekat Dagang Islam* (*SDI*- Union of Islamic Merchants), which was intended to coordinate efforts to promote Islamic trade, clashed with the Chinese amid rumors of trading rivalry. Competi-

Dutch language Chinese school, Kudus

tion in the batik and cigarette businesses in Kudus between Arab and Chinese businessmen had caused conflict which reached a peak on Thursday night, October 31, 1918, which is known as the "affair of the Kudus riots." That night many homes belonging to Chinese in Kudus were plundered and burned by thousands of SDI members who came from places around Kudus such as Mayong, Jepara, Demak and Pati. It was reported that 16 people died.[21] These riots had a traumatic impact on the Chinese. They represented the peak of the anti-Chinese feelings which were already evident in riots in Surabaya and Solo in 1912 and which continue until now.

After becoming acquainted with Christian teachings, Tee experienced changes in his life that made him feel more at peace. His wife and children supported him to the degree that they began to take religious matters very seriously. This common faith within the fam-

ily brought an extraordinary and visible recovery. Tee began to feel at peace, and his restlessness was replaced by an overflowing joy. Lieutenant Tanuhatu, who became his spiritual guide, happily came to Kudus to serve Tee Siem Tat and his family. Tee had found what he had been looking for. He was like a man freed from heavy spiritual shackles. He marked this change one day as he sat in front of his house when a man passed by selling

Tee Siem Tat and
Sie Djoen Nio

birds. Tee bought all fifteen birds in the man's cage

and released them. As Tee recalled this event he said, "Freely you have received, freely give." (Matthew 10:8).

Tee became a power-filled evangelist. He was asked to pray for the daughter of his close friend Sie Giok Goen because she had a serious eye disease. Tee witnessed to his experience and prayed for the daughter. The power of God worked to heal her eyes and his friend's eyes were opened to faith. The whole family of Sie Giok Goen became believers in Christ.

This service which began from a real living witness bore the amazing fruit of repentance. Within a short time Tee had a gathering in his house of a group of Chinese he had won for Christ. Eventually Tee and his group began to look for a church or denomination that could provide support for their experience and faith. They tried to join the Salvation Army, but that didn't work out because the Salvation Army's baptismal ceremony used a flag. According to Tee, this was not biblical. The Adventists approached him, but Tee didn't agree with their teachings about the Sabbath and about food, which he considered too rigid.

The *Salatiga Mission*, an independent missionary organization in Salatiga, some 100 kilometers South of Kudus, visited and served his group several times.[22] But because of the distance and the obstacle of language, the representatives of the Salatiga Mission wrote to the Mennonite Mission (DZV). Nikolai Thiessen then contacted Tee's group. Tee was very happy because Johann Fast was serving in Kayuapu (Kudus) on behalf of the DZV mission.

Tee's group decided to join with the Mennonites, who were similar to the Salatiga Mission. Also the Mennonites were open and ready to serve the Chinese community. Aside from that, Tee and his group found teaching that fit with their beliefs stressing the Bible. Tee began to study Mennonite beliefs including the belief that the Bible was God's word, believer's baptism and a way of life that stressed practical living and peace and rejected violence. The church in Kudus was understood as a community that separated itself from political or government matters but strove to live with values of a liberating love.

Learning from the history of the sixteenth Anabaptist origins, on December 6, 1920 (three years after he had repented), Tee and twenty-five friends (sixteen from Kudus, three from Mayong and three from Tanjung) made their confession of faith and were baptized by Nicolai Thiessen at Tee's home. Membership in the Chinese congregation increased quickly, reaching the areas around Kudus like Tanjung

Karang (five kilometers from Kudus) and Mayong (fifteen kilometers from Kudus). They were known as the "Kudus group."

On September 27, 1925 this Kudus group took the brave step of forming a congregation by choosing candidates for leadership of the church council. They requested permission from the Indies government and two years later, on February 3, 1927, a decision entitled *"Chineesche Doopsgezinde Christengemeente"* was handed down from the governor of the Dutch Indies and acknowledged by Tan King Ien and his secretary Ang Mo Sam. They also made a request to the government that Tee Siem Tat and Oei Tjien Gie be given the right to serve as church leaders in the Semarang Residency (including Jepara and Rembang). This request was granted on August 21, 1927 on the basis of a government regulation no. 177. After that the two of them were acknowledged as the pastors who led the congregation. There is no record that they were ordained as pastors in a church ceremony with the laying on of hands.

The Kudus group itself handled all preparations and requests for permission. They thought that the mission was too slow in pushing them toward autonomy, including in the matter of building a church building. The Javanese congregation at Margorejo had just become autonomous in 1928 and only in 1940 was a Javanese Church Association in the Muria area organized. So in 1926 Tee began trying by himself to gather money to build a church building, after a request for financial assistance from the Mennonite mission was denied by Johann Fast. Tee was of the opinion that it wasn't good for him to request funds from outside his group. What he had started on his own would be finished on his own. Tee sold some land and went around looking for money from members of the congregation and sympathetic Chinese in the Muria area and in several cities. Funds gathered in one year from 110 people amounted to 1,785 guilders, enough to buy a building.[23] The *Chineesche Doopsgezinde Christengemeente* finally owned a church building that was dedicated on February 16, 1928. This attitude of perseverance and independence was much talked about and the GKMI members have continued to be proud of it until the present.

The first meeting house, Kudus, 1928

A good thing happened at the missionary conference on March 20, 1930 at the home of missionary Schmitt, Johann Fast's replacement, when the missionaries discussed who was responsible to serve the Chinese Christians in Jepara, Pati, Juwana and Tayu. They decided that the Chinese congregations in the Semarang residency would be given over to Tee Siem Tat and Oei Tjien Gie. After that the Chinese in the Semarang residency were served by the Kudus congregation.

We should not forget the important role of Mrs. Sie Djoen Nio in propagating the Gospel. Because she often accompanied her husband during his evangelistic traveling, she was able to approach the women in their homes.[24]

Early Leaders of the Jepara Congregation

Tee made a visit to Jepara. Evangelism among the Chinese in Jepara was not easy. One reason was the strength of the organization known as *Tiong Hoa Hwe Koan* (THHK). This Chinese organization carried out religious and educational activities as well as organizing wedding receptions, funerals and burials. Tee's work resulted in winning several Chinese, among them Sie Giok Gian, nephew of Mrs. Sie Djoen Nio. Sie Giok Gian, better known as Gombak Sugeng, was respected in the THHK and served as THHK treasurer in Jepara.

Sie Giok Gian was converted by Tee and baptized on March 26, 1933 together with Thio Wie Jaw, Thio Gwan Sioe, Sie Lian Ing and Mrs. Sie Lian Ing. Two weeks after the first baptism eighteen people participated in a communion service. The work of the Holy Spirit was increasingly felt among the Chinese community as many people believed and were baptized. On July 23, 1934, fourteen people were baptized and on October 22, 1934, there were nine more. Three baptismal services were held in the Chinese Mennonite Church in Kudus which was served by Tee Siem Tat.

The first worship service at the home of Tio Ging Am on September 10, 1932, was attended by twenty-two men. Worship was once a month. It was held in homes and moved around from place to place. After several of these services, Sie Giok Gian had a vision while he was praying during the service. In this vision there was a *hio lo* (incense burner or place for the ashes of the ancestors where followers of Confucius worshipped) with another *hio lo* coming out of it. He interpreted that this meant that they would get a place of worship.

They obtained an old elementary school on the Post Office Street, now called Yos Sudarso Street. The building, which measured 7 by 21 meters, was repaired with corrugated iron sheeting (*seng*) so it is known as the "*seng* church." Dedication of the church building was on December 22, 1933, at 10 a.m. On July 1, 1954, this church building was renovated, and it was dedicated on December 22, 1954. This church building is still in use, and it has been renovated several times.

Opposition and pressure from Chinese in Jepara toward the Chinese Christians increased. Christian children in the THHK school experienced pressure. Some of the leaders of THHK were unhappy because this meant a decline in their membership since Christians didn't want to pay a required donation for religious ceremonies in Klenteng. Chinese Christians began to be ostracized from the Chinese community in Jepara. They were not allowed to borrow wedding and burial equipment. They didn't have the right to receive donations of money when family members died. In spite of opposition, the Christian congregations grew. Sie Giok Gian as well as other brothers and sisters visited from house to house to tell about the love of Jesus. God endowed Sie Giok Gian with the gift of healing and driving out evil spirits. He prayed for the sick and they were healed. "This is an advertisement for God," he said in his straightforward way.

Two stories from many miracles performed by Sie Giok Gian (Gombak Sugeng) can be told. One day he left home, heading toward Untung Suropati Street without realizing where he was going. He saw a house surrounded by many people and he asked what was hap-

Sie Giok Gian and his wife in Jepara

pening. He was told, "Demas Parni is in agony. He's about to die and people are already swarming around. All the neighbors are coming to pay their respects." Sie Giok Gian went into the room where Parni was lying. He uncovered him and greeted Parni who mumbled without turning toward him. Pastor Sie Giok Gian thought there was still a possibility of reaching him so he left the room to think about what to do. If water that is so clear (spiritual) couldn't enter his body, what is clearer (more spiritual) than water that could reach him? He thought of smoke so he lit a cigarette and puffed on it while he walked back into Parni's room. He said, "Parni." Parni answered "Heh." "I'm smoking a cigarette and I want you to puff on it as hard as you can. I'll stick it in your mouth and if you can puff smoke, tomorrow you'll be healed and can go back to work." He stuck the cigarette in Parni's mouth and he puffed as hard as he could till he started coughing. "Well, I prayed for you and tomorrow you'll be recovered and get up out of bed," he said. And the next morning Parni got up and said he was recovered. And he was totally recovered. It was a miracle that someone who was in agony and about to die was restored to health. All those who were coming to bring rice, sugar, coffee and other things for the funeral were amazed. When asked why he had to use a cigarette, Sie Giok Gian answered that he needed smoke in order to reach Parni. Think of it: for a week he hadn't been able to swallow water, let alone eat rice.

Sie Giok Gian had a little sundries shop that was always full of customers. His wife was irritated because he was always going out to do evangelism and she grumbled. "You're just hanging out, chatting here and there and the shop is full of customers and I don't have enough help." Then Rev. Sie Giok Gian said, "Be careful what you say. I'm doing God's work of evangelism. God will punish you and make your mouth crooked." Right after that his wife's mouth went crooked. She repented and he prayed and her mouth recovered.

On January 17, 1935, the Jepara church council made a request to the Dutch Indies Governor General in Batavia to get notarized recognition as a legal body known as the *Chineesche Doopsgezinde Christengemeente*. Sie Giok Gian was appointed as pastor in 1936.

Early Leaders of the Pati Congregation

There were leaders of the Chinese congregations in Pati and other areas in the Semarang residency as well as in Jepara. In Pati, for example, the group of Chinese Christians that had been started by Ambonese evangelist Leonard Silalily grew under the leadership of Tee and his friends. The work of the Mennonite mission in Pati and Juwana didn't grow because Leonard Silalily served both the Javanese community in Pati and also the Dutch Indies Church. The Chinese Christians felt that they didn't have a place where they fit because the Javanese congregations used the Javanese language, and in the Indies Church they didn't feel at home because they didn't get satisfactory attention and nurture. The efforts of Tee Siem Tat, Lie Liang Tjwan, Sie Tjien

Hay and Oie Tjien Gie were well received. Several Pati Chinese felt comfortable worshipping in Kudus and serving in the Kudus congregation.[25] But because of the distance between Kudus and Pati, they were advised to begin looking for a place to worship in Pati. Yap Tiang Hwat from Tlogowungu (5 kilometers from Pati or 30 kilometers from Kudus) responded and managed to find a place in a former cigarette factory, "Mintek" owned by Kwa Jan Tan.

Five people attended the first worship service led by Tee Siem Tat in 1935. This first congregation in Pati was very mission-minded and they energetically visited Chinese families in Pati to tell the good news and invite them to gather at a worship service for Chinese people every Sunday evening. One year later the Pati congregation had grown to twenty people and the worship was moved to the home of Sie Tiang Diwan. In 1938 the worship service was moved to the home of Kho Djoen Hong, until they finally got a donation of land from Ms. Nelly Tan.

"Mother" Nelly Tan

The existence of the Pati congregation cannot be separated from the role of Nelly Tan, a woman who loved the Lord very much. She was a part of Leonard Silalily's congregation which later joined with the work that was started by Tee Siem Tat; she was baptized in 1936. She remained single in order to fully give herself in service for evangelism. She was a team leader of the Pati branch of the Java Christian Evangelistic Band. This organization carried out a mission of bringing well-known preachers such as John Sung who was known as the "torch of Asia," from China to Indonesia in 1937 and 1939.

The Kudus and Pati congregations also brought Dzao Sze Kwang from China for evangelistic services. Mother Nelly rented the Union theater building and Dzao Sze Kwang preached three times a day for one week. As a result many Chinese heard the Gospel and believed in Christ. As a continuation of Dzao Sze Kwang's service, he left behind his interpreter, Job S. Liem, to shepherd the Pati congregation from 1939 until 1941.

Although not in a formal sense, Nelly Tan was the "mother" of the Pati congregation. Even in the matter of building the church, her service was commendable. As a seller of batik cloth she had limited means, but she bought a piece of land (formerly a place of

prostitution and gambling) in order to
donate it to the church. With a strong
commitment she collected contributions
by visiting twenty five cities in Central
and East Java.[26] Mrs. Tee Siem Tat laid the
cornerstone in December 1940 and the
building was officially dedicated on June
2, 1940 with the name *Tiong Hoa Kie Tok
Kauw Hwe Pati.*

Dedication of the church at Pati,
June, 1940

After the church building was finished,
Nelly Tan sold her house in Cirebon in order to build a house on the
north side of the church building in 1950. She also included in her will
that when God called her, the home she lived in would be given to the
church with the understanding that it was to be a home for the pastor
who served the Pati church. Nelly Tan was very precise and prepared
everything. She had even prepared money to pay the fees for her own
burial and all the necessary equipment including her coffin.

Nelly Tan returned to the Lord on April 7, 1978 at the age of 92.
Just before her death, she asked to be moved to a room in the front
of the house that looked out on the street. She said, "I want to see
the way." This statement left an impression on the Pati congregation
because Nelly Tan to the end of her life was the way to the Lord. And
now when death was approaching she still wanted to see the way, the
direction in which she would see the people who were heading to the
house of the Lord.

Broadening the boundaries of Territory and Ethnicity

Tee Siem Tat began to see urban mission among the Chinese as the
point of departure for his service. After Kudus, Jepara and Pati, he
also served small cities or areas around Mount Muria, such as Tanjung
Karang, Bangsri, Welahan and Demak. Demak which had been served
by the Salatiga Mission requested to join with the Chinese Mennonite
Christian Community in Kudus on January 10, 1941, and on the following April 20, Demak was received into the Muria circle.

Tee began to develop his work across ethnic lines. He wrote a letter
in the name of the Kudus Mennonite Church to four Mennonite missionaries to request that the Kudus Church be given responsibility for
service to the Chinese, Ambonese, Menadonese and Javanese within
the boundaries of the Semarang residency. However, the Mennonite

mission did not agree with Tee's view and replied that they expected Tee to work only with the Chinese.

This disagreement between the Mennonite mission and the Kudus Chinese Mennonite congregation resulted in Tee separating himself from ties to the mission by declaring his independence in effort and funding. There were five reasons for doing this. First, it was difficult for Tee to have to report to Herman Schmitt who was still young. Second, he didn't agree with moving Javanese from the Chinese church to Schmitt's services. Third, Schmitt's presence in Kudus with good facilities showed that the mission had money so they wondered why it wasn't used for the Chinese congregation. Fourth, the Chinese congregation had developed on its own, including developing its assets, but still had to be under the umbrella of the mission. Fifth, Tee was aware that dividing the church along ethnic lines was not biblical, and thought that dividing the work according to territory could be better justified. Of course if the Chinese congregation could stand on its own, why did it have to be under the authority of the mission? Especially if the relationship wasn't based on a good mutual understanding, then separation was just a matter of time.

The Situation during the Pacific War

Tee Siem Tat died on October 2, 1940, leaving eight congregations in the Muria area as the fruits of his labor: Kudus, Tanjung, Mayong, Jepara, Bangsri, Welahan, Pati and Demak. He was replaced by his children and their spouses. As his death approached, Tee called his

sons Tee Yan Poen[27] and Tee Yan Siang with his son-in-law Tan King Ien who had been ordained as a pastor in 1936. According to a personal communication by Tan Hao An (Herman Tan) Tee's final message to his children and their spouses was "Feed my lambs" (John 21:15).[28] Tan King Ien together with Tee Yan Poen replaced Tee Siem Tat as shepherd of the Kudus congregation and also served the Chinese congregations around Mt. Muria.

The Chinese congregations gathered in 1941 to form a fellowship called the Muria Classis (or District) led by Tan King Ien. The need to form a regional structure showed the importance of

The church in Kudus, dedicated in 1941

communication and networking between the Chinese Mennonite congregations in the Muria area, especially because during these years the social, economic and political situation in Indonesia was not stable. On March 2, 1942, the Japanese landed on the coast at Rembang. The power of the colonial Dutch was replaced by Japanese domination from 1942 until Japan was defeated by the Allies in 1945.

The anti-Christian and anti-Chinese fundamentalist Muslim movement that rose up in Java affected the Tayu, Tanjungkarang, Juwana, Godong and Mayong congregations, among others. The situation was very traumatic for Chinese and Christians in the Muria area. Because of Chinese fleeing from these places, the Christian community experienced a drastic decline, especially the Juwana, Godong and Mayong churches, which eventually disappeared. The Tayu congregation tried to survive with supportive visits and financial aid from other Muria Chinese congregations.

The beginning of the GKMI congregation in Welahan (between Kudus and Jepara), recalled by Brother Partawiguna.

When pastor Tee Siem Tat came to evangelize, after Nkong Tjwa Eng Lim (at that time a local Confucian leader who later became a Christian) had agreed, the servants of the *klenteng* (the Confucian temple) became angry. They feared losses of income because they received a fee from all those people who came to the temple to ask for medicine or blessings or solving other problems. … So, when Tee Siem Tat and his helpers came by car, these temple servants started throwing stones at the car. However, Tee Siem Tat showed no anger, nor did he go to the police. The next Sunday, he brought along loaves of breads wrapped in paper. When the temple servants prepared to throw stones, Tee Siem Tat replied by throwing bread to them. Surprised, they stopped throwing stones! When they asked why he threw bread instead of stones, pastor Tee answered: "the Mennonite teaching tells us that we have to repay violence by doing well."

The Birth of the Muria Classis

After the war and the Indonesian declaration of independence on August 17, 1945, the formation of a district structure was one solution for uniting and caring for the community that had been threatened with being torn apart and scattered because of the cruel treatment they had experienced. On April 18-22, 1948 there was a meeting of the Chinese congregations in the Muria area to formalize the administrative structure that organized their Muria Association or Classis. The first article of the church order made during this meeting in 1948 was,

> Mennonite Church: *Tiong Hwa Kie Tok Kauw Hwee*. The Muria Classis is an association of Chinese Christian churches that is made up of members of Chinese Christian congregations in

Kudus, Jepara, Mayong, Pati, Bangsri, Welahan, Demak, Tanjung and other congregations not named here.

This meeting is considered the first session of the Muria Classis and at that time the Chinese congregations of the Muria area entered a new phase in their organization. They became independent and they began to distance themselves from the Mennonite mission. Also the political situation had changed. Several Dutch terms were replaced with Chinese, such as *Kerkeraad* or church council which became *tong hwee*. Classis became *khu hwee*.

The district structure *(khu hwee)* would play an important role in the growth of the Muria Chinese churches in the time that followed. All decisions that involved their life together would be discussed and formalized at the district assemblies. In 1958 the name Chinese Mennonite Christian Church became Muria Christian Church of Indonesia *(Gereja Kristen Muria Indonesia or GKMI)*. The name change became important in view of changes at that time. Using Chinese terms was not to their benefit, given the strong Indonesian spirit of nationalism which was accompanied by anti-Chinese feeling. The Muria Chinese churches had to change and become open beyond the limits of ethnic Chinese. The Chinese congregations in Kudus and surrounding areas were very conscious of this and tried to expand their service beyond the limits of ethnicity and territory. Also many Chinese were forced to use Indonesian family names from that time onward.

Awakening of the Muria Chinese Christian Congregations

The four clearest signs of the reawakening of the Muria Chinese Christian Congregations were first, the presence of young people ready to be prepared for service in the church. In 1946 the Kudus congregation began to send young people to study at the theological school in Yogyakarta. In December 1946 Sie Soen Jang and Goei Peng Djien were sent to study there and after that others from other Muria congregations followed. Then Tan Hao An (Herman Tan) studied at the Theological Seminary in Jakarta, and with the agreement of and financial assistance from MCC he continued his studies in America. The young generation who had theological education later assumed positions of leadership during the time of GKMI growth and development. Matters connected with the mechanics of work, style of worship, foundation of faith, basic structure, and even the publishing of a magazine and theological books equipped the GKMI to become an independent church ready to carry the Gospel to all corners of Indonesia.

Second, Pastor Sudarsohadi Notodihardjo was appointed as the first Javanese pastor to serve the Chinese congregation in Kudus. This was consistent with the path of Tee and those who followed him that the Kudus congregation's vision of service was not limited to one ethnic group but crossed lines of ethnicity and geography. Pastor Sudarsohadi was accepted not just as an assistant but as a valued pastor, and in 1960 he was chosen Secretary of the Muria Indonesia synod. Since that time, GKMI could not be called a strictly Chinese church but had opened up to a variety of ethnic and other groups.

Sudarsohadi Notodihardjo (r) is appointed pastor at Kudus

Third, by changing the name "Chinese Christian Mennonite Church" to "Muria Christian Church of Indonesia" in 1958, the names of the local congregations became Muria Christian Church of (city or area) and the Muria Classis or *khu hwee* became the Synod of the Muria Christian Churches of Indonesia. This was according to the advice of the leaders of the Classis. Because there were some people who didn't agree with this name change, an emergency session of the Classis was held on January 31, 1958 at the Jepara Church. At this meeting it was decided that the Chinese-language named Muria Classis should become Synod of the Muria Christian Churches of Indonesia, or Muria Indonesia Synod for short. Tan Hao An (Herman Tan) was chosen as chairman at that time. The new name was accepted officially by the government in 1965.

The fourth sign of an awakening was the development of the Basic Principles of Christian Faith which contained 20 articles. Herman Tan had formulated these principles as his thesis when he was studying at Goshen Biblical Seminary in Goshen, Indiana under the leadership of H. S. Bender. These principles grew out of the need to calm the disturbance in the Kudus congregation related to the conflict among the leadership (which had been going on for a long time) between pastor Tan King Ien and Pastor Liem Liong Tjoen. This conflict impacted the Synod and the unity of the Muria Chinese congregations at that time. The conflict came to a head when pastor Liem Liong Tjoen (whose background was in the Presbyterian GKI church) attempted to join the

Muria Chinese congregations with Chinese congregations in Central Java that had joined together with the GKI Synod. This was strongly opposed by Herman Tan. In one debate at a church council meeting at the Kudus congregation, Pastor Liem Liong Tjoen said, "Brother Herman always waves the Mennonite flag. The Muria Church is small. It would be better to merge with the GKI churches Chinese classis. The Muria church doesn't have money for pensions; the Muria church doesn't have a Bible school."[29] He also stated that the members of the church council had already agreed to join together with the GKI Synod which was in the Reformed tradition. We have to keep in mind that similar discussions occurred among Javanese churches as well. It was clearly a time in which ecumenical unity seemed to be necessary.

The tension was resolved by a discussion between two women participants in the above discussion, Mrs. Liem Liong Tjoen and Mrs. Herman Tan. Mrs. Liem said: "What if all the members of the Kudus church would agree to join together with the GKI?" Mrs. Tan answered, "All the members who agreed to join [GKI] would have to leave the Kudus Church building. The Kudus Church is Mennonite, not *Gereformeerd* or *Hervormd*."[30] The meeting ended tensely. And after that, Herman Tan published the Basic Principles of Christian Faith as the basis of faith for the Muria Christian Synod of Indonesia. It was similar in many ways to the Confession of Faith of the Mennonite Church (1921, Garden City, Missouri) and Herman Tan had consulted H. S. Bender in Goshen about

Herman Tan and his wife
Pouw Joe Nio

it. During a meeting on January 31, 1958, representatives of all nine congregations signed their names attesting to their loyalty to GKMI and to these principles of faith. In March 1959, Pastor Liem Liong Tjoen stepped down after serving the Kudus congregation for eight years.

The Earliest Conception of Theological Ideas

There were various theological ideas that undergirded the earliest GKMI movement. Tee Siem Tat's conception was not easy to define, as he picked a verse from Mark 16:16 to justify most of his teachings: "Whosoever believes and is baptized will be saved, but whoever does not believe will be condemned." He added a generic closing remark, "Anyone who listens should understand!"

For Tee and also for the Chinese people, salvation was very important both in the present and after death. Therefore, Tee stressed an understanding of life after death. He visited Chinese people and described to them the conditions for eternal salvation. He mentioned several steps on the stairway to heaven. First, he insisted that one should repent and turn away from his or her sins. Second, one should seek divine intervention from Jesus alone. Faith in His name was the key to salvation. Third, one should dwell in Jesus' presence practicing solemnity and prayer in order to enjoy shalom and His blessings which last into eternity. Fourth, one should be baptized as an adult as a public proclamation of one's faith in Jesus and a true sign of commitment and regeneration. Baptism was not cheap. It was not automatically conferred on anyone in a church as a formal act. One should humble oneself before God, asking for His mercy and pardon for sins as the beginning of a serious penitential life. Catechism was a must. Readiness to suffer worldly persecution (including mockery and exclusion from the rest of society) should be stated publicly before the congregation. "Costly baptism" was part of the identity of GKMI.

The Scripture, in Tee Siem Tat's tradition, was upheld as a moral cornerstone. In his view, the manifestations of true Christianity were as follows:

- A church should not conduct businesses in any form.
- No bowing to a coffin (this was a respected tradition among non-Christian people of Chinese descent)
- A rich man should share part of his wealth with the needy.
- No gender division, especially in the context of lay ecclesiastical participation
- No participation, agreement or support for warfare
- Ready to help anyone, including enemies

All of these principles were written in many separate booklets. They were principles of faith jotted down in practical sub-points. You may do this, you must do that, you should never do this, etc. They were indeed non-systematic, and many divergent interpretations arose.

The Articles of Faith set by Herman Tan

The twenty articles of faith adapted in 1958 replaced the principles prepared by the previous generation, i.e. Siem Tat's generation. In these basic principles of faith there were four that were stressed by Herman Tan, that is, a private relationship with God, evangelism, biblical authority, and departing from normally accepted attitudes.

Personal relationship with God. A close relationship with God is understood from a practical-spiritual viewpoint, not from a theoretical-physical one. Joy in the assurance of salvation is manifested in daily behavior where one is continually inspired by the Holy Spirit. Laypersons are worthy to serve various ecclesiastical ministries. They have opportunities for participation equal to the pastors. Regeneration of one's life is clearly apparent. Sensuous human nature is replaced by a thirst for His presence. A believer receives the Holy Spirit which has power to cleanse one's sins. Sanctity requires a conscious and continuous effort by the believer. The flame of the Spirit should be kept alive. The Holy Spirit moves a believer to pray, learn and interpret the Bible, and to witness to the saving grace of the Lord to "others who are jailed by the profane world and doomed to hell." Devotion, sanctity and purity are the internal conditions for perfection in Christ. Baptism and the Lord's Supper are given utmost consideration. A believer should take part in those rituals, in spite of their "outward" nature. The steps to be followed by a believer are: repentance, confession of faith and regeneration. Until these three conditions are fulfilled, one should not take part in the ritual of baptism.

Diligent evangelism, to reach new areas. The divine command as explained in Matthew 28:19-20 should be carried out in real life in one's individual context. A concern for practical evangelism should be among the basic concerns of the church. A church is defined as a communion among *disciples* (not saints). The sense of discipleship is strong here. The main task of the church are to tell others about the grace of salvation offered by the merciful God for all nations, and to make them His disciples. Furthermore, the church must testify to Christ's peace among the disciples. This testimony is an integral part of salvation. Disciple-like obedience to Christ should be manifested in inner changes and transformation. The "experiential" spirituality and acceptance of His teaching would be self-evident in a deep motivation to yield and follow the lead of Jesus and to carry His cross.

Biblical authority. Ultimate truth is based on the Bible. The Scripture is trusted to settle many problems for the individual and the congregation. Morality and ethics are based on Scripture. The root is Anabaptist. Some practical rules of conduct that need to be obeyed are: don't get drunk, don't wear over-stylish fashions, don't wear glamorous accessories, don't dance like heathen, don't hate anyone including one's enemies, don't defile your body, and many other prohibitons. But most of all, one should put his or her trust solely in the Bible and not in human teachings. The Holy Spirit's interpretation in one's heart should take priority over other forms of interpretation, even those delivered in sermons by educated clergy.

First edition of the Articles of Faith

Nonconformity to the World. Becoming a Christian should be "abnormal," i.e. one should be able to discern the difference between God's will and human will. The will of God is unchallenged, and with a free will the believer should always choose to glorify the name of Jesus by obeying all rules of conduct set by the Bible. When a brother or sister in Christ trespasses, the congregation should admonish or rebuke him or her with brotherly love. This is not solely a form of punishment, but on the contrary, is an invitation to purify oneself before re-entering congregational life. Exclusion is the gravest measure. Through discipline the members will see that they are different, separated from the world. However this does not mean that the "community of heaven" only cares about divine and holy things. It also mourns and weeps for the profanity of the world, and prays to God to save the worldly people "who march to hell."

Faith should manifest itself in many practical situations: separation from worldly matters, refraining from politics, refusing to enter civil service positions. A true, pietistic Christian should not interfere in any state affairs or join any political parties, particularly refraining from involvement in the military. Pacifism should reign as the basic principle in the life of the congregation. The only appropriate involvement for a Christian in government should be to pray for the well being of his or her country.

Widening the Area and the Network

Beginning in 1958, the leadership of GKMI shifted from the Kudus congregation (as the mother church) to the leaders of the GKMI synod. Replacing the classis with the synod structure raised many questions about leadership. In the seventh session of the synod in Jepara, January 20-21, 1960, it was decided that an executive committee was not necessary. Instead a six-person presidium was formed. This presidium chose one person to be chairman only when it was in session. This decision calmed fears that the power of the GKMI leadership was located in the Tee or Tan families. Pastor Soedarsohadi Notodihardjo, the Javanese pastor who served the GKMI Kudus congregation, was chosen to replace the temporary presidium chairman, Pastor Liem Liong Tjoen. Soedarsohadi stepped down due to health reasons in 1962, and the synod leadership returned to the former model whereby there was an executive committee. During the time of Herman Tan's leadership there were many positive new initiatives by the synods, including a new liturgy, building up the capacity of the staff through private courses, publishing a church magazine, using the perspective of the youth, developing a vision for work in Jakarta and the establishment of a board for evangelism and service (PIPKA), and the establishing of a network of relationships both within the country and abroad.

It can be said that at the same time that the church structure was reorganized to become a synod, the GKMI was not growing as quickly as it had in the first 20 years. This was definitely connected with the social and political changes that caused social disturbances between the years 1940-1950. And within the time frame of those ten years, the model of personal evangelism as exemplified by Tee in Kudus, Giok Gian in Jepara and Tan Nelly in Pati had moved to a model of spiritual revival worship with evangelists who were famous both within and outside the country. This model became more prominent beginning in the nineteen fifties into the seventies. At the same time the number of churches opening other churches began to decrease. From 1940 to 1960 there were only five churches that came to maturity: Tayu, Blora, Pecangaan, Semarang and Mlonggo. Tayu and Blora did not arise from within GKMI but rather joined the GKMI in 1951. Besides these five churches there were also several small fellowships in the vicinity of GKMI. These fellowship groups among others were in Keling, Tanjungkarang, Jekulo, Juwana, Gabus, Winong, Buyaran, Mlonggo and Sukodono.

Semarang

From the perspective of the movement to open new churches, the fellowship in Semarang that was started by GKMI Jepara was a strategic effort. The city of Semarang is the capital of Central Java with a promising future. Many inhabitants of the rural areas around Semarang sought their fate in Semarang including many GKMI youth in the area around Mt. Muria. The GKMI leaders in the Muria area were aware of that. Pastor Herman Tan and several other GKMI leaders saw that GKMI had to move quickly into Semarang if they did not want to be left behind by the youth. So they discussed who would be given the responsibility to open a fellowship in Semarang. The congregation that was the closest to Semarang was GKMI Demak, followed by Kudus. But in view of the fact that these two congregations were experiencing some internal problems, the responsibility to open a fellowship in Semarang was entrusted to GKMI Jepara.

GKMI Jepara in turn gave the responsibility to Djwa Sin Gie (Paulus Singgih Djajadihardja) to coordinate the opening of the fellowship in Semarang. Djwa, who was already known to the leaders of the Chinese

The Youth Camp movement, initiated by Herman and Jo Tan in 1956, yielded amazing fruit over the next 15 years recruiting new church leadership candidates. Pictured are the participants in the 1969 Youth Bible Camp.

Christian churches in Semarang, began to approach these churches as well as members of GKMI who lived in or had moved to Semarang. Djwa did these two tasks very well and the opening of the GKMI fellowship in Semarang did not cause any problems and was supported by the Chinese churches in Semarang.

The opening of the GKMI Jepara branch in Semarang took place on February 23, 1958 at the home of Sie Tiang Djwan. About 150 persons attended the opening worship service. There were representatives from the GKMI churches and from Chinese Christian churches in Semarang. This Jepara branch in Semarang developed satisfactorily. By 1959 it had

Djwa Sin Gie

fulfilled the conditions to become an independent church and became the tenth member congregation of the GKMI synod. The first five members of the congregation were baptized on April 24, 1960.

After moving several times, the Semarang church finally purchased its own place of worship, at 75 Pemuda Street. All the congregation's activities were officially moved to the new place on December 31, 1968. This place of worship has since been renovated at least five times.

The congregation grew in membership and in the number of activities. GKMI Semarang was blessed by God with the presence of many youth from the area around Mt. Muria who were very motivated to spread the Gospel and open new churches. Among them were many who became church leaders in GKMI or other churches. The missionary spirit to spread the news of the Gospel of the kingdom of God was carried out with great joy as they opened church branches in a variety of ways. GKMI Semarang has founded no less than six other congregations. The first was the GKMI Semarang branch in Salatiga, started in 1968 and declared an independent congregation in 1978. In the Semarang area itself four branches were founded which later developed into independent congregations: Lamper Mijen (1968, independent in 1981), Tanah Mas (1984, independent in 1990 as GKMI Gloria Patri), Sompok (1988, independent in 1995 as GKMI Sola Gratia), Progo (from 1973 on, independent in 1996) and Sidodadi (1980, independent on 2006). Finally, the Semarang branch in Yogyakarta was adopted by PIPKA in 1991 and became independent in 1998.

Aside from the branches which have become independent congregations, GKMI Semarang still has at least three branches which haven't become independent congregations yet. All in all, the present membership of the Semarang congregations is 850 members.

Establishment of the Foundation for Missions and Charities (Pengutusan Injil dan Pelayanan Kasih – PIPKA)

On May 15, 1965, Herman Tan, Tio Tjien Swie and Sie Djoen An, with the help of a notary, created a foundation for evangelism and service called Foundation for Missions and Charities (PIPKA). Three days later at the tenth session of the Synod, this foundation was officially turned over to the Muria Synod Commission for Evangelism. The

birth of PIPKA was influenced by the awakening of the GKMI youth through spiritual
revival services and youth camps which were
held for the first time in 1955. Youth who
were influenced by these Bible camps, among
others, were Sie Djoen An (Andreas Setiawan),
Sie Kiem Dong (Mesakh Krisetya), Tan Ing
Tjoe (Charles Christano), Albert Widjaja,
Yahya Chrismanto, Yesaya Abdi and Andreas
Christanday. In the years 1965-1975 many
forms of service were created by the GKMI

The founders of PIPKA (l to
r): Sie Djoen An (Andreas
Setiawan), Herman Tan and
Tio Tjien Swie

youth such as the music team All For Christ (which has become the
Christopherus Foundation); the non-profit Christian radio station
Alpha Omega (which changed its name to Radio Ichthus); Founda-
tion Sie Djoen Nio (the Dorcas Foundation); *Keluarga Sangkakala* (The
Last Trumpet Family), the forerunner of the church body JKI (*Jemaat
Kristen Indonesia*) and various others.

The Commission for Evangelism (1956), created by the synod
because of the enthusiasm of the youth for
evangelism, was not able to fulfill their aspira-
tions for carrying the Gospel to all corners of
Indonesia. There was criticism of the synod's
Commission for Evangelism in that it had been
formed to serve the churches internally with
spiritual revival services or lectures and seminars on mission. It was thought that a mission
organization was necessary for telling the good
news of the Gospel directly to many people and
ethnic groups who were not yet believers and
establishing churches in areas that could not be
reached by GKMI. For that reason they established PIPKA. Through PIPKA it was hoped that
the service of GKMI would become holistic with
PI meaning *Pengutusan Injil* (mission of evangelism – Romans 3:23, 6:23, John 3:16) and PKA

The leader of the Jepara church
since the beginning of that
congregation is brother Sio
Giok Gian. He owns a grocery
store, and has 12 children of
whom the youngest son is
now studying at the Baptist
Seminary in Semarang, Java.
Pastor Sie had only a 4th grade
elementary education, but God
has used him as His instrument.
Many Jepara church members
and also non-Christians have
felt the power and love of God
because they were healed
miraculously through the
prayers of brother Sie, who
obviously has received the gift
of healing.

meaning *Pelayanan Kasih* (service of love – Matthew 25: 31-46).

At the time of the birth of PIPKA in June 1964, the mission of
broadening the area of service and evangelism beyond Mt. Muria
had already been accomplished. At that time the Synod's Commis-

Herman Tan baptizes the first
believers in Surakarta

sion on Evangelism had begun a fellowship in Surakarta which was known as the Surakarta mission. After the birth of PIPKA, the Surakarta mission was handed over to PIPKA. In addition to Surakarta, they also pioneered the Jakarta mission at the end of 1965, exactly at the time Pastor Tan Hao An decided to leave Central Java to establish GKMI in Indonesia's capital, Jakarta. In 1967 Tan Hao An stepped down as Chairman of the GKMI synod demonstrating the seriousness of his intention to give more attention to the development of the church in Jakarta.

The first church in Jakarta became the focus and beginning basis for PIPKA's work to carry out the mission "Go into all the world and preach the good news to all creation." (Mark 16:15) Herman Tan, who saw great potential for service in Tan Ing Tjioe (Charles Christano), urged Charles to continue his studies at the Jakarta Divinity School (STT Jakarta). Tan hoped that Charles Christano would reach the GKMI youth who had migrated to Jakarta to continue their studies or to work.

Charles
Christano

Herman Tan and Charles Christano began their work by gathering together the young people. In less than one year on April 17, 1966, they began a fellowship with seventeen youth in attendance. Within three years this fellowship grew to seventy people. When Charles Christano and his wife left to continue his studies at the Disciples Training Centre in Singapore and Pastor Herman Tan left Indonesia to go to the USA, Pastor Sie Tjoen An (Andreas Setiawan) was designated to serve and care for the GKMI fellowship in Jakarta.

Andreas Setiawan arrived in Jakarta in April 1970 with great enthusiasm. The fellowship, located in Matraman, became independent with the name of GKMI Jakarta on March 17, 1971. This was the first fruit of the efforts of PIPKA after five years of work. At this time, PIPKA handed over the congregation with pride to the GKMI Synod. This was the beginning of the growth of PIPKA both in the Jakarta area and several other islands of Indonesia.

Leaders in the Work of the GKMI Churches in Jakarta

The development of the work in Jakarta became one of the cutting edges in the further development of GKMI after Kudus and Semarang. Within four years the number of members in the Jakarta congregation reached 130. Not only did the numbers increase, but the spread of new churches was also a cause for rejoicing. In 1974 a new fellowship in the area of Cempaka Putih Barat opened with about thirty people attending. Within three years the number at Cempaka Putih reached 120. Because the congregation at Matraman did not grow but actually declined in numbers, the place of worship for GKMI Jakarta was moved to 23 Cempaka Putih Barat Street, while the place of worship in Matraman became a mission post. Moving the congregation was followed by changing the name of GKMI Jakarta to GKMI Cempaka Putih in 1986. This change was made anticipating that the use of the name Jakarta implied that there was only one GKMI congregation in Jakarta. By that time there were already many other GKMI churches opening in Jakarta.

Enthusiasm for mission among the youth grew as did PIPKA's support of the work, and there was a longing to win the city of Jakarta. A new work in Kalibaru began in 1967 which became an independent congregation seven years later. At the same time meetings started in Depok where two congregations came into being, GKMI Petra in 1992 and GKMI Bukit Hermon in 1997.

Pastor Rudjito, who had opened GKMI Petra and GKMI Bukit Hermon, came back from Depok to open a fellowship in the area of Cipayung. The Cipayung branch started in 1970 under the wing of the Cempaka Putih Jakarta congregation. Two years later this congregation almost disappeared again, but the Lord moved the family of Dani Pribadi to help buy land and help build a church there. In 1977 church services were held again, and the following year seven people were baptized. The membership grew to fifty persons with thirty children, and in 1987 land was purchased to build a new church. In 1993 this group was declared a GKMI congregation with the name GKMI Immanuel. Now it has 250 baptized members from no less than 18 ethnic groups.

In the meantime in North Jakarta a meeting place was built in 1986, and two years later this branch, too, was declared mature. It became known as GKMI Filadelphia. In turn, this congregation felt a strong missionary call and in 1994 it adopted three PIPKA mission posts in Lampung, South Sumatra. Now these three mission post have become independent churches: GKMI Syallom (1996), GKMI El Shadday (2001) and GKMI Bahtera Hayat (2003).

Several GKMI members from Central Java started a branch in the western part of the capital city of Jakarta, assisted by PIPKA and by pastor Andreas Setiawan of GKMI Cempaka Putih in Jakarta. In 1986 the GKMI Synod decided to develop this GKMI Cideng group in West Jakarta as a pilot project of a missionary program called "Vision Jakarta." Its aim was to build a strong GKMI in Jakarta with 500 members. In 1988 this congregation was declared "mature," with 90 members. They first used a badminton hall as their meeting place. Later they met at the *Wisma Anugerah* (House of Grace) and chose the name GKMI Anugerah. Now it is one of the largest GKMI congregations in Jakarta with much potential and a strong missionary call. GKMI Anugerah nurtured at least three branches which became independent, such as Depok, Tangerang and Kelapa Gading and others which are still in the process of becoming adult congregations. GKMI Anugerah can be said to be a missionary church which has already raised many churches in Jakarta to maturity. It is active as the backbone of PIPKA's work in Lampung, Sumatra.

GKMI's Work Outside of Java

In 1968 PIPKA's work reached beyond Java to the island of Sumatra. In Lampung, south Sumatra, PIPKA began to serve Christians who had moved from Java to Sumatra in the transmigration program. At first the work in Lampung was a cooperative effort among the GITJ churches, GKMI and EMEK under the umbrella of the Sumatra Commission. The

GKMI church on the island of Batam

Sumatra Commission was formed to serve the small congregations in Mandailing and the members of GITJ who had moved under the auspices of the government transmigration program. During the nineteen sixties, seventies and eighties many thousands of landless Javanese farmers tried to build a new life in empty areas which were designated by the government, not only in Sumatra, but also in Celebes and Borneo. In 1973 this cooperative mission in Sumatra was ended as a result of lack of support and funds for opening new fields of mission outside of Java, though in the end a number of GITJ congregations came into being as a result of this early missionary cooperation. In 1968 GKMI, through

PIPKA and the support of the Board of Mission and Services (BOMAS) began to carry out work on its own on the island of Sumatra. Injections of funds from BOMAS motivated the PIPKA board to carry out the call to preach the Gospel to the ends of the earth. These steps by PIPKA can be said to be the key to opening new churches on other islands such as Borneo, Celebes, Batam and Bali.

PIPKA was an extension of the GKMI churches for opening new paths and serving areas that had not been reached by GKMI's mission which is known by the acronym 5M: *Mengutus* (send) , *Memberitakan* (tell the news) , *Menanam* (plant), *Membina* (develop/cultivate) and *Mendewasakan* (make adult). At the beginning, PIPKA experienced many difficulties. Among these were:

1. At that time many GKMI leaders thought that GKMI should give priority to consolidation and putting its internal affairs in order. This was natural because GKMI had solved the issue of identity and had just started working on organizational structure.

2. The awakening of the youth who were so enthusiastic was seen as a concern that they might make the church leadership ineffective. From the beginning of the 1960s into the 1970s many groups and organizations rose up that were driven by the GKMI youth, such as All for Christ, Radio Alfa Omega, Keluarga Sangkakala and others almost all of which separated from the GKMI to become independent organizations.

3. Economic problems and the limited wealth of the congregations at that time was also a problem for the support of PIPKA. The churches of GKMI which grew during the time of social, economic and political crisis definitely could not give real support.

Because of the above-mentioned problems PIPKA's work experienced stagnation. These conditions can be described as like a car that is out of gas and must be kept in the garage. The years from 1969 to 1973 were difficult for PIPKA. In 1973, PIPKA began to come back to life after receiving financial assistance from MBMSI. This reawakening was evidenced by putting its management affairs in order and also by the PIPKA vision for mission. Within a time frame of twenty years they had opened four service posts in large cities, 4 in small cities, two in villages and thirty-nine in remote areas. PIPKA's funds were from friends abroad such as MBMSI and EMM, and from within the country from GKMI churches, private contributions and fund-raising efforts. Support from GKMI churches was obtained with a commitment that five percent of all contributions that came in each month would be given to PIPKA; in the Jakarta area, GKMI's commitment is to give 15% of the contributions from the congregations each month.

PIPKA now has a better financial situation. Financial support from within the country has risen to 60%. GKMI churches and personal contributions are increasing. There are now 82 PIPKA mission posts consisting of 49 branches, 32 pioneering posts, and 1 foreign mission post. Seventeen former PIPKA mission posts have become adult member congregations of the GKMI synod, and in the future there will be still more that will be ready for independence.

In addition to starting new churches, PIPKA has developed a mission of service abroad. PIPKA is actively assisting and supporting the Mennonite Church of Singapore. Together with EMM (Eastern Mennonite Mission), the DZR (the Dutch Mennonite Mission), the Mennonite church in Hong Kong and Mennonites in the Philippines, PIPKA has sent female missionaries to serve among Indonesian migrant workers on the island of Cheng Chao, Hong Kong. PIPKA also sent Petrus Handoyo and his wife Yuliana as missionaries to Mongolia.

The Life of the Church

In many respects the GKMI is an expanding church. After independence, GKMI became a member of the Council of Churches of Indonesia (DGI), later Community of Churches of Indonesia (PGI), though not before 1959. In those years, but also in the 1980s, emphasis on Christian unity was necessary, in order that the voice of the Christians could be heard in the society. Also, the GKMI became a member of the CCA, the Christian Conference of Asia. Albert Widjaja served as a secretary in both bodies for several years. Later, the Muria churches also developed contacts with evangelical organizations such as the Lausanne Conference, the Overseas Missionary Fellowship (OMF) and the German-based *Christusträger*. This created a good balance between the ecumenical and evangelical wings in the church body.

In June 1947, after the Second World War, the Mennonite Central Committee was the first international Mennonite body to become active again in Indonesia. As has been mentioned above, the Muria church has cooperated since in a fruitful way with MCC and MCC workers, both in Central Java and Jakarta, and in Lampung, South

Sumatra. In several projects MCC had or still has a leading role, such as the scholarship program and the rural development program (through YAKEM). Also at least two North American Mennonite Mission organizations worked together with the Muria church: the Mennonite Brethren BOMAS. The contacts with the European Mennonites were rather limited in the beginning, both because of the history of the GKMI, which was separate from the Dutch mission, and because of the political circumstances. Later the contacts became closer, especially in theological education. Last but not least, the GKMI has always been an active supporter of the Mennonite World Conference and the Asia Mennonite Conference. Two MWC chairpersons came from GKMI: Charles Christano and Mesakh Krisetya. Through all these contacts, the GKMI became an internationally-oriented church. The MCC exchange visitors' program, study possibilities at several Mennonite colleges and universities in North America and even mission work among Indonesian immigrants in the USA reinforced all these contacts. After Herman Tan and his wife migrated to the USA, they became good ambassadors for the Muria church.

As we have seen above, originally the GKMI pastors did not receive formal theological training. Lay leadership through elders (*pinitua* and *boksu*) was preferred. However, a shift took place towards professional leadership during the 1950s. Some pastors were found in other churches. Students were sent to the STT in Jakarta and also to the Baptist Seminary in Semarang. From the 1960s onwards, several others studied at the *Institut Injili Indonesia* (Evangelical Institute of Indonesia – III) in Batu, near Malang, East Java, an evangelical institution, with a strong focus on church planting and evangelization.

Some of the renewal impulses which we find in PIPKA and *Sangkakala*, clearly have their origins in the faculties of the III and the Baptist Seminary. When the Javanese Mennonites started a theological school in Pati during the fifties, the GKMI at first was hesitant to participate. At the time of the reopening of the school, under the name *Akademi Kristen Wijata Wacana* (AKWW) in 1965, the GKMI became a full participant, together with MCC, EMEK and the GITJ. The number of students from the Muria church remained small, but Albert Widjaja and Mesakh Krisetya (after he finished his studies in North America) and others as well made important contributions as teachers. Mesakh served as a dean during the 1970s and early 1980s. Later, during the years of conflict within the GITJ, the Muria church decided to withdraw from the AKWW. Both at Duta Wacana Christian University (UKDW, in Yogyakarta) and at Satya Wacana Christian University (in Salatiga) theologians and others from the Muria church held or hold important positions. In Yogyakarta at UKDW there is an Institute for Peace Studies, led by Paulus Sugeng Widjaja. Nevertheless, at present the majority of the pastors working in the Muria church have a more evangelical theological background. In order to maintain possibilities for emphasizing its own theological identity, the Muria Synod started the Muria Academy to give additional training seminars to pastors and others.

As to the internal life of the Muria church and its congregations, it can be said that the Synod, especially since the late sixties, has been well organized. In 1967 and again in 1977 a church order was accepted. In the 1967 Church Order we find three levels of ministerial office: church worker, gospel teacher and minister. The order of 1977 clearly shows that the GKMI wants to be a congregational-synodal body. In general, consensus is preferred for decision-making, though especially during the earlier period, the voice of the older, influential leaders often was decisive. Also, the gap between lay leadership and professional leadership seems to have become smaller again. Since 1967 women have been eligible for all levels of church ministry, and today several women are junior or even senior pastors.

Though the congregations have much freedom of expression in their church services, nevertheless the liturgy shows a common pattern; a synodal liturgy committee prepared liturgical formulas a number of years ago. Also, the Muria Church has its own Hymnal, in which many hymns from North America can be found as well as some from Europe and a fair number of Indonesian hymns as well. Church

---

Mesakh Krisetya reflects on MCC

The work of MCC in Indonesia with GITJ was undergoing a lot of criticism from some people, including leaders of GKMI, during the early years of MCC. The purpose of evangelism continued to be debated. They believed that the role of the church is to convert, baptize and make members of the church; that the purpose of evangelism is to bring persons into personal relationship with God through Jesus Christ. For those people, evangelism meant preaching and conversion of the individual to faith in Christ. But now, they were introduced to a different kind of approach to evangelism from MCC. Namely, that the role of the church is to transform the world back to the intention of God, where God reigns and people live in peace and justice. And this is best done by deeds or actions to bring about change in society. Effective teaching is done by being, not by speaking. From MCC I found out this new meaning of "Mennonite." The uniqueness of MCC should not be changed, because I believe that evangelism approaching the third millennium will be the kind that MCC has been doing.

buildings in general are plain both inside and outside, though here and there we see churches in which art and decoration have found a place (such as in Yogyakarta and Pati). Many churches have been built or enlarged during the last decades; some church buildings (in Kudus, Jakarta and Semarang for instance) are very large.

The contacts between the congregations are maintained well by a monthly magazine, *Berita GKMI*, which has been published continuously since 1967. Perhaps the fact that among the Muria church membership there are several owners and employees of printing companies plays a role in this. A Literature Committee has worked on the publication of several books and booklets. Some of these are translations, such as Sjouke Voolstra's brief biography of Menno Simons (1997), and some are original Indonesian works. Unfortunately not many Indonesian Mennonite theologians have found the time and the opportunity to write basic textbooks or other theological works.

The Muria churches try to show a diaconial presence in the society at large by several means. In Kudus the *Mardi Rahayu* hospital has operated since 1970. It has steadily been enlarged and has several outpatient clinics. Medical doctors and nurses from the German *Christusträger* assist the work. In Kudus and Jepara and some other places there are also Christian schools which are under the aegis of the local GKMI congregation. The one in Kudus started long before the Second World War as a so-called *Hollandsch Chinese School*, founded in 1924 by missionary Johann Fast (in Kayu Apu, at that time). Together with MCC, EMEK and the Javanese Mennonite Church, the GKMI started a rural development agency in 1968, called KKEM, later continued as YAKEM (the Muria Cooperative Development Foundation). Unfortunately it had to be disbanded ten years later, due to conflicting ideas within GKMI and GITJ. Since then, the Muria Church has worked on development with local diaconal committees which often were active at times of crisis (serious floods, landslides and earthquakes). GKMI teams gave active diaconal and financial help both in Aceh after the dramatic tsunami which hit the coasts on Boxing Day 2004, and the earthquake in the Yogyakarta area on May 27, 2006.

Mardi Rahayu hospital, Kudus

Finally we have to mention the Radio Ministry *ICHTHUS* which has broadcast religious and educational programs from its Semarang station since 1971, in spite of many difficulties.

Jemaat Kristen Indonesia – JKI (Christian Congregation in Indonesia)

Athough the *Jemaat Kristen Indonesia* (JKI, Christian Congregation in Indonesia) is the youngest offspring of Mennonite movement in Indonesia, it has achieved the greatest growth. In the span of less than 40 years, JKI has planted over 50 churches with 45,000 members. The congregations cover cities around Mount Muria in Central Java, as well as in East and West Java. Several congregations are to be found abroad, such as in Los Angeles and the Philippines.

The chairperson of the JKI Synod, Rev. Adi Sutanto, confirmed his faith that now is the time for abundant harvest, as proposed by Donald Mc Gavran: The ultimate and most effective strategy used by by the modern church to enhance its growth is to multiply membership among open-hearted people in all nations on earth.

The Sangkakala Family

A great revival among the youth of (mainly GKMI) churches located around Mt. Muria (1960-1970) had produced various creative forms of

ministries, especially in mission undertakings. Many churches in Java invited foreign evangelists to initiate Revival Movements (*KKR*); especially Chinese-organized churches should be mentioned here, as they invited John Sung, Dzao Tze Kwang and many others. The GKMI youth also initiated many forms of fellowship. One of them was a fellowship organized by Adi Sutanto

Youth group in Jepara, 1960s

from GKMI Bangsri; his heart was moved to organize a unique group. The aim of the group was to generate funds and support for a friend named Chrismanto Yonathan who studied at the Baptist Seminary in Semarang. The group was named *Keluarga Sangkakala* (Trumpet Family), after the name of a GKMI choir in Bangsri in the fifties.

By early 1967, the membership had grown to 30 people. The Sangkakala Family wholeheartedly intended to bless more youth through its programs. A conference titled "Laborers of The Lord" ran for 5 days in December 1967 and was attended by 250 young people. 15 of them declared their willingness to become His servants.

Revival movements through youth conference sessions spread from Bangsri to other towns, and God worked many wonders and miracles among them. GKMI churches were swept by revival.[31] There were many GKMI members who pursued higher education in Semarang, Yogyakarta, Salatiga, Bandung and Jakarta, eager to initiate new fellowships. And in those very places new GKMI churches were built.

Since 1965 several new evangelizing organizations have been founded such as the *Evangelism and Charity Foundation* (PIPKA), the musical team *All For Christ*, a non-profit Christian radio broadcast *Alpha Omega* (later became Radio Ichthus) and many others.

The drive toward toward new forms of ministry was beyond GKMI Synod's working capacity, as in those years GKMI Synod concentrated efforts in making better internal structural and budgetary organization, and enhancement of human resources. Lack of appreciation of senior leaders of GKMI toward younger generation's movement was apparent. They showed reluctance to support many youth programs, which for them seemed to be unrealistic or non-urgent priorities.

In 1970, senior GKMI leaders proposed a merger between Sangkakala and PIPKA, as main and official mission bodies of Muria/GKMI Synod. The idea was rejected and a silent confrontation took place between the Synod office and both Sangkakala and PIPKA. PIPKA's activity came to a standstill and it suffered for a period, as the Synod office stopped any allocation of funds.

Finally Sangkakala joined with the Musical Team "All for Christ," with a new name: Christopherus (1972). Andreas Christanday was one of the motors of this interdenominational evangelistic ministry. This fusion recharged spirits to reach and minister to more youth. Christopherus carried on dynamic programs and made great strides in a relatively short span of time. Enthusiasm to re-kindle the "late 1967 flame" was still present in the hearts of Sangkakala's alumni.

In 1973 Adi Sutanto studied theology at Eastern Mennonite Seminary, Virginia, and completed the Master of Divinity program at Mennonite Brethren Biblical Seminary, Fresno and the Masters and Doctor of Theology degree (Missiology) at Fuller Seminary, Pasadena.

He came back to Indonesia in 1976 and the Muria Christian Church of Indonesia could only offer him a task to become a co-writer with Lawrence Yoder to write the history of the Muria churches. Two graduates of the Theology Academy "Abdiel" contacted Adi Sutanto to propose the installation of a new mission body, like the former Sangkakala. Adi Sutanto was confident that this was indeed God's intention and calling. *Keluarga Sangkakala* became a legal foundation on May 27, 1977. It started to work separately from PIPKA and Christopherus and by the end of the 1970s it had seven full-time staff members.

The first fellowship session in Semarang was attended by 80 persons from local churches of various denominations. The fellowship of *Keluarga Sangkakala* was opposed fervently by many senior GKMI leaders who regarded it as a competing evangelizing body. *Keluarga Sangkakala* had no established financial support. The *Keluarga Sangkakala* fellowship initially convened at Adi Sutanto's house in Semarang, but in mid-1978 it moved to another place. Fifty people were enlisted as members; all of them were young people.

Besides running fellowship meetings, *Keluarga Sangkakala* also actively supported many evangelistic events. Beginning in mid-1977 the group conducted evangelistic meetings in Ngaglik (a hamlet on the steep side of Mt. Merbabu), Sampetan (Boyolali), and Bondo (Jepara). In order to attract attention and support of villagers, Keluarga Sangkakala rented a projector and some Christian film titles. Through this program hundreds of people were saved; and in Ngaglik and Sampeten two little fellowships were planted, which later became churches.

In June 1978, an activist of *Sangkakala* named Billy Sindoro proposed evangelism by distribution of tape cassettes. He recorded sermons, and mass-reproduced them to be distributed for free to little towns. By this ministry many people were reached and touched by the Gospel. The cassettes served as an opening path for a yet bigger harvest through mass revival sermons.

Oikoumene Night was launched on March 1-3 1979 in Semarang, with 400 men/women declaring their willingness to receive Christ. Five months afterwards, a grand revival event was carried out in a big hall, with Ev. Yeremia Rim as preacher. The call for repentance was responded to by 2,186 persons. Spiritual fire incessantly drove Sangkakala team to move forward. The flame reached surrounding places like Kudus, Pati, Tayu, Jepara, Salatiga, Magelang, Yogyakarta, Surakarta and many other small towns.

In every vacation period, the *Sangkakala* activists launch city-tour evangelism all around Java, Bali, Sumba, Timor and Sulawesi. Since 1981 crusade teams have been dispatched to Singapore, Malaysia, Phillipines, Hong Kong and South Korea. In fact there are "core motivators" in the crusade team, i.e. permanent members. Other volunteers, however, are invited to join.

The movement grew bigger and bigger, necessitating a legally-recognized foundation to administer it. They could no longer use GKMI as their "umbrella," as the youth-driven movement (only part of them were GKMIs) had been actively working beyond the structure and coordination of GKMI Synod. *Sangkakala* was an inter-denominational body, with a strict, patterned and clear vision to be accomplished. However it was too big, a silent sign that it ought to lose its title as a "small fellowship"; it embraced an "amalgamated" church title, comprising multiple denominations. On November 1, 1979, the Sangkakala Foundation was registered officially as a foundation. Currently, the main purpose of the foundation is to evangelize people and carry out works of charity. The manifestation of its vision became readily apparent in the decade ahead: building new churches, schools, a polyclinic, geriatric care, etc.

Prayer Groups

Rapid growth made it necessary for the large gathering to divide into 7 smaller prayer groups. The seven groups soon became 14. By mid-1981 the number of prayer groups had climbed to 35, each attended by 20-60 persons. On May 1984 there were 40 groups with a total membership of 1,600; all of them resided within the bounds of Semarang. Outside Semarang some prayer groups were begun, but they grew more slowly compared to those in Semarang.

Activities within the prayer groups were similar with those of a house church, i.e. they practiced an informal liturgy. There was praise and worship, prayer, Bible reading, a sermon, witnessing, offering and a conclusion with relaxed fellowship (enjoying some tea and snacks). This kind of fellowship model was well-liked in the 1970s and 80s. People from non-Christian backgrounds did not feel like strangers and they were welcomed and embraced within the fellowship. A different situation was encountered in the formal and rule-laden churches.

The prayer groups were led by lay people; in 1981 some 35 lay preachers were actively sharing the Good News in the local dialect.

This was a definite advantage, as new members (they were common folk) were able to grasp new biblical ideas. Many testimonies of renewed spiritual vitality were shared. They could enjoy spiritual growth in a healthy atmosphere of edification and brotherhood.

Revival (KKR)

At first, the *Sangkakala Foundation* was recognized by churches in Semarang as an interdenominational body whose aim was to do evangelization and to promote revival: *Kebaktian Kebangunan Rohani* (KKR or Spiritual revival meeting). There were at least 5 revival meetings organized annually in Semarang and nearby cities like Jepara, Kudus, Pati, Magelang, Surakarta and Yogyakarta. Each revival was attended by thousands of people; many were reinvigorated, and many others did repent their sins before the Lord.

The first evangelism-oriented revival was organized in July 1977 in Ngaglik (*Boyolali*), at a local government's hall. Some 800 persons attended the event. The harvests were delivered to the Pentecostal Isa Almasih Church for stewardship. In Semarang there was a revival organized especially for high school students, called Oikoumene Night (Mar. 1-3, 1979), hosted by Ev. Damaris and Sister Yohana. Some 800-1000 students came each night; 400 people responded to the altar call and stated their readiness to follow Christ. The new believers were nurtured in the Imannuel Fellowship led by Mrs. Hanna Subagja, joining 700-800 other members. A similar activity was held in Jepara.

Speakers at these evangelization gatherings were not all renowned evangelists or preachers; many of them were lay persons or even young men and women. Some special KKRs were also organized for children of 5-12 years of age, in December 1983. More than 1,500 children came forward to respond to the altar call, and they showed remorse for their sins. A unique fellowship was later initiated for children.

Cassettes, periodical, bookstore and musical band

In those years many well-known domestic as well as foreign preachers came to Semarang and other cities on Java. Their sermons were recorded on tape. Direct and live recording on the site introduced the message of KKR; the listeners experienced the real situation of the evangelization event. By 1980 more than 1000 cassette titles had been recorded and distributed. This active ministry was suddenly discontinued when Billy Sindoro went to USA to continue his study.

Images and stories of ministries and harvests in various places were communicated through a monthly periodical, to be handed out for free, titled *Gema Sangkakala* (Trumpet Echo). The first copies of *Gema Sangkakala* appeared on July 1977, with only 4 pages. The number of pages of this bulletin increased as many readers were eager to obtain wider information on Sangkakala's expanding ministries. *Gema Sangkakala* carried current news along with stories of the impact of the Gospel. By the fifth year, *Gema Sangkakala* had been distributed to 20,000 addresses of Christian families nationwide; it now was a booklet of 28-32 pages.

The idea of opening a bookstore came up following a series of revival events in 1979, where so many people badly needed Bibles and faith-nurturing books. At that time Semarang was a city of 1 million people, and there was only one Christian bookstore to serve all the demand. Only Surakarta and Yogyakarta in Central Java also had Christian bookstores. Central Java Province presented a large opportunity to expand the Christian bookstore business. On April 1, 1982 a new Christian bookstore opened, named "Rhema." The store sold Bibles, exegesis books, testimonial stories, faith guidance books and numerous cassette titles. Rhema is still running to the present day, serving thousands of Christians who live in or near Semarang.

The Sangkakala Band was formed in 1977, with a strong motivation to minister to youth through popular music. KKR and evangelization in many places was accompanied by members of Sangkakala Band. The "Sangkakala" choir officially began on Dec. 7, 1978, led by Jimmy Oentoro. At first only guitar was available, but later many other musical instruments were also used. Through this band, many talented youths were given a place in a variety of ministries. The use of band music as an accompaniment for praise and worship was popular with the younger generation. From 1970 to1990, most churches used only organ and piano for their Sunday services. Band music was truly like fresh air for youth; since then it has become a trend both in cities and villages.

Social Ministry

The objective of the Sangkakala Foundation was to do evangelism and social work. In 1982, the Sangkakala Foundation Sangkakala projected a social ministry that would include the building of hospitals, a poly-clinic, an orphanage, a home for the elderly, etc. The commendable objectives were, however, not fully realized as most resources were concentrated in spiritual guidance programs and church planting. However, some social ministries are worth mentioning:

a. A scholarship fund for young people who enroll for Theology studies. The fund was generated from regular donors and various parties.

b. Aid to needy brothers or sisters. By 1979 Rp. 1,206,428 in aid had been disbursed.

c. Collecting used clothes for distribution in needy areas. In 1978 some 1,209 pieces of clothing were handed out in Demak, Salatiga, Wonogiri, Ponorogo and Magelang.

The founding of the Jemaat Kristen Indonesia

The necessity to take root as a new church became an urgent priority, because each person won by the *Sangkakala* crusade team had to be kept and nurtured "in a barn." On March 4, 1979, in Ungaran some new believers were baptized. This became the cornerstone of the Jemaat Kristen Indonesia (JKI) church. The name adopted for the maiden church was JKI Maranatha. There were 40 members in this congregation. By March 1983, the congregation was blessed; they purchased a big building, which has been used to the present. At the time, some 300 persons were listed as members of JKI Maranatha.

Fellowships of rural folk in remote locations (won through evangelization and movie nights) later became mature churches, such as in Sampeten (Boyolali), Banyumanik (Semarang) and Kelet (Jepara). The congregations at Semarang and Los Angeles have also been declared mature. The new churches adopted new evangelism models, namely through the formation of new house fellowships, the assignment of workers or servants to new places, and speeding up the transition from mission-post to mature church.

JKI developed a new strategy for planting new churches in villages. An example is the above-mentioned *desa* Sampetan at the steep side of Mt. Merbabu, 5 km from Boyolali. The first evangelism service was held in May, 1978 at an open field, after securing a local permit. Evangelization was carried out using a film about the Life of Jesus according to Luke, and a mass-revival sermon. Around 800-1000 people thronged the movie show each night. Copies of the Gospel according to John were distributed for free. Since there was a thirst for the Gospel, three persons were sent to the pioneer location to stay and to serve there. After a month, sufficient funds were collected to buy a plot of land on which to build a church. A simple building was erected on the site, with a maximum seating capacity for 100 persons. Lack of experience and coordination of the three commissioned persons, however, led to slow growth of the Sampetan church. At presently there are 60 baptized adults in Sampetan Church, with 80 people present at services.

The Sangkakala Family also pioneered a new church in Kelet. This village is considered isolated because it lies 50 km from Jepara. The church planting effort in Kelet was started by a theological school in Ungaran. Since September 1980, Puji Astuti, a young woman from Kelet, began a prayer meeting in her house once a week. The Sangkakala Team regularly came to help her ministry. Two years later the Kelet fellowship was handed over to the Sangkakala Family. Thomas HC was asked to continue and develop the Kelet fellowship. At the present time the Kelet fellowship is attended by 100 members with composition of 50 % Chinese and 50% Javanese.

Pioneering efforts

The focus of pioneering efforts in urban areas is in the outer urban areas and at housing complexes. If JKI can locate itself inside a city area, the suburbs will receive more support and be more feasible for development. Banyumanik (8-10 km away from Semarang's center) was the first outer region of Semarang which became a ministrial area of JKI. Banyumanik links Semarang with the neighboring town of Ungaran (the distance of Banyumanik-Ungaran is only 10 Km). Banyumanik was formerly a new settlement area. In the early 1980s the local government built 5,000 units of simple houses meant for lower-income people. In 1984, a few thousand more houses were provided by government. The church planting effort in Banyumanik is similar to former patterns where the starting point of evangelization is the establishment of house fellowships.

At first a simple building was rented to hold Sunday meetings. There were 10-20 people present at the first meetings. In a relatively short span of time the number of members grew to 40 (in 1984) and is now 150.

Factors of growth

There are three main factors which boost the growth of membership of the Sangkakala Family or Jemaat Kristen Indonesia: effective evangelism, effective pulpit-preaching and the establishment of new churches.

Adi Sutanto explains the success of "effective evangelization" as follows:

First, pay attention to the most urgent necessities of the local society. Each societal group has one or more urgent needs. Evangelists have to identify and give a proper answer to those needs.

Second, preach the Good News through networks of families, neighbors and friends. A newly-converted person needs attention, support and discipleship training, which in turn will move that person to spread Gospel to other family members, neighbours, and friends. This strategy has proven effective: seventy to eighty percent of present-day Christians attending the churches are fruits of this direct-preaching strategy.

Third, use other evangelism methods which prove successful. Avoid duplication of effort; do not work where other churches are active. Use effective methods. For instance, the Campus Crusade for Christ (*LPMI*) holds film festivals in many villages. A movie show is a well-desired commodity in villages, where many of the local inhabitants are more than willing to come and watch.

Fourth, contextualize evangelism to local conditions in order to avoid the misunderstanding that Christianity is a foreign and strange thing. If necessary, train local persons to become pastors or pioneers of new fellowships.

Fifth, keep in mind that effective evangelism has something to do with the conditions of local population; demographic research is necessary to understand local religious life, socioeconomic status, cultural patterns, and all the myths and traditional beliefs of the local people.

Sixth, each congregational member must pray to ask God's counsel, to understand His will in the course of church's ministry. Pioneering and ministry not only require good mapping of target areas, but also a good formulation of objectives, good timing, the adoption of a proper evangelism method, and placing the right man in the right place. The last factor has to do with appointing persons who are really consecrated to God's will. Spiritual discipline is the foremost important aspect for an evangelist or a minister.

Effective pulpit-preaching is a limited and focused effort to help people meet Jesus Christ personally, to help people attain a successful life, and to help people keep a passionate spirit to serve God. Conversion is the central objective of pulpit preaching. The love of God is explained in plain words and the power of God is offered and shown as the changing force in life. A preacher tries to respond to the main things desired by his lambs. If they want a successful life, the theme of preaching should invigorate faith and the expectation of God's capacity to change lives. Testimonies and illustrative stories about the ability of God to change lives are offered to help people believe in the living and powerful God. Good pulpit preaching uses simple words, clear and responsive to people's needs.

Evangelism in a congregational Pentecostal way

For the JKI, the creation and management of a new church is one of the most important things. The formation and management of a new church is easier than trying to change an old church already set in old patterns. JKI uses an approach model of evangelism usually taken by Pentecostal churches: to pioneer and simultaneously shepherd churches. The development of pastoral ministries is considered the core factor for the growth of a church and its eventual maturity. Old or conservative churches move slowly because of outdated liturgies, organizational rules and bureaucracy. In comparison with GITJ and GKMI, which maintain their historic backgrounds as well-designed and organized institutions, JKI chooses a pure congregational system where local churches and pastors determine the pace of growth of each individual church. The existing synod body within JKI has no authority to formulate and evaluate policies affecting local churches. Each local church develops its own pattern of ministry. They are to preach Gospel directly to assure good development of church, so as many people as possible are saved. The moving motto of JKI is "Win the Lost at any Cost." It doesn't matter how high the price is. The eyes are focused on the lost souls, with necessary sacrifices directed to this goal.

An example: the JKI congregation 'Injil Kerajaan' in Semarang

One of the pioneer churches in Semarang which became a large and deep-rooted church is JKI *Injil Kerajaan* (Gospel of the Kingdom

Church). This church was started by young persons who received Christ as their Saviour in a revival meeting in Semarang, held by the Sangkakala Family. The new converts formed the prayer fellowship "Immanuel," under the guidance of Mrs. Hanna Sebadja. God added to the membership of this fellowship; eventually 800 youths were registered, divided into 17 prayer groups. Most members were young persons or students; they were burning with a passion for evangelism and winning people for Christ. The grand theme of their every prayer was to accomplish the vision of Great Commission of Jesus Christ, as stated in Matthew 28:19-20. They claimed the spirit of Pentecost in every effort of church pioneering, racing to complete their work before the second coming of Christ. This ministry called for great sacrifices, although God gave them the sign of miracles to encourage them to stay steadfast in their belief and labor for Gospel.

This fast-growing fellowship had a difficult experience. They took out a loan from a bank to purchase a roller-skating building, but debt accumulated beyond their ability to pay. Petrus Agung Purnomo, one of the initiators of the fellowship and its most prominent pastor, realized his mistake. He had underestimated the impact of having such a big loan. A church should be founded on the offering of its mem-

The "Holy Stadium," the *Injil Kerajaan* (Gospel of the Kingdom) JKI church in Semarang

bers. Petrus and the other members prayed and fasted for a week and finally Petrus decided to offer his car to God; the sale of the car paid back the loan to the bank. In the following months God blessed the Sangkakala Fellowship with offerings by many others. In 1994 the building was renovated and the membership figures rose extraordinarily. In 1997, 200 people attended each gathering, and now the figure is 16,000! The members are new converts, the fruits of evangelization, not people "jumping on the bandwagon" from other denominations. On December 25, 2003, for instance, 246 people were baptized! Now every month between 50 and 100 people are baptized by immersion.

Although the hall is large, it can no longer accommodate the overflowing number of new members. Therefore JKI *Injil Kerajaan* purchased 2 hectares of land next to the old building and built another gigantic hall with 12,000 seats which they called the *Holy Stadium*. It was opened on July 7, 2007.

JKI *Injil Kerajaan* has developed a system of shepherding people in unique cell groups called "family altars." Each cell group comprises 6-12 members who develop a close fellowship for sharing love and exhorting each other in Christ. The mechanism of the cell groups was refined to fit the pace of congregational dynamics. In order words, the internal organizational structure continually adapts to the needs and levels of development of the congregation. God Himself gives wisdom over the best organizational structure JKI should have. The leaders of each "Family Altar" report regularly on the activity of their group, and a regional coordinator collects the reports every Sunday. The report contains figures of participation in the congregation and the quality of sharing. The emphasis is on stewardship. The cell group leaders are the spearheads of stewardship because they are the ones who responsible for the well-being of their sheep. The slogan of this "Family Altar" program is "Build inside to build outside." The character of each individual person is strengthened through the cell group's activities. The aim is to attain a quality of Christian practice so that the person blesses other people and brings the Good News to others.

The pyramidical structure of JKI Injil Kerajaan is as follows: the final responsibility is in the hands of the pastor, assisted by several area coordinators and assistant pastors. Under each area coordinator several regional coordinators are responsible for the "Family Altar" leaders. Then come the lay members. The congregation maintains a good and well-organized membership database system. JKI *Injil Kerajaan* is now the fastest-growing church in Semarang.

JKI *Injil Kerajaan* is aware of the gigantic burden of stewardship it has taken on. Thus JKI Synod developed satellites or branches in at least six different places in Semarang. The membership figure of each satellite is between 100 and 300. JKI *Injil Kerajaan* also has mission projects to areas outside Java, even to foreign countries. It sends mission workers to Kalimantan, Palau, Hong Kong, North India, Cambodia, North Vietnam, and the Philippines.

Bible School and social ministries

In order to prepare people for the future, JKI *Injil Kerajaan* organizes annually a short Bible course called The School of Acts (TSOA). TSOA teachings underline personal and simple spiritual experiences with God, in contrast to the teaching of complicated theological doctrines usually presented by conventional seminaries. The sharing of spiritual experience receives primary attention, in the so called "impartation." The school invites leaders from many other places in Indonesia or from foreign countries who have experiences of intimacy with God.

Along with a radio broadcast (Radio Rhema) and a literature department, the congregation recently opened a school (located next to the *Holy Stadium*) and a rehabilitation center for ex-drug addicts, named *Rumah Damai*. The vision for developing a good rehabilitation center is a response to the fact that there are more than five million drug addicts in Indonesia, among whom are 1.2 million late-elementary and high school students. The resulting death rate is horrifiying. The congregation is also very active in the field of charity, providing courses for unemployed people and pastoring a large group of transvestites.

Synod activities

There are now 194 churches under the JKI Synod including branches all around Indonesia; 11 international branch churches are operating in foreign countries: 6 in Los Angeles, 1 in New York, 3 in Australia, and 1 in the Netherlands. In total the JKI now has some 45,000 members. The churches are served by 136 senior pastors and 150 associate pastors. In order to train pastors, the JKI has opened a seminary near Kopeng, on the slopes of mount Merbabu.

Other Areas of Mennonite Presence in Indonesia

Besides the three churches which have been described above, western and Indonesian Mennonite mission and service agencies work in other areas as well. This has resulted partly in the founding of Mennonite, or Mennonite-related congregations, some temporary, others permanent. A brief description of these activities follows.

A new mission field in Mandailing, North Sumatra

At the end of the 1860s it became clear that no new mission field on Java could be opened, even though financial assistance from Mennonites in Prussia and the Ukraine made extension possible.[32] For that reason, the Dutch Mennonite Mission Board contacted the *Rheinische Mission* about possibilities in North Sumatra. After Heinrich Dirks (1842-1915) had completed his missionary training he was sent to South Tapanuli in the district of Mandailing in North Sumatra in 1870, a pagan area where Islam had a rather strong position

The Pakantan church, ca. 1908

already. A report by a missionary of the *Rheinische Mission* praised Dirks highly and called him "an Israelite without deceit."

Dirks's work among the Bataks in the village of Pakantan bore fruit. He managed to acquire woodlands from the pagan priests (*datu*) around the mountain Magogar, an area that was taboo for them. Both Dirks and his successors, such as Gerhard Nikkel, Nikolai Wiebe and Johann Thiessen (also Mennonites from the Ukraine) extended and cultivated this land and tried to reshape Pakantan and the other mission stations into modern colonies with a school, an orphanage, a hospital and even an old people's home. Original documents in the Amsterdam Archives show how *Raja* (sovereign) Goemanti Porang Dibata and *Raja* Mangatas of Pakantan handed over desolate woodlands to the mission in 1907 and 1909 "to be cultivated according to their own will to become a means of living for the community of the Christian congregation of Pakantan."

The missionaries took a certain risk by becoming landlords, coffee planters and shop keepers along with being missionaries,

Johann Thiessen (1869-1953)

Johann Thiessen was a member of the Einlage Mennonite congregation in the Chortitza Mennonite Settlement, South Russia. He studied for a time in the St. Chrischona institute near Basel, Switzerland. In July 1901 he began serving as a member of the Dutch Mennonite Mission Association (*Doopsgezinde Zendings Vereeniging* [DZV], now *Doopsgezinde Zendingsraad* [DZR]) on the island of Sumatra, taking the place of Nikolai Wiebe and Gerhard Nikkel. He worked at both Pakantan and Muara Sipongi until 1912. The board of the DZV was dissatisfied with Thiessen's work, since he was more Baptist-minded than Mennonite (he had been baptized in a Baptist congregation in Berlin). In 1921 he became the founder of a Pentecostal church in Bandung, West Java, Indonesia, and editor of a church paper, *Dit is het*. Thiessen, who was married to a Dutch woman, A. Vink, was a well-known and gifted photographer.

although missionaries from other denominations in North Sumatra did the same. However, Dirks, and especially Thiessen ran into financial debts which made Thiessen's dismissal in 1912 inevitable.

A Christian family in Pakantan, ca. 1908

In any case, their congregations grew. When Dirks left the mission field in 1881 to become a travelling *Missionsprediger* among the Mennonite settlements in the Ukraine, his congregation counted around 100 hundred souls, 51 of them baptized. Because of pressure from Muslims, further growth was slow. Therefore, in 1890 Nikolai Wiebe started a new mission station in Muara Sipongi, where the pagan Ulu's lived. Unfortunately, relations with the Bataks in Pakantan were sometimes strained and there were some debates about whether the congregations had to be divided along tribal lines. In the meantime, no less than four young men from Pakantan had trained as teachers and evangelists in the well-known interdenominational seminary of Depok, south of Batavia. At least three of them, Jonathan, Johannes and David, became important congregational leaders.

From 1912 until his early death in 1928, missionary Peter Nachtigal worked with relentless energy on this mission field, first in Huta-Godang, later in Pakantan. He even worried about the fate of Christian transmigrants from the Toba area, who faced serious difficulties in this new, Islamic context. When he died, there were 470 Christians in the congregations belonging to the mission field in Pakantan and Mandailing (200 of them belonging to the Toba church).

Teacher Jonathan (cntr), at the celebration of his forty years of service

Unfortunately at that time the DZV had neither money nor personnel to continue the work. Funds from the Ukraine congregations had dried up after 1917, and so had potential missionaries. North American Mennonites were unable to take over the mission field, both for ideological and financial reasons. Although the DZV continued to carry the final responsibility, for the time being the field was handed over to the *Rheinische Mission*. In the meantime the congregations had to stand on their own feet. Under the capable leadership of the old Jonathan, and later, of Zacharias Gelar Djasahata Nasution, they succeeded in carrying on during the 1930s and 40s.

During the Japanese occupation this church suffered in ways similar to Christians elsewhere, sometimes threatened by Muslim gangs. Many fled to the mountains or to larger towns; others became Muslims. By 1950, 150 Christians (adults and children) were left, most of them living in Dolok Siantar near Panyabungan.[33]

After Indonesia received its independence, this small group started to renew contacts with brothers and sisters in Central Java. In April 1953 Soehadiweko Djojodihardjo, together with the MCC worker Johan van den Berg visited the suffering congregations. According to a report by Djojodihardjo, he asked one of the people there: "Why didn't all of your people become Muslims again?" He looked at me with amazement and answered: "We could not leave Jesus Christ because of that situation, because Jesus Christ was present with us and guided us."[34]

As a result of this visit, a Javanese pastor from the GITJ, Soedijoso, worked in the Mandailing area from August 1956 until early 1958. Martin Nasution was sent to Pati to study at the theological school but worked later as a farmer in his home area. In the 1970s, several other young men studied at the AKWW in Pati and in 1968 Julianus Nasution, who had finished his studies at Jakarta Theological Seminary, became a teacher at this seminary, his main field being Islam.

Contacts between Mandailing and the churches in the Muria area were intensified in these years by the so-called Sumatra Committee in which the GITJ, GKMI, MCC and EMEK participated. This committee was, on the one hand, responsible for the economic and spiritual well-being of landless Javanese migrants (including church planting) in Lampung, South Sumatra. A large number of congregations came into being in this area, as we have seen above in describing the work of

Rural church in Lampung, South Sumatra

the GITJ and the GKMI. On the other hand this committee also was responsive to the needs of the small congregations in the Mandailing area. Several delegations visited the area. The Javanese pastor Parwoto worked in Panyabungan for some time and MCC even sent Keith and Sharon Waltner and later Jim and Cathy Bowman to Panyabungan to assist in economic development. However, in 1975 MCC decided to move its personnel to Lampung.

After another visit to Pakantan by Soehadiweko Djojodihardjo, Charles Christano, together with Julianus Nasution and Lawrence Yoder in December 1975, the four small congregations decided to join a larger regional church, the *Gereja Kristen Protestan Angkola*, in which they form, till today, a *classis* (sub-department) while preserving a certain identity.[35] The hymnal of the GKPA contains some hymns written by missionary Johann Thiessen; during his stay he had brought together a number of hymns to be used in his own congregations. In fact, the case of the Mennonite congregations in Mandailing proves that interdenominational and ecumenical cooperation can be a fruitful solution in Indonesia, where Christian churches are a minority. Incidentally contacts both with the Muria churches and with the Dutch Mennonites remained. The latter sent some help in 2006 and 2008 when earthquakes claimed several victims and caused much damage.

Mennonite Presence in the Bird's Head of West Papua

When World War II ended in Indonesia with the capitulation of the Japanese forces, the churches were mature and independent. The

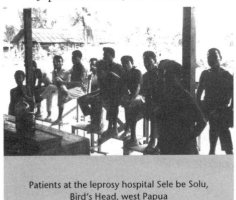

Patients at the leprosy hospital Sele be Solu,
Bird's Head, west Papua

future tasks for western mission agencies seemed limited. Consequently, the Dutch Mennonite Mission looked for other areas in which to work. They decided on the Bird's Head of West Papua (then called: *Nieuw Guinea* and later *Irian Jaya*). When the Dutch government and the Republic of Indonesia finally came to an agreement in 1949, West Papua was not part of the deal;

it remained a Dutch colony. The Reformed mission had been working in Bird's Head since 1924. After rounds of serious negotiation this mission board handed over the district to the DZV in 1950, an area half as large as the Netherlands. The aim was to work together with others towards the founding of an independent Christian church in West Papua as a whole; this became a reality in 1956.

This mission project was a complex and interesting exercise in ecumenical cooperation. Mennonite ecclesiology had to find ways to co-exist with a Reformed type of church.[36] Founding an Anabaptist kind of church has never been an option. Yet, in the organization of the new Evangelical Christian Church of West Papua, space for basic Anabaptist convictions has been guaranteed to this day.

Several Dutch missionaries (such as Herbert Marcus and Lieuwe Koopmans), medical doctors, nurses and teachers worked in the area under difficult political circumstances. Next to them we have to mention especially two Swiss nurses, Ruth (Watopa)-Bähler and her sister Lydia (Mambor)-Bähler, who for many years worked in the leprosy clinic *Sele be Solu* near Sorong. They were the only ones who were allowed to stay in 1962 when a political and military conflict forced the Dutch to pull out entirely and to hand over West Papua to Indonesia.

When Dutch presence was made impossible, the Javanese Mennonites made pastor I. Siswojo of the GITJ available, at the request of the DZV, to continue the work of the missionaries from 1964 until 1970. Also, Papua church leaders such as reverend Ruben Rumbiak played an important role. Rev. Herman Saud, one of the pupils of the Mennonite missionaries, even became chairperson of the Evangelical Church of West Papua. Both European Mennonite agencies and the MCC have had personnel in the area or in other parts of West Papua since the 1980s. Contacts between Dutch Mennonites and several Christians from Bird's Head have continued to the present day.

MCC and PIPKA efforts elsewhere in the archipelago and in Asia

From 1948 onwards, MCC not only cooperated with the young Mennonite churches on Java and Sumatra, but also with other Protestant denominations and Christian organisations elsewhere.[37] In 1948 MCC started relief work near Kisaran in Sumatra. The unit was transferred to Java, however, the next year. From 1956 to

1968 several couples and single men worked in the field of agricultural development on the island of Timor, Eastern Indonesia, in cooperation with the (Reformed) church of West Timor. At the same time, from 1957 to 1967 medical teams and agricultural development experts worked in Tobelo, Halmahera. Nurse Anne Warkentin Dyck reported in a humorous way about the long and difficult journey through government offices to get permission for five young people (Muslims and Christians) from Tobelo to study at the Bethesda Christian Hospital in Yogyakarta, in 1960. Eventually, two graduates settled down in Tayu to work in the Mennonite Hospital there. During the 1970s and 80s MCC was active on the large island of Kalimantan, and on Sulawesi. In Tentena, a Christian town in Central Sulawesi (one of the places where in the late 90s Christian-Muslim conflicts caused hundreds of victims) they worked side by side with the Christian Church of Central Sulawesi (GKST) and with development NGOs, partly in behalf of Javanese migrants who settled there.

Later, MCC workers also came as university teachers at the Cendrawasih University of Manokwari (West Papua), at the Universitas Kristen Satya Wacana in Salatiga (Central Java) and in Jakarta. In cooperation with the GKMI a peace and reconciliation research centre was opened at the Duta Wacana Christian University. MCC increasingly began using local Christians as staff. Together with his wife, one of them, Subandi Kernowidjojo from Pati, even served several years with MCC in Bangladesh. Beginning in 1969 exchange visitor programs (including study facilities in the USA) had a significant impact and were helpful in broadening the horizons of hundreds of young Indonesians.

In the meantime the mission board of the GKMI (PIPKA) spread its wings also all over the archipelago.[38] Here church planting remained the main aim, but development and charity programs were started as well. From 1975 on PIPKA planted churches in Kalimantan and Bali, as well as in Yogyakarta, Surakarta, Malang, Surabaya and Bandung, partly in cooperation with Eastern Mennonite Mission and the Mennonite Brethren Missions and Services. Both agencies had personnel in Indonesia for a number of years. In the 1990s, Mesakh Krisetya and others emphasized

> Even though the receivers of the Message are considered poor, they have their freedom and are not foolish. They have their own culture, habits and characters that need to be considered.
> — Mesakh Krisetya

the need to work in an innovative way in the big cities, seeing the recipients of the Gospel as subjects.

In West Kalimantan the work among the Dayak people originally started as social work together with MCC. However, after a survey made by Charles Christano and Eddy Paimoen, it was decided to begin church planting as well, in spite of the fact that several foreign mission agencies claimed the area as theirs. Charles Christano made a bold statement after their visit: "We as Indonesians are more responsible for the salvation of this nation." Beginning in the mid-80s PIPKA opened no less than twenty mission posts in Kalimantan.

Maranatha church, West Kalimantan

A final step was taken when PIPKA opened a congregation in Singapore and around 2000 social work and evangelism began among female migrant workers from Indonesia on the island of Cheung Chau, Hong Kong.

Even though the efforts of MCC, PIPKA and other partners in Indonesia were only partly successful in the end, they prove that the globalisation of the mission of Christ is continuing in spite of rather difficult times in their pluralist society.

Translation: Janet Umble Reedy

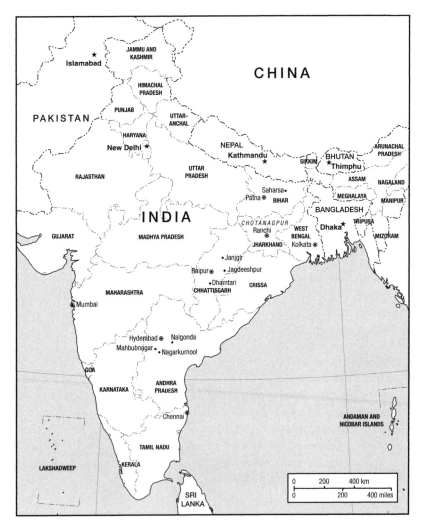

India

The Mennonite and Brethren in Christ Churches of India

CHAPTER
IV

by I. P. Asheervadam

The Mennonite and Brethren in Christ churches of India are the largest body of this communion in Asia, second-oldest to the Javanese Mennonite Church of Indonesia. The first Mennonite Brethren church was established in the 1890s. Others soon followed. Mennonites in India from these beginnings have been closely linked to the rich heritage of Christianity in India.

Introduction

India has a unique cultural and religious history. It is the birthplace of four of the world's major religions – Hinduism, Jainism, Buddhism, and Sikhism – and home to the world's second-largest population of Muslims. India welcomed Christianity, Zoroastrianism and Judaism long before Europe did. Through Hinduism, Buddhism, Jainism, and Sikhism India not only influenced the philosophy and thought of Asia, but also of the world.

Present-day India comprises 28 states and seven union territories with a population estimated at 1.21 billion people (2011), making it the world's second-most populous country, after China. It has been noted that about 400 significant dialects and 1,645 languages are spoken in India, of which there are 22 major languages such as Bengali, Hindi, Tamil, Telugu and Oria. These languages and dialects are spoken in over 4,000 ethnic communities. Such a wide variety of ethnic groups and castes give India its own character, with a rich cultural heritage and history. India is diverse, multi-religious, and multi-cultural and can only survive by being a truly pluralistic country.

Christianity has its own early history in India, with the planting of the gospel seed in Indian soil dated traditionally back to the first century. A strong and persistent tradition holds that the Apostle Thomas came to India (Malabar in Kerala) in 52 CE, was martyred in 72 CE, and was buried in Mylapore (Chennai) after establishing seven churches. Today there is a shrine to St. Thomas in a basilica which is built over the tomb where he was believed to have been buried. This is one of three basilicas built on the tomb of an Apostle. The other two are built on St. Peter's tomb in Rome, and St. James's at Compostela. Recently the Shrine of St. Thomas Basilica in Chennai has been declared a National Shrine and receives visitors and pilgrims from all over the world. There are large Christian communities – Syrian Orthodox, Mar Thoma, Indian Orthodox, Roman Catholic, Church of South India – that trace their lineage to the early Christian centuries.

Historical Overview of India

Geographically, India is the seventh largest country in the world, set off from the rest of Asia by the Himalayas on the north and seas on the other three sides. Myanmar (Burma), Bhutan, Nepal, Bangladesh, China, Pakistan and Sri Lanka are neighboring countries. Before Independence, Pakistan and Bangladesh were part of greater India.

India has four well-defined physical regions – the northern Himalayan Mountains, the northern plains including the deserts, the peninsular plateau, and the coastal areas. These regions provide almost all the variety of land forms for the balanced development of the country. Each region has its special features and has played its own part in the history of the country.

The Himalayas have some of the highest peaks in the world, including the famous Mount Everest. Important north-Indian rivers like the Sutlej, the Ganga and the Brahmaputra irrigate the land and are the source of prosperity. The fertile Ganga and Indus basins made India prosperous and were the main attraction for the invaders from the west.

Indian civilization is among the oldest in the world, contemporary with Egypt and Sumer in Mesopotamia. The discoveries at Harrappa and Mohenjodaro in the 1920s established that Indian civilization goes back to at least 3,000 BCE. Already in 1,500 BCE Harappan traders had dealings with the west by land and sea. India's agricultural products, spices, precious stones, textiles and handicrafts were exported to the countries of central, west and east Asia. Ships sailed into the Persian Gulf and the Red Sea, especially from Mauryan times (300 BCE). One of the land routes was connected with the famous silk route of China through Takshashila and the Khyber Pass. The Silk Road was an extensive interconnected network of trade routes across the Asian continent connecting Asia with the Mediterranean world, as well as with northern Africa and Europe. Already a thousand years before Christ, the Silk Road was the most important path for cultural, commercial and technological exchange between traders, merchants, pilgrims, missionaries, soldiers, nomads and urban dwellers from Ancient China, India, Tibet, Persia, and Mediterranean countries. India's natural features and economic riches proved tempting to invaders, from ancient times down to the modern period.

Indians began spreading their influence to other countries before the first century CE. During Ashoka's reign (273 BCE) many Buddhist missionaries visited Myanmar. The first Hindu kingdom in Java was established in 132 CE, although Hinduism was subsequently supplanted by Islam. Bali was also a Hindu sphere in ancient times and remains so. Hindus also reached Cambodia in the first century CE. Angkor Wat, a Hindu temple in Cambodia, is a masterpiece of Hindu architecture, dedicated to Lord Vishnu.

Indian culture greatly influenced the cultures of all the south-east Asian countries. During Kanishka's reign (230 BCE) many Buddhist missionaries went to China, Afghanistan and the central Asian countries, and there were Buddhist converts soon in Korea and Japan. In some countries like Afghanistan, Buddhism continued to be a dominant religion until it was replaced by Islam in the 8th century CE. In 2001, the Taliban destroyed huge Buddhist sculptures in Afghanistan, in the name of Islam.

Buddhist universities in the Indian sub-continent were famous schools, attracting students from China, Korea, Japan, Sri Lanka, Afghanistan, Baluchistan, and Nepal. Nalanda was the most important of these schools. It is said that between 414-445 CE it had 10,000 students. India played a significant role in spreading Buddhism to Tibet. A large number of Tibetan students acquired higher education at the Indian universities of Nalanda and Takhashila. King Ashoka in the third century BCE did much to promote the spread of Buddhism.

After the rise of Islam in 7th century Arabia, it soon spread to other countries in Europe, Africa, Asia and even reached India with Arab traders. Some Indians embraced the new religion, and many of the Arab traders settled in Kerala. In the 8th century CE, Muslim rulers began to occupy India, in spite of strong resistance from the Rajputs. However, Muslim rulers kept control over Sind for 300 years. With the decisive battle of Panipat, near Delhi in 1526, Babar established a new Muslim rule in north India. With the arrival of the Muslim religion, new cultural influences entered the country, including a beautiful style of architecture. Perhaps the most famous of these buildings is the Taj Mahal in Agra.

In 1498 Vasco Da Gama, the Portuguese explorer, reached Calicut in South India. The discovery of a new sea route to India was a remarkable achievement and paved the way for European companies to begin trading directly with India. The coming of the Portuguese also brought India and Indian Christians into an enduring contact with western Christendom and the Roman Catholicism that entered India and put down strong roots.

Throughout the 17th and 18th centuries various European trading companies established themselves in India. The Dutch East India Company was the first to break the Portuguese monopoly early in the 17th century. The British soon followed, with the Danes and the French also establishing trading centers for a time. With the battle of Plassey in 1757, the British established their supremacy over Indian Territories. The British controlled India until its Independence in 1947.

The long struggle for independence from British rule under the nonviolent leadership of M. K. Gandhi resulted in the establishment of India and Pakistan as independent countries. Following independence, the 562 independent native states of India were absorbed into a central government. The division of states was made mainly along linguistic lines. It is estimated that there are 2,209 major people groups in India. Although there are differences from state to state, there are also similarities: the poverty and marginalization of many, the opulence of the few, issues relating to the caste system, globalization, unemployment, child labor, and corruption are some of the issues shared by all regions.

Religion is an integral part of the Indian way of life. Religious laws govern peoples' lives, their clothing, food and marriage. As noted above, all the world's major faiths have met on Indian soil. For Indians a guest is equal to god (*Athidhi devo bhava*); hence, Indians received visitors hospitably. In turn, each religion welcomed into India has taken on distinctively Indian characteristics.

Hinduism is not only the oldest living religion of the world but the most complex of all religions. The term Hindu is said to have been invented by foreigners to describe the inhabitants of the country to the east of the river "Sindu." later known as the Indus. Hinduism has grown gradually over a period of 5,000 years, absorbing and assimilating different religious and cultural currents. Hinduism shelters monotheism, polytheism, pantheism, worshipers of the great Shiva, Vishnu and female counterparts, as well as the spirits of trees, rocks, and village deities. Absolute monotheism goes hand in hand with extreme pluralism: many paths are said to lead to the same goal.

The Vedic scriptures, written between 1500-500 BCE, have shaped the entire Hindu tradition. They teach that all living creatures will have many lives on earth, their souls transmigrating to new incarnations after death. The teaching of Karma holds that all acts in this life will receive an appropriate reward in the next.

Hinduism and the Caste System

The caste system is the social foundation of Hinduism, an everyday reality for the majority of Indians regardless of age, gender and regional, political and religious affiliations. The word caste derives from the Portuguese word *casta*, meaning breed, race, or kind.[1] Among the Indian terms that are sometimes translated as caste are *varna* (color) or *jati*.[2] Although many other nations are characterized by social inequality, perhaps nowhere else in the world has inequality been as elaborately constructed as in the Indian institution of the caste system. M. N. Srinivas defined a caste as a hereditary, endogamous, usually localized group, having a traditional association with an occupation, having a particular position in the local hierarchy of castes.[3] A person is considered a member of the caste into which he or she is born and remains within that caste until his/her death. This cannot be altered by any talent or wealth of the person. In Hindu society, caste is still the most powerful factor in determining a person's dignity and identity.

The four castes from top to bottom are the *Brahmins* (priests and teachers), the *Ksyatriyas* (rulers and soldiers), the *Vaisyas* (merchants and traders), and the *Shudras* (laborers and artisans). Within the four principal castes, there are thousands of sub-castes, also called *jatis*. These endogamous groups are further divided along occupational, sectarian and regional lines. These are sometimes referred to as 'caste Hindus' or people falling within the caste system.

A fifth group of people falls outside the *varna* system, and they are known as "untouchables." These untouchables (Dalits) were given tasks considered to be ritually polluting, so they were considered an "unclean" people.[4] B. R. Ambedkar, a champion of the Dalits, wrote in 1932 that it was immaterial whether an untouchable caused pollution by touch or by use of the common well. "Both are outward registers of the same inward feeling of defilement, odium, aversion and contempt."[5]

The Dalits were prohibited from entering temples, using wells from which the "clean" castes drew their water, and even from attending schools. Dire punishments were prescribed for Dalits who read or even heard sacred texts. Thus, they were reduced to the periphery as untouchable, unspeakable and unapproachable people. Economically, they comprised the poorest of the poor, confined to traditional jobs prescribed by the caste system. Their children were the undernourished and malnourished, without educational opportunities, the child laborers and victims of sexual abuse. Dalit women were subjected to rape, molestation, sexual harassment, assault and scorn, subjected to rejection, deprivation and denial of justice and right to live. A. P. Nirmal, a pioneer Dalit theologian, wrote that Dalits in the sight of caste people were not just "no people" but "non-humans."[6]

The caste system was useful for the ruling classes and so it was continued under Muslim[7] and British rulers.[8] Thus, the Hindu institutionalization of caste and subsequent political, economic and socio-religious historical forces had trampled the identity of these "untouchable" people by the time the colonizers and Christian missionaries arrived in the 19th and 20th centuries. [9] Today, these "untouchables" have chosen to call themselves "Dalits." The term is not a mere name or title but used now as a badge of honor, much as the word "Black" is used today in the United States.[10] Dalits, oppressed in every way by the evil caste system, are now seeking a spirituality that endures conflict and provides hope for a new identity and a new future.

Tribal people and Tribal Conversions in India

While Dalits of South and Central India were converting to Christianity, north-east India, Jarkhand and North Bihar witnessed a substantial conversion of tribal peoples to Christianity. India is home to the world's second-largest tribal population in the world, after Africa. There are over 400 tribes living in India with a tribal population of about 80 million, according to 2001 statistics. Together, Dalits and tribal people constitute 25% of India's population. Tribal communities come from three racial stocks: Mongolian, Austroloid and Dravidian. They are divided into four major sectors on the basis of their geographical location.[11] They are indigenous people who have maintained their distinct social, religious and cultural identities. Unlike Hindus, tribal people have no caste system. However, the British census commissioners and British government anthropological advisers of the 19th century classified both Dalits and tribal people as untouchables, outside the four-fold caste system.

Tribal people and Dalits share a common history of oppression and displacement.[12] Wati Longchar, quoting Peter Haokip, describes the Hindu treatment of Tribal people:

> The hill tribes in Manipur (till recently or still today in some places and by some) were *hao* (a derogatory designation) and were not allowed to enter the houses of Manipur Hindus. It was considered to be a defilement. If a tribal [person] wanted to meet a Manipuri Hindu, he could only shout from a distance in front of the court yard of the house.[13]

Tribal people, however, argue strongly that they are not Hindus.

Like the Dalits the tribal people were described by derogatory terms such as "animist," "primitive," "backward," "uncivilized," and so on. The tribal people themselves preferred to use the terms "ethnic," "indigenous," "primal/primordial," or following India's Sanskrit-derived terms, *adivasi* (first inhabitants), *vanavasi* (forest people), *girijan* (hill people), etc. They have decided to use the term "Tribal"[14] for themselves, even though the term can carry a negative meaning. By accepting the "tribal" designation they are asserting that they are the indigenous people, the first people of India, retaining their primal traditions. Secondly, the term reminds them of their own history of suffering, humiliation and alienation, and of the way God has liberated them from that situation. Thirdly, the term affirms the distinctiveness of tribal tradition, which affirms the centrality of land/creation or space as the foundation for their understanding of culture, identity, personhood and religious ethos. And finally, the term affirms a common identity.[15]

The Constitution of India has given official identity to these communities who are not fully assimilated in the general population.[16] North-eastern tribal people strongly argue for their geographical, political, cultural and racial difference from Hindus. Most north-eastern Indians describe their identity as politically Indian, and racially and culturally Mongolian, placing them outside Hindu culture with its caste-ridden social system.[17]

Women in Hindu Culture

Until recent years, women in India were systematically limited to a secondary role in society. Women were confined to performing household chores, bearing children and caring for the entire family. Women, regardless of religious background, geographical location or linguistic background, were the most oppressed people in the patriarchal structures, in practice allowed no rights at all either in education or property.[18] M. N. Srinivas has written that "the husband was not only the wife's master but her deity. In his service was her salvation. He might be a wife-beater, drunkard, gambler and womanizer but her duty was to serve and obey him."[19] In short, the caste system and Brahminical patriarchy[20] are the twin oppressive institutions which have relegated Indian women to a submissive position.

In the modern period Christian missionaries and Indian women reformers like Pandita Ramabai and Savitribai Pule have fought for women's rights. The Indian constitution has declared equality between men and women as a fundamental right, and guarantees equal protection before the law and equal opportunities in public employment. Subsequently, the social realities have been changing, even though the rate of change is slow. Hundreds of thousands of women now go to work, and educated and successful women have acquired a remarkable confidence.[21] There are now women employed in education, health, banks, industry, in the social sciences, engineering, and aviation and even in the Police Services.[22]

Despite their long struggle, women have not yet been able to attain a rightful position in politics. India was proud when Indira Gandhi became the first woman Prime Minister of India, but since, no one has been able to reach such heights. Women have been accepted as voters but not as policy formulators and decision-makers, although at the time of this writing, the President and Speakers of the *Lok Sabha* (literally, "House of the People," that is the Lower House of Parliament) are women.

Christianity in the Indian Context

Modern Indian church history can be traced to the arrival of Roman Catholic missionaries in the 16th century. The first Protestant missionaries – German Pietists – arrived on the southeastern coast in 1706. William Carey, the first English-speaking missionary, arrived in Bengal in 1793. Throughout the 19th century European and North American missions established churches throughout the sub-continent. Most churches practiced a form of "comity," or agreements not to interfere or overlap with Christian work already established in a town or region. When they arrived, Mennonite and Brethren in Christ followed the patterns of evangelization and church development already present in India.

O. L. Snaitang and Dick Kooiman have rightly observed that religion has been an important agency for acquiring a better and more dignified place in Indian society.[23] It is thus not surprising that tribal people and Dalits, who were victims of Hinduism and its caste system, converted to other religions that granted them self-respect and dignity along with a new religious identity. Tribal people of north-east India, Chotanagpur, in the present states of Bihar and Jarkhand, have chosen to convert to Christianity.[24] Among the Dalits there were also conversions to Islam. Dalits in the Punjab chose Sikhism; Maratha Dalits chose Buddhism; the south-Indian Dalits chose both Christianity and Islam.

After Independence in 1947 there was a five-fold increase in the number of Christians in the tribal regions. Christianity was widely accepted among the Mizo and Naga people, with conversion rates at close to 100 percent, while among the Khasi, Jaintia and other Tribal groups there is a sizeable Christian following.[25] Independence did not result in mass conversions among the Dalits, however, since Dalits who converted were denied the same benefits the tribal people received.

The historian Frederick Downs has observed that generalizations about Tribal people are not appropriate because each tribe has its own distinct history, heritage, culture, language and identity.[26] However, a recent study argues that Christianity provided the north-east communities with the means of preserving a distinctive identity.[27]

Downs also writes that Christianity provided the tribal communities with an ideology that helped them "maintain their identity in the face of the erosion of their traditional religious, social and political institutions."[28] For Downs, identity is the key interpretive category for the conversion of tribal people to Christianity. In fact, there is a consensus among scholars who have studied north-east India that in the twentieth century, the gradual enculturation of the Christian message in various segments of tribal cultural diversity has succeeded in giving Tribal people a new identity. [29]

The Mennonite witness in India began in the last decades of the 19th century. The Mennonite arrival in India was part of a large movement of Christian missions from Europe and North America between 1850 and 1950. Today the Mennonite and Brethren in Christ Churches are well-established particularly in Andra, Chhattisgarh, and Bihar states. Many of the missions in India came from the west, but the Mennonite mission in India came first from Russia in 1889. Although Mennonite Brethren in America began supporting Baptist missions in India as early as 1883, it was the Mennonite Brethren Church in Russia who sent the first missionaries to India in 1889. Several Mennonite and BIC churches followed with their own mission efforts, but the Mennonite Brethren are the oldest and largest Mennonite group in India. Another important Mennonite witness in India is that of the Mennonite Central Committee (MCC), first present in India in 1942 in Calcutta (now Kolkata).

The majority of Indian Mennonite adherents came from the Dalits,[30] from poor landless farm laborers, or from tribal and Satnami[31] backgrounds. Not surprisingly, the Mennonite and BIC missions began their work by establishing orphanages and educational and medical institutions to empower these marginalized communities. In the fashion of the time, they established mission compounds in which to locate these institutions. Linguistically

Mennonite Missions to India

American Mennonite Brethren (AMB), 1889 to Hyderabad, Andhra Pradesh

Mennonite Church in India (MCI), 1899 to Dhamtari, Madhya Pradesh (now Chhattisgarh)

Bharatiya General Conference Mennonite Church (BGCMC), 1900 to Champa, Chhattisgarh

Brethren in Christ Church (BIC), 1914, to North Bihar

Bharatiya Jukto Christian Prachar Mandali (also known as United Missionary Society, UMS), 1914, to West Bengal, *Bihar*

Mennonite Mandali (BMM), 1940 in South Bihar (now Jarkhand)

Brethren in Christ Church, 1982 in Orrisa

A fellowship association of these Mennonites groups in India, called Mennonite Christian Service Fellowship of India (MCSFI) came into existence in 1963.

the Mennonite and BIC churches established in India are a hetero-geneous group, speaking more than a half-dozen languages; officially they correspond with each other in English as the common language of communication. Geographically the Mennonite churches are at great distances from each other, spread out in several states in India.

India welcomed Christian missionaries of various denominations, and as a result the foreign missionaries who came to India planted their denominational divisions along with the Gospel. In fact, many Christians carry various denominational labels (divisions) in India without knowing the reasons. In India the denominational labels are only historical accidents; therefore, the relationship between denominations in the post-missionary era has been very cordial. The denominations work together in regional, national church councils such as the Andhra Pradesh Council of Churches (APCC), the National Council of Churches in India (NCCI), etc. What is most important and challenging to an Indian Christian is having faith in Jesus Christ.

The Mennonite Brethren Church in India

The Conference of the Mennonite Brethren Church is the official name of the Mennonite Brethren Church in India (CMBCI), pioneered by Mennonite Brethren missions to India in 1889. In the 120 years since the first Mennonite Brethren missionaries came to India, the Mennonite Brethren Church of India has become one of the largest denominations in the Telangana region of Andhra Pradesh and also, one of the largest conferences in the Mennonite World Communion. The MB Conference has a membership of two hundred thousand persons, worshipping in nine hundred and sixty four congregations.[32] The gratitude of Indian Mennonites for the work of foreign missionaries is expressed by Karuna Shri Joel:

> I am one of the products of missionary work here in India... if no missionaries had come to India over one hundred years ago, I would not have been what I am now. To put it briefly, I became a Christian, because I believed; I believed because I heard. I heard because someone preached; someone preached because they decided to come to India with the Gospel of Jesus Christ. It was the strong convictions of the missionary workers that led me to become a full-time minister.[33]

Through their committed services the missionaries took the Gospel to remote and inaccessible places. As a result of the many faithful Mennonite missionaries and nationals there is a strong Mennonite presence today in India. Dr. Arnold, president of the CMBCI, reflected in January 2010 at the celebrations of the 150th anniversary of Mennonite Brethren, saying:

> These celebrations are a celebration of MB Missionary services in India and worldwide. But it is also a celebration of the faith journey of our great grandparents, grandparents, our parents and us. This celebration is extremely significant for us here in India. Today we are not the people just saved by the blood of Jesus Christ but we are also the people evolved to a higher status in faith, in Biblical knowledge, in interpretation of the scriptures, in culture, in social status, in economical status, and in political status. Once our ancestors were blind, now we see. Once we were objects of mission and now we are sufficiently evolved and empowered to be the agents of mission.[34]

This expression of gratitude was spoken on behalf of all Indian Mennonites who have been transformed and empowered as a result of Mennonite missions and ministries in India.

Historical Background of Andhra Pradesh

Andhra Pradesh is historically called "the Rice Bowl of India." It is the third-largest state in the Indian union and the largest of the south-India states both in area and population. Telugu is the predominant language of the state and the second-largest spoken language in India after Hindi, the national language.

Christianity did not come to the Telugu region until the sixteenth century. The first Christian missionary to bring the Gospel to the Telugus was Father Louis, a Franciscan priest in 1535 CE. In 1597 the Jesuit Fathers came to Chandragiri and remained 18 years; they left in 1615 when could not convince anyone to convert to Christianity. The Jesuit fathers then made Machilipatnum and Bheemlipatnam their centers of activity. The Jesuits undertook more missionary activity in Chittoor and other parts of the region in the early eighteenth century.

The first Protestant mission to propagate the Gospel among the Telugu-speaking people was Benjamin Schultze of Germany with the Danish-Halle Mission. As early as 1716 the Danish-Halle missionaries had opened schools for Tamil children in Madras and Cuddalore,[35] which brought them into contact with Telugu-speaking people. The nineteenth century saw numerous missions among the Telugu people with the Mennonite Brethren coming from Russia in 1889, and the American Mennonite Brethren in 1899. These missions bore fruit. The 19th and early 20th centuries witnessed substantial Dalit conversions to Protestant Christianity in Andhra Pradesh, with the highest percentage of group conversions to Christianity in all of India.[36]

The first Mennonite Brethren missionary to India, Abraham Friesen, arrived in Hyderabad from the Ukraine in 1889, less than thirty years after the emergence of the Mennonite Brethren as a new denomination in Russia. Ten years later, American Mennonite Brethren (AMB) missionaries, on the invitation of Friesen and the Baptists with whom he served, also arrived to serve the Telugu-speaking people of Andhra Pradesh. The American Mennonite Brethren missionaries decided to work independently in and around the Mahabubnagar District and soon achieved remarkable success among the Dalits.

Abraham Friesen

Like many other early missionaries to India, the Mennonite Brethren missionaries did not understand the complex socio-religious and cultural issues of India, particularly relating to caste and "untouchability." Many Protestant missionaries first sought to convert high caste people, and when they failed to convert them began to concentrate on the Dalits. Unlike those missionaries, the Mennonite Brethren missionaries concentrated on Dalits as soon as they arrived.

John Everett Clough of the American Baptist Mission is considered the "Apostle of the Madigas" (one of the sub-castes of Dalits). At the time of his arrival in 1865 the mission had only one station at Nellore, called the "Lone Star Mission," with a church membership of just 30 people.[37] When John Everett Clough came to Andhra Pradesh in March 1866, he was easily convinced that he should work among the Dalits (Madigas) even though he had intended to work among higher caste people. He had outstanding success and initiated a mass movement of conversion. One day in 1868, Clough is reported to have baptized 2222 Madigas (Dalits) near Ongole and subsequently there were mass baptisms of nearly 9000 persons in six weeks in and around Ongole.[38] In 1882 alone 20,086 baptisms took place.[39] It is possible that the group conversions to Christianity in this region were supported by a revolutionary sentiment of which the Christian missionaries were probably quite unaware.[40]

The mission station in the Mahabubnagar District area of Andhra Pradesh, which became the center of Mennonite Brethren mission work in India, was an extension station of earlier Baptist missionary work. Albert Chute, a pioneer Baptist missionary in Mahabubnagar District, had shared Clough's ideology and policies, and the American Mennonite Brethren who followed generally adopted the strategies of the American Baptists who had preceded them in their work among the Telugus.[41] Daniel F. Bergthold, one of four pioneering missionaries among the Mennonite Brethren, concentrated his work among the Dalits when he reached Nagarkurnool, the first American Mennonite Brethren mission station in the Mahabubnager District.

Abraham Friesen and his wife arrived in Hyderabad in 1889. Clough's success at Ongole had led Friesen to opt for India and the Telugu region.[42] However the young Russian Mennonite Brethren church was not in a position to start its own work due to lack of resources. Therefore, Friesen began his work in collaboration with the American Baptists. In May 1890, Friesen and five native missionaries from the Ongole Baptist mission moved to Nalgonda, to take over the station founded by Campbell as an out station in 1885. The Mennonite Brethren Church in Russia sent around half a dozen missionary couples to meet the growing needs of the mission work in India. They established stations at Suryapet, Bohnigir and Janagam. They continued their mission until the First World War and the Russian Revolution, after which it became difficult to receive funding from Russia. The Baptist mission organization in Boston took over these three mission stations, which by then had an approximate membership of seven to eight thousand people. The American Mennonite Brethren mission, which began its mission work in the same area, did not show any interest in adopting these stations,[43] but Abraham Friesen did motivate the American Mennonite Brethren (AMB) to come to India.

Abraham Friesen spent the years from 1897 to 1899 in America, where he encouraged the American Mennonite Brethren Church to start mission work among Telugus. There had been considerable interest in foreign mission work among the Mennonite Brethren Churches as early as 1883, and many members had contributed privately and through the conference to various mission efforts in India and Africa.[44] At Friesen's urging, the American Mennonite Brethren Church decided to start its own mission, and chose India and the Hyderabad area as their first destination. Choosing India was made easy by Friesen's successful work at Nalgonda, and the American Brethren had heard of the Dalit conversions (Madigas) under John Everett Clough at Ongole during the previous decades.[45]

The first missionaries sent by the AMB mission were N. N. Hiebert, his wife Susie Wiebe Hiebert and Miss Elizabeth Neufeld, who arrived India in 1899. This group of three was soon joined by Miss Anna Suderman, who had gone as an independent worker to Ahmadabad, Gujarat in 1898. The Hieberts chose Hughestown, in the city of Hyderabad to begin their work, but unfortunately, he had to return to North America within eighteen months due to illness.

In 1902 J. H. Pankratz and his wife arrived and purchased three acres of land and a few buildings in Malakpet the following year. This was the first mission property owned by the AMB in India. Several native evangelists from Nalgonda now joined the missionaries in the proclamation of the Gospel. On 27th March, 1904 the missionaries, some native workers and a few new converts organized themselves as the first Mennonite Brethren Church in India. In 1904 Miss Neufeld began a School for Children, which gathered initially under a shade tree. Miss Suderman found open doors ministering to the sick and suffering and also doing personal evangelism among local women.

In 1904 D. F. Bergthold and his wife arrived in India. At first Bergthold stayed with Pankratz at Malakpet, Hyderabad. According to the "comity" agreements, the district area in and around Mahabubnager district area was reserved for work by the American Baptists and Albert Chute had established the first American Baptist Mission station in the district in 1885 at Mahabubnagar town. Since the area was too large for Chute to handle, he invited American Mennonite Brethren to share in the work. As a result, in 1906 Daniel Bergthold of the AMB entered the Mahabubnager district and began by opening a mission station at Nagarkurnool.

American Baptists and American Mennonite Brethren carried on simultaneous activities until 1937.[46] In 1937 the two big Baptist Mission stations, Mahabubnagar and Gadwal were added to the American Mennonite Brethren Mission. The purchase of the Mahabubnagar and

Gadwal mission stations also included 65 acres of land at Jedcherla. The oldest church at Jadcherla had been started by the Society for the Propagation of the Gospel (SPG), but after organizing the church they handed it over to Chute and the Baptist Mission, who had used the land for industrial training. [47] The policy of Mennonite mission was not to enter into industrial training. Instead in 1952 they started medical work there resulting in a hospital still famous in that district.

The "Telugu Village Mission" at Makthal and Narayanpet was added in 1954. D. P. Musabaye of Srilanka had started independent mission work here with Chute's permission, in 1913. After serving for seven years Musabaye decided return home, but learned that Billington of the Church Missionary Society (CMS) was interested in beginning a ministry in India. Musabaye wrote to Billington to come and carry on the work he had begun. Thus Charles Billington came and occupied the field in 1921, founding "The Telugu Village Mission," which experienced many conversions in a 15-year period. [48] When the Mennonite Brethren added the Telugu Village Mission to their work, they became responsible for the entire district. Later the South India Missionary churches in the Adoni area also joined the AMB.

Thus, the present-day Mennonite Brethren Church in India is the amalgamation of the work of American Baptists, the SPG, the Telugu Village Mission, and the South Indian Missionary Church. Although the Mennonite Brethren Mission came late to the district, today it is the major denomination in the Mahabubnagar district.

Protestant missionaries who came to India in the colonial period lived a comparatively luxurious life style, leaving much of the evangelistic work to the native people. The Mennonite missionaries were no exception. However, Mennonite missionaries did introduce some Anabaptist views, particularly the concept of non-violence, not rendering military service, and political separation. Ironically, most of the Mennonite missionaries kept guns, saying they needed them for protection (their mission compounds were far from the towns) as well as for hunting.

Many missionaries, like white *sahibs*, adopted the style and methods of colonizers. As soon as they arrived, they began to build huge bungalows and compounds. The missionary house was called a "bungalow," but it was not the small cottage implied by the American usage of that term. In India a bungalow was a large structure built of red bricks and with a red tile roof that reached down over wide, sweeping verandas. Seen from the outside, the missionary bungalow appeared to be a two-story dwelling, with windows located in the walls above the veranda roof. But it was just a one-story building with a high ceiling in the central rooms. The central concern of bungalow design was to combat the severe summer heat, which could rise to 110 or 120 degrees F. (43-49 C.) in the summer. A large rug-like fan hung from the ceiling which could be

Mennonite Missionary Bungalow at Wanaparthy

moved by a servant on the veranda pulling a cord through the wall. Missionary dwellings were in their own way as impressive and imposing as the lavish houses of the local Indian elite – the landowner kings. J. H. Voth at Devarakonda built a commodious two-storied building at the center of the mission compound, covering 3720 square feet on the ground floor. Missionaries used to report that if they did not build such bungalows they might possibly die from the heat.

The coming of electricity and electric fans made the high ceilings unnecessary, while the coming anti-colonialism and national independence made the disparity in life-style between mission and church a potential source of conflict. With the departure of the missionaries in the 1970s, some of these bungalows became white elephants, empty and deserted reminders of a day when the relationships between missionaries and nationals were vastly different.[49] Missionary Janzen at Wanaparthy began building a huge two-storied bungalow and a compound during a time of extreme famine, from1919 to 1921. The walls inside the huge bungalow were coated with a lime mix made with thousands of egg whites to make a smooth, shiny finish similar to the palace walls of the Raja.[50] Janzen justified building such a huge bungalow saying that the local Raja wanted to have a suitable house in which to stay when he came to the compound.[51]

The huge mission compounds included schools, dormitories, and a hospital. Missionaries had their attention diverted to the administration of these institutions, rather than being able to concentrate on evangelism. They would supervise these institutions until the summer vacation, and they would then retreat to the hills for rest for three months. Therefore A. E. Janzen, then executive secretary of the Mission Board, who visited India in 1948, wrote the following in his report.

> I am convinced that we must strengthen this phase of our work. Our missionaries are not getting out into the 2,000 villages like they should, or would if it were possible. This neglect is no fault of theirs. Our staff is inadequate. Our present missionaries are tied down by station work. The one who has charge of the Bible School cannot tour during six months. The one who supervises the High School cannot tour for nine months of the year. The one who needs to supervise two main stations has no time to tour because of the many station duties.[52]

Mennonite Missionaries also enjoyed sufficient financial support from the mission board. For example the salaries for an MB missionary couple in 1912 were $1,000 annually, and for each child, an annual allowance of $100. A single missionary got half of the above amount. These salaries were about 30 percent of what an experienced British collector of a district was paid. Nevertheless, missionaries complained that it was difficult to make ends meet on these allowances.[53]

On the other hand nationals received much less, in spite of the fact that their contribution to the work from the beginning was significant, with a remarkable commitment to the growth of the church. Missionaries depended on local preachers from the beginning. The evangelists, Bible women, and village pastors were particularly effective witnesses to Christ in the villages. From the beginning the Indian Mennonite Brethren have been uncomfortable if they are not engaged in mission outreach and evangelism.

The missionaries in the field knew from the beginning that India could be evangelized "only by her own sons and daughters." Thus they realized the need for theological training. However, having no school of their own, they sent their

Panzagulla Church dedication, 1964

brethren to the Ramayapatnam Baptist Theological Seminary, until they began their own Bible school in 1920 at Nagerkurnol.[54] Even then students were sent to Ramayapatnam and later to Union Biblical Seminary, United Theological College, Bangalore etc. V. K. Rufus was right in his observation that the early leaders were not trained in Anabaptist environments of higher education.[55]

Since most of the converts came from Dalit background, the Baptist Theological Seminary introduced 6 years of training, with 3 years of early education, followed by 3 years of seminary training. By 1970 the MB Conference had stopped sending candidates to Ramapatnam Baptist Seminary and began sending students to Union Biblical Seminary. In the 1990's the MBs developed their own College and began training their own candidates, granting B.Th and B.D. degrees.

The Mennonite Brethren Church in India started a "Home Mission" in the Avurpally village of Kalwakurthy Field in 1924, with R. Rathnam as the first native missionary. Rathnam and his wife labored for many years with good results. Over the years the Kalwakurthy Home Mission carried out its mission program in thirty-four villages, sent additional missionaries into the field and selected students for studies at the Conference's Bible institute. The Telugu Convention supported the Kalwakurthy Home Mission until 1959, at which

Village Outreach, n.d.

time it was merged into Kalwakurthy Field. M. B. John, the first Indian president of the Governing Council of the CMB Church and a pastor who worked alongside some of the pioneer missionaries, claims that many conversions resulted from the work of village preachers who went from village to village preaching and witnessing.[56] Even in the hot summer seasons these native pastors, preachers, teachers, paramedical staff, and other leaders formed groups to go on evangelistic tours and often reported massive evangelistic campaigns and many baptisms.

Several early missionaries noted that it was the "natives" who did much of the work of evangelism, but the work of these "natives" has never been adequately recorded. In the reports of the time they

Fellowship meeting with pastors, 1963

were often referred to only as a "national" or in passing, without mention of their name or identity. P. B. Arnold, President of CMB Church in India, in his inaugural address at the one hundred year celebration of the birth of Mennonite Brethren Church in India in 1989, gave full recognition to national workers, stating that "the sacrifice and selfless service of the nationals was in no way less important. The missionaries gave the support, leadership and guidance, and the nationals worked in the field facing many tribulations. Together they accomplished far beyond their capacity."[57]

Village Sunday School class, Amrabad Church, 1964

Local preachers could make a great impact because they had easy access to their own communities. Like most of their listeners, they were Dalits who had no education or social status and were even forbidden to enter temples. Such "social lepers," now transformed, came to their own people with the power of the Gospel, the message of equality, the message

that the God they had found would love them all equally. This made a remarkable impact on fellow Dalits as it was not just a verbal message with which they came, but also a message based on personal experience and real change – in clothing (previously denied), in Bible reading (education), in association with missionaries (status) and in reference to a message of equality and love.

Workshop with Deverakonda preachers before beginning a month of evangelistic campaigns, 1966

The MB Convention was the yearly spiritual gathering of the Mennonite Brethren churches in India, generally held in April/May in a central location. It started in 1918 with the name Andhra MB Telugu Convention. This convention used to bring together people from all the fields of the MB church in India. Its most important contribution was to support the "Home Mission" that started in 1924 in Kalwakurthy Field. The last Convention was held in April, 2004 in Parllepally village of Yemiganur Field.

The missionaries felt the need to use printed materials to reach the masses with tracts, books, pamphlets and other kinds of literature. The first printing press was brought to the Mahbubnager district by A. A. Unruh from Russia in 1931. This printing press produced the Conference periodical *Suvarthamani*, an MB spiritual magazine that was started in 1920. By the 1960s many theological books had also been printed and published.

Publishing house staff at work, 1970

Radio Evangelism began in the 1950's, when it was discovered that in India the entire family would listen to radio programs. The first Telugu Christian radio program had a three-fold aim: to disseminate the Gospel as widely as possible and thus serve as a supplement to evangelism in the Telugu area; to penetrate homes in order to reach families with the Gospel of Jesus Christ; and to present the Gospel to the high caste people (Caste Evangelism), Muslims, educated professionals, and government workers.

Henry Krahn and the John Wiebe began recording half hour radio programs which were sent to the Philippines and Ceylon to be broadcast back to India. R. R. K. Murthy, a Brahman convert, was one of the main speakers. Correspondence courses were offered, with J. Paramjyothy doing follow-up work. In the 1970s R. R. K. Murthy and Henry Poetker began working independently of the Indian Mennonite Brethren Church, although they still depended upon the

S. A. Jyothy, radio broadcast technician, 1979

Recording "Ghar Sansar," a women's radio program, 1976

Mission Board for most of their financial support. The radio ministry produced some good results. It was reported that 36 new places of worship were established in the Kavitham and Nididevolu coastal areas in 1979, with a total attendance of 1,170. The MB radio staff used to visit these places to encourage and strengthen the new believers.

Transition from Mission to Church and Rapid Growth in the Post-Missionary Era

In 1954 the Indian Government established "The Christian Missionary Enquiry Committee" to look into foreign missionaries and their mission work in India. Hindus were considering initiating a movement called "Missionaries Bharat Chodo" (missionaries leave India). The report by the Committee in 1956 complicated the status of missionaries and raised the issue of conversion, and many missionaries subsequently left India, beginning the process of handing over church leadership to Indian leaders.

The transition of the MB Church from mission church to national church took place in 1958 when the AMB mission transferred administrative power to the "Conference of the Mennonite Brethren Church of India." The first national leader, M. B. John, became chairman in 1960 and served a few more terms into the 1970s. However, no Governing Council meetings were held without a missionary presence until after Dan Nikkel, the last missionary, left in 1973. In the 1970s the government of India began restricting visas to missionaries, and in 1972 the parliament of India passed the Foreign Exchange Act to regulate and control the purchase, holding, sale or transfer of property by foreigners in India. This law was expected to come into force in March, 1973. The biggest challenge for the mission was the transfer of property to the trust, an issue that was resolved in 1976 when the properties of AMB mission were transferred to M. B. Property Association of India (P) Ltd.

The official membership of the Indian Mennonite Brethren Church (IMBC) in 1949 was 12,443.[58] There has been continual and substantial growth since then; in fact, the IMB has become one of the largest churches in the Mennonite World Conference.

India Mennonite Brethren Church Governing Council meeting. D. J. Arthur is at podium; M. B. John is standing

In the 1980s, the IMB Conference established two separate mission fields, one in Mumbai, and the other in Gangavathy, Karnataka District. The CMBCI is also extending its services into the Sholapur area and into North India, particularly in Delhi and Punjab. Over the last two decades, the MB church has also received converts from other castes, creeds and religions because of its emphasis on evangelism and church planting through Church Extension Workers, Inter-Faith Ministries, and Disciple Making International members (formerly CPE). The Mennonite Brethren Church leadership has emphasized Biblical knowledge, Evangelical Spirituality and the Peace position. Therefore it was observed that from the early times Mennonite Brethren were uncomfortable if they were not engaged in mission and evangelism. Subsequently they have engaged in vibrant missionary activity, and gave first priority to it.

A good number of independent churches have recently merged with the Mennonite Brethren church from the Districts of Nizamabad and Cuddaph. In addition, 27 Baptist Churches in Tripura state of North Eastern India are seeking to affiliate with the Mennonite Brethren. Thus CMB Church in India continues to grow steadily by continuing mission and evangelism, and receiving independent churches. Apart from the Conference Church Extension Workers (CEWs), who are our native missionaries involved in evangelism with the support of MBMSI, many local churches are engaged in evangelism in their nearby villages, leading to tremendous church growth. Some of the larger churches are spending as much as 30% of their income supporting pastors and undertaking missionary activity.

The MB Women's Conference, established in 1958, has contributed a great deal to the growth of the church. The major contribution of the MB Women's Conference has been in the area of evangelism, fund raising for the conference activities, and in recent times for relief and rehabilitation. Mrs. Sarada Arnold has provided leadership to this church body.

Minister P. B. Benjamin leading his family in worship, 1966

The leader of the MB Church over the last three decades has been Doctor P. B. Arnold. He is the son of P. Benjamin, a village pastor. By profession he is a medical doctor who did his Masters in Surgery (MS) at the Christian Medical College, Ludhiana, Punjab, a famous medical college. Dr. Arnold, who is known as a skilled surgeon, was ordained to the ministry in June 1976. The following year he became Chairman of the MB Church. Except for a period from 1979 to 1980, Dr. Arnold has been the Chairman (now President) of the Governing Council, more than 33 years of service. Dr. Arnold has represented the IMB Church at numerous national and international conferences, has helped govern MB properties in India, and currently (2010) also serves as President of the Andhra Pradesh Christian Council (APCC).

The emergence of trained theologians since late 1970s with the scholarship and support from MBMSI has been a strength of the

Dr. P. B. Arnold and his daughter, Dr. Margaret Arnold, at Jadcherla Medical Centre, 1999

Conference ministries. By the 1970s 14 persons had received leadership training in Mennonite Brethren Biblical Seminary in Fresno, USA. In recent years two Indian MB students were sent abroad for specialized studies: E. D. Solomon, for PhD studies in Missions and Christina Asheervadam for Peace and Conflict Resolution Studies. Other church leaders have pursued theological studies in the UBS, Pune and UTC, Bangalore.[59]

The Mennonite Brethren Centenary Bible College (MBCBC) in Shamshabad is also an important Conference vehicle for preparing Bible centered, and missionary oriented pastors.

The Mennonite Brethren Centenary Bible College (MBCBC) was established in 1989, but its beginning goes back to 1920 when Rev. D. F. Bergthold, a Mennonite missionary, started the Bethany Bible Institute at Nagarkurnool. Later the school was moved to Shamshabad where it has remained ever since. Bethany Bible Institute offered a Certificate in Theology (C.Th) and introduced the Graduate of Theology program (G.Th) in 1958. It has trained hundreds of men and women to serve the church and its educational and health institutions. In 1967, the school's name was changed from Bethany Bible Institute to Mennonite Brethren Bible Institute, or MBBI.

Groundbreaking at Mennonite Brethren Bible Institute, Shamhabad, 1975. Dr. P. B. Arnold digs with the shovel; Rev. M. B. John and Rev. N. F. James (Principal of the MB Bible Institute) are to his right.

The Mennonite Brethren Centenary Bible College (MBCBC) grew out of the MBBI and remains located at Shamshabad, 18 kilometers south-west of Hyderabad, Andhra Pradesh. This College has been affiliated with the Senate of Serampore College since 1995. At present it is the only Mennonite Bible College in all of south Asia that offers degrees at the B.D. level. The B.D. program is designed to equip persons for essential functions and ministries of the church, persons who can commend their faith with relevance, in a pluralistic world. B.D. studies attempt an integrative and interdisciplinary approach in biblical, theological, historical and religious studies, with the added involvement in the practical life and ministry of the sub-continent. Beginning in 2003, MBCBC has offered the Bachelor of Theology degree and a Diploma in Christian Studies, as well as the Bachelor of Divinity degree.

Student and daughter, MBBI, 1983

Om Prakash

Om Prakash is a final-year student at MBCBC. He comes from Siddartha Nagar, the birth place of the Buddha, in Utter Pradesh, located on the border of Nepal. This area is a very strongly Hindu, and there is not a single church in the whole district of Siddartha Nagar. After beginning studies at the College, Om Prakash was attracted to Mennonite Brethren life and teachings, and became a member of the MB church. He now goes to his birthplace during the holidays and engages in mission. As a result, this Hindu area is responding to the Gospel positively. He feels that very soon he will see Mennonite Brethren churches emerging in this place. He wants to "live and die as a Mennonite Brethren."

B. V. Bushanan in 1996, at the time, the oldest living MBBI graduate

Peace has been a core biblical value for the Anabaptist-Mennonites since the sixteenth century. Nevertheless, before 2003 no courses in Peacemaking and Conflict Studies had been offered in theological colleges in India. A few secular universities did offer Gandhian studies. This changed with the offering of a course at MBCBC entitled "Anabaptist Mennonite History and Peace Theology," at the B.D. level. As the news spread, other affiliated colleges in the Senate family invited MBCBC to conduct Peace Workshops. This led to the development of a curriculum in Peacemaking and Conflict Studies at the B.D. level, and the founding of the Center for Peace and Conflict Resolution Studies (CPCRS) at MBCBC, attracting students from other denominations, from all over India and even from neighboring countries such as Myanmar and Bhutan. Most post-secondary graduates become pastors and evangelists.

The CPCRS aims to promote reconciliation and forgiveness in communities, not just by achieving absence of conflict, but by establishing Shalom, the right relationship between individuals, the community and God. CPCRS programs aims to build peace at all levels of society through educational efforts. If one pastor/theologian is equipped as a peacemaker, the whole congregation and community can benefit.

Old MBCBC Students Quarters, as seen in 2006

The Historical Commission came into existence in 1999 with the goal of strengthening the historic Anabaptist-Mennonite Brethren roots of the MB Church in India. The India Historical Commission has been able to organize seminars and exhibitions, photo exhibitions and "Historical Consciousness" Sundays in the Conference. A significant event was the inauguration in 1999 of the Historical Library and Archives, meant to serve as a research center for Mennonite Studies in India. The Historical Library and

History Writers' Workshop, Shamshabad, 2006

Archives began to serve as the official deposi-
tory of documents, the place to preserve the
records of the rich history of our conference.
I. P. Asheervadam's association with both the
Historical Commission and the Mennonite
World Conference's Global History Project
paved the way for the collecting of historical documents of the other Mennonite and
Brethren in Christ groups in India. Thus in a
short time the Historical Library has become
center for Mennonite studies in India, preserving unique and rare books, files, letters,
pamphlets, photographs, anecdotal stories
of Mennonite church pioneers, records of
church activities, and annual reports.

> **Motto and objectives of the MB Historical Commission**
>
> **Motto**: "Preserve and pass on the MB Church Tradition for the next Generation in India"
>
> **Aims and objectives:**
> i. To collect and preserve the historical documents of the activities of churches, conferences, boards, and institutions.
> ii. To record and interpret this history.
> iii. To recover and tell the story of the churches,
> iv. To bring awareness of the importance of history.
> v. To publish historical literature.

The Mennonite Brethren Development
Organization (MBDO), the branch of the Mennonite Brethren Church in India concerned
specifically with social concerns, was registered in 1982 as a welfare
society. In 1983, MBDO successfully completed 69 Food-for-work projects in 4 districts of drought-stricken Andhra Pradesh, with 211 tons
of wheat made available by Mennonite Central Committee/Commit-
tee on Social Action of the National Christian Council (CASA). There
were 70,400 laborers who benefitted from this aid – 80% of them
Dalits. Other activities included a program of subsidies to feed poor
children, community development activities, and assistance during
natural calamities with the help of MCSFI-MCC. The involvement of
MBDO helping the recent flood victims in Mahabubnager was well
appreciated.

The Mennonite Brethren Medical Centre was established at Jadcherla in 1952 by the Mission
through the vision of Jake and
Ruth Friesen. In 1973 Dr. Arnold
became its superintendent and
chief surgeon. Till late 1990s it
was the only large hospital in
the region that continued to
serve as a non-profit making and
charitable institution. The Cross

Eighth graduation class of nurses' training
school, Jadcherla, 1970

Culture Mission Service (CCMSM) has been the only major donor to the medical center in recent times. At present the medical center is being developed into the MB Christian Institute of Medical Education and Research, with the establishment of a Nursing College and various allied professional courses, thanks to the work of Dr. Arnold and all the staff, past and present, at the Medical Centre.

Recent Significant Events in the Mennonite Brethren Church

The Church of South India (CSI) has played a pioneering role in opening the ministry to women in the church. The CSI first ordained a woman as a presbyter in 1984, and by 1990 the CSI had ordained twenty women presbyters. Other congregations – among them the Church of North India, the Methodist Church of India, and the Lutheran Church in India – have similarly ordained women in their congregations and organizations.

The situation in the Mennonite Brethren church has been somewhat unique. Even though the women have played a significant role in the MB church from the beginning, participating actively in the ministry with commitment and dedication, they were not ordained until recent times. November 8, 2008 was an historic day for the CMBCI. For the first time 26 women were ordained and 34 women commissioned in the Mennonite Brethren Church. On this day, which marked the Golden Jubilee Celebration of the formation of the Governing Council of the MB church in India, a total of 236 men and women were ordained and commissioned for Conference mission activity, to empower local congregations and ministries.

The Constitution of the MB Church was revised in 2007 to allow women to participate in the leadership and admin-

---

MB Church practices in India

MB churches practice immersion baptism.

In cities worship is held in the mornings; in the villages, in morning, evening, or night.

MBs use their own hymnal called *Suvartha Keerthanalu* (Gospel Songs)

The Lord's Table is observed the first Sunday of every month.

Foot Washing is no longer a common practice.

Shagapuran MB Church baptism, 1967

istration of the Conference and Church. Now women may officially participate in the church and field Governing Councils. Rev. Sarada Arnold is the first woman to be elected Vice-President of the Governing Council.

In recent days the leadership of the Conference came to feel that uniform clerical dress is essential in Indian context, particularly in today's changing world, in order to give identity and witness to Christian pastors as the servants of God in the multi-religious, multicultural and multi-ethnic Indian context. The aim of this clerical dress code was not to identify a hierarchal structure but rather to stress pastoral service. The pastoral dress code was introduced to the clergy during the celebration of the 150-year anniversary of MB Church held in January, 2010.

An Indian Theology of Dalit Christian Identity

"Once an untouchable always an untouchable" has been the rule for Hindu social life, with "untouchability" still rampant in the villages.[60] The vast majority of Dalit Christians continue in their traditional occupations with fellow Dalits of the same jatis. Conversion into the new faith has not redeemed them from their "Dalitness," and from the stigma of "untouchability." Furthermore, because of legal decisions taken against Christian Dalits, injustices against them cannot be redressed in the courts. Dalit Christians have come to realize that their specific *Jati* identity is equally important, and politically more effective than having just a Christian identity.[61]

Indian theologians in the 19th century felt that the theological articulation that had been brought to India was "ineffective and had little relevance" for the Indian context. Keshub Chandra Sen (1838-1884) argued that Christ should be presented in India in his Hindu character, as an Asiatic ascetic. Brahmabandhab Upadhyaya (1861-1907) considered Christ as the perfect fulfillment of centuries of Hindu longings. Many subsequent "upper caste" Indian thinkers made significant contributions towards the emergence of a new Indian Christian consciousness, attempting to harmonize Hindu philosophical thought with Christian theology in their quest for an authentically indigenous theological expression.[62]

Theologians of the post-Independence era focused on the nature of mission in the Indian context and on inter-religious and interfaith dialogue. M. M. Thomas adopted an empathetic approach to the

Hindu-Christian encounter, affirming that the core of Christian faith is the message that God has acted in a unique way in a secular historic event.[63] In the past two decades there has been a reaction against the so-called "Hindu Brahmanic" interpretation of Indian Christian Theology, with one of the responses being "Dalit Theology."[64]

Dalit Christian theology developed in the wake of liberation theology in South America and Black theology in the USA. Dalit Theology differs, however, in that it focuses the question of caste oppression, which is unique to India. The source of Dalit theology is the affirmation that God is preferentially intertwined with the lives, experiences and struggles of the Dalits, thus positively affirming Dalit identity.[65] Dalit theologians have come to reflect theologically upon the oppressive situation of Dalits in India.[66]

One of the major sources for the emerging Dalit theology is the lived experience of Dalits, which has been one of suffering and pain.[67] Dalit theology expresses the shared longing and efforts by the Dalits to abolish their unjust situation in the light of their faith. Consequently, a church serving the Dalits should be a community living an option for the poor, accepting poverty in its own life-style.

George Oommen writes that the ultimate function of Dalit theology is two-fold: to act in solidarity and to act for liberation. Liberation is envisaged as the liberation of Dalits from historically oppressive structures, both religio-cultural and socio-economic. The concept of solidarity has also emerged in this school of theology. The Christian values of sacrifice, charity and commitment to others are all intertwined in this profound understanding of solidarity. In transcending one's creed, ideology and religion, a Dalit is invited "to lose oneself for the sake of the other." Incarnational theology is the basis for such a two-sided solidarity with God and with fellow Dalits.[68] Dalit Theology affirms the identity of the Dalits before God as people among whom God is working against oppression, and many Dalit communities are beginning to feel empowered by claiming their "Dalitness."

Mennonite Brethren Institutions

According to some estimates, IMB membership today may be as high as 200,000 members attending 964 churches in forty-one Mennonite Brethren Field Associations.[69] While some of the church's ministries have been downgraded or diminished over the years, such as the radio programs, a film ministry, and hostels, there remain other ministries that continue to function effectively. Among these can be named the Bible College in Shamshabad; the Medical Hospital in Jadcherla; the Mennonite Brethren high schools in eight of the

Mennonite Brethren High School at Shamshabad, 1982

former mission fields; a Junior College in Mahabubnagar; a Historical Commission; a Center for Peacemaking and Conflict Resolution Studies (CPCRS); the Mennonite Brethren Development Organization (MBDO); the Mennonite Brethren Women's Conference; the Future MB Church of India Board of Evangelism and Church Ministries.

The Board of Evangelism and Church Ministries coordinates a number of ministries, including ministries in evangelism (Church Extension Workers), urban and inter-faith ministries (reaching out to Muslims and others), literature, *Suvarthamani* (the conference's Telugu language magazine since 1920), the Partnership in Discipleship Making International ministry and the Partnership in Global Youth Ministry. Thus the Gospel has brought changes in the religious and socio-economic lives of converts, and has given a sense of meaning, security, status, dignity, hope and purpose to the Indian believers.

The Mennonite Church in India (MCI)

In 1899 the Mennonite Board of Missions sent three missionaries to India. Dr. William and Alice Page and Jacob A. Ressler were advised to locate at Dhamtari, Madhya Pradesh, in what is now Chhattisgarh State. There they were legally recognized as the American Mennonite Mission. This mission became known as the Mennonite Church in India (MCI), the designation we will use in this chapter. Since the MCI carried out its mission with Dhamtari as headquarters, they also are known as the Dhamtari-Mennonites.

The motivation for both of these missions was the famine of the 1880's and 1890's in India, of which the famine of 1896-1897 was the most severe. This latter famine led American Mennonites to respond in a manner resembling the response one decade earlier of the Russian Mennonite Brethren to the Dalit situation in Andhra Pradesh. It happened that George Lambert, a Mennonite pastor and a member of the Mennonite church in Elkhart, Indiana, visited India in 1894-95 on his trip around the world. On his return he provided a full account of the miseries he had witnessed in India in an exhaustive 417-page book entitled *India: the Horror-Stricken Empire*. It contained a full account of the famine, plague, and earthquake of 1896-97 and included a description of relief work being done by the Home and Foreign Relief Commission. The book, published by the Mennonite Publishing Company in 1898, was read widely. Lambert visited congregations across the Midwest, appealing to the Mennonites to give money for the humanitarian cause in India. This resulted in the formation of the Home and Foreign Relief Commission in 1897. That same year the Home and Foreign Relief Commission sent George Lambert to India again, to supervise the distribution of funds and food. A committee was constituted to supervise the distribution of aid in India, chaired by the prominent Methodist Bishop T. M. Thoburn.

When Lambert returned, he reported that 20,000 famine orphans in mission orphanages required continual support. Lambert's reports and letters pointed out that the famine was due not only to the failure of the monsoon, but also to the evils of the *zamindari* (feudal) system.[70] Philanthropic work opened a whole new missionary enterprise for the Mennonite Church in North America; India became their first foreign mission. Although Mennonites seemed to have little preparation for mission work, yet they were able to establish a strong mission in India in the following years. It appears that the North American Mennonites were not much aware of the Russian Mennonite Brethren Mission that was already working in Nalgonda of Andhra Pradesh.

Mennonite missions began in the present state of Chhattisgarh, formerly the State of Madhya Pradesh. Chhattisgarh State is gifted with natural beauty and bountiful resources. Its rivers provide sufficient water for irrigation, power generation and industry. This region is rich with minerals such as bauxite, copper ore, manganese ore, rock phosphate, asbestos, mica, iron ore and coal. Due to its abundant natural resources, the region has experienced an industrial explosion with the coming of steel, aluminum, cement, gunpowder and paper industries, as well as power plants. These industrial developments have encouraged people to migrate from rural regions to the cities.

Chhattisgarh is called the tribal belt of central India, with many caste and sub-caste, different racial groups and migrants residing together in this area. There are 42 tribes in Chhattisgarh, the principal ones being the Gond tribe and the Satnamies. The Satnamies originally are Chamars, one of the Dalit groups of North India. Later many Satnamies converted to Christianity when Protestant missionaries arrived and preached about the love of Jesus Christ.[71] Prior to the coming of the Mennonites, mission work in this area had been carried out by the Gossner Lutheran Mission, the Methodist Episcopal Mission, and the Evangelical Reformed Church.

Jacob Andrew Ressler and Dr. and Mrs. W. B. Page, pioneer MCI missionaries, chose to begin work in the vicinity of Dhamtari of Chhattisgarh state, where they arrived in November, 1899. Dhamtari is situated 48 miles south of the new state capital of Raipur on a national highway which runs from Delhi to Madras. Dhamtari has been a political center since the days of the struggle for India's independence.

MCI Church, Dhamtari

Mahatama Gandhi visited Dhamtari twice during the height of the independence movement. The Mennonite mission became a pioneer in education as well as medical and vocational training in this area. When mission work began

Testimony of Aaron Massy of Dhamtari, 77 years old.

I was a beggar in the past. Today my son is a doctor. This is the blessing of the Mennonite mission in this area.

in the region, local people were living in seriously depressed conditions.

Jacob Andrew Ressler was a school teacher and Dr. Page was a medical doctor. Their plan was to start an orphanage; the immediate priority of the sending mission was feeding the hungry rather than doing evangelism. They agreed with Lambert who wrote that "this was the quickest and best way to build a church."[72] The idea was fitting in the Dhamtari area, where the government had recently opened public work projects. It was easy for these pioneer missionaries to get involved and begin their work. Soon Ressler became the Honorary Famine Relief Officer and Dr. Page took a position in the government hospital. Ressler reports that in 1900 there were 14,000 people fed twice daily. The famine kitchens served rice and dhal to the needy and children were given milk 3 times a day in Dhamtari. In a few years, the missionaries were involved in even more relief efforts and public works, such as digging reservoirs and wells and constructing roads.

Ressler and Page built their first mission station at Sunderganj in Dhamtari in 1900. Sunderganj means "beautiful place." Soon the station included an orphanage for boys, an elementary school, a school for training evangelists, a major hospital (established in 1910) and a large church building; some industrial work was also done there. By 1903 the missionaries were able to purchase another station at Rudri, four miles southeast of Sunderganj. Here they built an orphanage for girls. When the government purchased this property to construct a dam for irrigation and a canal, the Mission purchased the entire village of Balodgahan in 1906, a few miles away, and built their largest station. The missionaries took over the village for farming, dug ponds and became the *malguzars* (landlords). They built

MCI church at Shantipur, near Dhamtari

a big bungalow on the 845 acres of village land, along with a home for widows and two large orphanages for boys and girls. All these properties had been sold by early 1970's.

The MCI mission in India established a series of stations and outposts. The mission programs included orphanages, hospitals, health centers, homes for the widows, a leprosy asylum, schools for girls and boys, a short-term Bible school, a vocational school, and agricultural farms. The original members joined the church through conversion and the baptism of orphan boys and girls, as well as families who came from other areas to work at the mission stations.

Stephen Solomon and his wife Phoebe Sheela are outstanding examples of people who developed and matured in MCI Mission institutions. They grew up in Mission hostels, and in fact, the missionaries arranged their marriage.

Stephen Solomon was born in Jagdalpur, Bastar District. His father died when Stephen was very young and his mother took him to Dhamtari, where he was admitted to the boys' orphanage of the Mission. Stephen completed high school and taught for two years in the Mission normal school, as well as tutoring new missionaries in language. In 1946 he received BA and B.Ed degrees from Kolkata; he was the first MCI orphan university graduate. He returned to Dhamtari and taught Hindi at the Mennonite Higher Secondary School until his retirement in 1976.

Garjan Bai

Garjan Bal ("thunder") was born to a humble family, about 10 miles from Dhamtari. She was brought to the Mennonite mission orphanage in Dhamtari in 1900, covered with sores, and near to death. The other members of her family had died in the famine of 1900. After she completed the 6th class in school in 1905, the mission sponsored her for teacher training in Jagdalpur. After training she was appointed to teach in the mission school for girls in Dhamtari. Later she became a matron at the orphanage in Dhamtari where she continued until her death. She was known for gifts of leadership and spiritual maturity. She left the good testimony of a disciplined and dedicated life. The middle school in Balodgahan was named in her honor as the Garjan Memorial Middle School.

Solomon was a prolific writer and a good musician who composed songs, wrote dramas, and translated texts into Hindi. He translated about 60 books and booklets for the North India Christian Tract and Book society and the *Masihi Sahitya Sanstha.* He also edited the Conference paper, *Mennonite Mondli Samachar Patricka* for several years, and was a regular member of the Mennonite Literature and Audio Visual Board. He served on the panel of translators for the Bible Society of India's new Hindi translation of the Bible. In 1947, he was ordained deacon in the Sundarganj congregation and in 1970 was ordained as a minister to serve as co-pastor. He has also worked as a pastoral assistant in several congregations and served as conference secretary for two terms.

Stephen Solomon and Phoebe Sheela married in 1942. Phoebe also completed her primary and middle schools in Mennonite Mission schools at Balodgahan and her high school in Jabalpur. She graduated from Isabella Thoburn College, Lucknow, Uttar Pradesh, and she was the first woman university graduate in the Mennonite Church in India. Phoebe taught in the Garjan Memorial Middle school in Balodgahan from 1940 until her marriage to Stephen Solomon in 1942, when she transferred to the mission schools in Dhamtari. There she taught both in the high school and in the normal school. In 1954 she began teaching in the municipal higher secondary school where she remained until her retirement in 1972.

Both Stephen and Phoebe were ordained as Deacon and Deaconess in the Mennonite Church. Phoebe was the first woman deaconess in 1942. In 1962 she represented the Mahila Sabha of the Mennonite Church in India at the Mennonite World Conference in Kitchener.

Members of the Mennonite Church in Mangal Tarai, Chhattisgarh, stand in front of their church building, under construction, 2008

The Mission station at Mangal Tarai, established by George Lapp, was a unique station. The village is situated far in the jungle, established for the rehabilitation of cured leprosy patients from the Shanthinagar and Dhamtari areas. There were 150 families in the village, of whom 32 families were church members. The first families to come to Mangal Tarai were given 15 acres of land; a later group got 5 acres, and a third group received only 2 acres. Consequently, the background of the members of the congregation varied; some of the members also had Adivasi background.

MCI was a member of National Christian Council of India (NCCI) right from its formative years. NCCI had units concerned with the Rural Church, Christian education, Medical work etc. George Lapp was the chairman of the Committee on the Rural Church. He wrote a book "The Rural Church in India" which was published by the YMCA, Kolkata.

By 1910 the Mennonite Mission took deliberate steps to integrate Indian brothers from each congregation into evangelical teams, which were strengthened as a result. In January 1912, the missionaries and visiting Mission representatives drafted the constitution for the Mennonite Church, bringing a conference structure into existence. There were four MCI congregations at the time, all of whose ministers were missionaries, with a total membership of 488. In 1929 the constitution was revised. At this time there were 7 ordained missionaries, 9 ordained national delegates, together with 53 lay representatives from 7 congregations who were voting members of the conference. Church membership in 1929 stood at 1,279 church members with an additional 735 unbaptized persons participating. The first four native deacons were ordained in 1913 and the first Indian pastor in 1927. The first deaconess was ordained in 1947.

P. J. Malagar was ordained bishop of the MCI in May, 1955, the first Indian bishop to hold the office. A second Indian bishop, O. P. Lal, was ordained in 1965. Bishop Malagar's father was a first generation Christian and his mother was a Bible woman. Both of his parents were from orphanage background, and both became teachers. Malagar completed the certificate course at South Indian Bible Seminary (SIBS), Bangarpet, South India, and then began his carreer as an evangelist, planting 7 churches in the North

Bishop Malagar in retirement, 2004

Baster district. He was the first MCI member to study abroad, attending Goshen College from 1948 to 1950, where he received the BA degree in History. One of his most significant achievements was facilitating the formation of the Mennonite Christian Service Fellowship of India (MCSFI) in 1963, involving all of the 6 Indian Mennonite groups in the project. He subsequently served 18 years as director of MCSFI and also served as chairman of the Asia Mennonite Conference.

The MCSFI became an important inter-Mennonite institution, opening doors for mission work, fellowship and leadership training. MCSFI sent R. S. Lemuel and his wife to Bangladesh as the first Indian missionaries, with good success. R. S. Lemuel served as MCSFI Director from 1981-1993. M. B. Devadas was also sent to Vietnam as a service worker. These three Indian missionaries were from the Mennonite Brethren Church. MCSFI also started a Visitors Exchange Programme (VEP), with MCSFI providing the workers and MCC sponsoring them financially. As many as 70 persons from all Mennonite groups participated in this program. P. K. Singh of MCI,

R. R. K. Murthy speaks at a pastors' conference, 2006

who became one of the leaders of the church in the 1990s, was the first person to go on a visitor's exchange to the United States. The MCSFI also sponsored exchange programs for doctors, church leaders and women. Dr. Sunil Chatterjee, Dr. Veena Chatterjee and Dr. Das, all of MCI, went to Vietnam and Cambodia with MCC. R. R. K. Murthy visited Indonesia and the Philippines, Mrs. O. P. Lal went to Japan and one lady came from Japan to Dhamtari on a women's exchange program. Such exchanges helped Asian people meet and integrate into a larger Mennonite brotherhood.

In 1970 the MCSFI invited the Asia Mennonite Conference [AMC] to India and hosted the first Asia Mennonite Conference in Dhamtari that year, attended by 218 delegates from all over Asia. MCSFI also organized Reconciliation Camps in Asia, initiated all-India student camps, youth camps, all-India women's conferences, etc. When R. S. Lemuel of the Mennonite Brethren Church replaced Bishop Malagar as MCSFI director he continued the momentum and strengthened relationships. During his tenure a cordial relationship was maintained between MBs and other Mennonite groups.

Musicians at AMC, 2004

The Mennonites, Mahatma Gandhi and others

As the national Constitution was being drafted in independent India, the India Mennonite Church realized that it had a very definite interest in matters of religious liberty and conscientious objection. Accordingly two representatives were chosen to approach the appropriate authorities on these matters. Rev. P. J. Malagar was chosen by the conference and J. N. Kaufman was chosen by the Mission. Upon the advice of a highly placed Christian official in Delhi they wrote identical letters in 1947 addressed to the men who were preparing the constitution: Dr. H. C. Mukherjee, Acharya J. B. Kripalani, Mahatma Gandhi, Dr. Rajendra Prasad and Sardar Vallbhbhai Patel. The letters set forth, in brief, Mennonite faith and practice and particularly the issue of nonresistance. The letters included a plea for religious liberty and a consideration of the scruples of conscientious objectors, offering civilian service of national importance in lieu of military service. The letter argued:

It is our understanding that the constitution for independent India is now in the making. While there is opportunity, we wish to make petition on behalf the Mennonite Church, asking for a provision in the new constitution guaranteeing to us, as well as to other religious groups holding views similar to our own, a degree of religious liberty.

We as a Mennonite people are conscientiously opposed to militarism in general and to war in particular. This position is made clear herewith for your information and reference. We do not seek to evade the duties of responsible citizenship. On the contrary we hereby express our willingness at all times to render civilian public service of national importance in lieu of war service should the calamity of war again overtake our country. We feel all the more encouraged to make this appeal in view of the fact that Mr. Jawaharlal Nehru and other highly placed officials in their private capacity have expressed their personal convictions favoring the safeguarding of the religious convictions of the several groups in India.

Although no replies were expected from these men, some replies did arrive. Acharya J. B. Kripalani stated, among other things, "I do not think that in independent India conscientious objectors will be compelled to do military service."

A reply also came from Mahatma Gandhi, in his own handwriting. In a card from New Delhi dated June 30, 1947 he wrote:

Dear friend,
Your letter, why worry? I am in the same boat with you.
Yours sincerely,
M. K. Gandhi.[73]

Mennonites might interpret Gandhi's reply to mean that he and the Mennonites were in the same ideological stream of love and peace as a means and an end. Gandhi was the only one who responded directly, and something of his deep vision and dreaming is contained in his brief postcard message. The Mennonite church was grateful to Mahatma Gandhi for taking time to affirm for Mennonites that he was "in the same boat" as they were.

The Mennonite missionaries gained more and more respect for Mahatma Gandhi from the 1930s on. However the problem for Mennonite pacifists lay with Gandhi's nonviolent techniques. In several

articles George Lapp pointed out the difference between Christian
nonresistance (the Mennonite term for pacifism) and Hindu nonviolence. Lapp was sure that

> He (Gandhi) is rabidly and stubbornly revolutionary and his pro-
> gram of non-violent opposition thru picketing, obstructing offi-
> cial fulfillment of duty by stubbornly lying across roads in relays,
> recruits quickly filing in ranks where obstructionists were arrested
> and taken to jail.... Very clearly while advocating bloodless means
> he is belligerent and has declared a stubborn non-violent war on
> the British Raj.

Missionary J. D. Graber saw a more positive side of nonviolence,
predicting already in 1930 that "his revolution will likely not be a
particularly dangerous one."

The missionaries feared Gandhi's criticism of missionary activity.
In 1933 Gandhi visited Dhamtari and gave a gift of Rs. 1,000 to aid
the outcastes in the community. J. N. Kaufman, then secretary of the
mission, was invited to serve on the reception committee but refused
because of its political implication. By the time of Gandhi's death
the Mennonite Board of Missions and Charities could send a letter
of condolence to the Indian Embassy in Washington and also issued
this statement:

> No one interested in India could help but be profoundly sad-
> dened by Gandhi's tragic death on January 30. Although not a
> Christian, he held Christ and His teachings in great respect. He
> was always a restraining influence on violence in that country.
> Let us pray that even after his death Christ's people in India may
> lead a quiet and peaceable life so that the purposes of God may
> be realized who will have all men to be saved and to come to the
> knowledge of the truth.

MCC administrators, J. Lawrence Burkholder and J. N. Byler carried
on discussions with Pandit J. Nehru in Kolkata in 1945 concerning
the value of non-violent social change. Another early MCC worker,
William Yoder, walked with Gandhi as he went from village to village
in East Bengal as Gandhi was searching for a peaceful transition to
power.

After independence, the Indian government strongly objected to
evangelization that made use of foreign funds. In response the Mission Board formed a unification commission in 1950 comprised of six
missionaries and six nationals to work on a new church constitution.

According to this new constitution, which took effect on July 1, 1952, mission and the church were merged into one. According to Malagar, 90% of the members came from low caste, Satnami or tribal background, although a few also were from high caste background. Many received special privileges and government benefits related to their caste. After independence, Christians noted their religion, but took their original caste and tribal names as their surnames in order to receive government benefits.

In the new constitution the official name of the Mennonite Church was changed to "The Mennonite Church in India." In 1952 the MCI comprised 10 congregations with a membership of more than 1,470 persons, with 1,205 unbaptized children and youth. The church had 5 ordained missionaries, 8 ordained national pastors, 6 deacons, and 1 deaconess.

In 1956, the church retired a number of lay evangelists, providing them with pensions. Evangelism was supposed to become the responsibility of every church member, but the results proved quite ineffective. In 1960, autonomous boards for education, medicine and literature services were registered and the church became fully responsible for congregational and evangelistic services in accordance with the constitution registered with the government. The church became self-witnessing, self-propagating,

Marriage and Weddings in MCI churches

Mennonite weddings are usually simply done, without recordings, bands, dancing or dowry demands. Today the groom wears a suit and dress shirt in place of the *dhoti*; most brides still prefer to wear a white *sari*, since gowns are not common.

Some traditional ceremonies are celebrated during the week. A traditional tent made up of bamboo is shaded with mango and black berry leaves under which the celebration takes place. A few days before marriage the *haldi* preparation ceremony takes place: a paste of turmeric, sandal wood powder and other ingredients is prepared and this is applied to both bride and groom, in order to beautify their appearance. Songs, Bible readings, and a sermon precede the exchange of vows and the joining of hands and the declaration that they are a couple.

In the south, the bridegroom ties *tali* or *mangalsuthra* around the bride's neck as is Indian tradition and there is also an exchange of vows and rings. A feast follows wedding ceremonies and gifts are given to the couple at dinner.

Marriage is a lifelong bond and divorce is not allowed under any circumstances. Though marriages do break up, divorce is not granted, nor is civil marriage or civil divorce accepted by the church.

Mennonite Church at Sankra, Chhattisgarh

self-supporting, self-governing, independent, and indigenous. The Mission Board continued to cooperate in partnership and funding for new projects. When education became the main responsibility of the Indian government, church-sponsored village schools were closed, although the large schools in Dhamtari city continue to serve hundreds of students.

The missionaries were fully phased out in 1975, but beginning in 1947 there were increasing numbers of trained national members available to give leadership in administration, education, evangelism, medicine and pastoral services. A national leadership emerged over the years, sharing responsibilities. Institutions were important organs of the Mennonite mission and before independence missionaries used to be the heads of the various Boards. After independence, the Education Board and the Medical Board became indigenous and independent. They received funds from the government and ran their respective institutions.

Dr. H. S. Martin, 2008

A third-generation Dhamtari Mennonite, Dr. H. S. Martin (d. 2011) trained in London and became a Fellow of the Royal College of Surgeons (FRCS). In 1966 he became director of the Dhamtari Christian Hospital and developed the hospital's modern facilities. The hospital was affiliated with large Christian research and teaching hospitals in Ludhiana (Punjab) and Vellore (Tamil Nadu). With the help of retired missionary S. Paul Miller, the hospital received a USAID OHSA grant for new equipment and refurbished and expanded facilities.

Dr. Martin served on numerous medical boards in India. Beginning in the 1990s he began to phase out of hospital leadership. His successor, Dr. Lhondi died in 1993. Dr. J. Das then served until his untimely death in 1998, and was replaced by Dr. Sunil Chatterjee.

Nursing Students,
Dhamtari, 2004

The well regarded "Dhamtari Christian Hospital College/School of Nursing" trained professionals who have worked throughout North India since the 1940s. Under the aegis of its Mennonite Medical Board, the MCI also operated a major program for people with leprosy at Shantipur and a network of regional hospitals and dispensaries.

Mennonite English Senior Secondary School, Dhamtari

Under the management of its Mennonite Education Board, the MCI also founded and sustained an impressive number of schools. There was a teachers' training program for staffing elementary schools at the various stations. There were also middle schools in Dhamtari and Balodgahan and the high school in Dhamtari has a notable reputation for training Christian

Principal Amy Jiwanlal with student performers

teachers and leaders. J. W. Samida was the first Indian headmaster. The current principal, Mrs. Amy Jiwanlal, is active beyond the MCI as well as being a Deaconess in the Dhamtari congregation.

From the beginning the missionaries taught their adherents to practice the Mennonite distinctive of separation of church and state, which involved being good citizens and remaining loyal to the government of the day, praying for that government. When India achieved independence special services were held in Dhamtari. The missionaries discouraged army and police service, since the Mennonite Church is a peace church. Some members did join the military and police services, but those who did were excommunicated from the church.

The period from September 1984 to December 1990 was a time of conflict and division in the church, a difficult time of struggle for the church. The conflict was triggered by disagreements over church administration. But like many church issues in India there

Harishchandra's story

Harishchandra was the son of Mennonite parents. Before he began work as a school teacher he was selected for service in the Indian Army. The missionaries discouraged him, saying that this was against Mennonite doctrine. Nevertheless, he joined the Air Force. When he visited home his mother used to weep for him and pray for him to resign and return. His position in the Air Force was a good one, and he was earning handsome money, but his mother's tears and teaching led him to resign and return home. The reason he gave was that his church was against what he was doing. The missionaries were pleased, and appointed him a mission school teacher at Dhamtari. Later he became headmaster, a position he held until his retirement.

were competing visions, rival personalities, widespread poverty and ethnic competition. Often, as in this case, there have been lawsuits in the civil courts. These two groups, led respectively by P. K. Singh and M. K. Nathan, were separated for six years. During these years of conflict the Mission Board in North America sent reconciliation teams, but reconciliation was not achieved. On December 9, 1990 the estranged groups were reconciled and united once again. P. K. Singh led the reconciliation process, after which M. K. Nathan became the secretary of the MCI. After he had served 10 years in that office, P. K. Singh took his place as secretary.

In 1960 MCI began sending pastors for theological training to the Union Biblical Seminary (UBS) for B.Th and BD level studies. By 1986 nine young men had graduated from that seminary. Bishop Kunjam, who was the third director of MCSFI and an important leader of MCI, studied at the UBS. Kunjam's father had been a first-generation Christian. He worked for the missionaries as a mason at the Sankra station. After studies at AMBS in Elkhart, Indiana (1980 to 1982) Kunjam became director of MCSFI (1993) and served in that position for 12 years. In 1997 the assembly of the Mennonite World Conference took place in Kolkata under his leadership, with over four thousand people attending. Kunjam wrote a well-received song for the occasion.

Bishop Kunjam

In the year 2000 MCI numbered about 3,700 members who worshiped in 19 churches with most members speaking Chhattisgarh and Hindi. Seven out of 19 MCI churches are located in the jungle. The large, relatively wealthy Sunderganj congregation in Dhamtari contributes much to the support to these churches. In 2000, MCI was served by 45 ordained ministers and a senior bishop who is the chairman of the assembly of ministers. There are also ordained deaconesses serving the churches. Bishops are called "inactive ministers" after the age of seventy. Congregations may call them for preaching, baptizing or other functions but they cannot hold office. Deacons function as helpers for pastors, but if there is no pastor, the deacon may give the blessings. At present MCI is served by nine ordained pastors (Reverends), two active bishops, and two inactive bishops.

Worship Service, Dhamtari, 1999

Worship in the Mennonite Church of India, including Sunday school and women's meetings, is held weekly, on Sunday mornings. Sunday school is limited to children, held when they are excused from the worship service. Typical worship services feature singing, responsive reading, Bible reading, a sermon, the taking of an offering and announcements. The sanctuaries are full when there are special services with outside speakers and music programs, healing activities or competitions,

Baptism is performed by pouring. At the time of baptism, persons have to provide affidavits, that they are accepting Christ and are ready to face any difficult situation. Traditionally, communion services are held three times a year (spring, fall, winter). There was a rule that those who do not partake at least once a year should be excommunicated, but it has not been enforced. Communion services are led by a bishop or a minister after regular worship, and the elements are distributed by ordained members.

Foot Washing is customarily practiced before Holy Communion. It is unique to the Mennonite Church, as other churches do not practice it. Therefore, in every MCI church there are small tubs built at the back. The hymnal used for worship in MCI churches is the *Masssiah Geet* (Messiah's Songs). The local *panchayat* (church adminsitrative council) deals with all issues and takes decisions for the church. The local pastor is the chairman and all local ordained persons, such as deacons and deaconess, are permanent

Footwashing in an MCI church, 2001

members, along with six more elected church members making up the local *panchayat*. MCI pastors are supported by the conference.

The Balogdahan church

Each MCI member has to pay a certain amount of per year to retain church membership. Every year in October or November the Conference holds an assembly called *jalsa* (making merry). It is attended by delegates and all ordained persons.

The Mennonite Church in India is not large, but it is quite stable. A persistent issue for the more-than-100-year-old conference is the tension between congregational growth and the strong institutional base. MCI currently supports the Dhamtari Christian Hospital, the Mennonite Higher Secondary School (Hindi) and the Mennonite English Senior Secondary School. The schools and the hospital in themselves are strong centers of Christian witness. Already in the 1930s, however, church growth strategy questioned whether strong institutions might overwhelm evangelistic interests. The tension continues into the second century of the MCI.

Bharatiya General Conference Mennonite Kalisiya[74] (General Conference Mennonite Church—BGCMC)

The official name for the General Conference Mennonite Church in India is "Bharatiya General Conference Mennonite Kalisiya" (BGCMC). Like the MCI, the General Conference Mennonite mission began work in Chhattisgarh state. The same severe famine that motivated the Mennonites in Indiana to send George Lambert to India also prompted the General Conference Mennonites from Newton, Kansas to send David Goerz in 1899 with a shipment of food for distribution in India. David Goerz challenged his home churches to feed the Indian people with "more than physical food." This motivated General Conference churches to send missionaries to India. The first BGCMC missionaries were Peter A. and Elizabeth Penner and John F. and Susanna Kroeker, sent before David Goerz returned to America in 1900.

From the beginning the Mennonite Church in Dhamtari (MCI) and the General Conference mission cooperated well with each other. The BGCMC missionaries lived with the MCI missionaries in Dhamtari for a year, learning the language and locating their own field of service. After that period of preparation and exploration, the BGCMG missionaries opened their first station at Champa in 1901. MCI and BGCMC missionaries continued to meet frequently for retreats and conferences.

Remains of the Champa church

The BGCMC mission in Champa opened in the midst of hostility and rejection by the native rulers. The Champa region had a number of local princes who were not friendly to strangers in their midst. The Penner family continued in Champa while the Kroekers went 8 miles further to Janjgir, and opened a mission station there in 1901. The Penners began their work with leprosy patients; the Kroekers worked at Janjgir among the Dalits, taking care of children orphaned by the famine. After four years three persons were baptized, two of whom were orphans and one who was suffering from leprosy and who died soon after being baptized.

Members of the Janjgir church in front of a church property being used as a school, 2007

The main focus of the BGCMC mission was providing social services, medical assistance and education for the people in their territory. In 1903 Mohan Rufus Asna came to Janjgir to teach in the school there, and continued in that work for the next 45 years. In 1906 Amardas and Manohar Nad also came to Janjgir to teach. Peter Penner received an award from the government in 1912 in recognition of his services to the lepers.

The mission stations in Champa and Janjgir progressed well and a third station was opened in 1910 at Mauhadi, some twenty five miles south of Champa. In 1915 a fourth station opened in Korba, a small village surrounded by dense jungle. Korba was first visited by

C. H. Sukhan, a native evangelist. In 1940 Ratan Singh became the first Indian pastor there. The fifth station was opened in the Basana

BGCMC pastors and church members in front of Korba Mennonite Church, 2004

village now known as Jagdeesh-pur in 1912, in an area that had originally been designated for work by the Baptists.

By 1916, the mission included Janjgir, Korba, Mauhadi and Jag-eeshpur with a membership of about 9,500 persons worshipping in 20-25 churches. Jagdeeshpur became the most important station due to the presence there of the mission hospital, a school and a residence for boys.

Around 1930 an important mission station was opened in Saraipali. The mission station was opened in response to a call received from a Christian named Gopal from the English Baptist Church. Saraipali had been the center for the English Baptist Church in the area, but the Baptist mission found it difficult to administer the work from their headquarters in Balangir, Odysha (Orissa). Therefore the Baptists resolved to transfer the work to BGCMC. A group of Indian evangelists accompanied by a missionary made a tour of the area. At the end of their tour they met Gopal, a convert from the village of Sukhri. He informed them that there were some seven families who wanted to receive baptism. Isa Das, the first BGCMC evangelist to be stationed in the territory, was sent to Sukhri. Through these contacts churches were established.

The tragic death of Annie Funk

Annie Funk came to India as a missionary teacher in 1906, from Pennsylvania. That same year she started a school for girls in Janjgir and was active in other work with the women and girls. In 1912 she traveled home to attend to her ill mother. Tragically, she boarded the Titanic ocean liner and perished when it sank, giving up her place on a lifeboat to a mother with children. After her death the school was named after her; it continued to function until 1960.

In 1938, when the English Baptist Churches merged into the BGCMC, there were four churches: Denaia Church, Shalem Church, Bethany Church and Sirco Emmanuel Church, with approximately 400 members in total. In 1950, around 10 to 12 Baptist villages close to Saraipalli joined the BGCMC.

In 1951 the Sarguja mission station was started by P. A. Banwar, son of the early evangelist Joseph Banwar of the BGCMC. The church is known as Calvary Mennonite Church, located geographically in the middle of Chhattisgarh, with the Janjgir, Korba and Sarguja missions stations to the north and the Jagdeshpur, Sukhri, Saraipali and Basna mission stations to the south. These stations were at the center of mission activities for the General Conference Mennonites. From these mission centers, mission work operated through medical, educational, industrial and social work, and as a result, churches were established. Most of the BGCMC converts came from Dalit background, but also many Sathnamies in that area became Christians through mass conversions in the villages.

> **A conversion story**
>
> Ibrahim Nand, a senior BGCMC pastor, tells his grandfather's conversion story. His grandfather was a worshipper of Krishna. A Baptist missionary met with him and preached that "Krishna came to kill sinners, Rama came to kill sinners, but Jesus came to this world to save sinners." His grandfather was curious to know more about it, and had discussions with the missionary for the next two years, in search of the truth. Finally, one day he decided to become a Christian, joining the Baptist church, becoming a Mennonite when that mission replaced the Baptist mission. His wife Esther Nand became a deaconess in the church.

Given the various denominational emphases of early native evangelists (Lutheran, Methodist, Episcopal, Reformed) the BGCMC missionaries felt the need to teach Anabaptist-Mennonite principles by initiating short-term Bible schools and annual Bible classes. The Bible School, begun by S. T. Moyer, was located in Janjgir. Other denominations, such as the Disciples of Christ, also sent their people to this school for Bible training. For higher theological training, students were sent to Union Biblical Seminary, now located in Pune. Many Indian BGCMC pastors received their theological training at UBS. At the time of this writing, Rev. Dr. Shehar Singh of the BGCMC serves as the Principal of this seminary.

Although educational, medical and industrial work had its place in the overall program of the BGCMC, it did not displace the primary purpose of the mission, which was preaching, teaching and planting churches. By 1940, the BGCMC had 22 congregations with 2,196 baptized members. There were two Hindi high schools, two English high schools, and five mission stations had primary schools.[75]

Dr. Shekhar Singh

Commissioning BGCMC
governing body members, 2007

In 1938 the General Conference Mennonite Church of India organized the *Sammelan* (conference or assembly). At the same time the *Palak Saba* (administrative council) of the *Sammelan* was organized. This administrative body consisted of all ordained ministers, church leaders and deacons of the church. From this point onwards, Indians began to share in the leadership of the church. In 1942 a new draft of the constitution was presented, officially adopted the next year. The conference went through several name changes, finally adopting the name "Bharatiya General Conference Mennonite Church" in 1967, the name this conference continues to use this as its official title in India.

BGCMC members participated very little in the independence movement, although they supported it. The American missionaries also supported the movement, but did not participate in it. On the first day of independence, August 15, 1947, the Hindus, Christians and others who had not sat or eaten together before, sat and ate supper together. The whole village of Jagdeeshpur participated. The event was arranged by the Mennonite Church leaders. When the invitation was extended for the meal "everybody responded positively." On that Independence Day the first flag in Jagdeeshpur village was hoisted by Samuel Stephen and John Thiessen, the missionary.

Samuel and Helen Stephen

Samuel Stephen, one of the members of the constitution-making body, became the first chairman of the Indian Mission Conference. He served for four years. Samuel Stephen also served as Head Master of the Janzen Memorial School in Jagdeeshpur; his wife Helen was a teacher. In 1956, Samuel and Helen traveled to the USA for further studies. Mrs. Helen Stephen represented BGCMC at the sixth MWC Assembly in Germany. She was the only Indian present there.

There was a BGCMC magazine called *Bandhu*, first published in 1944. J. Walter was its first editor, followed by S. Kumar and then Helen Stephen. The magazine continued up to the mid-1960s when publication stopped. The journal contained spiritual lessons, news, messages, poems for children, a women's section, an editorial and some spiritual stories.

Phasing out the Mission and the transfer of property to BGCMC and Trust

On the 26th of August, 1957 the Gass Memorial Centre, a reading room and center of Christian social and beneficent activities in Raipur, was burned and destroyed by a mob of around 9,000 people. The Centre had been founded by the Evangelical Mission. Missionary reports suggested that the attack had an anti-Christian character and was encouraged by organizations such as the RSS (*Rashtriya Swayam Sevak*) and the *Hindu Mahasabha*, organizations which consider Hinduism an integral part of India's national identity. As a result, the BGCMC conference began its "New Vision." It decided not to ask for any more missionaries from America, and said that it would take care of its own mission.

In the 1970s the missionaries began to leave India. Edward and Ramoth Burkhalter were the last long-term missionaries to leave in 1989. In the mid-1970s, during the missionaries' final phasing out, the conference had a total membership of 4,246. However, the biggest challenge for the mission had to do with mission properties. In 1973 Lubin Jantzen was called back to India to help with the transfer of the properties. He was instrumental in that process, receiving help from Indians such as Victor Walter, a government official with specific training in land matters, Subhash Ben, and Din Bandhu Nand. The Evangelical Trust Association of North India (ETANI) had been organized in 1960, and in March, 1973 the properties were successfully transferred from the mission to ETANI. The properties included hospitals, mission compounds, reading rooms and various plots of land.

The mission schools started by the missionaries were handed over to the Menno Christian Education Society, and this also contributed to the growth of the church. MCES managed the Beacon English School system in the Korba area, a well-developed network of schools which provided an opportunity for Christian pupils to acquire their education in English, and at the same time the Jyoti Higher Secondary School, also in Korba, a Hindi medium school known for the quality of its educational program. Along with better education, schools also provided job opportunities for the Christians in the region. As a result, the church gained educated and

New Building, Champa Christian Hospital, 2007

employed members, and the social and economic stability of local people improved.

In the post-missionary era the BGCMC continued its work independently. The church was responsible for the leadership of the church and evangelism; some mission schools were handed over to the government in 1974, and the hospitals were transferred to EHA (the Emmanuel Hospital Association, with headquarters in Delhi) in 1975. With the schools and the hospitals being administered by other organizations, church members had fewer opportunities for employment. The institutions began hiring non-Christian employees, and the link between the church and the schools and hospitals has weakened. In 1976 the BGCMC wanted to strengthen its evangelistic efforts, so the COM (Commission on Overseas Mission) agreed to fund this program. With this a new era of cooperation between North American Churches and the BGCMC in India began.

The Conference divided itself into the Northern region, the Southern region and the Sarguja region in Chhattisgarh. The Conference appoints directors for all three regions to oversee the church work.

The 1980s brought tremendous changes in the northern region, particularly in the Korba area, due to industrialization and urbanization. When the missionaries began their work in this region, there was little economic development. The people were poor, not well educated, and the area was covered with dense forest with no proper means of transportation. The Champa, Korba and Janjgir stations were established by the missionaries. The coming of the coal industry SECL to Korba brought an increase in population. At the same time, enormous power stations, the Aluminum Industry (BALCO), and other manufacturing industries were established in and around Korba. As a result the Christian population in the area also increased. Members of BGCMC were also able to find employment in these new industries. Soon some of these industrial areas were turned into big townships, and the Korba Mennonite church gained some prominence. This strengthened church has helped the BGCMC grow, with four new churches established in the region.

The 15 churches in the southern region are virtually all rural churches. Therefore the Rural Economic Development and Community Health program (REACH) has been introduced. REACH is a rural development program focusing on teaching vocational skills such as driving, handicrafts, electrical work, tailoring, agriculture, etc. REACH has been successful in training many young people.

The Sarguja region is populated primarily by tribal groups. In the early years the missionaries were not welcomed in this region and Christians faced opposition, but this changed over time. Evangelism was carried out among the tribal group called the Oraons. As a group the Oraons are very poor and earn their living as day laborers. Work among this group began with adult education, friendship, care for the sick and the poor and health education. Gradually people began to accept Jesus Christ and new fellowships were started. The outcome was that BGCMC churches were established at Ambikapur, Kharadang, Neempara, Khaparkhela, and Mahuapara.

The church established a boarding school for the poor children of the region and primary schools were established later. These continued until the COM stopped funding the work of evangelism; at that point the lack of funds forced their closure. In response to the cutting of overseas funding, the local church constructed a commercial complex which was rented to raise funds for evangelistic work. The income from this complex went into the central church treasury.

BGCMC Churches, Institutions, Ministries, Organization & Administration

At present the number of BGCMC members is approximately 8,800 with some 6,000 children and youth participating. The area churches have 15 seminary-trained pastors and three pastors trained in Bible school. There are 24 BGCMC churches including one in Raipur and one in Odyssa (Orissa). There are also more than 50 "worshiping groups" such as in Sarguja, Raighad, Bilaspur, Raipur, Basthar, all districts of Chhattisgarh State. The headquarters of the BGCMC is in Jagdeeshpur and Basna.

The conference rarely ordains laymen, with ordination reserved for those who are theologically trained and who are in full-time ministry. Theological training for the conference is approved only at UBS and Allahabad Bible Seminary because these are considered evangelical colleges. Although peace is a central teaching for Mennonites, Premanand Bagh observes in his thesis that peace is not much discussed or preached by BGCMC preachers. After the Mennonite missionaries left, the teaching of Mennonite history lapsed. However, MCI Bishop

Malagar, when he visited congregations, did used to talk about the Mennonite peace position.

A practice started by the missionaries was to prepare sermon texts for use in the whole conference. This meant that they had many years of teaching/preaching curriculum. The teachings in these sermons stressed a peaceful way of life and living biblically. The practice of preparing these sermons stopped when the missionaries left. In terms of clerical garb, only a few pastors wear the "cacique" in spite of a resolution passed in the elder's committee. It appears that this resolution was passed without adequate consultation with all pastors.

The BGCMC established a literature committee in 1953. The committee cooperated with MCI to develop Sunday School Curriculum. This committee produced material for students, from beginners to intermediates, which was taught in the churches for several years. The BGCMC also printed their first hymnal book, the *Massiah Geet*, which was also used by MCI and other churches.

Although the BGCMC generally does not ordain lay people, it does give leadership opportunities to the laity. It is customary to have two to five lay leaders in each local church, functioning as deacons or deaconesses. Christian education is carried out through Sunday Schools, Christian Endeavor groups for youth, women's fellowships and annual Bible courses in which one book of the Bible is studied systematically for a month.

There is a conference-level youth organization known as the Annual Youth Conference (*Yuvak-Yuvati Sammelan*). All the local Christian Endeavor groups send representatives to this conference. The annual conference is held yearly for four or five days in order to provide the youth representatives an opportunity to share, pray, and have fellowship together. The youth customarily take active part in worship services and in leading church choirs. One Sunday in the year is celebrated as "Youth Sunday" in which the youth share their vision and hope. The Christian Endeavor groups meet every week for Bible Study, singing, fellowship, discussion and planning.

The BGCMC churches are led by a Conference chairman, a vice-chairman, a secretary and a treasurer. There are also three agents from each of the three regions to deal with the church properties. The three agents also sit on the executive council. Each church has its own representative who represents that church on the Governing Council. The executive secretary of the Conference keeps in touch with all the

member and local churches. He is responsible
for co-coordinating and executing conference-
approved programs. The executive body of the
Conference is elected in the Annual General
Meeting. An open election takes place in the
Annual Meeting where one name is put forward by the nomination committee and then
the floor is open to more nominations by the
delegates. Due to this method of open election, most of the elected Conference leaders
are lay leaders; ordained ministers have had
to work under this lay leadership. Conference

Pastors sing at the BGCMC
governing body meeting,
Champa, 2007

decisions are taken in the Governing Body. The Governing Body consists of one representative from each church unit; the representative
is also a lay leader from the church. In the BGCMC church structure,
the authority of decision making about the church and pastors is
primarily in the hands of the laity.

In 1946 a central fund was established from which pastors were
paid. Each local church administers its own affairs. Of the total income
of a local church, 70% goes to the Conference and 30% remains in the
church to be used for local church activities. In 1967 the Conference
passed a resolution that every member of the Church should give 6%
of his/her salary towards the growth of the church. This resolution is
still followed today.

The BGCMC churches practice baptism by sprinkling. Except for
those who join from Roman Catholic background, the baptisms of
other churches are accepted by the BGCMC church without difficulty.
The BGCMC churches do not practice Foot Washing.

From the beginning, the BGCMC emphasis was for members not to
perform military service, to maintain peace-
ful personal relationships, and to resolve
disputes outside the courts. The BGCMC did
not suspend anyone's membership, even if
they joined the army, but very few did.

Concerning the role of women, it has
been said by some women in the Conference that "Equality is the talk, but there has
been no woman president so far." Women
are not ordained, although there are women

"Bible Women" in the early
days

deaconesses. Women also are allowed to preach the Gospel, as long as they do not do it from the pulpit. In the early missionary period there were "Bible women." Three to four women would gather together and visit Hindu homes and share the Gospel, distribute tracts and sing songs. Today women have their own conference, the BGCMCWC. This is an autonomous body of women within the BGCMC structure. The Women's Conference has its own governing body and organizational structure which regulates the activities of Conference.

In the early years many women went for theological training, but none of them got adequate ministerial opportunities. Only a few who stepped out were able to make the most of their training. One of them is Rachel Bagh, who did her BD at UBS and served as BGCMC women's project coordinator for a few years. When this work was closed down she and her husband Rev. Dr. Prem Bagh served in the Allahabad Bible Seminary for several years. Both now teach at Union Biblical Seminary.

Today many women are getting opportunities to be a part of the church governing committee which is called *Panchayat*, and many women are also serving the church as deaconesses. Many women from BGCMC are also giving leadership to the women's conference at the national level. Mrs. Clementina Nand, for example, has served the BGCMCWC as president for many years and has also served as president of the All India Women's Conference.

The BGCMC has good relationships with other denominations. In the Raipur area there is an interdenominational clergy fellowship in which BGCMC pastors participate. Rev. Subodh Kumar was its chairman in 2000. The pastors meet regularly for prayer, fellowship and evangelism. Just as the Mennonite Church in India (MCI) is a member of the NCCI and works closely with the Churches' Auxiliary for Social Action, in the same way BGCMC is a member of EFI and works with the Federation of Evangelical Churches of India. There has been regular interaction with the Ambassadors for Christ, who conduct seminars for pastors and youth and invite participation from other denominations. BGCMC is also working with Compassion India, a para-church organization, in its program for child development in the southern area.

A Difficult Decade: the Division of 1991-2001

In 1991 a conflict emerged in the BGCMC, primarily between the churches of the northern region and the Jagdeeshpur area churches in the southern region. The conflict was not new, having roots as far back as the 1977 church conference.[76] The northern churches objected, legitimately, that all primary Conference officers came from the south. The Conference resolved to divide into two groups, north and south, which would meet annually in a general conference. The church worked out a plan of equal representation in the Conference, in the governing body and in the committees. Although a short reconciliation took place at that time, the power struggle continued between the two regions and was quite visible during church elections. In spite of this struggle, the church continued all of its activities very successfully, including the nurture and evangelism programs.

In 1991, the Champa church went through a dispute which ultimately resulted in the division of the Conference. The Champa church split into two competing groups. One group separated itself from the church Conference and took over the Champa church building; the other group remained with the church Conference and continued to meet in the old Mennonite Church which had been handed over to the Champa Mission School.[77] The 1993 church conference decided that a committee should be formed consisting of the Conference president, vice president, secretary, and treasurer, that this committee would combine with the Elders' Board (*Rakhwal Samitee*), and that together the leaders would initiate the process of reconciliation between both the separated groups.

The tension between the president and the secretary continued and ultimately brought division in 1994, at a time when the COM secretary Larry Kehler and Rev. L. W. Jantzen were visiting India.[78] The issue became the location for the Annual Conference of BGCMC. The president called the churches to Janjgir for the yearly conference, but the secretary summoned the churches to Jagdeeshpur, which is also the headquarters of the BGCMC. This caused great confusion in the local churches, and division resulted. Some churches went to Jagdeeshpur and some attended the Janjgir conference with the result that the BGCMC divided into three groups: the Janjgir Conference, the Jagdeeshpur Conference and a third group who simply separated themselves from the conflict and functioned autonomously. The Janjgir Conference was cancelled due to the lack of a quorum, but the Jagdeeshpur conference went ahead with the election process and elected new officers for the Conference. This exacerbated an already-existing problem, and the unity of the church was completely destroyed.

These actions not only divided the Church, but also divided the people who joined one group or another on the basis of history, favoritism or location and instinct. Even though the major groups started functioning on an autonomous basis by electing their own officers, reports were made to the police and government officials against the other party with blame and recrimination coming from both sides.

The division rocked the structure of BGCMC completely, resulting in bankruptcy, litigation, division in local churches and a decline in every aspect of church life. This situation prevailed until 2001.[79] A Silver Jubilee was celebrated in December, 1996 in Champa, but the conflicts prevented large centenary celebrations; a small celebration was held nevertheless.

Reconciliation and the Beginning of a New Era: 2001-2005

After ten years had passed, and conditions in the church had gone from bad to worse, leaders and pastors began to recognize the need for reconciliation. Not only was the church divided, but there were also hard feelings in the congregations. In the year 2000 the presidents from both of the primary groups met in Raipur to talk about reconciliation. In this meeting each of the respective presidents said

Sant Masih, officer of BGCMC in recent years, and his wife

that although God had called them to lead these two groups, now God wanted the groups to be reconciled and united in the body of Christ. In the same year, pastors from different churches gathered together in Parapath for a time of prayer and fasting. In this meeting the pastors decided to be united with each other and also to unite the church. After many discussions and meetings it was decided to call a joint conference in Jagdeeshpur, Chhattisgarh.

The reconciliation conference began in November, 2001 under the supervision of Rev. Dr. C. S. R. Gier, a former member of BGCMC now based in Delhi, who had been asked to chair the conference. As the session started the chairpersons of both the groups were called along with their executive members, and in unison they promised to be united and work towards the welfare of the church.[80] The Council of Elders, committee members, and pastors also promised to maintain the solidarity of the church. The whole congregation supported their decision by giving a round of applause to God Almighty.

Many good things happened in the process of unity and reconciliation and one of them was acceptance of the alienated churches into the fold of BGCMC. Some churches that had separated from the BGCMC, such as Korba Mennonite Church and Champa Mennonite Church, were accepted back into the fold. In November, 2001 new officers were elected to lead the church in the fear of the Lord, maintaining the solidarity and sanctity of the church. The 2001 conference marks the beginning of a new era for the BGCMC, even though it was not the end of problems and hardships for the church. There was reconciliation on one side, but on the other side there were many who were not happy with the decision. Of the many challenges ahead, the first was to restore all the property of the church which had not received the proper care and protection. The conflict also resulted in many court cases being filed against the conference and conference officers; many of these cases are still pending in the courts.[81]

In 2004 the governing body of the Conference passed a resolution that its name should be changed from "General Conference Mennonite Church" to "Bharatiya General Conference Mennonite Church," a change brought into effect the following year.

Bihar Mennonite Mandali in Jharkhand

While Dalits of South and Central India were converting to Christianity, the tribal peoples in north-east India, in South Bihar (also called Chotanagpur) and North Bihar began converting in substantial numbers to Christianity. The Brethren in Christ Church established its first mission station in the northern part of Bihar in 1914. The other mission working in Bihar was the Bihar Mennonite Mandali church (BMM), which established itself in the South Bihar area. In the year 2000, Chotanagpur (South Bihar) was made Jarkhand state with Ranchi as its capital. This has separated from BMM from Bihar leaving the BIC as the only Anabaptist church in present-day Bihar.

The main language spoken in Jharkhand is Hindi along with local tribal languages such as Kodoku, Koruku, and Sadhari. Jarkhand is bounded by Madhya Pradesh in the north, Utter Pradesh in the west, Orissa in the south and Bengal in the east. The land is extremely fertile as it is constantly watered by the rivers Sarayu, Ganges, and Gandak. The large two plateaus, Ranchi and Hazaribagh, are situated almost at the center of the Chotanagpur plateau.

Northern India has been called the "graveyard for the mission movement," but the conversion of tribal peoples in Chotanagpur negated this argument. The people of this region responded positively to the Gospel with the coming of Christian missions in the late 19th and early 20th centuries. The tribal peoples of Chotanagpur were the original inhabitants of the region. They had taken the land from "the fangs of the snake and from the claws of the tiger," but after many centuries raiders came up from the plains and plundered their lands. Although the tribal people defended themselves with their hunting weapons, they were overcome and lost most of their land.

At the time the missionaries arrived these tribal peoples were in an acute agrarian crisis. They were being gradually alienated from their land by moneylenders, the Zamindars. Many were forced to become bonded laborers. They were exploited, oppressed and isolated from the Hindu or Muslim inhabitants of Chotanagpur.[82] It was in this context that the missionaries arrived and preached the Gospel of liberation.

The first Christian missionaries to arrive in Chotanagpur were four missionaries of the Gossner Evangelical Lutheran Mission, who came in November 1845. They settled at Ranchi, and for the first few years there was not a single convert. Then a strange incident occurred. One day four men of the Oraon tribe came to the mission house asking to see Jesus, of whom the missionaries had been preaching. They were asked to attend the church service. Having done so, they were deeply impressed but still unsatisfied. "They wished and said to see Jesus with their own eyes." One of the missionaries took them into an inner room and prayed fervently that they might be guided to the light. They went away quietly. Later the same men reappeared and asked again to be allowed to participate in the worship service. At its close they came forward with great joy on their faces saying now they had found Jesus. Now they were satisfied and they desired to become Christians. After further instruction and teaching they were baptized in June 1850. From then on the number of converts rapidly increased. Within ten years mass movements among the Oraons and Mundas brought many converts, and baptized Christians numbered about 10,000. Thus the mission work continued, spread, and flourished. Sometimes entire villages came to the missionaries, asking for baptism. The Lutheran mission was followed by an Anglican mission (1869) and a Roman Catholic mission (1887).

Although the early missionaries came from a background of evangelical awakening, they began to give serious attention to economic and social problems, as well as providing spiritual guidance. They sided with the peasants in their struggles against exploitation, providing them with lawyers to plead their cases, giving them advice, and helping them financially. The missionaries founded a mutual help society and co-operative credit societies for the mutual benefit of the converts. The schools and educational institutions that were established led to the intellectual awakening of the converts. Their tribal superstitions regarding spirits disappeared. According to C. F. Andrews, body, soul, and spirit were raised after conversion to Christianity. Since the missionaries supported the cause of the oppressed tribal peoples in this area and helped them in their struggles against their economic exploitation, it was natural for the tribal peoples to convert to Christianity in large numbers.

The Beginings of the Mennonite Church in Chotanagpur (BMM)

In the 1930s, Mennonite Church of India missionaries in the Dhamtari area were frustrated by the slow growth of their church and were looking for new ways in which to work, possibly in a new area. J. W. Pickett's book *Christian Mass Movements in India* (1933) had shown that 80 percent of Indian Christians had become Christians in groups.[83] Many of these conversions were among tribal people and Dalits. In May 1934 Pickett presented his findings to the Mid-India Christian Council. G. J. Lapp rose and asked: "Dr. Pickett, why does not that sort of thing happen here [in Dhamtari]?"[84] Dr. Pickett observed that the American Mennonite Mission approach was heavily institutional, attempting to establish Christianity through a program. This created a Christian community that was isolated from the larger community and that lacked evangelistic zeal.

From the start Mennonite missionaries were hoping for many converts, but with little result. Their mission stations such at Sankra and Ghatula seemed to be strategically located to cultivate a tribal group movement, and the missionaries were expecting this in the near future. There were some small caste movements at Durg in 1937-38, but in spite of much money and effort, there were no substantial conversions such as other denominations were experiencing. Eventually the missionaries realized that the mission-station approach was the problem. With some disillusionment and with a sense of failure they proposed establishing a new mission field, and investigated the possibilities in Bihar.

In response, the British Disciples of Christ invited the Mennonite Mission to work in the southwest corner of Bihar, close to the prospective mass movement area. After careful study, the mission decided to occupy Kodarma and Patna, a former Methodist station between Kolkata (Calcutta) and Benaras. The S. J. Hostetler family moved to Kodarma in January, 1940. They discovered a group of Turi (basket weaver) caste persons who were responsive to their message, and the mission was underway.

The first baptism took place in October 1940, marking the beginning of the Bihar Mennonite Church. In 1941 the Hostetlers were joined by the M. C. Vogt family and two Indian co-workers, D. M. Lakada and A. M. Dokono. Soon a second congregation developed at Harila, 20 miles from Kodarma, but local people were hostile and forced the Christians out of the village. The British Disciples of Christ Mission then offered part of their mission field, where there was receptivity among the Munda and Oraon tribes. In March 1947 the Mennonite mission decided to move to Chandwa in south Bihar, some 100 miles south of Kodarma.

The new mission was near Ranchi, the center of the large Gossner Lutheran Church mission. After resolving several comity conflicts through the Bihar Christian Council, Mennonite mission stations were established at Chandwa and Latehar. The latter station was purchased from the British Churches of Christ in 1949. The new buildings were erected on a more modest scale than those in the Dhamtari area, since the thrust in Bihar centers was to be a non-institutional evangelization program, with missionaries concentrating more on preaching and personal contacts than on medicine and education. Mission secretary J. D. Graber reminded the Bihar staff not "to feel that unless you are managing something of an organizational or institutional nature you are not getting anything done."[85]

According to a policy statement written in 1944, the aim of the Mission in Bihar was to "lead men and women to the new birth in

Christ and to organize them into village churches, sound in doctrine and practice as understood and believed by the Mennonite Church." Members were to be "integrated as much as possible into the economic structure of their original communities so that they may be more nearly self-supporting and may escape the weakening influence of a paternalism that uproots them economically and makes them dependent on the mission." "It has been observed," the policy statement concluded, "that where the church has taken strongest root in India this policy has been followed."[86]

Initially, the new mission was regarded as an extension of the Mennonite Mission in Madhya Pradesh. But by 1944 the Bihar Mission was able to maintain its own structures and budget. It became a separate mission in less than four years. A church conference was organized in 1951. By 1955 there were project committees for education, evangelism, and economic development. In 1955 it opened a Bible school at Chandwa, to offer intensive training for Christian leaders, and also opened a hostel at Latehar for Christian students attending public high school. In 1962 it also built a hospital at Satbarwa where Mark Kniss was stationed.

In October 1940 six people converted from the Turi tribe (basket-making people) at Kodorma. In 1941 ten more converted from this same tribe, and with 20 members a church was established. When the BCC (British Church of Christ) decided to leave the Palamau area in 1946, missionary teams of Mennonites came to take over the BCC fields. In 1947 this mission came to be known as the "Bihar Mennonite Mission" (BMM). After the move to Palamau, the church at Hazaribad was neglected; some members transferred to other

Daniel Tirky, Balamuth Chattaq

churches, and some fell away. Mission work came to be concentrated mostly in the rural areas.

The Chandwa Bungalow

The Bihar Mennonite Mission initially made Latehar its mission headquarters because the BCC mission bungalow and buildings were there. Soon land was purchased at Bathet and a mission station begun. Initially there were 25 people in the Mennonite church, some of whom had been BCC members. Although there was initial reluctance, BCC members began joining the Mennonite Church.

In 1947 construction of a mission bungalow at Chandwa began, in the same year that Daniel Tirky and his cousin Joel Tirky were baptized. They would become prominent leaders in the BMM. By 1950, the BMM was able to establish 8 evangelical centers, and 3 mission stations at Chandwa, Lather and Batad. In 1952, Bihar Mennonite Church had 150 members.

In 1955 BMM opened a small Bible school and offered a 2-year course of study, training 22 people in two classes. The Bible school would remain open until 1959. During this time 9 preachers went to the BIC church area in Purnia for 15 days under the leadership of Paul Kniss to help evangelize among the Oraon tribe. The BIC church members were all from the Santal tribe. Thanks to this mission in Purnia, 11 people were baptized. In the same year (1955), a women's fellowship called Mata Samaj was founded. In 1956 the Kuru church began; it came to have 64 members and became the main mission church, with a large church building. In 1955 the BMM also established reading rooms in Chandwa, Latahar and Bathet which functioned up to 1963.

In 1961/62 Evangelist Minj, known as a good speaker, was ordained. He served in Kushanpuri. In 1961 the Nav Jivan Hospital and reading

Chandwa Mission Station

room were opened at Thummanagada. The 1960s saw the arrival of Rev. Sushil Kaka, H. Kujur and his father. Both father and son served as senior pastors.

In response to the severe famine of 1966-67 the BMM undertook relief work with the help of MCC and the Committee on Social Action of the National Christian Council (CASA). Free meals were served in many places. The membership of the BMM was 450 in 1962, but after the famine membership had grown to 700. Among other activities the BMM started a dispensary at Lathehar and in 1967 Good Books was begun in a house rented by Paul and Easter Kniss; by 1972 Good Books had built their own building. Meanwhile, Paul Kniss began the Ranchi congregation. In 1968 nine people were ordained to the ministry, among them, H. Hujur, Manohar Ekka, Sushil Ekka, Boaz Ekka, and Das Gupta. The official name for the conference was changed in March, 1968 to the Bihar Mennonite Mandli.

The years 1972-73 were a transition period for the BMM, with the departure of the missionaries. Daniel Tirky became the first Indian chairman of the BMM, succeeded by Boaz Ekka. Membership in the conference dropped to 500 persons, meeting in 20 congregations with 17 church leaders. The church began to implement measures for independent support, but it appears that many who had joined the church because of its relief work left the church after the relief work was done.

Emmanuel Minj calls the period 1975-1990 the dark period for the church; the leadership grew older. In 1990, new leaders stepped forward. George Kaka began his work by visiting congregations and encouraging them, attempting to bring a new spirit to the churches. Unfortunately, he was given only three years to work before health problems led to his death. Sushil Kaka tried to continue in the spirit of George Kaka, but Sushil was also an older person, and died of cancer in 1992. V. Toknu took up the same kind of work, visiting and encouraging congregations.

During this time Emmanuel Minj joined the Conference. Minj had a good job, serving as a manager at Bharat Petroleum in Bombay. However, he did not have peace in his heart. Eventually he resigned, motivated in part by the deep needs of the church, and devoted himself to the ministry. He felt that God had called for him to join the church. From 1995 onwards Minj began to work in full-time min-

Emanuel and Malti Minj, 2003

istry. He also began visiting and encouraging congregations.

The first thing he wanted to do was to train the leaders, and so he began a training program in Chandwa, conducting two-day seminars.

On the first day students would attend classes and on the second day they would visit one congregation and spend time with them. The program elicited a good response. It succeeded in motivating congregations to take part in evangelism. He also began the Association for Theological Education by Extension program for Conference pastors (TAFTEE), because the majority of them did not have Bible training. Minj himself did not have Bible training, but after he left his managerial post he devoted himself to deep Bible study, and prepared himself to train others. The Mennonite World Conference's Global Sharing Fund was a blessing for the church: with the money Minj secured from this fund he was able to start new programs for the church.

BMM missionaries used to say *Dhamtari ka Galthi nahee karenge* (we will not make the same mistake as we did at Dhamtari – building so many institutions). But Emmanuel Minj felt that the situation could have been different if the Mission had developed different kinds of institutions. For example, Minj noted that while other missions flourished because of their educational institutions, the BMM suffered for lack of education. When the missionaries were about to leave, they considered buying some land for the church, but in the end they decided not to, thinking that if there was land, leaders would work in the fields rather than doing church work. It may be that because of the lack of property, the BMM so far had had no conflicts, divisions, or court cases as the other conferences have had.

The organizational structure of the BMM is headed by an executive body consisting of a president, a vice president, a secretary and a treasurer. They are selected by a nomination committee to serve for a period of two years. A meeting is called every three months to discuss Conference matters; this meeting is called *Kalasiya Sabha*. Participating in the *Kalasiya Sabha* are the members of the executive as well as one pastor and one delegate from each church in the conference.

In partnership with MCC India the BMM has opened two hostels, one for girls at Latehar and one for boys at Chandwa, enabling these students to attend local public schools while they stay in the hostels. BMM is also associated with Compassion India, a para-church organization concerned with child development. Through this project many children from Chandwa are being helped and 10 young men and women have been able to find jobs.

Culturally and linguistically this church has the closest affinity to congregations in the Banmankhi and Purnea districts of the BIC conference and with those of the Purnea District of the United Missions Service. In the year 2000, the BMM counted 21 churches and 11 pastors. Most of the pastors serving in BMM churches have completed their Certificate Course in Theology; two pastors have Bachelor degrees. BMM pastors are not paid by the conference, and receive only a minimal amount as an honorarium. They must earn the rest of their salaries from different sources. BMM does have some land which is cultivated to support mission work. In spite of scanty financial resources and in the face of serious challenges, the BMM continues to give attention to evangelism.

BMM churches practice immersion baptism and partake in the Lord's Supper four times a year. Foot Washing is practiced when the Lord's Supper is celebrated. They sing hymns in Kodoku, Koruku, Sadhari and Hindi, using a song book called *Jeeven Sangeet* (music of life). They practice a typical Protestant Christian's way of greeting in this area: they say *Yesu Sahaya* (Jesus Helps). The Roman Catholics greet by saying *Jai Yesu* (Hail Jesus). Interestingly, when non-Christians see Christians, they greet them in this way since they know that this is how Christians greet each other.

Marriage in the church is reserved for those who have been baptized. The consent of the parents and families is very important, and the process follows well-established steps. The young man's family visits the young woman's family and puts forward the marriage proposal. If the proposal is accepted by the bride's family the groom's family gives some gifts to the bride's family. This is called *Suth bandhani* (the marriage is fixed). Later the bride's family also visits the groom's house with some gifts for him. Following this, engagement takes place, which consists of two ceremonies. The first ceremony is called *Lota pani* (water in a tumbler), in which the bride and the groom stand with two of their friends facing each and exchange this *Lota pani* three times, each time confirming their wish to engage and marry each other. Once this ceremony is done the actual engagement takes place. This is called *Vacchan Daat* (taking vows) where the bride and groom promise their commitment to marry each other. It is compul-

Golden Jubilee celebration, 2009

sory for there to be a three-fold announcement in the church before the marriage ceremony takes place.

For the marriage ceremony itself, the groom's family goes to bride's house with the *Baarat* (the groom's family with a musical group). When they reach the bride's house all are welcomed with traditional music and dance, after which the ceremony takes place with marriage vows and the exchanging of rings. The marriage ceremony is followed by a reception in which the bride's family is invited to the groom's place for the ceremony called *Sharat*.

In 2009, the BMM celebrated its golden jubilee at Chandwa; Paul Kniss participated in the celebration. Daniel Tirky was the first member from this area who went to North America, representing the conference at the MWC meeting in Winnipeg in 1990. Rev. Sushil Kaka, Walter Kaka, Luks Lakada and Emmanuel Minj also visited abroad and participated in MWC Assemblies and other meetings. Emmanuel Minj continues to provide leadership not only to his church but also to all the Mennonite groups in India as director of the Mennonite Christian Service Fellowship of India (MCSFI), following Bishop Kunjam in this position.

Brethren in Christ Churches in Bihar

The Brethren in Christ Church established its first mission station in India in 1914 in North Bihar. The creation of Jarkhand state out of South Bihar in 2000 has left the BIC mission the only Anabaptist-related nission in the present Bihar state.

Bihar has a renowned ancient history. It was the home state of the Mauryan Empire. Under the great king Ashoka, the capital city Pataliputra (Patna today) became famous for its wealth and splendor. Bihar subsequently lost its independence, reduced to the official status of a province in 1936 under British rule.

The population of Bihar is dominated by tribal groups, sometimes called Adivasis. They were the original inhabitants of the region.[87] According to a 1991 census close to 90 percent of the people of Bihar live in rural areas, making Bihar one of the most rural states of India.

The Brethren in Christ Church, which began around 1780 in Lancaster county, Pennsylvania, took a progressive approach to evangelizing and witnessing for Christ across the globe. In 1904 the General Conference of the Brethren in Christ Church created a Foreign Mission Board which decided to send missionaries to India as soon as possible.[88]

The first attempt to establish a BIC mission station in India in 1904 did not succeed. The first BIC missionaries arrived in Bombay in January 1905, and worked for a time in Andhra Pradesh, moving later to North Bihar, near the border between India and Nepal. Although they won a handful of converts, this first group of BIC missionaries returned home in 1912 without being able to establish their own mission station. However, they provided needed information for the Mission Board to send missionaries later.

The second group of BIC missionaries sent to India included Henry L. Smith and Katie Burkholder and Henry and Effie Rohrer. They reached Kolkata in November 1913. They spent a month observing the work of the Mennonite Mission in the central provinces and the Church of the Brethren mission in Bombay, after which they began searching for their own field, eventually deciding on North Bihar. The missionary party moved to their chosen field eight miles south-east of Saharsa railway. They began their mission work in May 1914 staying in a mud-walled house in the village of Sour in an area that had no Protestant missions. In the same year Henry Smith was chosen BIC superintendent for India. Later the missionary team moved twelve miles north-east of Sour to the town of Madhipura and took up residence in a dilapidated building which had been used by the villagers as a shelter for goats and cows.

Henry Smith was able to secure land immediately adjoining the railway station compound in Saharsa, where a small bungalow was erected in 1916. Mr. and Mrs. David Rohrer and Ruth Byer came to join the mission team in 1916 which allowed Smith to move to Saharsa with Ruth Byer while the Rohrer family moved to Supaul and established another center for outreach. As the mission field widened the missionary staff continued to grow. By 1919, three mission stations had been established and there were twelve missionaries in the field. These early missionaries preached the Gospel with great zeal, and were hopeful of extending their mission to the unreached in North Bihar. Soon after their arrival in India they started learning Hindi and began studying the local culture. This enabled the missionaries to communicate the Gospel to Hindus and Muslims by direct evangelism, medical work, relief work and orphanages.

Apart from the evangelistic campaigns led by Smith, they were able to meet local medical needs because Effie Rohrer was trained as a practical nurse. Ruth Byer took charge of the dispensary work in Saharsa. When Leona Yoder, the first registered nurse arrived, thousands of people came for treatment. As the medical work developed, a hospital was established in Madhipura in 1953. Dr. George Paulus was the first BIC missionary doctor to India. Within a few years the Madhipura Hospital was treating thousands of patients.

According to Alvin and Leona Buckwalter, orphanages and schools were also an integral part of the mission from the beginning. Mission schools were started at Saharsa in1918 and later in Bazaar. The orphanage for boys in Supaul, the orphanage for girls and the home for widows in Madhipura were opened in1940. As the orphans were nurtured in this Christian atmosphere most of them accepted Jesus Christ as their Lord and Savior. During the time of famine (1916-1920), the BIC mission also was involved in relief work, presenting clothes and food to the hungry. Relief work was carried out later by the Mennonite Relief Committee of India. In 1958, the Saharsa station alone distributed weekly rations of wheat to more than 3,000 people.

Ragu Murmu's father

Ragu Murmu's father was a Hindu tribal priest, as his grandfather was also. As a priest he used to perform sacrifices and solve village problems. But Ragu Murmu's father had no peace in his life. One day he met a missionary in Balmanki, and began to search for truth and peace. One day he went to the church, where he found peace in his heart. As a result, he left the priestly job and he and his family converted and accepted baptism. From that day on the villagers persecuted him. People in the village said that he had chosen a low-caste religion, and they disassociated with him and his family. Ragu Murmu's father owned land which he donated to the church in the village.

The BIC mission's first baptism took place in August, 1917. He was a young Muslim man by name Sitab Ali. But progress was slow: after five years of ministry at Sahara and Madhipura stations it was reported that there were only two converts, while Supaul reported sixteen adherents. Many new converts helped the missionaries in this early mission and were appointed as village evangelists, namely Andreas, Daud, and James Biswas, Arthur Singh, Emmanuel Henry, and Isaac Paul. Some native women also helped in carrying the Gospel to nearby villages. Over the next 35 years mission stations were established at Bajora, Monghyr, and Banmanki with hostels and orphanages. The descendants of the orphanage children were the beginning of the BIC Christian communities. Saharsa served as the headquarters for the mission until it was transferred to

Purnia where there was a Hindi-speaking church with converts from Dalit origin.

In 1940 the BIC mission began working among the Santal people in the eastern part of Bihar, in the Purnia district. The church experienced a great harvest in that place. The first BIC missionary to reach the Santals was Charles Engle who baptized a Santal named Budhu (Paul) in April 1945. Budhu Paul wanted to witness to his own people, and began to work among them. The missionaries also began learning the Santali language, but they realized that Santali Christians would be much more effective working among their own people. According to William Hoke only Santal Christians were involved in this mission to the Santal people, not the missionaries. Applying the principle of "each one, win one," Santal Christians carried their mission even into Nepal.

Along with Patras Hembrom, a key leader among Santals, God chose Benjamin Marandi, who had been a guru, a witch doctor and an influential village head man. He played an instrumental role in establishing the church among Santals. Today people call him the "forefather of the Santali Christians and the church" and "the patriarch of the Brethren in Christ Church."

> **Benjamin Marandi**
>
> Benjamin Marandi was a Santali from South Bihar. He became ill with "plague of blood" disease. He went to a witch doctor but was not healed; Christian prayers did heal his illness, and he became a Christian. Benjamin Marandi began a small "people movement" among Santali tribal people. He had a true heart for the Lord and for his people, and a willingness and an ability to travel on the dusty roads, live with his people and model the Christian life. He had a successful ministry thanks to his natural gift of preaching and his musical ability. His preaching was said to be so powerful that nobody could oppose him or challenge him. He was a good singer and also played the mandarpin (a kind of instrument). He would begin singing and when people gathered around, he would begin to preach. He was tireless in preaching. Although the missionaries gave him a horse, he preferred walking, carrying a big bag on his shoulder. He liked tea, and always carried tea and biscuits, along with his mandarpin. He ministered in this way for many years until his death. He was buried beside the church in Purnia. His daughter Deena Marandi was also a Bible teacher. She remained unmarried and traveled from village to village, teaching the Gospel.

By the early 1950s the church realized that it needed leaders who had seminary or Bible college training. There was also a felt need to develop lay leadership. Persons like Hem Paul who attended Union Biblical Seminary, Surendra Nath Rai who attended Allahabad Bible Institute, and Luke Murmu who attended the Carey Bible School in Kolkata became important teachers for the BIC church.

The first church among the Santal people was established at Khanua village, south of Banmanikhi mission station. Benjamin Marandi

BIC church in Purnia, Bihar

was asked to serve as preacher among the Santals. Once he was well settled at Khanua he began to search for his relatives. At Donkhora village he made contact with Patras Hembrom who accepted the Lord, received baptism, and became very active in the Lord's ministry.

The formation of an executive committee in 1954 further strengthened the Santal church. Three Indian and three missionary representatives served on the committee which formed three church

districts. Each district committee was responsible for the finances and evangelistic work in its district.

An interest in education led to the opening of a lower primary school in Khanua village where Deena, the daughter of Benjamin Marandi, was the appointed teacher. The school could accept only a limited number, so children were also sent to the Barjora School which had a hostel.

The mission had a vision for childhood education, and set up a scholarship program and organization (SPICE) to further education. Some of the beneficiaries of these programs have become the leaders of the church. Rev. Samuel Hembrom, the first General Director of the BIC church in Bihar and Rev. Moses Marandi, the present Director of the BIC church, both benefitted from the BIC scholarship program. Both of their fathers (Patras Hembrom and Stephen Marandi) were early leaders in the Santal church. Since 1970 the church of the tribal peoples has continued to grow in the Purnea District and beyond, with new villages contacted and new churches established. The BIC mission saw Indian and American missionaries joining hands and working hard together to established a "mini kingdom of God" in Bihar. Their mission work was not confined to Bihar, but also extended to new areas such as Nepal and Orissa.

In the early 1980s, native BIC preachers crossed the border into Nepal and went from village to village, witnessing to the Lord. They were instrumental in establishing the church in Nepal. Some migrant

Santal people found affordable land in nearby Nepal and began to establish new churches. This church planting has been the result of lay pastors, who have provided much of the leadership for the churches in both Purnea and Nepal. In 1982 a new ministry was initiated in Orissa, and in the late 1980s, church planting began in West Bengal and Assam.

In 1976, there were 22 churches in North Bihar with about one thousand baptized members. By 1987 there were 1,944 communicant members recorded, meeting in 48 different worship places, fewer than half of which were church buildings. Church planting and growth was a direct result of having reached new villages, both in the area of the established churches and beyond.

The church maintained only one literature center, Jeewan Jyoti in Saharsa, but many people benefitted from it, doing the correspondence courses offered by the center. Besides the courses offered, a 1973 report states that Jeewan Jyoti enrolled 13,073 in its reading room ministry, out of which 1,319 were given free literature. The reading room was not only a blessing to Christians in the area, but also to non-Christians across the state of Bihar.

A significant transition took place in 1973 when the church's constitution was registered with the Bihar government. The last missionary to preside was R. V. Sider, and the first Indian chairman was Surendra Nath Rai, with Luke Murmu the first Indian secretary. Samuel Hembron continued the radio ministry that had been run earlier by the missionary William Hoke.

The BIC in America broadcast a radio program called "Gospel Tide," and they wanted to begin broadcasting also in India. The radio program in India began in 1978. Samuel Hembron preached in Santhali. William Hoke, the BIC missionary who was teaching in Allahabad, was instrumental in facilitating the radio ministry. He would take the radio team to Delhi to record the programs. The first radio program was in Hindi and was called *Aap ke liye* ("For You"). Several other programs followed. Bijoy Roul did a program in Oria and then in Bengali. Bijoy's brother-in-law did a separate program in Hindi. All in all, the BIC radio ministry broadcasts programs in seven languages. Broadcasting transmission was done by Trans World Radio.

The BIC church has been involved with Mennonite World Conference over the years. Samuel Hembron attended the MWC Assemblies in Strasbourg, France (1984), in Winnipeg, Canada (1990) and in

Kolkata, India (1997). One hundred people from Samuel Hembron's church participated in the 1997 Assembly. In his view, the Assembly in India was a great witness to non-Christians about the Christian faith; for other Christians, it was a witness to our Mennonite faith. The church contributed Rs. 10,000 toward the great Assembly. In 1997 an International BIC Assembly was also held in Purnea, in conjunction with the MWC gathering. The BIC church enjoys good fellowship with other conferences, is a member of the National Christian Council of India and also a member of the Bihar Christian Council.

In the year 2000, BIC churches could be found in Saharsa, Sepol, Madhyaapura, Purnia, and Banmaki districts. In that year the BIC church numbered 57 churches in the Conference in 7 regions, with an approximate membership of 7,000. Some churches own up to 5 acres of land, the income from which goes to support the pastors. In addition, the Mission Board gives Rs. 1,000 to each pastor which is supplemented in some cases with income from their churches. The church also gets funds from the Mission Board for support of the hostels, with the church providing scholarships for bright and needy students. Most of the rural congregations are poor. Not many of these churches have their own land and only about 10 percent have government jobs.

The *Mahasabha* is the decision-making body of the BIC church led by a chairman who is selected for a term; secretaries are elected. The church board is the chief governing body. It consists of one ordained and one lay leader which meets twice a year. There are also regional councils which select the regional superintendents. There is a General Director who is responsible for mission work as well as all the properties for all the regions.

The BIC church has a rule that members must attend at least 40 Sundays in a year in order to qualify for any church position. In addition to regular worship, BIC churches commonly have mid-week prayers and women's fellowship on Wednesdays. The women's fellowships of the local churches take care of the poor. Until 1990 it was the practice to celebrate a Galghat convention for fellowship during Christmas; now the BIC churches hold regional conventions during October (*Durga puja*) holidays.

The BIC operate two schools, in Saharsa and Baljora. They also operate a hospital in Madhyapura which is run by the Emmanuel Hospital Association (EHA). The church is now associated with Compassion India and many church members volunteer with that organization. The BIC church is also running a child development project in association with Compassion India. This project is dedicated to the physical and moral development of children. The BIC in Bihar is also working closely with MCSFI addressing the issue of HIV/AIDS in their local area. The Mission Board has continued supporting evangelism but does not give priority to schools or education.

The BIC churches practice immersion baptism, during which those being baptized confess their faith. The Lord's Table is usually observed 4 or 5 times a year, although some churches celebrate the Supper only 2 or 3 times a year. Foot Washing was practiced initially in the BIC churches, but it has slowly fallen into disuse. Although teachings on peace and non-violence are a distinctive of the BIC, there has been no systematic teaching on these principles in the local churches. As a result, some church members have joined the police and the army. The BIC believe that Christians should not go to the court, and so far they have not had any court cases.

There are no BIC women pastors in Bihar, the USA or Canada; women can become teachers and hold other offices, such as serving on church councils, but they have not been ordained to pastoral ministry. There are few women Bible teachers in the present BIC church. The youth among the Santals have become very active in the church, sharing the Gospel in new places and helping believers build their churches.

In terms of marriage, members follow Santali customs. This includes the ceremony of *Baraat*, welcoming the bride or groom with candles, accompanied by the washing of feet. The *Manduva*, i.e. a thatch with green branches, is constructed. The couple does not exchange rings or *Mangala Suthra* as a sign of marriage nor do they use *Sindhur* (red colored powder put on the forehead, used by married women), but they do exchange garlands. They also practice *haldi*, a custom in which they apply turmeric powder mixed either with water or oil on the body, and rice mixed with turmeric powder is sprinkled over the heads of the couple as a blessing. The bride wears a white *sari* while the groom wears the *dhothi* or a suit. Marriage to a non-Christian is grounds for excommunication.

According to Santali custom, young men and old men show respect for each other by bowing down with folded hands. The older man gives the younger man a blessing; in the case of women the younger woman touches the elderly woman's feet.

The BIC Mission to Nepal

For much of its history Nepal has been virtually closed to outsiders, but political changes in 1950 led to openings. In 1951, Christian missionaries were permitted to visit Nepal and shortly thereafter the United Mission to Nepal (UMN) was founded (1954). The UMN is an cooperative agency through which various mission groups work together. By 1987 the UMN numbered about 400 missionaries from more than 20 countries, sponsored by 39 mission boards. The assignments included medical, educational and economic development work. In 1956, Rudolf Friesen was sent by the Mennonite Central Committee (MCC) to work in Nepal. Later that year two PAX volunteers joined him. In 1957 Lena Graber became the first mission worker sent to Nepal by the Mennonite Board of Missions (MBM). Since then numerous MCC and MBM workers have served under UMN in professional, administrative, and clerical roles. Maynard and Dorothy Siemens have been supported by the Mennonite Brethren BOMAS since 1960. They are engaged in medical work under the Evangelical Alliance Mission (TEAM) in western Nepal. In 1986 the Christian church in Nepal numbered about 20,000 members; it has continued to grow in spite of persecution.

Nepal is the only Hindu nation in the world which has not been colonized. In 1992 Nepal achieved political independence from its former traditional monarchy, but before this time Christians found it very difficult to preach the Gospel and even to worship. Conversion was strictly prohibited in Nepal, although these took place with the BIC members who went there to share the Gospel. Like the mission work in Orissa, mission work in Nepal was carried out by native BIC missionaries, not by foreign missionaries. The church of Nepal was started by persons who had relatives in Bihar; because they shared a place of origin the development was organic. Many Santal people had settled on the Nepalese plains, beginning their migration from India about 200 years ago.

The work of the BIC in Nepal began when Benjamin Marandi and Petrose Marandi went to Nepal in search of a girl who had once attended the BIC church in Purnia. They went from village to village and inquired whether there was any preacher. When the reply was "no," they said *Yesu Prachar* (preaching about Jesus), but the answer still was "no." Later in the 1960s, Samuel Marandi started traveling regularly to Nepal from Purnia. Gradually, the Santal people of Nepal received the Gospel and began to spread it. Benjamin Marandi,

Petrose Marandi, Stephen Marandi, and Luke Murmu were the pioneering missionaries to Nepal. As a result of these connections, the Nepal BIC church became a branch of the Purnia church. The BIC church in Nepal is a fast-growing church with a membership of 1,000 meeting in 11 congregations in the year 2000.

The first known baptism in Nepal took place in 1962. Hati Ganga was the first village to be evangelized; the first gathering was held as a small house church. Whenever there was a Santal festival, or a Hindu festival, believers used to meet to worship together. To other people their worship looked Hindu, because the Nepalese did not know the language or the festivals of the Santal people. Baptisms were not done in the open, but were held in jungles and rivers where no one could see them. Those baptized do not change their names after baptism, although those named Rama or Krishna sometimes do want to change their names.

A Baptism continued

Once when Petrose Marandi was baptizing a believer in the river on a Hindu festival day, the police arrived. Everybody ran except Petrose Marandi and the person who was being baptized. When the police asked what was going on, Petrose Marandi said "Just as the Hindus do, we are doing our ceremony." During Hindu festivals people commonly go to the river to take a dip in the water. The police said "OK, go ahead" and they left. That is how Petrose Marandi escaped on that day.

When the independence movement began in the Nepal in 1990, the government suspected that the movement was due to Christianity, and persecution became more severe for Christians. The police began to check up on Christian activities and homes. When the police came to Shamlal one of the members home, they found Santali books and English books and they took those books thinking that they were Bibles. Shamlal's father and his sister were arrested and many in that village were badly beaten. Some men were taken to the temples and were forced to worship Hindu gods and idols.

There are no Hindu militant groups such as the VHP or Shivasena in Nepal, but there is a militant group called *Pasupathi Sena*. There are 17 denominations present in Nepal and many of their people have suffered in the recent years. It is estimated that Christians make up around 2 percent of the population of Nepal. At present the BIC have 22 churches in Nepal, including some small congregations. The Biratnager congregation purchased property in late 1990; since that time the church has grown substantially.

In terms of structure the Nepalese churches are still under BIC Purnia. Nepal is one of BIC church's 7 regions, but since Nepal is a separate country, the Nepalese church has its own director and chairman. Although the church has freedom to act on its own, for major decisions leaders consult with the Purnia Church. The Nepalese church has members from different tribal groups such as Orov, Santal, and some Nepali people of Biratnagar. The church recently started a mission in Katmandu. The Nepali language is commonly used for worship and preaching, although the Santalis and Oraons use their own language. There is a women's fellowship in Biratnagar, and women are allowed to preach in the Nepalese BIC church. There is one case of a woman leading a congregation.

Deepak Sharst is the director of the BIC church of Nepal. He did his B.Th. at the Allahabad Bible Seminary. Although crossing the border was not allowed, nevertheless he traveled to Bihar for leadership training. After democracy was achieved in Nepal in 1992, Deepak Sharst moved to Nepal where he conducted open air evangelistic meetings. In 1994 a small piece of land was purchased and a church and hostel in Biratnagar were constructed. The church there began with two people but today it has 70 members. The church has opened a small theological school which currently has 53 students. The church has begun a Theological Education through Extension (TEA) program, the first of its kind in Nepal. The material used came from the Allahabad Seminary and was translated into Nepalese.

The BIC is a member of the NCF (Churches Fellowship of Nepal). Although the BIC church has organized some medical camps, the focus of the church is primarily church planting. The church has already attempted reaching into Tibet and Bhutan from its mission location in Katmandu. MCC recently opened a center in Nepal and will be working directly in the country. Fifteen church members from Nepal participated in the MWC Assembly in 1997, and many MWC participants visited Nepal as a site of "Assembly Scattered," something that strengthened and encouraged the Nepalese churches.

The BIC Mission extension to Odyssa (Orissa)

The BIC church stepped into Orissa in 1982, long after other missions had discovered the area. The Lord used Bijoy Kumar Raul to establish the church in Orissa. Bijoy worked for twenty two years for the Brethren in Christ church with a church planting organization called "India Every Home Crusade." The BIC never had a foreign missionary in Orissa; all work was done by native Indians. However, in just over two decades the BIC were able to start over one hundred churches in Orissa, even though there were prohibitions against conversion from one religion to another.

Orissa, although geographically small, is an important state in India. The Hindus have an important temple called *Puri Jagananth* here. The state is rich in natural resources, inhabited mostly by Dalits and Adivasis. The Baptists were the pioneer Protestant missionaries to Orissa. In the Northern coastal part of Orissa, which was influenced by the Baptist mission, Serampore developed into a focal point. The Lutheran church of Germany followed in 1882 when two young volunteers came to the Koraput District of Orissa and began work in that area.[89] By 1896, 203 people from 29 villages had been baptized, and the figure multiplied to 14,026 baptized members by 1939. This great mission continues bringing many people to the Lord. The Canadian Baptist Mission was the third mission to arrive, in 1902, coming first to Paralakhmundi. By 1922 seven churches had been founded and had formed the rural Ganjam Baptist Church Association.

Bijoy Kumar Raul

Bijoy Kumar Raul came to study at the Allahabad Seminary as an independent student. He was from ECI (Evangelical Church of India) church background. He was a good student, but did not have the financial resources to continue his studies. When the BIC missionary William Hoke came to teach at the Allahabad Seminary in 1971, he met Bijoy Raul there and raised the funds Bijoy Raul needed to complete his studies.

When William Hoke began work in Bihar Bijoy joined him briefly, but soon began work with the BIC in Purnia, after which he studied at the UBS (Yeotmal) where he received his B.D. and taught in a small seminary in Ruky for a year. After working in Delhi for three years, Bijoy shared his burden about his people in Orissa with the BIC missionary in Delhi (Sider). Bijoy's brother Pramod was the first to work in Orissa. Bijoy was assigned under the Every Home Crusade – not of the BIC – and began work in Cuttack.

Bijoy and his brother Pramod made contact with MCC and began doing some development work; eventually the BIC purchased a tractor for development work in the villages. The church began to grow even in the midst of persecutions. After Bijoy was ordained in Orissa by William Hoke he become Chairman and Secretary of the BIC work in Orissa, and the church grew steadily.

Even through many mission agencies were already in Orissa, the BIC church that began work in 1982 expanded its mission quickly. By 1985 it had organized as its own conference, separate from BIC Purnia. Most people in Orissa are tribal people and live in rural areas where there is no electricity, no proper drinking water, and no educational or medical facilities. The BIC's targeted these tribal people, of whom the Bondos are one.

BIC church, Orissa

The Bondos have contin-ued to inhabit their traditional dwelling places in remote areas deep in the forest. They are fiercely independent and aggressive. The BIC church decided to start with social work among the Bondo people; evangelistic efforts began later. In spite of limited finances, the church has attempted to help the Bondo people with an edu-cational program for children and adults, hostel facilities for students, agricultural help in planting and digging wells and ponds, along with medical help, vocational training and relief work. As a result of these activities, a good number of Bondo people joined the BIC church.

The situation for Christian evangelism is difficult in Orissa. There are strong anti-Christian elements, and churches have been demolished or set on fire. Some pastors and believers have even been killed. In spite of

Worship in a village church

such unfavorable conditions, the BIC church has continued its ministry in Orissa. In spread-ing the Gospel message, the Orissa BIC church has used film ministry, story-telling, Christian drama, radio ministry, literature distribution, home visits, and social work. The results have been very positive, with the BIC establishing more than 100 churches with approximately 6,000 believers.

The BIC church practices immersion bap-tism of members. Worship revolves around fixed times for spiritual activities. In order to encourage spiritual growth, the mission encour-ages every new believer to attend all church activities. Worship fol-lows an indigenous style, using indigenous music and dance. At the same time the mission guards against importing elements from the former religions of the new members.

The BIC radio program called "Gospel Tide" was recorded origi-nally in the Oriya language. Bijoy recorded this program in both Oriya and Bengali, and also did the follow-up work. The radio mission began in 1977, and eventually Bijoy took the broadcast team to Delhi for recording. The first recording in Hindi was called *Aap ke liye* (For You), which then grew into several programs. Bijoy's brother-in-law, a Methodist pastor, recorded the programs in Hindi. When the Gospel Tide studio moved to Cuttuck, Bijoy supervised its construction. It is now the only studio used.

The Bharatiya Jukta Christo Prachar Mandli

The Bharatiya Jukta Christo Prachar Mandli church (BJCPM) is the offspring of the United Missionary Church (UMC) of North America. Its official registered name in Bengali means "The Indian United Christ Evangelistic Church." Its headquarters are in Kolkata. It has become part of MCSFI and has identified with the Mennonites in India.

Kolkata, the capital of West Bengal, is situated on the banks of the river Hoogly; the local language is Bengali. Although the sea is 150 kilometers away from Kolkata, it is an important port city, connected to the sea by the deep and navigable Hoogly. Kolkata has a tram system and is one of the only cities in India (along with Delhi) to have an underground railway system. For the past three decades the state of West Bengal has been ruled by the Communist party, which has emphasized religious freedom. Christian programs have not suffered or received any opposition from the government. The Communists were defeated in the state elections on May, 2011.

The first United Missionary Church missionaries to reach India were Francis Matheson and Ruby Reeve. In 1903 the UMC mission moved to Raghunathpur in the Purilia district, where the Mission bought a spacious lot with already-existing buildings. The buildings were renovated and converted into hostels for boys and girls. In 1907 a new station was opened at Adra, about four miles from Raghunathpur. A bungalow was built there for the missionaries and a school for the children. This bungalow was sold again in 1942.

When a famine broke out in 1920 in Orissa the missionaries returned with a number of orphaned boys and girls, as well as some aged people, hoping to provide them with home, shelter and Christian nurture. Later many were converted and have served faithfully in church ministries. In 1924 the denomination acquired its own territory in the Purilia district of West Bengal, where a mission station was opened at Balarampur. W. E. Wood was instrumental in this work.

In an interesting development, the Hephzebah Faith Missionary Association eventually was incorporated into the work of UMC (or BJCPM). The Hephzebah Faith Missionary Association had begun its mission work in Balarampur in 1914, and expanded to Ahmadabad in response to the severe famine there. The mission began an orphanage and schools for boys and girls, providing education and Christian nurture. Eventually, the Hephzebah Faith Missionary Association received faithful workers from the original group of orphans. These native workers moved from Ahmadabad to the West Bengali mission, where the Hephzebah Faith Missionary Association also worked in Anara, Domonkiyari, and Adra. When the original missionaries of Hephzebah Faith Mission returned to the United States, the search began for persons to look after the work. Eventually the BJCPM (UMC) was approached with the proposal that BJCPM take over the Hephzebah Faith Missionary Association without any strings attached. In 1948, all properties belonging to the Hephzebah Faith Missionary Association were handed over legally to the BJCPM mission.

The first Annual Conference following the 1948 merger was organized in 1951. Rev. Satyen Hembron served as the first national District Superintendent of the expanded BJCPM conference which also became self-governing. Beginning in 1958, John Gamble designed a successful program to reach every home in the area with the Gospel. Although a Bible training program had been carried on for years, it was recognized that a standard Bible training school was needed to prepare workers for the future. This resulted in the foundation of the Bengal Bible Institute in 1963.

In the late 1950s Pronoy Sarkar became an important leader in the BJCPM church, providing leadership over several decades. Pronoy Sarkar graduated from UBS in 1956 and began working with Alfred Rees, a Canadian missionary who was just beginning his ministry. Together they began an expansion program. They secured a location for the first English-speaking house of worship, named "Emmanuel Chapel." A location was also found for Bengali-speaking services. By 1959 both English and Bengali congregations had been organized and enjoyed growth. The work has since expanded to other areas in Kolkata. A Telugu-speaking church has also opened in conjunction with Emmanuel Chapel, with Mr. Devadson as its first lay pastor.

In 1956 a correspondence course opened in the Emmanuel Chapel facilities. Pronoy Sarkar began working with the correspondence courses, designing courses for non-Christians that could be read and understood easily. Eventually the Calcutta Bible Institute was opened with Pronoy Sarkar as its principal. The correspondence course was advertised in the leading Bengali paper as follows: "If you want to study the life of Christ then please send your name and address." Some one thousand people sent their names in response, and the number grew substantially over time, at one point numbering 10,000 students enrolled in one year. Bible classes were conducted in 8 centers, with enrolled students coming to the centers to study the Bible; there was follow up work with the students after the courses were completed. In 1962 John Blosser was appointed the full-time director of the Bible courses. Every year 30 to 40 students would be baptized into the church, helping establish the Bengali Church in the city of Kolkota. So far, two Bengali-speaking churches, three English-speaking churches, and one Telugu-speaking church have emerged in that city.

Acquiring the historic Hastings Chapel in Kolkata was a big achievement for the BJCPM church. Pronoy Sarkar tells the story of how God led them to the Hastings Chapel that had once belonged to United Church of the LMS mission. The chapel was built in 1862, but was not well maintained. The roof collapsed and the chapel lay empty and unused. Pronoy and Alfred Rees visited the area to distribute tracts, and they would see this old building. They prayed, "Lord, give us this building, and we will make it a house of prayer." The Lord heard their prayer. One day in 1958 they read an advertisement in the local newspaper saying that the LMS was ready to lease the building. Pranoy applied, along with many others, but the Mission chose Pronoy as tenant, renting the building for Rs. 30/per month. There was no money for the repair, and there still was no roof, so they again began to pray "Lord help us build the church."

One of the pioneer BIC missionaries, W. E. Wood, who was working in the Balampur area, died and left enough money to rebuild the church. The mission board sent this money to the BJCPM to rebuild the church. It was rebuilt and re-dedicated on December 23, 1962 in memory of W. E. Wood. John Blosser served as the first pastor of Hastings Chapel under the United Missionary Society. In Kolkota the rule of tenancy seems to be that once you are a tenant you are always a tenant. That is how the BJCPM church continues to this day. The main offices of the church are located here, along with offices for the

Correspondence Course; an English Medium school has been opened. Pranoy Sarkar was the first Indian pastor to serve there.

In 1973 all the foreign missionaries were withdrawn, and the entire church and mission work came into the hands of national Indian leaders. By this time there were seventeen organized churches and seven unorganized congregations along with two high schools (one for boys and another for girls), with hostel facilities for fifty students. There is also one residential vernacular Bible school with a hostel facility for twenty students. A Bible correspondence school operates from the city of Kolkata and thousands of students are enrolled. A recording studio was constructed in 1975 to prepare gospel messages for broadcast.

The BJCPM conference was strengthened when the Purliya conference of Santal Christians joined. The Purliya conference was a bit hesitant about the merger because BJCPM members did not speak Santhali. Finally the Purliya conference decided to join and form a separate conference within the BJCPM, which was called the East India Conference. The BJCPM helped build new churches and in the 1990s also established the North Eastern Conference which included 29 churches in the tea-growing area. The Purliya conference was the third conference to join the BJCPM.

In 1998, a group of 35 churches in Orissa, under the leadership of Mr. Pramod Nand, negotiated to join the BJCPM. This group officially joined the BJCPM in 1999, and was called the South East Conference.

The United Missionary Church or BJCPM is organized around separate geographical districts. This has enabled the larger body to incorporate new regional groups from rural Bengal and neighboring Orissa. The 1970s and 1990s were times of rapid growth. By the year 2000 the BJCPM had 95 congregations with 6000 baptized members. Ten of these congregations are in greater Kolkata. The BJCPM is served by 77 pastors out of whom 20 are theologically trained; the rest have had some Bible school training. The Conference is in the process of establishing its own training center to meet this need.

The United Missionary Church in North America, now headquartered in Mishawaka, Indiana, no longer considers itself to be part of the Mennonite "family," but in India the BJCPN church does. It is autonomous in nature but follows the same doctrines as the Mennonites, with baptism carried out by immersion.

The BJCPM is a part of MWC, and in India the conference participates actively in MCSFI. Paul Kniss, who has served as construction manager for the building of churches and has helped raise funds, was a Mennonite Church missionary in Ranchi, but helped the BJCPM for a number of years. Conference churches observe the Lord's Supper twice a month; once a year, during Passion Week, they practice Foot Washing, and the conference opposes military service for its members. The ordination of the pastors is done by the conference, not by the individual churches, although the pastors are supported by their local churches. The Calcutta Bible Institute in Kolkata continues to receive support from the overseas mission, the United Missionary Church in North America.

According to the BJCPM constitution, the Executive Secretary is the leader of the Conference. The Governing Committee of the BJCPM approves all projects for all the regions in an annual conference. At the conference, one delegate represents 50 members from the churches. Each of the four districts has a District Superintendent who is an ordained person. The Governing Committee also looks into disciplinary matters, ordinations and other such matters. Ordination takes place only after candidates have completed theological studies and have served 3 years.

BJCPM churches minister in English, Bengali, Oria, Telugu, Santhali, Bodo, and Hindi. There also are three Telugu-speaking churches. At Raghunathpur in Tata Nagar, the Conference has a huge mission station. The Conference aims to construct 3 new churches every year. The church did publish its own magazine, but when the Calcutta Bible Institute began to publish its magazine, the church stopped publishing its own, since the latter served both purposes. BJCPM members don't go to court to settle their issues, but will attend if a case needs defending. More than half of its members are poor and work as daily laborers; some have small land holdings. Therefore the church provides help for the education of members' children. However, each member is committed to paying Rs. 1/- per month to the church. One Sunday a year they observe a "Conference Sunday" to raise money for the Conference. The conference runs seven schools and one medical clinic.

Although the BJCPM follows many Mennonite practices, Pronoy Sarkar feels that the MCSFI should provide literature on Mennonite faith to all the BJCPM churches, because the congregations are not aware of the Mennonite positions. He also feels that MCC and MCSFI should work on promoting peace, since all churches are very weak in this area, and pastors do not preach on the subject. In his view, church disputes take place because of a lack of teaching on peace values.

Margaret Devadason

The role of women in the BJCPM is somewhat limited. They are allowed to pray publicly, but they are not allowed to preach from the pulpit. However, there are some exceptions, such as Mrs. Margaret Devadasan, who was treasurer of her church; she sometimes even preached in the church. Mrs. Cynthia Peacock, who rendered her services to MCC for several years as office manager, has provided leadership to the BJCPM Women's Conference since her retirement, and also to the All India Women's Conference. Today she is providing leadership to the MWC, as she serves as chairperson of the MWC Deacons' Committee. In her view, the BJCPM should be open to women and invite women preachers.

BJCPM associates with EFI and has a seat on the executive committee of the EFI. Pronoy Sarkar was also chairman of UBS, and served on the organizing Committee of the MWC Assembly held in Kolkata in 1997. The current Chairperson of the BJCPM is Joram Basumata, who is theologically trained and the pastor of three churches.

The BJCPM (the India United Missionary Church), though one of the smallest churches in India, is known for its missionary work in rural areas, particularly for taking the Gospel to the borders of Assam, Bihar, West Bengal and Orissa. It has become an essential participant in the Mennonite and BIC family of churches in India.

The Gilgal Mission Trust

The Gilgal Mission Trust was founded in 1979 by Pastor J. Paulraj and Mrs. Arputhamani Paulraj, originally under the name Operation Biblical Counseling Center (OBC) in Tirupur District, Tamilnadu. In 2005 its name was officially changed to the Gilgal Mission Trust. From the beginning the OBC was an independent para-church movement with a three-fold emphasis on establishing colleges for biblical counseling and theological training, promoting intensive and extensive evangelism, and planting indigenous inter-State churches.

Gilgal Mission Trust's head office is located in the Tamil Nadu state in South India, in the foothills of the Western Ghats near the Indira Gandhi National Wild Life Sanctuary. This border region is home to Tamilians, Malayalis, tribal people and nomads. There are various caste groups living together, such as Brahmins, Gounders, Adi-Dravidis, Narikuravars (gypsies), Nadars and Dalits. Although this mission was not born of Mennonite mission work, it was attracted to the Mennonite fellowship and the MCSFI family in 2005. Church planting is the main goal of the Gilgal Mission Trust. The mission sends evangelists to remote villages to preach the Gospel. As a result, the Gilgal Mission Trust has established twenty seven churches.

In 2005 Paul Phinehas of the Gilgal Mission Trust requested affiliation by means of a letter to Mennonite World Conference, which was then forwarded to Mennonite Christian Service Fellowship of India (MCSFI). As a result MCSFI Director Emmanuel Minj and vice-Chairman Bijoy Roul visited GMT pastors and consulted board members. The request for affiliation was subsequently approved, and the GMT recognized as an affiliated member of the MCSFI.

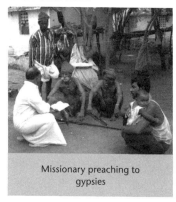

Missionary preaching to gypsies

In addition to its work in evangelism, the GMT is involved in social work. In particular, it has initiated a program for the feeding and education of rural children. The GMT offers free tuition to school-going children and a midday meal program for children below the age of five. Since poverty has compelled many children to miss school, this program is helping transform lives, giving many poor children hope for a bright future. The GMT also provides service to senior citizens and provides free medical camps in slums and rural areas, including camps for eye and dental care for the needy. Finally, the GMT conducts AIDS awareness and Peace and Justice programs, as well as seminars on liberation from drugs and alcohol in rural India.

The Mennonite Central Committee (MCC) in India

MCC came to India in 1942 at the encouragement of Mennonite missionaries who wished to respond to the tragic Bengal famine. Once in the country, MCC continued relationships with development agencies and church-related bodies, the Mennonite Service Agency (MSA) and the Brethren in Christ Development Society (BICDS). With the establishment of MCSFI in 1963, MCC began to support a variety of inter-church programs as well as development committees in each of the church regions. "MCC's work in India has always operated under the umbrella of the church."[90]

In 1999, Dr. Ron Kraybill of Eastern Mennonite University, USA, joined the faculty of the Henry Martyn Institute for an academic year. Dr. Kraybill helped develop the HMI mediation program and, along with an MCC staff person, conducted training programs in conflict resolution for local NGOs, schools and police departments. In the same year Dalton Reimer of Fresno Pacific University, USA conducted a three-day workshop on Conflict and Reconciliation for the faculty and staff of Mennonite Brethren Bible College at Shamshabad, in Andhra Pradesh.

Although the concept of peacemaking was always at the forefront of MCC's mandate, in India the direct program of peacemaking in church and society began in 1997. Initially mediation training was provided to the national staff of MCC and then to several people from Kolkata and other places in India. The core focus of this program is to provide skills in mediation efforts through appropriate skills in listening, paraphrasing and then helping disputants come to a conclusion. In 1997 ongoing training for one staff and initial training in mediation and networking with NGOs was the prime effort for the year.

In 1999 an active phase of the Peace and Justice program began, with numerous conflict-mediation training workshops conducted by MCC staff, both within and outside the Kolkata community. This Peace and Justice Program provided training, workshops and seminars to many NGOs, institutions and individuals in areas of reconciliation, mediation and conflict resolution skills. MCC's partnership with the Henry Martyn Institute for Interfaith Relations and Reconciliation (HMI) in Hyderabad and with the Social Unit for Community Health and Improvement (SUCHI) in Vellore proved to be helpful in developing mediation and conflict resolution skills at the grass root level.

In the year 2004, MCC, MCSFI and Mennonite Brethren Bible College organized a workshop for all Indian Mennonite Church leaders, in Shamshabad. As a result, Christina Asheervadam was sent to EMU to be trained in the peace education, with the eventual aim of strengthening peace studies in India.

Mennonite Christian Service Fellowship of India (MCSFI (by Earl Zimmerman)

The foreign missionaries who came to India did so out of a deep sense of spiritual dedication and at enormous personal cost, yet they lived in rural India in a way that set them apart from the surrounding communities.[91] The foreign missionaries were completely in charge of the churches and mission stations. After the first generation, considerable emphasis was placed on nationalizing the churches and mission institutions and on making them self-supporting. This was done under the prevailing mission paradigm of "self-propagation," "self-government" and "self-support" known as the "three-self movement."[92] It was a process filled with many pitfalls and no easy solutions.

The movement toward self-government and self-support was well underway in the 1960s and was part of the impetus behind the creation of MCSFI, which was conceived as a national Mennonite service agency. The emphasis on self-support may partly explain why MCC administrators were reluctant to give too many external funds to MCSFI in the following decades. By the middle of the 1970s, all the former mission churches and institutions had been turned over to national control and the foreign mission boards had almost completely phased out their work. MCC was the only remaining North American-based Mennonite agency with a significant presence in India. The speed and scope of the transition was traumatic for the Indian churches. A secure, albeit paternalistic world had passed away and an independent but a less secure world had emerged.[93]

Bishop P. J. Malagar, a gifted and competent Indian church leader in the post-colonial era, was appointed as the first director of MCSFI, a position he would hold for the next eighteen years. MCC would give MCSFI an annual grant of US $2,500 to cover the director's salary and related expenses.[94] The annual grant continued throughout the next decade with the understanding that the Indian churches would gradually assume this financial obligation. Although MCSFI was conceptualized as a national organization, its first board had five North American members and only three Indian members. The chairman, vice-chairman, and treasurer were all North Americans.[95]

The four-fold agenda for the new organization was: (1) to promote Christian service in the spirit of Christ, (2) to work at disaster relief and the alleviation of human suffering, (3) to strengthen the fellowship of its associated churches, and (4) to promote evangelism and a Christian peace witness.[96] It was a bold and perhaps impossible task for a newly created entity representing six different church conferences spread across a huge geographical swath of India, speaking different languages and dialects and with no prior experience of working together.

The initial plan was for Bishop Malagar and his family to move to Kolkata for his work as director of MCSFI. The family, however, found it impossible to adapt to life in Kolkata. When their youngest son required emergency hospitalization, the family moved back to their home town of Dhamtari. Bishop Malagar would subsequently make endless overnight train journeys between Dhamtari and Kolkata to do MCSFI errands.[97]

The following several years involved a flurry of joint disaster relief work in various parts of India. MCC India and MCSFI worked with volunteers from different Anabaptist-related churches and pooled funds and personnel with other international aid organizations. A significant disaster relief project responded to the devastating cyclone that struck the Chittagong area (present-day Bangladesh) in 1963. Bishop Malagar reports that when MCC sought the help of the churches, "the response of the churches was immediate and intense."[98] In response to a request from the Bengal Refugee Service and in cooperation with the West Bengal Health Department, a hospital was established north of Kolkata through an MCC and MCSFI partnership. A separate MCSFI medical board was formed in 1964 to oversee the enterprise and the Shyamnagar Christian Hospital was finally opened in 1971. Bishop Malagar was the only Indian serving on the medical board; all the others were North American missionaries serving in the various Mennonite and Brethren in Christ hospitals. He mostly listened and did not say much during board meetings. The plan had been to involve the Indian churches directly, but getting people to move there to serve the hospital and the surrounding community proved difficult. The hospital functioned as a Mennonite-run ministry for ten years before it was eventually turned over to the West Bengal government in 1981. A final indignity took place when Bishop Malagar was appointed secretary of the medical board so he could perform the task of signing the legal transfer papers, even though he was adamantly opposed to this action.

Various Indian Mennonites took international service assignments through the MCSFI partnership with MCC. In the 1970s a husband and wife team served in Vietnam under Vietnam Christian Services. Another family served as missionaries in Bangladesh. In the 1980s a medical team from the Dhamtari Christian Hospital went to Cambodia and a doctor couple from the hospital served there for several years.

The peace witness of the Mennonite and Brethren in Christ churches was another major MCSFI undertaking over the years. Bishop Malagar arranged for Norman Kraus, an American Mennonite theologian, to come to India to teach at

Clothing distribution

Serampore College in 1966-67. During that year Kraus traveled and spoke in various Mennonite and Brethren in Christ churches throughout India. He kept returning on peace education assignments with the Mennonite churches at various times in the following years. Reflecting on these experiences, he wrote, "I have a feeling that 'peace witness' in India means first of all sharing God's infinite loving patience with people who think of almost everyone as a potential enemy."

Such a peace witness was close to Bishop Malagar's heart and he devoted much of his energy to promoting and strengthening it in Indian churches. He thought it needed more radicalism and involvement in real life situations. He lamented that no Mennonite or Brethren in Christ missionary in India ever became nationally known for his or her peace stance. The mission boards and MCC never saw fit to help Indians establish a peace center. He wrote:

> We have undertaken no "peace mission" and joined no "peace march" protesting against nuclear holocaust. We have not espoused the cause of the poor and downtrodden for social justice. We have lacked passion for the redress of injustices and the cessation of exploitation. We have accepted too easily the corruption in the government and society. We have been too placid and acted in a withdrawn manner. Possibly the Indian Mennonites need to develop their own genius in this field rather than just become too intelligent in Anabaptist history and theology.[99]

The most highly valued activity of MCSFI has been its building fellowship between the various Mennonite and Brethren in Christ churches by organizing all-India church conferences, trainings, and retreats, thus helping the churches in India through a difficult period of their history. MCSFI has also hosted international meetings and conferences, including the 13th Mennonite World Conference Assembly held in Kolkata in 1997[100] and the Sixth Asia Mennonite Conference in 2004.

Reviews and assessments of the role and viability of MCSFI as an organization go back to a self-study that was conducted in 1975 after its first decade of existence.[101] Representatives from each of the member conferences expressed their appreciation and support for MCSFI and affirmed its objectives. Two expressed concerns were that too much of the director's time was taken up with other responsibilities, and that member church conferences were not giving adequate support. There was considerable concern that MCSFI was not as active as it had been in the beginning, with the hope expressed that MCSFI should "remain largely a fellowship of churches, sharing needs and resources and seeking to strengthen each other."[102]

The MCSFI self-study did not bring substantial changes to its objectives or to its organizational structure and capacity. Bishop Malagar resigned as director in 1981. He was succeeded by Rev. R. S. Lemuel of the Mennonite Brethren (director 1981-1993), who was followed by Bishop Shant Kunjam of the MCI (director 1993-2002).[103] These leaders had even less success in reactivating the ministry of MCSFI or in developing it as an organization. They needed to relate to a far-flung, bickering church constituency and, on the other hand, had to deal with often-critical MCC India directors.[104] Yet MCSFI continued to bring Mennonite and Brethren in Christ representatives together on a semi-annual basis to discuss common interests, and organized events that kept the churches in relationship with each other. That in itself was quite an accomplishment.

A major consultation was held between MCSFI, MCC and CIM (Commission on International Mission) in 1991 with the purpose of reviewing the work of MCSFI. It explored: (1) questions of funding for MCSFI, (2) the relationship between MCSFI and its member churches, and (3) the challenges and opportunities for future cooperative work between the three organizations. In retrospect, the consultation failed to address the real constraints to the growth of MCSFI and its ministry.

One way of assessing the inertia in MCSFI during these years is to understand the shifts in external environment. The traumatic transition from a colonial world to a post-colonial world created organizational and leadership challenges that many were not able to handle. During the 1960s MCC was MCSFI's major partner and source of funds. During this era MCC implemented relief and development projects, often in communities where there were Mennonite and Brethren in Christ churches, but this relationship also shifted.

In 1978 Bert Lobe, who was then serving as the MCC India director, told the MCSFI annual general meeting that MCC was changing its method of operation in India. It would no longer administer programs itself and would instead move toward partnerships with indigenous organizations. According to Lobe, "Our objective is to provide consultative advice and financial assistance to projects which are well organized, committed to true development, and work towards self-reliance with the support of the surrounding community."[105]

Circle dancers, Asia Mennonite Conference, 2004

MCSFI did not have the necessary staff or organizational capacity to implement projects itself. This meant that MCSFI could not compete with other organizations that became major MCC India project partners in the 1980s and beyond. It became more expedient for MCC India to work in partnership with larger or better organized Indian service agencies that had the capacity to respond to disasters in an efficient and timely way and could handle large projects in accordance with external planning, monitoring, and evaluation requirements. Eventually only a small fraction of the total MCC India program in India would be done in partnership with MCSFI or the Mennonite and Brethren in Christ churches.

Another challenge was that MCC India had formerly done projects with small conference level Mennonite and Brethren in Christ service agencies. At some point the decision was made that all Mennonite and Brethren in Christ projects in India should go through MCSFI because these conference level agencies were often unable to administer projects in a way that met the expectations of MCC or its international donors. This, in turn, put MCSFI into a double bind because its member church conferences were reluctant to relegate such service projects to MCSFI.

All the above has constrained MCC's ability to do quality relief and development work with the Mennonite and Brethren in Christ churches in India. Yet MCC sees itself as the service arm of the global Mennonite and Brethren in Christ churches. One response has been to help MCSFI develop its organizational capacity to do credible relief, development, and peace-building programming. Rev. Emmanuel Minj, who became the director of MCSFI in 2002, had prior experience as an administrator in a major Indian company and was deeply committed to the life and service of Indian churches. This background was a real gift to MCSFI at this juncture in its history.

Under Rev. Minj's administration, MCSFI has been able to establish an office at a church center developed in cooperation with Bihar Mennonite Mandli in Ranchi, Jharkhand.[106] MCSFI has been able to recruit a small staff that has successfully managed projects including a rural water project in Jharkhand, peace training for Mennonite and Brethren in Christ churches, HIV/AIDS training, and vocational education scholarships through the church conferences as well as several disaster relief projects. When the Kosi River flooded and displaced two million people in the state of Bihar in 2008, MCSFI organized a major disaster relief response that included the efforts of local Brethren in Christ volunteers. In addition to these efforts MCSFI has also organized various all-India retreats and conferences for Mennonite and Brethren in Christ churches.[107]

MCSFI did an organizational assessment in 2009 where participants affirmed that it would relate to its constituent church conferences in mission work through a partnership model rather than through a top-down model. MCSFI will function like any other partner of MCC in India with special consideration for MCSFI's ability to do holistic mission work. MCSFI will also work independently of MCC and build partnerships with other organizations. Its newly-focused mission includes the following activities: (1) intra and inter-conference fellowship, (2) meaningful engagement with other communities and religions, (3) peace and justice interventions, (4) facilitating the empowerment of vulnerable and marginalized communities, (5) disaster relief and rehabilitation, and (6) working to enhance and revive the Anabaptist and Mennonite movement among its constituent churches.[108]

Today MCSFI is not only involved in relief work, conferences and retreats but also in community development and peace and conflict resolution. Under the leadership of Rev. Emmanuel Minj, MCSFI has taken up three social development projects in Jharkhand and Bihar and is working for peace and conflict resolution with the nine constituent Mennonite and BIC Conferences in India and Nepal. Engag-

The following programs are run by MCSFI on a regular basis.

- Quarterly meeting of Executive Committee and Annual General Meeting.
- Pastors Conference, Triennial Conference for church leaders.
- Training/Seminar on Peace and Conflict resolution.
- Disaster relief program – drought, flood, tsunami and fire.
- Vocational Training Program
- Women's Program – All India Mennonite Women's Conference (AIMWC) was formed in 1977 as a women's wing of MCSFI. It holds its Executive Committee Meeting. Triennial Conference and other programs of training and fellowship from time to time.
- Youth Program - All India Mennonite Youth Conference (AIMYC) was formed in October 1987 as Youth wing of MCSFI. It holds its Executive Committee Meeting. Bienneal Youth Retreat and other programs of fellowship among Mennonite Youths.
- MCSFI also functions as hosting agency for international conferences: MWC 13th Assembly, 1997, Kolkata; India Mission Consultation, 2002, Secundrabad; Global Discipleship Training Alliance Annual Meeting, 2003, Delhi; Global Mission Fellowship Planning Committee Meeting, 2004, Hyderabad; Sixth Asia Mennonite Conference, 2004, Shamshabad.

ing in social development has enlarged the world view of MCSFI, relating now not just with churches but also with the people of other communities. Today many BIC and Mennonite churches are actively engaged in integral mission in partnership with MCSFI.

In Jharkhand MCSFI is working on a Water and Food security project, even though there are difficulties. In the Ulahatu village of Lather district in Jharkhand, for example, the people were very suspicious. This village is populated mostly by a group called Taana Bhagat, a strong Hindu tribal group. This group hates Christian people because Christians eat meat and try to convert Hindus. The village people were uncooperative initially, but later realized that MCSFI had come for their betterment and benefit. They welcomed MCSFI to their village and today this people group has tasted the sweetness of Christ from life-testimony. Though MCSFI was not engaged in direct evangelism, people have come to know our Heavenly Father through good work.

MCSFI also supports many students in their vocational training; this work has been a big blessing for MCSFI. Although the amount which is given to students as scholarships is very small, the blessing counts very much in the life of these young people. Many young people give testimony to life-transforming experiences. Through this scholarship they have tasted the love of Christ in their lives.

Chinese-speaking Areas

The Mennonite Churches in Chinese-speaking Areas

by Chiou-Lang (Paulus) Pan

"Walking into Nandajie (*South Main Street*) of Daming, it seemed as if we stepped back in time 100 years." This was the common impression of participants of the Mennonite visiting mission to China in 1997. In October of that year the China Educational Exchange (CEE), a Mennonite service agency working in China, invited representatives from Mennonite churches in Hong Kong and Taiwan to join a visiting mission to Daming, Puyang and Caoxian (Tsao Hsien), the former "Mennonite mission fields" in China. This new connection marked an important moment in the history of the Mennonite Church in Chinese-speaking areas on both sides of the Taiwan Strait.

Christianity in China

The first Christian body in China was *Jingjiao* during the Tang Dynasty in the 7th century. In 635 C.E., the Nestorian missionary Alopen arrived at the capital *Zhangan*. He built churches and translated the Scriptures with the support of the Emperor, Taizong. For the next two hundred years, the Nestorian Christians worked to establish themselves among the Han Chinese, with the support of the government.[1] As symbolized by the "cross out of the lotus" – the decoration on the top of *Jingjiaobei*, the Nestorian tablet found in Xian – *Jingjiao* assimilated the terminology and practices of Taoism and Buddhism. However, *Jingjiao* was classified as a foreign religion and was driven out of China, along with Buddhism, when Emperor Wuzong ordered the elimination of such reli-

Nestorian inscription, 781 CE. The cross out of the lotus is at the top

gions for political and economic reasons in 845 C.E. Because the Nestorian *Jingjiao* had relied on the support of the government, the church was not able to survive.[2]

221

Christianity came a second time to China during the Yuan Dynasty in the 13th century when the Mongols ruled China. The Mongolians called the Christians *Erkeun*, a Mongolian transliteration of the Hebrew term Elohim, which means "those who believe in God." Nestorian Christianity returned to China with the coming of Mongol rule because some of the members of the Mongol royal family and high officers of the government were *Erkeun*. In addition, the Catholic missionary John of Montecorvino came to China in 1289. The Mongol rulers helped him build churches and granted him privileges to evangelize the Buddhists. However, because the *Erkeun* churches (both Nestorian and Catholic) had grown among non-Chinese residents from Middle Asia, and were identified as the rulers' religions, they could not survive after the strongly anti-foreign native Ming Dynasty overthrew the Mongols in 1368.[3]

Christianity entered China a third time with the arrival of Jesuit missionaries in the sixteenth century. Jesuit missionaries such as Matteo Ricci recognized the important connection between Confucianism and Chinese culture and were able to distinguish the differences between contemporary Confucianism and the original Confucian teachings; they enthusiastically adapted the proclamation of the Gospel to Chinese culture. Looking like Western Confucians, with their clothing and teachings, the Jesuits dialogued with the Chinese intelligentsia and tried to supplement Confucianism with Christian theology.[4] Nonetheless, because of the intrinsic differences between the Gospel and Confucianism, members of the Chinese intelligentsia who had accepted the Jesuit teaching because of misunderstanding gradually separated, as they came to a better understanding of Christian teaching. In addition, the Rites Controversy among the Catholics finally resulted in an edict by Emperor Kangxi in 1720 which forbade the practice of any foreign religion.[5] With this decree the church lost its ability to function. Although at one time there had been around two hundred thousand church members, only a few members of the lower class remained Catholic after 1720.

This was the dilemma of church-state relationships in monarchical China: since Chinese rulers considered religions to be educational organizations that needed to be regulated, the church could not operate freely without the permission of the regime in power. But if the church relied too heavily on the support and protection of the government, it would not survive when the regime changed, which occurred frequently in China.

The arrival of Robert Morrison of the London Missionary Society in the nineteenth century marked the fourth entry of Christianity into China. Even at this time, Christianity could not avoid the complicated political situations in China. Morrison and his fellow missionaries could only do some publishing and Bible translation work at Macao, Hong Kong and Malacca because of the closed-door policy of the Ch'ing Dynasty. In 1842 China and Great Britain signed the Nanjing Treaty following the so-called Opium War. The treaty and its Five Ports Trade Article opened a door into China for Christianity. Then a series of lopsided treaties followed that favored Great Britain, with the result that Christian missionaries entered China under the protection of a naval fleet and cannons.[6]

Because of this, Chinese nationalists condemned Christianity as a cultural arm of Western imperialism. Missionaries were in a difficult situation, and encountered frequent hostility in nineteenth-century China.[7] The Chinese found it difficult to welcome a Jesus who "rode on an artillery projectile flying into China." Christian clergy and converts who abused their privileges were abhorred, and Christianity was strongly opposed by the Chinese officials and the upper classes.[8] The weakness of China's rulers led to a variety of reform movements until there was a strong conservative reaction with an anti-foreign and anti-Christian focus, culminating in the Boxer Uprising in 1900. Following the Uprising, however, the Chinese attitude toward foreigners changed radically from despising and opposing foreigners in the nineteenth century, to worshipping foreign things and fawning on foreign powers in the twentieth. The failure of the nineteenth century reform movement and the international humiliation subsequent to the Boxer Uprising helped create a readiness for change in China.[9] With the intent of "saving China," western democracy and science became the prevailing academic focus.

Mennonites in China

The Boxer Uprising also put China on the mission map. A great number of missionaries were sent to China, even though anti-foreign sentiment was still strong in some areas. The Mennonite

Church was one of the denominations that sent missionaries into mainland China during this period, beginning in 1905. During the Mennonite Church's decades-long stay in China in the twentieth century, four Mennonite conferences were established in different areas: the *Christian Church Gospel Association* in Shandong Province, which was later supported by the China Mennonite Mission Society, associated with four denominations in the United States; the *General Conference Mennonite Church in China* in Chili (now on the border of Henan and Hebei Provinces); the *Hakka Mennonite Brethren Conference* in Fujian Province, and the *Inner Mongolia Krimmer Mennonite Brethren Conference* in Inner Mongolia. In addition to these four conferences, the *Mennonite Board of Missions and Charities* also contributed to the work of evangelism in inland China for a short period of time.

The Mennonites came to Taiwan and Hong Kong after World War II to do relief work and to carry out a medical ministry; from this work mission fields developed. However, the Mennonite churches there did not directly relate to the Mennonite churches in China.

The Christian Church Gospel Association

The first Chinese Mennonite church, named *Ji Du Jiao Fu Yin Hui* (the Christian Church Gospel Association, or CCGA), was established by Henry C. and Nellie Schmidt Bartel in 1905. Together with a few

co-workers and only 50 dollars, they started a new mission in Caoxian (Tsao Hsien) in Shandong Province. Their mission was to establish an independent Mennonite Church, emancipating the Chinese from the suffering of ignorance and impoverishment through education and charity. Because of financial difficulty and the lack of the foreign institutional resources, from

Orphanage workshop, Tsao Hsien

the beginning the church realized that it had to rely on the native Chinese, and sought self-sufficiency. From the beginning the goal was to establish an indigenous church. Therefore, the Mennonite Church's Chinese co-workers played a leading role from the start and carried much of the responsibility for raising funds. However, since financial resources were small, it was difficult to carry out evangelism in so large an area with such a large population. On October 21, 1906 seven experienced and trained social workers came from the United States to help the team's work, especially in the places where medical care and material support were much-needed. They brought Gospel tracts into the countryside and preached the Good News from one village to another.

The first Mennonite church with the capacity of 1,000 persons was begun in Tsao Hsien, which later became the headquarters of CCGA. Like other Christian bodies at that time, the mission strategy of CCGA was to establish mission stations and carry out itinerant evangelism. After the Revolution in 1911, the administration of the new republic practiced a tolerant

Tsao Hsien church building

policy toward Christianity which opened a door to the development of Christianity in China. When the *China Mennonite Mission Society*

Colporteur selling Christian materials in Tsao Hsien

(which became the supporter of the CCGA) was officially founded in 1913 in the USA, there were already 100 Christians baptized into congregations in Tsao Hsien and in Shan Hsien. Some new churches and meeting places had also already been established in different cities of Henan Province.[10] The mission was expanding with the cooperation and work of 30 missionaries and 100 indigenous co-workers. The first Sunday of each month was called "Full Sunday." All church members of the country gathered to worship God in Tsao Hsien station.[11] During breaks from farming they did "tent work" evangelism in a huge tent.[12]

The training of indigenous co-workers had always been important for the *Christian Church Gospel Association*. In 1908 a short-term Bible school was officially started; sessions were held every other month, lasting for ten days.[13] The main reason the church was able to grow under per-

Bible Women

All CCMA pastors and evangelists gather in Tsao Hsien, 1930s

secution was that the indigenous Christians had been educated and prepared for leadership.[14] Some Chinese Christian members played important roles during 1920's. For example, Wang Hsuen Ch'en became the pastor of the congregation of Heze and leader of the Bible College.[15] He also was a member of the Executive Committee of the *Zong Yi Hui* (church conference), called the *General Council of the Native Church* which was established before 1927. According to the "Word of Testimony," the official news letter of the church, in April 1932 the leaders of the Council were three missionaries and five Chinese workers.[16]

In the 1920s some Chinese Christian leaders, responding to anti-Christian movements and to the government's Rural Village Reconstruction Movement, called for an incarnational model of mission and for mission efforts to go into the countryside.[17] The Mennonites, however, had already been present in the villages. The indigenization policy and the village strategy of "going out to where the people are" put the native workers in an important position and helped Christians spread around the villages, living close to the people. Because of this, the mission continued to develop and the churches were ready for the large-scale social change that came when the Communist Party took over the China Mainland in 1949.

A Chinese depiction of the parable of the Prodigal Son, early 20th century

In order to get total control of every aspect of Chinese society, the Communist government began a series of political campaigns, such as the Land Reform, the Oppose-American-Aid-Korean Movement, and the Suppression of the Counterrevolutionary Movement soon after it took over China. Consequently, the entire country was plunged into a difficult situation. The Denunciation Campaign that began in 1951 was directed against Christianity to "eliminate the toxins of the imperialistic ideology." The closest friends or colleagues of the foreign missionaries and Chinese pastors came forward to accuse their own coworkers as "imperialists wearing religious clothes" or "the running dogs of foreign secret agents."[18]

Consequently, missionaries fled or were deported, and many local pastors were put into jail. As a result, the government-sponsored Three-Self Patriot Movement Committee was able to control most of the Christian institutions. The number of Christian churches in China dropped from around 20,000 in 1949 to less than 100 in 1958.[19] Loyal H. Bartel, the eldest son of Henry Bartel, did not run away. Rather, he stayed with the Chinese Christians to participate in their sufferings.[20] During the One Hundred Flower Movement (1956-57) and the Cultural Revolution (1966-1976), many people were required to write a "confession and prosecution." Those whose confessions and prosecution were considered insufficient in the eyes of the authorities were publically humiliated, forced to wear tall paper hats in parades and in mass meetings. Christians were not excepted. Similar actions were carried on for several years.[21] All church properties were occupied and all church activities were forbidden. All Christian denominations were dissolved.

The Chinese Communist government later allowed Christians to gather legally under the Three-Self Church institution after the Cultural Revolution.[22] A three-room building was returned in 1978 by the government at the request of the some former Mennonite Christians; they then organized the Tsao Hsien Christian Church, a registered body of the nationwide Three-Self Church. In 1987, the official number of Christians in Tsao Hsien was 15,400. Later in 1993, the Communist government compensated the Tsao Hsien Christian Church with 6 *Mu* of land (a Chinese acre; 1 *Mu* is about one-sixth of an

Leaders of the Caoxian (Tsao Hsien) church, 2001

American acre). A new church building, constructed by the Chinese believers in a week, was inaugurated in August of the same year. By the year 2000, 46 meeting places had been established throughout the county of Tsao Hsien, and the number of the believers reached 30,000.[23] From a historical perspective, the Christian church in Tsao Heien was actually an indirect product of the Mennonite mission task, yet it officially was no longer called Mennonite, although several senior Christians there missed Pastor Loyal Bartel very much and recognized the contributions of the Mennonites.

In 1941, after a visit to their son Paul Bartel in Sichuan Province, Henry and Nellie Bartel started a Mennonite mission there. They were forced to remain in Sichuan Province due to the Japanese attack on Pearl Harbor. With the invitation of the *China Inland Mission* and the *Christian and Missionary Alliance*, they established a church in Shuang

Shih Pu of Guang Yuan county, near the Sichuan-Shanxi-Gansu border area. By 1949, 20 people had become members of the church. During the 1950's, however, all missionaries were forced to leave China because of the Communist government's hostility toward foreign-

Shuang Shi Pu Church welcomes Henry Bartel, May, 1949

ers. Chinese co-workers took over all church responsibilities. However, Chinese church leaders were persecuted from 1957 on, and all leaders were condemned during the *Damingdafang* movement (One Hundred Flowers, 1956-1957). Ministers were forced to flee, and the churches were finally closed in 1963.[24]

The General Conference Mennonite Church in China

The *General Conference Mennonite Church in China* was founded by Henry J. and Maria Miller Brown in the spring of 1911, after they had studied the Chinese language with the help of Henry C. Bartel and Jonathan J. Schrag. While the Chinese Revolution stirred all of China the Browns, as independent missionaries, started their mission in the area around Kai Chow of Chili (now Puyang of Henan Province), just west of the mission field of the Christian Church Gospel Association, home to more than 2 million people living on the banks of the Yellow River. The Chinese name for the General Conference Mennonite Church in China was *Qing Jie Hui* (The Society of Purity). It is said that the name was given because of Henry Brown's Chinese name, Qing-Jie Bo (Purity Bo), a memorial to his great contribution.[25]

The Browns established a small church, a medical center and an adult reading class soon after their arrival at Kai Chow. Eight people were baptized into the church in the second year. This location later became a large mission station of 112 *mu*. In 1915, the General Conference approved the Browns' mission in China and dispatched many missionaries to aid the evangelism effort.

Kai Chow, Pu Yang church, built in 1917

The May Fourth Movement in 1919, in response to the Treaty of Versailles, was the beginning of a series of the anti-Christian and anti-foreign movements in the 1920s. Patriotic sentiment was everywhere in China. The scholars and their students supported "the New Tide and New Culture."[26] The government forbade Christian courses in schools in 1924. In an effort to "re-take the sovereignty of education" in 1925, many Christian university students demonstrated and condemned the mission schools as a cultural invasion of the West; Chinese Christians were criticized as "running dogs" of Western missionaries.[27] Ironically, most of the leaders of the revolutionary movements were products of mission schools.[28] A Communist slogan of the day, "One more Christian, one less Chinese," was particularly harmful to Christianity. The students of Hua Mei High School and of the Bible School also demonstrated in the streets. The church leaders could do nothing but close the campus until 1931.[29]

In the Mennonite church in Puyang, the different value systems of the indigenous leaders and the missionaries soon resulted in a church conflict. Indigenous leaders demanded autonomy in certain church functions such as weddings, funerals and other Chinese customs and asked for participation in managing the treasury of the church. S. F. Pannabecker noted that there was too much inter-missionary and inter-Christian controversy.[30] A new way of encouraging cooperation among the indigenous churches was needed. After much work, the Constitution of Church Independency was officially issued in 1935.[31]

Pu Yang city church primary school

The contest between the missionaries and the indigenous Chinese for decision-making power in the General Conference Mennonite Church in China intensified throughout this period of anti-Western movements. The conflict could be seen as a response to the call for indigenization. The indigenous Christians' criticism of the missionaries, who lived in big and beautiful residences with good food and drink, seemed to be a kind of jealousy.[32] The missionaries' lifestyle could be justified as being necessary for hygienic reasons,[33] but unfortunately, the living conditions of the missionaries were "far above that of the best-trained employees."[34]

There were also some theological-cultural differences which created problems. Ancestor worship was an unavoidable problem for Chinese

Christians. It was also a big problem in dealing with the call for indigenization. H. J. Brown once threw the memorial tablet of a deacon's ancestor into his house and reproached him for idol worship. The deacon was offended and argued that ancestor worship was a way of respecting ancestors and was an act of filial piety.[35] This problem became more troublesome when church leaders held different opinions about this practice because of their different backgrounds. However, ancestor worship has ceased to be an issue because

This Bible woman in Daming had suffered foot binding. A man was hired to transport her to a village where she was going to preach at a remote church.

the atheist Communist party has removed the custom from Chinese cultural life.

Nevertheless, the Gospel changed the structure of Chinese society at its root. The Gospel broke down the patriarchal power structure symbolized by the undesirable custom of foot binding. Ms. Qing-Feng Lee was the church moderator in Daming for several years during the late 1930s through early 40s, which was history-making in China. Both male and female members respected her during her term there.[36]

Ms. Pauline M. Goering also set up the Women's Missionary Society in Daming.[37] Having female leaders became a characteristic of the General Conference Mennonites in China.

The preaching of the Gospel did not stop even during the chaotic situation of the 1920s. There

Women's meeting

were ten well-organized churches already established by 1923. The number of church members increased from 850 in 1927 to 1,450 in 1936. Many people rushed into the church when the Japanese aggression began in 1937. According to church reports, there were 2,273 church members and 24 churches in 1940 in the General Conference Mennonite Church in China. In addition, 1,474 people requested baptism into the church and five Chinese co-workers were ordained in the same year. The new General Conference Committee was also established in this year to supervise the work of the whole Mennonite church in Chili.[38] During the disorder caused by wars in the 1940s, the contributions and services of the Mennonite Church to the Chinese people finally earned its due approval.[39] The Mennonite Church also learned how to survive in difficult times: some experience had been gained in the art of accommodation, the skill of adaptation needed to resist while obeying the political authorities.[40]

The Communists took over the Daming-Puyang areas in January of 1946. The next year, all church meetings were forbidden and the visible denominational institutions disappeared. However, Christians in Puyang still gathered together to worship God privately throughout the following decades. Pastor Qing-Xuan Liu continued to make circuit visits to believers during those years. Christianity was legalized after the Cultural Revolution. In 1993, the building belonging to the former Mennonite Church *Dong Quan Fu Yin Tang* (East Suburban Church) was given back to the Puyang Christian Church. Believers volunteered to repair the building and offered a lot of rice in support of the work. There were still more than 1,000 kilograms of rice left when the building repairs were done. Currently, there are more than ten thousand Christians in Puyang.[41]

The multiple changes in the use of the South Main Street church building of Daming, built by Peter J. Boehr, 1927-29, show the church's difficult experiences. The building was confiscated during the Cultural Revolution. Later it became a public activity center, and after reconstruction it became a theater. Because few people went to the theater, the building was returned to the Daming Christian Church in 1992 under the Executive Religion Policy and then

Daming Mennonite church, 1935

became the church's headquarter. All the Christians in the county, about 1,000, attended the restoration ceremony on Easter of the same year. Since then, hundreds of youth, eager for the knowledge of God, have rushed to the building to attend the annual Winter Bible Training Class. Baptisms were held here annually during the summer because there was only one pastor in the county. The young Pastor Liu once stood in water for over seven hours, pulling new believers from the pool, more than a thousand times on that one day.[42]

Due to the civil war in eastern China immediately after World War II, Peter J. Boehr, his wife Frieda and Ms. Elisabeth D. Goertz had to escape westward. They arrived at Baoji of Shenxi Province in 1947. They started evangelizing with the help of Chinese co-workers, people such as Ling-Sheng Wang (Paul Wang) and his wife Ai-Xin Zhang. However, they had to move to Chengdu, the capital of Sichuan Province the next year, because of the spread of the civil war. There they established two churches at Si-Dao Street and at Flower Gateway (Hua Pai Fang) on the west side of the town. Around 20 believers joined the churches at the beginning. When these churches were closed in 1958, there were already 70 Christians in Si-Dao Street, and 96 Christians in Flower Gateway.[43]

The Hakka Mennonite Brethren Conference

The Hakka Mennonite Brethren Conference was established by Frank J. Wiens in 1912 in the Hakka areas of Fujian Province. "Hakka," meaning sojourners, is a special community in Chinese society. They treasure the value of education and farm labor as well as their identity as a people. They maintain their unique language and customs and prefer to live independently from the rest of society. Many leaders of the Tai Ping Rebellion (1851-1864) and the Chinese Revolution were from the Hakka community.

As independent missionaries, Frank J. and Agnes Harder Wiens conducted a survey in Guangdong Province and Fujian Province in 1912. They decided to start their mission in the Shanghang area of Fujian Province. They rented a house, rumored to be haunted, and started to evangelize. In October, they bought a bigger house to be their meeting place because of an increase in church members. The local governor and administrators participated in the opening ceremony. At about the same time, Frank and Agnes Wiens also bought a piece of land suitable for constructing a big church building, a Bible school and dormitories for students and employees, a medical center, and their own residence. The series of construction projects created large conflicts between the missionaries and the local gentry. The Chinese argued that the construction projects destroyed the Feng-Shui of their ancestral graves, which was believed to be very important to the well-being of offspring. Fortunately, the disagreement was resolved in the end.[44]

After the conflict had been settled routine street evangelism and evening Bible studies began. In 1913, Wiens held two baptismal ceremonies in which 15 people were baptized into the church. The indigenous Christians in the church, including Wiens' Chinese teacher Mr. Liu, all committed themselves to the work of the church. They arranged church services and created their own regulations. Local believers donated a substantial amount of money for the construction of a large church building in Shanghang, with the capacity to hold 600 people; construction was completed in 1917.[45] The Hakka Mennonite Brethren Conference was not officially inaugurated until 1920, at which time eleven full-time Chinese pastors were leading about 450 church members in eleven different meeting places.[46] From 1920 to 1922, nine missionaries were dispatched to assist the mission in Shanghang. They expanded the work of education to the high school level and set up a women's job training and a Children's Bible study community. They also built up a new mission field in Yongding, a city forty miles away. A few years later the church in Yongding appointed its own pastor and established three schools and a clinic. Because new medical professionals and nurses participated in this team to enhance the quality of medical care, the church was able to help more wounded soldiers during the period of civil wars.[47]

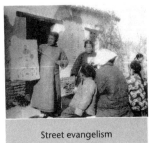

Street evangelism

The Hakka Mennonite Brethren Conference was reorganized in 1926. An Executive Committee composed of 21 Chinese church members was established to manage all the administrative duties of the church.[48] This committee became a sign of the indigenization of the church. It led the church through the difficult time from 1927 to 1928, when Chinese nationalists reacted against "western" Christianity and most missionaries had to be evacuated. Most of the church buildings and schools were destroyed by the civil war, and many Christians left the church. By 1940 there were around 400 formal church members, gathered in ten meeting places, shepherded by four pastors in the Shanghang area. Some faithful Christians continued to hold church services and carried on with the training programs for co-workers, even after the Pearl Harbor Attack in 1941.[49]

In the early 1950s the Shanghang area was taken over by the Communist Party. The churches there gradually lost connection with the outside world. However, according to some information from the China Educational Exchange, the church there is still developing within Hakka in Fujian Province.[50]

The Inner Mongolia Krimmer Mennonite Brethren Conference

In 1922, Frank and Agnes E. Wiebe and Miss Margaret Thiessen were sent to China by the Krimmer Mennonite Brethren Conference (KMB). After one year of language training in Tsao Hsien, Henry C. Bartel accompanied them to Inner Mongolia. At the invitation of the Swedish Alliance Mission, they started a mission in the Zhouzi (Chotzeshan) area in the Sui-Yuan Province (now the Inner Mongolian Autonomous Region).[51] The first Sunday service was held on October 24, 1923.[52] Their mission goal was to establish an independent Krimmer Mennonite Brethren Conference in Inner Mongolia, to introduce the Krimmer Mennonite Brethren confession of faith and fully conform to conference regulations in all church practices.[53]

The Krimmer Mennonite Brethren Conference was established in a small, poor city in a difficult time, in the midst of the anti-Christian movement and anti-foreigner sentiment. The villages in Zhouzi were distant from each other. Bandits and the troops also caused the church severe problems. Preachers held circuit evangelical activities around the villages. They had regular Bible studies every week and engaged in large evangelistic efforts during the summer and spring vacations.[54] The number of Christians increased. Ten were baptized into the church in August 1924, and three more in the next year.[55] Missionaries encouraged the indigenous Christians to start a new church whenever each village had ten Christians, and they appointed one of them to be the leader. Some trained pastors made circuit visits to help the new converts.[56]

Evangelism, education, and medical care were the main activities of the church in Inner Mongolia.[57] The most numerous admissions to the church clinic were for surgical trauma, skin and eye diseases, and midwifery. The church also established a drug-abuse clinic. The clinic was able to help 15 out of 55 people overcome opium addiction.[58] After the civil war during 1926-1927, the church started to distribute flour and blankets, which attracted many people to the church. Forty people were baptized in 1931, four of them becoming church leaders. Around 150 Christians joined in the Holy Eucharist and Foot Washing ceremony.

Evangelism became more difficult during the period of Japanese occupation. The Japanese authorites forced all Protestant missions and churches in this area to unite into one body in order to fully control the society. The Pacific War in 1941 ended this Japanese practice. The Communist takeover caused much hardship. Missionaries had to leave by the end of 1948 and most native workers were dismissed and had to earn their own livelihood. Inner Mongolia Krimmer Mennonite Brethren Conference gradually ceased to function. Nevertheless, this small Mennonite conference was able to recruit around five hundred new converts during its short presence in this area despite the difficult situation.[59] No information about this church's situation was available even after China re-opened its door in 1979. Nevertheless, the churches in neighboring areas were growing rapidly according to reports in 1981.[60] It was most likely that the seed of faith was preserved and grew up silently in the area of Zhouzi.

The Mennonite Church (Min Ai Hui)

In February 1947, at the suggestion of the Methodist church, the Mennonite Board of Missions and Charities decided to receive Hechuan in Sichuan Province as a Mennonite mission field.[61] In 1948, Don McCammon and four other co-workers arrived at Hechuan. They bought the property from the Methodists and took over the congregation. They established the Mennonite Church at the gate of the county and began teaching English classes and holding Sunday schools. In addition to evangelism, they also set up a clinic for newborn babies and hygiene classes for women in 1949. They invited the governor and administrators of the county to assist with the activities.[62] Later, when Hechuan was taken over by the Communist Party, restrictions were placed on foreigners; unfortunately, the indigenous Christians were not yet ready to be independent. By the end of the next year, Don McCammon was arrested and expelled from the country. There has been no information from the Mennonite Church in Hechuan since then.[63]

The Mennonite mission in China tried to be a holistic ministry, not only involved in evangelism, but also in relief, education and healing. The Bible Schools of the Christian Church Gospel Association were formally established in Heze in 1922. In 1930 the schools were moved to Tsao Hsien. There the schools enrolled more than 70 students. However, this ended with the Japanese attack on Pearl Harbor.[64]

The General Conference Mennonite Church in China started a Bible School in 1925, but it was suspended already in 1927 because of student demonstrations against Christianity; the school was restarted in 1930. In addition to theological education, students also were equipped with skills in printing and needlework. Pastor Chang Ching later took charge of the Mennonite Bible School. The Bible school played an important role in educating pastoral co-workers in the villages where the elite were moving out to the cities.[65]

When the first church of the Hakka Mennonite Brethren Conference was established in Shanghang in 1913, the Shanghang Bible Institute also began to recruit students. Three years later, four students had graduated and became church leaders.[66] Although the scope of the school was limited, it did train some indigenous church leaders for the future of the church.[67]

Kindergarten in Daming

The Mennonite churches set up many mission schools for cultivating the coming generation, in preparation for the growth of the church. Education freed the Chinese villagers from ignorance and impoverishment. The first residential primary school of the Christian Church Gospel Association was opened in 1912 in Tsao Hsien. In addition to formal lessons, students had to study the Bible and were obliged to do manual labor. Later, commuting schools were also established. All of these schools were suspended during the war of the Northern Expedition in 1927[68] and never reopened. The Hua Mei (Sino-American) primary school was established in Puyang by the General Conference Mennonite Church in 1916. From that time on, many other

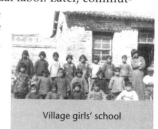

Village girls' school

primary schools were gradually set up in villages, although the number of students never exceeded 1,200. In 1924 E. G. Kaufman inaugurated the Hua Mei High School. The students of the school organized a fellowship called the "Love the Lord Society," with more than one hundred members. They also organized weekly worship and regular short-term evangelistic and social service trips to the countryside.[69]

Hua Mei High School students do relief work, 1935

James Liu was one of the bright alumni of Hua Mei High School. After his studies in the USA, Liu became principal of the Hua Mei High School.[70] He was the first chairman of the General Conference Committee when it was founded in 1940. He moved to Hengyang, Hunan Province and administered an MCC orphanage

Hua Mei HS building

there after WWII. These ministries provided an excuse for the Communists to jail him in his own school for three years during the Cultural Revolution while he was an English teacher in Hengyang high school. He was released in 1971 and later became a freelance English tutor at his home in Hengyang.[71] Nowadays, Hua Mei High School is managed by the government, without any change in the school's name or building.

In the second year after arriving at Shanghang, Frank and Agnes Wiens established a school. The school was financially independent thanks to donations by members of the local gentry.[72] With their support, 15 schools with 30 teachers had been established by 1920, supplemented in 1924 by a high school. The schools were suspended due to the chaos brought on by the Northern Expedition during 1927-28, when nationalism dominated people's hearts and missionaries became the target of hatred. The suspended schools resumed operation, but were soon closed again because of the invasion by Japan.[73]

The mission schools in China, as K. S. Latourette concluded, bridged the West and the East, opened a window for the Chinese, and helped the Chinese see the world from a different point of view.[74] The view, however, was not always welcome.

Western medical science was far more advanced than contemporary Chinese medical science. However, in village areas it was seen more as magic than science. Rumors spread that the westerners kidnapped children in order to make magical medicines by using their hearts and eyes. Missionaries such as Henry Bartel, Henry Brown and Frank Wiens were not trained in medicine; however, they still had to bring medical

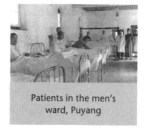

Patients in the men's ward, Puyang

services and hygiene education to the villages.[75] Doctors and nurses from the General Conference Mennonite Church were dispatched to join the General Conference Mennonite Church in China team in 1921. In 1927 a new, large medical facility was inaugurated and became the pioneer and best hospital in Puyang area. It signaled the acceptance of new medical science. In 1940 the number of people receiving outpatient care increased to 28,000. War contrib-

uted to the increased number of patients.[76] A nursing school was opened in 1930, headed by Ms. Elisabeth Goertz.[77] After finishing his studies, Paul Wang came to support the nursing school. He moved to Chengdu of Sichuan Province in late 1940s and started a medical evangelism program by opening the "Evangelical Health Office."[78]

Nurses' graduation, Puyang, 1930s

The areas where the Mennonite Church was located were places where people lived off the land. Most of them did not have enough food and had many material needs. The series of wars worsened the situation for the impoverished villagers. Northern China experienced

Women's class, Daming

droughts and floods in 1909, throughout the 1920's, and from 1933 to 1935. In addition to offering food and asylum, the General Conference Mennonite Church in China provided refugees with job opportunities. In 1929 poor women were rewarded after they took lessons in weaving, reading, and listening to the message of

the Gospel.[79] The Hakka Mennonite Brethren also opened a widows' home in the late 1930s.[80]

Henry C. Bartel established an orphanage in 1906, the second year of his arrival in Tsao Hsien, Shandong Province. The missionaries used their experience of organizing the "Light and Hope Orphanage" in

North America to organize a similar one in China. There were more than 400 orphans who were called "Bartel's children." The orphanage had an ancillary job-training school to equip the orphans with work skills. Some of the children from this orphanage played important roles in the church when they grew up, a few becoming ministers after receiving theological education.[81]

Orphanage boys at Tsao Hsien

The Mennonite Central Committee (MCC)

In September 1945, MCC opened an office in Zhengzhou as the center for their mission in China. MCC cooperated with two Mennonite churches in Changyuan and Dongming to start a charity program as well as to promote the cooperation sentiment among the local people under the title "Of Cooperation."[82] MCC opened a clinic for medical care and also supported the development of agriculture by offering cotton seeds and soybeans to the peasants, free of charge. Nonetheless, the team was forced to move to Shanghai due to a local battle in 1947. When Shanghai was taken over by the Communists in 1951, all foreign workers were gradually evacuated.[83] The work of MCC ceased at that time.

Re-connection of Mennonites in China

After Liberation in 1949 Mennonites in China lost contact with Mennonite bodies abroad. In the late 1970s China gradually began to open its doors. The China Educational Exchange (CEE) was established in 1982 to facilitate mutually beneficial exchange relationships between Chinese universities and Mennonite colleges in North America. Chinese teachers of English came to North America for further training in teaching English while North American teachers were invited to teach English in Chinese universities. Eventually, CEE workers were able to make contact with former Mennonite members in China. Many descendants of missionaries from North America visited former Mennonite mission fields. These interviews helped the Mennonites reconnect with believers and their local congregations. A leader of Daming observed, "The Nazarenes came, then left; the Bethelians also came, then left; but the Mennonites came, and stayed." The Mennonite church respects the independence of the Chinese church and the particular conditions in China, and does not intend to set up a Mennonite denomination in China. Instead, as a faithful partner, the Mennonite church is helping Chinese believers see the world from an international perspective. The Mennonite church intends to play a continuing role in the modernization process in China.

Retrospect: A Critical Epilogue

The history of the Mennonite Church in China is divided by three major wars: the Northern Expedition War in 1926-1927 when Chiang Kai-shek led the People's Revolution Army north from southern China to try to unify the country, the Japanese invasion from 1937-1945, and the civil war between the Nationalists and the Communists which resulted in the so-called Liberation of China and the establishing of the People's Republic of China on October 1, 1949. During these disorders and wars, some Christians were killed or made homeless, and missionaries were evacuated. The church faced a great shortage of leaders. In addition, the majority of Christian bodies in China adopted the confessional approach, that is, conversion followed by a period of catechetical training and probation before baptism was granted. This model relied heavily on stable organizations and leaders. Social unrest deeply affected the growth of the Church. The wars forced the church to transform its mission strategy and to become indigenous. Jessie Lutz correctly observed that after entering the Communist era, "Christianity in all its variety had taken root in China and possessed the strength and techniques to survive decades of hostility and/or persecution."[84]

The theological and cultural baggage which the missionaries brought into China sometimes resulted in the accusation that the mission was an arm of American foreign policy. For example, the use of military terminology, such as the phrase "conquer China for Christ" used by many missionaries, gave the nationalists ammunition to attack Christianity as the agent of Western imperialism. Moreover, the fundamentalist interpretation of mission work as a "spiritual battle" led missionaries to take a confrontational position against Chinese culture. This is why the arguments about the customs of weddings and funerals happened in Puyang.[85]

The modernization of China is another issue and has become the only politically-correct Chinese ideology. Patriotic sentiment has pervaded the hearts of the Chinese for one-and-half centuries. Christianity was welcomed because it was considered to be a path to national salvation in the first quarter of 20th century. However, it was rejected when it was considered to be a method of harmful cultural imperialism.

Christian missions appeared to fail completely because the denominations disappeared after the Liberation of China in 1949. But in fact, Christianity in China cast off its Western colors in that period. Christianity has proven itself able to accommodate, to assimilate, and to integrate into Chinese culture.[86] All of the registered churches in China were integrated into an umbrella organization, the China Christian Council, for political and theological reasons after the Cultural Revolution. Since 1980, the growth of Chinese churches has surprised the global Christian community. An all-new Chinese church witnesses that the Gospel of life has overcome the power of hell. It has been proven that one more Christian does not result in one less Chinese. "Chinese Church for China," the goal of the Convention of the Centennial Anniversary of Mission in China in 1907, was forged in the fire of the Cultural Revolution. To date, as Jessie Lutz says, "Chinese understanding and appreciation of many Western ideas and institutions were not separated from their experiences with Christian missions."[87]

Nowadays it is possible for Christian churches to legally register outside the China Christian Council. More and more intellectuals explicitly demonstrated their academic and spiritual interests in Christian thought, and many research centers of Christianity are being established in the universities. The future of Christianity in China is brighter than ever.

Is it true that Mennonite churches ceased to exist in China after the Cultural Revolution? The elders in Puyang answer with a definite NO. "Although the assembly no longer takes place, Christian meetings are always held in alleyways and believers' houses. The Mennonite church never vanished from China."[88] The elders in Puyang still identify themselves as Mennonites. They say "God had called us to this work. Didn't God keep His promises?"[89] God has proven his faithful-

Liu Shiu Mei
Elder Liu Shiu Mei of Puyang, Henan Province is the leader of the Puyang church, a former General Conference Mennonite Church. "Mennonites never disappeared," she said. "Although the church buildings were confiscated, the believers still gathered to worship God in their houses."

ness in China. The Apostle Paul's statement that "the Word of God can never be bound" may be the best interpretation of the history of the Mennonite church in China.

The Mennonites in Taiwan

A brief history of Taiwan

Taiwan is the small island that is located in the middle of East Asia, between Japan and the Philippines. The Portuguese praised it as Formosa in fifteenth century because they were fascinated by the landscapes. The diversity of the people on this island also creates the diversity of the cultures in Taiwan. There were more than 20 tribes of aboriginal peoples living on this island long before the Han Chinese ventured onto it.

From 1626 to 1666 Spanish Dominicans from the Philippines built some churches among aboriginal peoples in northern Taiwan. From 1627 to 1662 Dutch Reformed chaplains came to southern Taiwan. However, neither group managed to survive when Ch'eng Cheng-Gong of the Post-Ming Dynasty took over Taiwan in 1662.

In 1865 Scottish Presbyterians sent their first missionary to Taiwan. The Presbyterian Church in Taiwan has established many Taiwanese-speaking churches since the nineteenth century. By the end of World War II there were four Christian bodies in Taiwan: the Presbyterian Church, the True Jesus Church, the Taiwanese Holiness Church, and the Catholic Church.[90] After fifty years of Japanese rule at the end of World War II, Taiwan became a province of the Republic of China (Nationalist China). However, the excitement of the Taiwanese about returning to the "Patriarch Country" on October 16, 1945 soon turned into disappointment. The 2-28 Incident[91] on February 28, 1947 led the Taiwanese to question deeply their sense of belonging to the Chinese people.[92] In the years that followed the civil war between the China Nationalist Party (Kuomintang, or KMT) and the China Communist Party, more than one million refugees and 600,000 Mandarin-speaking soldiers were exiled to Taiwan together with Nationalist Party members. At about the same time more than five hundred missionaries who belonged to more than sixty denominations were also expelled from their missions on the Chinese mainland and sent to Taiwan. The interaction between the diverse Taiwanese and the Mandarin-speaking imigrants radically changed Christianity in Taiwan and also society at large.

The religious policy of the KMT was relatively free, except that no criticism of the government was tolerated, in order to cultivate the friendship and sympathy of the international community.[93] Therefore Christians in Taiwan were given freedom to pursue their ministries as long as their activities and public preaching did not counter government policies.[94] However, the tragic 2-28 Incident separated the Taiwanese from the mainlanders. As a result, Christianity in Taiwan naturally split into two major groups: the Taiwanese-speaking churches and the Mandarin-speaking churches. Mennonite churches in Taiwan could be classified as Taiwanese-speaking.

The Origin and Development of the Fellowship of Mennonite Churches in Taiwan

In 1948, MCC was invited by the Presbyterian Church in Taiwan to establish the Mennonite Mountain Medical Team for mobile service in the mountain areas. MCC envisaged its work as Christian service "in the Name of Christ" and its programs built up a respect for Mennonites throughout the island.[95] This team was directed by Glen D. Graber, and set up provisional clinics in some places. They made circuits around the mountain areas every year diagnosing and treating illnesses and providing food and hygiene education. Under the leadership of Dr. Roland Engle and Dr. Roland P. Brown, the mountain clinic at Hualien finally expanded in 1954 to become a hospital with

Mobile medical clinic, 1959

a 35-bed capacity.[96] The Mennonite Christian Hospital (MCH) became a milestone of the medical care of the Mennonites in Taiwan.

Mennonite Christian Hospital, 1954

Due to the expansion of medical work, the General Conference Mennonite Board of Missions (later the Commission on Overseas Mission, or COM) decided to take over the work of MCC and to plant churches in 1953. The Mennonites did not initially plant churches among the indigenous people, who were more recep-

Capping ceremony at Nursing School, Mennonite Christian Hospital, early 1960s

tive of the Gospel, because of an agreement that had been reached with the Presbyterian missionary James Dickson. But in the end, the Mennonites decided to preach the Gospel to the Taiwanese-speakers. The first Mennonite church in Taiwan, the so-called Bamboo Church, began in November 7, 1954 in Glen Graber's garage, which had been built from bamboo. The church, Linsen Road Mennonite Church, was officially formed on March 12, 1955 in Taichong. Some Presbyterians members transferred to the new Mennonite church. Church members took turns leading the prayer meeting once a week in the church. The prayer meeting has been held for fifty years.

Hugh Sprunger and his family were dispatched to Taiwan to help establish the church and later founded other churches.[97]

The Bamboo church, 1954

Lu Chun-Tiong, called Uncle Peng-Hu, a Presbyterian pastor with a folk-like charisma, attracted many Taiwanese people who were baptized. He was the most important contributor in the early period of the Mennonite church in Taiwan.[98] The quality and quantity of the Mennonite church in Taiwan eventually improved because of new social services such as the extension of hospitals, the establishment of nursing schools, the airing of the English radio program "Daily Thoughts" and the "Christian Literature Center" bookstore.

Together with these social services, the Mennonite churches also cooperated with Missions-Pax to deliver milk powder and flour to

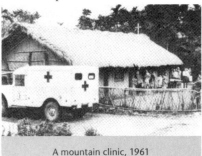

A mountain clinic, 1961

the countryside wherever material support was needed. From 1954-1964, seven local churches were established and shepherded by indigenous pastors spread across three areas: Taichong, Hualien and Taipei.[99] Harold Bender's classic work, *The Anabaptist Vision*, was also translated and some intense courses were held to introduce the nature of the church from the Mennonite perspective.[100]

The Fellowship of Mennonite Churches in Taiwan, FOMCIT, was officially established at the 5th Annual Conference in 1963.[101] Socio-logical studies show that the churches in Taiwan grew quickly during this period, among both the mainlanders and the indigenous tribes. The Protestant commu-nity shot up from about 37,000 members after the war to over 200,000 in 1960.[102] The unstable political situation for Taiwan resulted in a feeling of uncertainty among both Taiwanese and mainland people. Thus, they became "fertile soil" for the Gospel.[103] The percentage of Christians on the island rose from one percent in 1945 to five percent in 1965.[104] The Mennonite

FOMCIT conference, 1964

Church in Taiwan also grew rapidly during this period. With the sup-port of COM,[105] new Mennonite churches were gradually established. According to the annual report of FOMCIT, there were 16 congrega-tions with a total membership of 903 in 1978.

The manner of opening new churches has been debated, however. The church never started with believers, but rather with a building. Children's Sunday school or English classes were held in a rented apartment or in a living room of a missionary's house. The location of the church was chosen on the basis of the need for Christian witness.[106] The special significance of gathering places is a characteristic of Mennonite church planting in Taiwan.[107] In early Taiwanese society, proper worship places were very impor-tant: people were accustomed to going to temples for religious services. The temple court was also the meeting place where people chanted, shared, and fellowshipped. Territory and religion are tightly combined in Taiwanese society.[108] This Taiwanese

Typical Taiwanese shrine

feeling for a gathering place did not change even when Taiwanese society was transformed from an agricultural society to an industrial one. The desire for "a place of our own" still deeply marks Taiwanese identity.

GPS: The Ten-Year Mission Program

On November 20-22, 1972, FOMCIT enthusiastically responded to the GPS program of COM to hold a seminar on the development of three criteria: Goals, Priorities and Strategies (GPS) for church work. COM's GPS program was adopted as the vision for FOMCIT. They focused on problem of the shortage of pastors and members in Taiwanese Mennonite churches, and set up ten top goals.[109] On September 19-21, 1976, when the second seminar on GPS was held, two more goals, the training of Anabaptist theologians and at least one overseas missionary, were added to the project.[110] Because of the GPS project, FOMCIT decided to plant a new church every year. FOMCIT also recommended and supported many pastors for further study at the Associated Mennonite Biblical Seminary in the USA. Since 1977, 13 Taiwanese pastors have studied at that Seminary. However, most of these pastors were not involved in educational ministry after returning to Taiwan. Their time and energy have been drained by pastoral ministry in their own congregations, and some have even left the Mennonite church. The training project of Anabaptist theologians has not yet succeeded. The goal of supporting a proper overseas missionary not yet been reached either, although one missionary did serve one term overseas.

The response to GPS also displayed FOMCIT's attitude toward COM and the relationship between FOMCIT and the mission: harmony along with some dependence. When Hugh Sprunger was transferred from Taiwan to Hong Kong in 1980, Taiwanese pastors interpreted the reason as being the continuous requests that he be the chairperson of FOMCIT. The missionaries never accepted that position because of mission policy and the lessons learned in the Chinese mission. COM has stated that its principle is "the founding and strengthening of the indigenous church."[111]

In 1994, COM announced that its task in Taiwan was finished.[112] FOMCIT became a mission partner of COM from then on. In the meantime, FOMCIT also achieved its Economic Independence Project which was begun in March 1983. FOMCIT now is self-supporting, self-governing, and self-propagating. But the more difficult task, becoming self-theologizing, is still in process.

Challenges and Prospects in the New Millennium

The series of projects in planned economics and land reform which were set up in Taiwan beginning in the 1950s improved Taiwan's economic development, the quality of life and the annual income of Taiwanese. In the late 1970s the Taiwanese performed a surprising economic miracle. The churches in Taiwan gradually broke away from their dependence on American aid. The Mennonite churches were able to fulfill their desire for unity with the global Mennonite community, reflected in a fever of "pilgrimages" in the 1980s. Many church members organized travel groups to attend the Mennonite World Conference assembly in Kansas, USA in 1978 and at Strasbourg, France in 1984 in order to strengthen their Mennonite identity. However, materialism, the side effect of the economic development, immediately followed. The spiritual enthusiasm of communal relationships gradually disappeared. Some scholars argue that when Taiwanese society became affluent, people began to pursue material gain rather than spiritual well-being. Being rich and successful means that church members' time and energy are consumed with their jobs. The church then became a place where church "activities" were organized for church members. In addition, material supports such as milk powder and flour were less needed by those outside the church.

Sociological studies show that church growth reached a plateau in the mid-1960s.[113] It seems that the church lost the ability to say "in the name of Jesus Christ of Nazareth, walk" when the era of "silver or gold I do not have" passed away. In comparison with the churches in Tsao Hsien in the beginning of the twentieth century, poverty seems to have been a blessing.

From 1977 on, the social services of FOMCIT kept developing. Otto Dirks founded the New Dawn Retardation Developmental Center in 1977 in Hualien for taking care of those suffering physical or mental disabilities. In 1992, the Taiwanese government allocated 126 million Taiwanese dollars (about four million US dollars) to reconstruct its office into a seven-story building because of New Dawn's respected service. Now New Dawn, with a progressive vision, is a pioneer in professional skills-training for the disabled in east Taiwan. In 1986 the Good Shepherd Center was established in

The New Dawn Building

Hualien for rescuing child prostitutes, sexually abused young girls and women who are victims of domestic violence; it now runs a halfway house in support of these people.

After a series of expansions with the support from Christian organizations in North America and Germany, the Mennonite Christian Hospital became a 206-bed regional hospital in 1981. It later gained its fine island-wide reputation when Dr. Roland Brown's story was broadcasted on television in the mid 1990s. The Taiwanese were surprised that a "Taiwanese Schweitzer" had been living among them for forty years. Large donations from Taiwanese completed the third expansion project, making MCH a modern hospital with a 500-bed capacity with the newest equipment. These three organizations are still expanding. However, at the same time that social services were expanding, FOMCIT opened only four new churches, two of which have already closed. There were 1,150 active members of the Mennonite churches in Taiwan in the year 2009. It is obviously far behind the first goal of the Ten-Year Project of GPS, to achieve 1,500 church members by 1983.

From 1971 on, the churches in Taiwan began to pursue revival, with church leaders holding a number of church growth lectures, seminars and conferences. Actually, all religious groups in Taiwan

Street Bible class for children

have called for the increase of believers, especially since the late 1990s. Unfortunately, Christianity in Taiwan is not exempt from End Times fever. Many churches have tried church-growth models imported from North America, Singapore and Korea, including the example of the Full Gospel Central Church of Seoul under Paul Yung-chi Cho. They also have tried the new Cell Group Church model strategy developed in Singapore, and the models of Top Ten Growth Churches in America. There are a lot of slogans such as "10,000 churches, 2,000,000 Christians" proposed by the Year 2000 Evangelism Movement. Responding to this movement, FOMCIT held a seminar on "The Mennonite Ten-Year Project Toward the Year 2000" on June 23-24, 1990. There were five issues dealt with at this seminar: extending the function of the FOMCIT, encouraging the training of the laity, strengthening the existing churches and opening up new churches, enhancing theological education, and shoring up FOMCIT's finances. There were different goals and strategies for the different issues.[114] However, because of the difficulties in executing these strategies, most goals of the "Third GPS" were not accomplished.[115]

Taiwanese culture has had an impact on the church. Taiwanese society is a complex composition of clan and folk religions. There is a strong emphasis on living in the religio-familial web. Individual decisions extend beyond that person: if a family member becomes Christian, that person and his or her parents will be criticized.[116] In addition, Christians unavoidably conflict with neighbors when it comes to the offerings and animal sacrifices associated with the rite of the rain-request or the peace ceremony which are connected with the destiny of the whole village. Paul Lin has pointed out that the task of the church in Taiwan is "to paint over a heart which has already been painted by heathen religions... For although an idol has no real existence, yet it does have a power to control people and to occupy human hearts."[117] Ancestor worship is a more difficult problem. In 1981, a young man was baptized into a Mennonite

Lin Shen Road church building, 1994

congregation. One of his parents was very angry and asked him, "Will you let me be a starving ghost or provide food to me after my death?" Nobody in the family talked to him from that moment on, as if he were invisible. There are similar stories all over the island. A Taiwanese person runs the risk of becoming a social outcast after conversion, especially when the Gospel is interpreted in a soul-winning way as a psychological, spiritual salvation. FOMCIT has had to pay attention to the question which James Juhnke has raised: "What would it mean to be a faithful Christian and a Mennonite in Taiwan in the 1980s and beyond?"[118]

At the end of twentieth century, a national and racial identity crisis became the most important social problem in Taiwan. The indigenous Hakka and the different Han Chinese groups who came to Taiwan in different periods, divide Taiwan's society and produce disharmony around the country as well as among the churches. The use of languages reflects this situation. Speaking mother languages has become a label of political identity. For example, although the Meilun Church in Hualien traditionally has an oral interpreter during the Sunday service, because of its international and multi-group church members, many Mennonites are reluctant to speak Mandarin.

Taiwanese Mennonites began to reflect on language usage because young people did not like to attend Sunday services in Mennonite churches. Taiwanese is the official language of Mennonite churches but young men and students are not familiar with Taiwanese since Mandarin has long been spoken in much of Taiwan. Linsen Road Church began a Mandarin service following the main service in September, 2002 to deal with this problem. The "second round" service has attracted forty participants since then.

FOMCIT was established at the invitation of the Taiwan Presbyterian Church. Mennonites, in turn, have helped the Presbyterian Church establish about 400 mountain churches among tribal people. Many Mennonite pastors and believers have come from Presbyterian background, bringing some of their Presbyterian background with them. Moreover, the procedure of worship, the hymnbook and even church regulations are similar. Therefore, some Mennonites cannot distinguish whether FOMCIT is "Mennonite Presbyterian or Presbyterian Mennonite."[119] They wonder whether the Mennonite church is going to be assimilated into the Taiwan Presbyterian Church, using the same hymnbook, worship procedure and the same dialect.

When the Presbyterians in Taiwan increasingly indentify with the land and with the people, the Mennonites have to look for their own traditions: nonconformity, and non-compliance with the mainstream.[120] Mennonites identify with Jesus Christ who has identified with us. "The church's identity as God's people of faith is sustained and renewed as members gather regularly for worship."[121] As a response to the voices from member congregations and a reflection on the effectiveness of the institutional administration in the past two decades, FOMCIT held a summit conference on October 8, 2009 in order to find out Mennonite core values and FOMCIT's identity in contemporary Taiwan. FOMCIT is now urgently working to rediscover the Anabaptist vision to "let the Mennonites be Mennonite." They dream of an Anabaptist Study Center in Taiwan to help members communicate the Gospel to the churches and the society in Taiwan from the Mennonite perspective. The Mennonite churches in Taiwan are seeking new insight from their theological origins, hoping to show the world a sample of life under the lordship of Christ.

The Mennonites in Hong Kong and Macau

Mennonites in Hong Kong

Located on the east side of the Pearl River Delta in southern China, Hong Kong is famous as the Pearl of the East, a typical immigrant city. After the Sino-British War in 1842, Hong Kong became a British colony and a free port. Its cultural identity, however, is stronger than its political identity. The churches that were planted in Hong Kong were the product of 19th century Mission Movement. Generally, the churches in Hong Kong were subsidiaries of the churches in Southern China. Many refugees fled from China when there was political unrest on the Mainland, such as the Tai Ping Rebellion and the Revolution of Dr. Sun Yat-Sen. The number of churches in Hong Kong increased because of these immigrants. At the beginning of the twentieth century there were nine major denominations and seventy-five congregations in Hong Kong.[122] However, the fluid population did not dramatically increase the number of Christians, of which there were about eight thousand in the 1930s.[123]

Many refugees rushed into Hong Kong after World War II. Following the Communist take-over in China in 1949, Hong Kong became a fortress and missionaries continued to pursue their China vision.[124] The population of Hong Kong jumped from 600,000 in 1945 to 2,100,000 in 1950. It kept increasing at the rate of one million people every ten years. The rapidly increasing population and turbulent society brought along uncertainty and severe social problems. Relief charities and evangelism were successful in helping the churches grow. According to one statistic, the number of the churches increased from 188 in 1955 to 344 in 1962, and the number of Christians grew accordingly, from 53,917 to 112,200 in that period.[125]

Under the government of the United Kingdom, Hong Kong became one of the most competitive cities in Asia. However, Hong Kong also became one of the most expensive cities for expatriates. As of 2009, Hong Kong was the fifth-most expensive city in the world. Hong Kong's high cost-of-living made it difficult for missions to work there and became the foremost obstacle the Mennonite Church needed to overcome. It cost $136,363 US for a one-unit apartment when the Mennonites decided to buy a property in 1983.[126] With the generosity and support from mission boards, all 3 Mennonite churches in Hong Kong finally became owners of their church properties.

Mennonites came to Hong Kong after World War II. When missionaries were forced to leave China after Liberation in 1949, some

The Hong Kong Mennonite Center

MCC workers and Mennonite missionaries went to Hong Kong to set up relief work such as hot meals and a reading room for refugee children. During the mid 1960's, Dr. Andrew Roy of Chung Chi College suggested that Mennonites open a mission in Hong Kong. The Eastern Mennonite Board of Missions and Charities (EMBMC) dispatched a missionary couple, Ira and Evie Kurtz, to take over the leadership of the MCC reading room in 1966. Through friendships, English classes, and Bible studies they turned their ministry into more church-related activities. However, a formal church was not started until February 1976 when some young people believed in Christ.[127] This was the Lok Fu Mennonite Church, the forerunner of the first Mennonite Church, Agape Mennonite Church. Evangelism was done gradually through English classes, family Bible study groups, and the distribution of books and Gospel tracts. However, relying on temporary facilities had a "negative impact on the growth of the church and hindered development of its ministries because of the time and space limitations imposed by the temporary facilities."[128] After several changes of locations, the church finally moved to Tin Sum Village, Shatin in 1991. Church members began to sponsor the Agape Arts Center, in order to attract people. The pastor then was Paul Wong. In 1998, Jeremiah Choi came to serve as the pastor in charge, and Agape moved to Sun Tin Village, Shatin in 2008.

In 1980, The Commission on Overseas Mission (COM) of the General Conference Mennonite Church joined with EMBMC in a united mission program. These two organizations cooperated in supporting the mission in Hong Kong. Rev. Hugh Sprunger came from Taiwan to assist in church planting in Hong Kong. He also initiated a theological education program for believers in Hong Kong.

A second Mennonite church, the Homantin Mennonite Church, was established in 1986, responding to the pastoral needs of overseas students who had come back to Hong Kong. This church is now called

Grace Mennonite Church. In the following year, the East Kowloon Mennonite Church was closed because of difficulty in developing at Kowloon Bay. Church members of East Kowloon Mennonite Church joined Grace Mennonite Church. The church gradually grew and the number of its members reached eighty in 1996 when Rev. Daniel Ngai was leading this congregation..

After the retirement of Daniel Ngai and the departure of the missionaries, Grace Mennonite Church has been finding its identity by connecting with the communities in the church's area and using the Natural Church Development to build up the church in a guided approach. In June of 2011, Grace Mennonite Church will move into a new area to start a new phase, and at the same time, the leadership team will join a course using one year to find the vision of the church. The pastor in charge now (March 2011) is Alde Wong.

The Mennonite church in Hong Kong is small but quite active and enthusiastic. The Asian International Reconciliation Work Camp of the Asia Mennonite Conference and the Assembly of the Asian Mennonite Conference stand as a record of the great work of church members. They also hold regular outreach ministries to the street-people, where food and clothing are distributed. Later, when this ministry was expanded as "Helping Hands Ministries," Eastern Mennonite Missions dispatched Youth Evangelism Service teams to assist the ministries in Hong Kong.

The Helping Hands Center opened in July, 1989 in Kwai Fong to help children, youth and families, with an emphasis on tutorial help for students. On June 4th of the same year, Hope Mennonite Church was established. Under the supervision of Hugh Sprunger and Tim Sprunger, Jeremiah Choi served as the first Chinese pastor of Hope Mennonite Church while his wife Wendy Choi served as the first tutor at Helping Hands Center. Some parents became Christians because of this service. Ms. Faena Tjung is a good example. She came to Hong Kong from Indonesia, raising two children alone after an unhappy marriage. She became a Christian because of the educational assistance in the church. She came through a difficult time after her broken marriage. The church members and pastor Simon Szedu took care of her children when she went out

Helping Hands computer class at Hope Mennonite Church

to work. She is now a happy woman of faith in Jesus, having a meal with church members every Sunday.

Hope Church had engaged in outreach activities among the newly arrived immigrants from China in a suburb called Tuen Mun since the 1990's. After some years of labor, a group of Chinese immigrant mothers came to Christ via a mother's group in a local kindergarten. In December 2007, with the help from the Kauffmans (a missionary family sent from EMM) and the vision of some church members, Hope Church was moved there to nurture the evangelistic fruit. To continue the outreach work, the church premises are used as an activity center (under the banner of Helping Hands Ministries) during weekdays. The pastor in charge (March 2011) was Mr. Fu.[129]

In 2007 the three churches considered merging to form one church in order to share resources more effectively. But after consultation this idea was abandoned in favor of separate development of each congregation. The ordination of Pastor Jeremiah Choi is to take place on Aug 14th of 2011.[130]

Christianity in Hong Kong gained respect from the people of Hong Kong in the 1970s and 80s because of its social service and standing for the good of the people. However, Christians became more and more dissatisfied with the established church and began supporting para-church institutions which also served the churches and society.[131] Therefore, the churches did not grow but the para-church institutions developed rapidly.[132]

In addition, the issue of returning Hong Kong's sovereign right had become unavoidable and influenced the churches from the time that negotiations started in 1982 between the United Kingdom and Mainland China. The "June Fourth Incident" in 1989 caused many people to emigrate from Hong Kong due to the fear of violent suppression by the Communist party. According to one report around 100,000 church members, about one fourth of all members, left Hong Kong from 1982 to 1997.[133] Some scholars called for revising the Christian attitude toward the church, advocating that the church take on the nature of a suffering servant and Messianic victim.[134]

The Mennonite church in Hong Kong also went through a difficult time when many church members emigrated to other countries.[135] In 1997, one of the congregations began to organize into cell groups in case their facilities were confiscated and they needed to abandon larger, centralized meetings.[136] In 1985, the Hong Kong Mennonite

Conference registered as The Conference of Mennonite Churches in Hong Kong Limited (CMCHK) in order to protect church property and reduce the possible impact due to the return of sovereign rule. Although the CMCHK still relies on overseas personnel and financial support, without any independent help to provide theological opinions on the politics and society in Hong Kong, they do support mission work in northern Thailand and the work of the Industry Evangelical Fellowship. In addition to the CMCHK, Nora Iwarat from the Integrated Mennonite Church of the Philippines, and Timoria Gurning sent by the Indonesian Mennonite Church (GKMI), supported by Mennonite Mission Network and Mennonite Church Canada Witness, started an outreach ministry, the Cheung Chau Christian Center, mostly to Filipino and Indonesian domestic workers on Cheung Chau Island. As the ministry was growing, the All Nations church was started by missionary Andrew Wade together with Nora on June 4, 2006.

Since the 1997 handover, Mandarin has become more popular as immigrants from mainland China increase and there is greater integration with the mainland economy. Additionally, the self-censorship by journals whose owners have close ties to the People's Republic of China and the worsened income gap all created a feeling of insecurity among the people. However, together with all Christian bodies and in the face of future uncertainty, the Mennonites are witnessing to the seven million residents in Hong Kong, that only in Christ is there eternal shelter.

The Macau Mennonite Church

Located on the west side of Pearl River Delta, since the sixteenth century Macau has been a beachhead for Christian missions to China. However, Macau is now known as the gambling capital of East Asia. Gambling casinos are everywhere and prostitution, organized crime, and drug abuse have resulted in many social problems. In addition, the worship of idols, ancestors, and the presence of cults is pervasive in Macau. These socio-spiritual strongholds have caused the church in Macau to remain weak.

In 1996 an international team of Mennonite mission workers began the mission in Macau with the Commission on Overseas Mission taking the lead. George Veith and his family moved to Macau from Hong Kong in 1996 as did Shirley Liem from Indonesia. Bill Tse from Hong Kong, who was a student at the Macau Bible Institute, also joined the team. The work began in the Veiths' apartment. Isaiah 61:1 became the guiding principle and focus.

In 1999, Macau returned to the rule of China and is now seen as a gateway to China. Through cell groups, English classes, children's classes, street evangelism, prayer walks, and a prison ministry, the Macau Mennonite team seeks to win working-class people to Christ. A Family Life Center was established in 2001. Workers on the team included one person from Indonesia, one from Hong Kong, and one family from Canada. The Taiwan and Hong Kong Mennonite churches participate with financial support. Macau Mennonite Church grew slowly but surely. On June 7, 2009, this small peace church celebrated its first ordination of local leader, Treasure Chow. As a sign of passing on the authority to lead this church, the Veiths washed the feet of the Chows, and then each believer in attendance was anointed with oil to signify the kingdom work of the church being handed over to the body of believers during the handover ceremony on June 14, 2009.[137] This ceremony marked the beginning of a new era of Macau Mennonite Church.

Conclusion: Being a Community of Faithful Disciples

The century-long presence of the Mennonite Church on both sides of the Taiwan Strait has meant being in the shadow of large-scale changes in China. The root of the Mennonite churches has been planted into the soil of far-flung areas. In facing the new century, the uncertainty of the relationship between the countries on the two sides of the Taiwan Strait brings challenges as well as opportunities. It is a "challenge of change," said Hugh Sprunger in 1966. "The Mennonite churches in Taiwan are facing the challenge of change. They also challenge the people with a change of life through faith in Jesus Christ as Savior and Lord."[138] The Mennonite churches in Chinese-speaking areas, especially in Taiwan and in Hong Kong, are minor Christian groups; however, just as at the beginning of the Anabaptist movement, they are not afraid of big changes in the world because they believe that "the one who is inside us is bigger than the one in the world." They intend to continue being the community of faithful disciples, witnessing to their Lord, Jesus Christ. They also intend to keep Christ's example and teaching to call the Chinese-speaking people to Christ and continue their lives of holiness and purity by surrendering themselves to God while heading into the new, coming world.

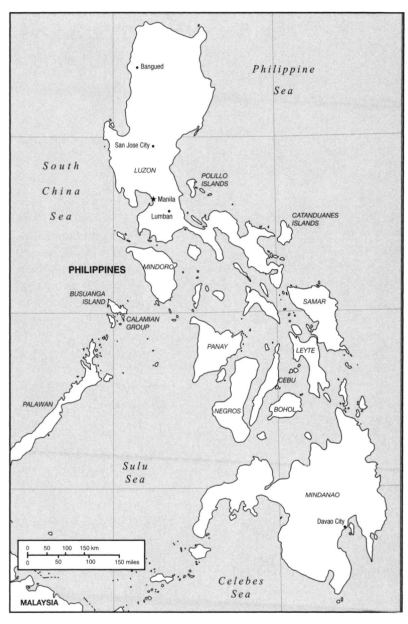

Philippines

The Mennonite Church in the Philippines

CHAPTER
VI

by Regina Lyn Mondez

The Philippines: An Introduction

Geography

The Philippine archipelago consists of over 7000 islands, only 7% of which are larger than one square mile, and only two-thirds of which have names. The total land area of the Philippines is 115,830 square miles. The largest island is Luzon, which is located in the northern part, followed by Mindanao in the southern area. There are over 30 active volcanoes across the mountainous topography, where bamboo, orchids, and a huge variety of trees grow. The country is rich in flora and fauna, which is the main source of livelihood for the majority of the people. Although the country is rich in natural resources, it has unfortunately been exploited by logging and mining companies who destroyed millions of hardwood trees. Deforestation has led to serious problems with soil erosion.

Filipino ethnicity and culture

The aboriginal inhabitants of the Philippines were the Negritos who came from Borneo, Sumatra and Malaya. They reached the area in 25,000 BCE via land bridges connecting the islands. In 3,000 BCE, Indonesian and Malayan settlers followed. During the 14th century, extensive trading with India, Indonesia, China, and Japan was conducted, with wood and ores the primary products traded.

In 1521, Ferdinand Magellan arrived and claimed the country for Spain. He was killed by a local datu (chief) named Lapu-lapu, who refused to accept Spanish rule and Christianity. In 1542, however, more Spanish expeditions followed, including a decisive one under

259

Lopez de Villalobos from New Spain (Mexico), after which the country was named for the Spanish king, Philip II.

Early Filipino religion

Early Filipinos believed in gods, spirits, creatures, and men who guarded the streams, fields, mountains, forests, and houses. They worshipped Batala or Bathala as the creator and savior of the world. They believed that he was the most powerful god among all the other gods and deities they worshipped. Aside from this, ancestral spirits were revered through wood and metal images, although no distinction was made between the spirits and their physical symbols. In the 14th century, Islam was introduced to the southern islands of Sulu and Mindanao by Arab traders from Malaya and Borneo. This remains the major religion in Mindanao until today.

During the Spanish regime (1521-1898), Christianity was introduced and embraced by the Filipinos. They learned to pray, hear mass, and read the Bible. They accepted the Catholic tradition of giving high value to the altar, paying homage to different images and sculptures of saints, and honoring their patron saints. Until now, celebrating fiestas in honor of patron saints has been part of the Filipino culture in every town throughout the whole country. Although Christianity was widespread during the Spanish occupation, there are still a number of Filipinos who refuse this religion. The Muslims in the southern islands are among those who resisted Catholicism.

During the American period (1898-1935), education and democracy were promoted. Most of the teachers who came to the Philippines were Protestants, some of whom were Protestant ministers. The arrival of these Protestants resulted in the birth of denominations such as Seventh-Day Adventist, Presbyterian, Episcopalian, Methodist, Lutheran, and United Brethren. Although the Americans emphasized the separation of church and state, religion in Filipino culture always had a significant influence on kinship ties, patron-client bonds, and other relationships outside the nuclear family.

Today, Filipinos have the freedom to worship and to choose what religious group to join. But still, the more than 300 years of Spanish influence in the country had a great impact, because 85 percent of the Filipinos are Catholics. The remainder of the population adheres to Buddhism, Protestantism, El Shaddai, Jesus is Lord Movement,

Jesus Miracle Crusade, United Methodist Church, United Church of Christ in the Philippines, Mennonites, Ang Dating Daan, Seventh-Day Adventist Church, Aglipayanism, Iglesia ni Cristo, Jehovah's Witnesses, Mormonism, Islam, Judaism, Sikhism, Hinduism, Atheism, Agnosticism, among others.

History of the Mennonites in the Philippines

The Mennonites first arrived in the Philippines after World War II, when the Mennonite Central Committee (MCC) assisted war victims by sending 17 workers to the country. Their ministry began in Bangued, the capital of Abra province in Northern Luzon, which had been destroyed by bombing. The program of MCC was not focused on evangelism and church planting, but the Anabaptist conviction of mutual aid became widely-known and respected. To this day, Bangued Christian Hospital, which was founded by MCC in 1948, is still known and respected in Abra as a "Mission Hospital." MCC left the country in 1950 after establishing the hospital. This private Secondary General Hospital is now owned and operated by Protestant doctors.

Meanwhile, in the same year (1950), Felonito A. Sacapaño, together with Marcelo Masaoay, were called by God to do mission work in the municipality of San Quintin, in the province of Abra. Sacapaño and Masaoay were Baptist missionaries who started weekend Bible Studies among the Tingian tribe and other indigenous people in the area. They used their personal resources to conduct and support their mission in the foothills of Northern Luzon. The tribal people heard the message of salvation for the first time, and they believed and received the

Felonito A. Sacapaño

Savior Jesus Christ and were baptized. In 1955, the congregation put up a chapel where they held their worship services.

In September, 1956, Masaoay felt the need for Christ's workers. He resigned from his good-paying job and went to the hill tribes of Abra where he worked with Ilocano lowlanders who spoke his language. There he focused on God's work, leaving Sacapaño as a one-man mission board. Sacapaño, on the other hand, was then holding a key position at the International Nutrition Products, Inc. He personally provided for the ministry expenses while receiving reports, and conducting Bible studies on weekends.

On March 6, 1965, Sacapaño organized a brainchild Missions Now, Inc. (MNI), which was duly registered and approved by the Philippine government. The vision of MNI was to "serve the total need of man whom the Savior Jesus Christ loved and died for and rose from the grave to give full justification." The mission of MNI was: 1) to serve the spiritual fulfillment of believers and 2) to meet their temporal needs.

Missions Now, Inc. (MNI) reached out to economically disadvantaged people and started to develop and expand small cottage industries in seacoast fishing, inland fishponds, agricultural production and rice processing, carpentry and furniture shops. Shell crafts, wood crafts, and handicrafts were exported. Hand in hand with church planting and MNI, the Mennonite Economic Development Associates (MEDA) extended Bro. Sacapaño a loan to establish the Faith Woodcraft shop in Paete, Laguna. The loan made it possible for this small-sized cottage woodcraft business to flourish. Later, MEDA provided more loans which paved the way for the success of their projects. Some of the hand-carved woods were exported to North America and Europe.

The beginning of Mennonite work in the Philippines, through MEDA and the MNI became successful and helped serve a lot of people who were poor in spirit and economic resources.

MNI and the EMBMC (the 1970's)

On October 1970, Sacapaño resigned from his job and in 1971 went to the United States. There, he had the opportunity to share

Students at the Philippine Mennonite Biblical Institute with their teacher, Leon Stauffer, 1979-80

God's work in the Philippines. Different churches invited him to speak and he was given significant love gifts to help the ministry in the Philippines. By July 25, 1971, Missions Now Inc. (MNI) was officially endorsed by the Council of the General Conference Mennonite Church in Eureka, Illinois.

In God's own time in December 27, 1972, the Eastern Mennonite Board of Missions and Charities (EMBMC) in

Salunga, Pennsylvania sent James E. Metzler, an American Mennonite missionary. He went to the Philippines to establish contact with Sacapaño and his group, the Missions Now, Inc. (MNI). This undertaking resulted in twenty-two pioneer churches and mission points around the country.

In 1978, MNI already had an estimated number of 2,000 believers in 22 congregations. Eight of these congregations consist of members among the poorest in Filipino society. During this same year, 48 students in secondary schools and colleges were being supported in their studies. In 1979, MNI and EMBMC established the Philippine Mennonite Biblical Institute (PMBI) in Lumban, Laguna. This Bible

Students at PMBI, 1979-80

school trained a lot of young people in different areas of ministry work. Leon and Nancy Stauffer served as teachers in this Bible school from 1979 to 1980.

MNI and MCC (the 1980's)

In the middle of the 1980's, the Mennonite Central Committee (MCC) opened a new program in the Philippines, which focused on peace-making and justice concerns. A group of experienced workers engaged in community and agricultural development, research, and writing. In 1985, MCC reported 10 persons in its program. These people were committed to nonviolence despite the increasing conflict around them. MCC worked with and channeled some resources to other Filipino groups who shared the same goals, such as dealing with political detainees and their families, and working with prostitutes who lived near the huge US military bases.

The approach taken by MCC workers, however, experienced its own problems since North American supporters and their church leaders did not totally understand the position of the team. The team felt it must work in partnership with the people and allow them to define methods of relating to the community. The results of their work were not always easy to measure. The rise of the "People Power" movement in 1986, however, suggested that MCC objective had been well-suited to the situation. The People Power revolution enabled a nonviolent ouster of then-President Ferdinand Marcos, putting Corazon Aquino into presidency.

Meanwhile, MNI continued its ministries throughout the country, until the death of Felonito Sacapaño in October 6, 1987. After Sacapaño's death, MNI faced difficulties that led to division among its leadership and members. Sammy Sacapaño, the son of the late Felonito, took over the leadership of MNI. He changed course, left the Mennonite church, and a number of congregations in the provinces of Nueva Vizcaya, Nueva Ecija, and Laguna followed him. They retained the name of their group as MNI. The other faithful members, however, continued their connection with the Mennonites and organized themselves in 1991 as the "Integrated Mennonite Churches of the Philippines, Inc."

The birth of IMC (the 1990's)

Members of the Lumban Mennonite Bible Church in front of their new building, 2006

On October 23, 1991, the Integrated Mennonite Churches, Inc. (IMC) was registered as a religious, non-stock and non-profit organization at the Securities and Exchange Commission (the Philippine government accreditation agency). The IMC main office was in the Lumban Mennonite Bible Church in Lumban, Laguna, which was also the first church founded by Sacapaño.

The newly-registered IMC, under the leadership of the then-president Gervacio Balucas, continued its ministries of evangelism, discipleship, and church-planting throughout the country. Camps and conferences were organized, as well as leadership trainings, which produced a number of pastors and workers that have served IMC until today.

Through thick and thin (the 2000's)

The first ordination of bishops of the Integrated Mennonite Churches, Inc. (IMC) was held on April 12, 2000 in the municipality of Castañeda, province of Nueva Vizcaya. On that occasion, bishop Howard Witmer, Secretary of the Lancaster Mennonite Conference, installed four Filipino bishops. Bishop Ambrocio Porcincula was ordained for the Southern District Conference; Bishop Ramon Bansan for the Central District Conference; Bishop Jose Basa for the Northwestern District; and Bishop Adriano Fernandez for the Northeastern District. Bishop Porcincula was installed as the first Moderator of the IMC Board of Bishops from April 2000 to December 2009.

IMC Bishops in 2011 (l to r): Ambrocio Porcincula, Edgardo Docuyanan, Ramon Bansan, Adriano Fernandez, and Jose Basa

IMC churches flourished, especially in the northern and mountainous parts of Luzon. On April 9, 2004, the Ordination Council, under the leadership of Porcincula, ordained Edgardo Docuyanan as the Bishop of the IMC Northern District Conference. Docuyanan, at that time, had already been doing mission work with the tribes in Dupax del Norte, province of Nueva Vizcaya.

In January 2006, a Filipino-Canadian missionary couple, Dann and Joji Pantoja, came back to the county to serve as Mennonite missionaries after spending 20 years in Canada. They were sent by Mennonite Church Canada to do peacebuilding work in the war-torn island of Mindanao. They began their ministry by embracing their Muslim neighbors in the name of Jesus Christ. They opened a small coffee shop in Davao City and advocated for Fair Trade Arabica Coffee, while also addressing different issues of injustice and conflict in Mindanao.

In September 2006, IMC hosted the Holy Spirit in Mission Conference and the International Missions Association business meeting held in Lumban, province of Laguna. Forty-five international guests from 16 countries participated during the event. Together, they prayed, fasted, shared testimonies, reports, teachings, and workshops for three days. The IMC members were encouraged as they witnessed and heard testimonies of Mennonite brothers and sisters from different parts of the world. The Pantoja couple also participated in this event and began to establish their first connections with IMC.

By the year 2008, some of the members of the IMC Board of Trustees decided to split from IMC due to issues of finance and leadership. Together with their families, they formed their own group which they registered as "Integrated Mennonite Conference of the Philippines, Inc." This issue of separation was later addressed by the officials of IMC. Eventually, some of them requested to be part of IMC again.

Today, IMC continues to be strong despite the storms and trials. It continues to grow and bear fruit as it acknowledges the prayers and support of our brothers and sisters in the global Anabaptist church.

Mennonites in the Philippines Today

Church Organization, Polity, and Order of Worship

The Integrated Mennonite Churches, Inc. (IMC) is currently under the leadership of the Board of Trustees (BOT) which is the highest deci-

IMC bishops and trustees, 2011

sion-making body of the organization. Seven of the trustees are elected by the entire body every three years: the President, Vice-president, Board Secretary, Treasurer, Auditor, and two Board members. In addition, the Men's representative, Women's representative, Youth representative, Socio-economic Committee head, Education Committee head, and Mission Committee head are also automatically members of the BOT. The five bishops are ex-officio BOT members.

The Board of Bishops (BOB) serves as the spiritual adviser of the organization. The BOT and BOB meet regularly every quarter to report, decide, and plan their activities. On November 2010, IMC appointed a National Coordinator to centralize all communications on behalf of IMC. Regina Mondez, the appointed National Coordinator, also serves as the secretariat, who works hand in hand with the Secretary of the Board in dealing with office work, coordination tasks, and filing system.

Like most evangelical churches, IMC churches meet regularly every Sunday to worship and praise together. In the middle of the week, they gather for prayer meeting, and conduct Bible studies on weekends or on any day of the week as scheduled by the members. Sunday School for Adults, Children, and Youth are conducted simultaneously on Sunday mornings before the Worship Service.

Regular worship service includes singing, preaching, prayer, and testimonies. In some churches, testimonial

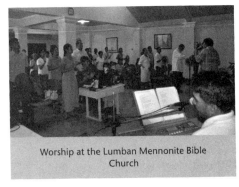

Worship at the Lumban Mennonite Bible Church

nights are held every Sunday so that the Sunday morning worship service will not take too long. As for singing, most of the churches choose either hymns or contemporary Christian songs, and other songs composed by Filipino Christian singers. Some churches use no instruments, others use only a church organ, while most churches have a complete set of musical instruments for their Praise and

Worship leaders and members are free to raise their hands and dance during worship

Worship singing. However, regardless of the songs they sing or what instruments they use, IMC churches are united by the idea that the Heart of Worship, Jesus Christ, is the most important element in singing and not the song itself, the singer, or the instruments.

At present there are 21 local congregations affiliated with IMC. Most of these churches are located in the Northern provinces of Luzon, while the remaining members are in the Southern province of Laguna and in the Metro Manila

An improvised drum kit accompanies worship at the Ginautan Mennonite Church

area. IMC congregations can only be found on the island of Luzon, located in five provinces and one city: Laguna, Nueva Ecija, Aurora, Nueva Vizcaya, Pangasinan, and Pasig City.

Meanwhile, Peacebuilders Community, Inc. (PBCI), a Mennonite mission organization supported by Mennonite Church Canada and dedicated to peacebuilding work throughout the country, is affiliated with IMC as a mission organization, and can be found in Davao City in Mindanao island. Dann Pantoja, president of PBCI, is also the head of the IMC Technical Working Group, which was formed to do tactical planning for the development of the IMC vision for the next few years.

Summary of Membership Profile

IMC currently has a total of 701 baptized members in 21 congregations. Among the 701 members, 295 participated in a survey conducted for

the purpose of this chapter. Stratified random sampling was used in selecting 50% of the total members of IMC. Among the IMC members, females (62%) outnumber the men (38%). A greater number of the population belongs to the age group 20-29 years old (22%), followed by ages 30-39 (14%). Members that belong to age group 70-79 and 80-89 are the least in number.

IMC General Conference, Bongabon, Nueva Ecija, 2008

Twenty-nine percent of the members have completed elementary education, while only 21% were able to finish a college degree. A significant number (27%) finished high school education. Almost half of the members (52%) are employed and the rest are either unemployed, or have unstable jobs. The majority of the members are farmers and laborers, while a significant number of the members are working for the local government unit of their municipality or province. The employed members are teachers, pharmacists, midwifes, managers, and government employees. IMC has only a few full-time missionaries and pastors.

Among the members, the highest number (18%) have 6-10 years in the faith, followed by those (14%) who have been believers for 0-5 years. Only 2% have been in the faith for 56-60 years already. A significant number of members are involved in the Music ministry and Youth ministry. There are also a considerable number of members involved in Sunday School ministry, Discipleship, Evangelism, and Intercession.

Aside from the individual members, a mission organization, Peacebuilders Community, Inc. (PBCI), is affiliated to IMC. This mission organization serves as the peacebuilding arm of IMC. It promotes the ministry of Peace and Reconciliation (PAR) throughout the whole country by training and equipping leaders in each province in peace theology and peace-building skills. At present, the Anabaptist theology of peace is widely-known and embraced by different denominations and religious groups in the country, through the efforts of PBCI. The PAR movement was also embraced and is being promoted and supported by the Philippine Council of Evangelical Churches, the largest network of evangelical churches across the country.

IMC Leaders and their journey with the Mennonite Church

One of the oldest members of IMC is Bishop Adriano Fernandez. He was first connected to the Missions Now, Inc. in 1968 and worked closely with Sacapaño and Masaoay. Before joining the Mennonite group, he had finished his army training and was ready to pursue a career in the armed forces. However, he was called by God and entered into a Protestant Bible School. Later, he transferred to a Mennonite Biblical school under Sacapaño and embraced the Anabaptist teachings of non-resistance and adult baptism. To this day, he is actively serving the Lord through his church in Pantabangan, Nueva Ecija.

> "I joined the Mennonite Church because of my belief in non-resistance and in believers' baptism as a Biblical teaching of Jesus."
> *Adriano Fernandez*

Anabaptist Mennonite Community Church, Pantabangan, Nueva Ecija, pastored by Bishop Adriano Fernandez. Yda Villa, former youth leader, stands in front of the church building that is currently being expanded.

Bishop Jose Basa also met Sacapaño in 1968 and decided to join this group because he believed that the Mennonites had a sound biblical teaching and practice, especially when it came to baptism. He pastors a congregation in San Fabian, province of Pangasinan. As one of the oldest in the faith, he has experienced a lot of struggles in his ministry but God continues to be faithful to him. He experienced how God answers prayers and provides for our needs – especially the needs of the church. Through the ministry of Bishop Basa, a young man came to know Christ and dedicated his life to the ministry. Pastor Felix Sotto got involved in church ministry in 1987, and decided to

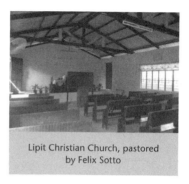

Lipit Christian Church, pastored by Felix Sotto

study at the Mennonite School of Theology in San Jose City, Nueva Ecija. Later, he passionately served the Lord and followed wherever he was led to serve. In 2004, he was assigned as Assistant Pastor of Bishop Basa at the Lipit Christian Church. By the year 2007, Bishop Basa had to resign as the Head Pastor of their church and Felix Sotto was unanimously appointed by the members to become the Head Pastor. Until now, he continues to serve in Lipit Christian Church while opening other outreach ministries in different areas of their town.

In 1971, Bishop Ramon Bansan became a part of what was then Missions Now, Inc. He was pastor of a small independent church in Castañeda, province of Nueva Vizcaya. He decided to join the Men-

Grace Anabaptist Mennonite Church, San Jose City, pastored by Bishop Ramon Bansan

nonite group because he saw Mennonites as peaceful and loving people. Aside from this, he felt that they respected the principles of other Christian groups and were free to have fellowship with other groups of believers in the name of Jesus Christ. He embraced the doctrine of non-resistance, which is a biblical way of loving your enemy. He is now the overseer of the IMC Central District and pastors a small church in San Jose City, Nueva Ecija. The church that Bishop Bansan led in Castañeda, Nueva Vizcaya is now being pastored by Pastor Jomedes Eusebio. Eusebio first connected with the Mennonites in 1992. Before this, he was a member of another church but was not actively involved in the ministry. He was a violent trouble maker, but longed to have peace. When he met the Mennonites, he decided to become part of them. He joined the Mennonite group because they were not involved in any destructive or violent acts that destroy love, peace, and unity.

In 1981, Bansan introduced the Mennonites to his friend, Edgardo Docuyanan. Docuyanan was then doing ministry work among the ethnic groups in Dupax del Norte, Nueva Vizcaya with another evangelical group. He noticed that the Mennonites had a strong emphasis on the equality of believers and servant leadership which is characterized by walking and serving God together in the way of Jesus. In 1988, he officially became a member of the Missions Now, Inc. (MNI). To this day, he has been faithfully serving the Lord through IMC as pastor of the Friendship Christian Church of Pasig, and is overseer of the Northern District churches. He is the current Bishop Moderator of IMC and is actively involved

> "Being Mennonite now, I have no regrets, instead grateful to God for through it I and my fellow Filipino pastors are linked to a Mennonite World Conference"
>
> *Edgardo Docuyanan*

with the global gatherings of the Mennonite World Conference (MWC). He is also a member of the MWC General Council.

In August 1986, a teacher-politician in Lumban who was dreaming of becoming mayor of the town was prompted by the Holy Spirit to attend a Sunday service at the Lumban Mennonite Bible Church, where Sacapaño was ministering at that time. Ambrocio Porcincula was just reading his Bible when he heard a voice telling him that he would not become a mayor, but that God would use him as one of His servants in His vineyard. Right then and there, he cried hard, repented of all his sins and asked God for forgiveness. Later on, he was baptized with water as a true believer of Jesus Christ. Six months after he was baptized, Sacapaño assigned him to pastor an outreach church in Barangay Lewin, Lumban, Laguna. He was hesitant because he did not have any Bible School training, but the Holy Spirit insisted that he take on the task. After a year in Lewin, he was called to serve in the Lumban Mennonite Bible Church as an Associate pastor, where he has served from 1988 until the present. In 1991 to 1993, he was appointed Secretary/Treasurer of the IMC and was elected IMC Chairman from 1995 to 2000. On April 12, 2000, he was ordained as a Bishop and was the first installed Bishop Moderator of IMC from April 2000 to December 2009. He joined the Anabaptist Church simply because of its radical adherence to the teachings and lifestyle of Jesus Christ as Son of Man.

As a young man, Eladio (Ely) Mondez received Jesus Christ as Savior and Lord on April 7, 1976 as a response to an evangelistic message in a Summer Youth Camp conducted by MNI. He was a former Roman Catholic and came to know Christ through the Mennonite Church. He embraced the Mennonite doctrine of baptism, peace, and non-resistance. He studied at the Philippine Mennonite Biblical Institute (PMBI) in 1979-1980 while at the same time working on his college degree in a secular school. From 1984 to 1998, he was a member of the Philip-

Eladio Mondez and his family when they were with the Conservative Mennonite group

pine (Conservative) Mennonite Church. He was ordained as a pastor in 1987 and served on the Board of Trustees of the Association. In 1998, he and his family peacefully left the Conservative Mennonite Church and decided to re-unite with the Lumban Mennonite Bible Church (LMBC) in June 2000. Since then, he has been assigned as Associate Pastor of LMBC until May 2010 when he took over as pastor of the Lacao Mennonite Bible Church, one of the daughter churches in Laguna. He is currently the IMC Treasurer of the Board.

IMC Ministries

The IMC youth organized themselves as the Philippine Menno Youth (PMY) and regularly meet for camps and fellowships. They conduct an annual youth camp which is held in different IMC churches. Although

Philippine Menno Youth Camp, 2010

it is geographically challenging, the PMY sees the importance of worship and fellowship together as young believers of Jesus Christ embracing the Anabaptist doctrine. There is a deep connection among the IMC youth despite the geographical distances. One of the biggest challenges the youth face is expanding their activities because of the lack of funding. They independently raise their funds, although the IMC lends financial support for their activities whenever it can. The PMY officers are young professionals, students, and Bible School students who are dreaming of a radical transformation among the youth in the Philippines.

Philippine Menno Youth leaders conduct ministry outreach in Dupax del Norte, Nueva Vizcaya, 2011

The IMC women and ministers' wives meet every three years during the General Conference. Meanwhile, the women's groups also meet regularly (quarterly or yearly) per district or province. They encourage and strengthen each other in the faith while also sharing their joys and experiences of being wives and mothers. They are also active in sharing the Gospel with other women who are not yet in the faith.

One of the most important ministries of IMC is community service. Youth, women, or other members all see to it that part of their activities involve making an impact in their community. For instance, IMC is one of the religious groups in the country that responds to disasters and crises, feeling the need to respond to people who are in dire need. When IMC receives extra funding, it can extend more help to neighbors in the community. Even when there is no funding, IMC members work hand in hand to respond and help anyone that needs their help and prayers.

Church members come to assist flood victims, 2009

Current IMC Vision

The Integrated Mennonite Churches, Inc. (IMC) envisions a Mennonite Church at the Global City in Metro Manila that will be an active Peace and Reconciliation catalyst in our land.

It envisions a strong structure for national representation, strategic planning activities, corporate financial management systems, and competency-based leadership development programs that must be established in the National Capital Region.

IMC consists of a number of congregations from the Northern part of the country, down to the Southern part. It has established several churches in the rural areas, even to the remotest parts of the country. It has since been faithful in worship, fellowship, service, and witnessing.IMC believes that it is time that as the Body of Christ, it becomes an active catalyst for Peace and Reconciliation in the country. IMC envisions planting a church in the National Capital Region, which is where the center of power and authority in the government, military, business, and religious sectors lies. It seeks to actively make the Gospel of Peace known to the top leadership of the country. With this, the IMC prays for committed workers who will be part of this church planting vision.

IMC seeks to have a National Office in Metro Manila where the National Director will stay and serve on a full-time basis. It envisions the office to be able to house pastors and workers from the provinces so they can meet and together pray and listen to the voices of their people. This office will also serve as a home for committed workers who will undergo leadership trainings and seminars based on Anabaptist conviction.

Affiliations with the Global Anabaptist Church

The Integrated Mennonite Churches, Inc. (IMC) belongs to the Mennonite World Conference (MWC), and some of the IMC leaders and bishops are members of the General Council. IMC is linked with other MWC churches and is part of the community of fellowship, worship, service, and witness.

Beginning in 1972, the Eastern Mennonite Missions (EMM), formerly Eastern Mennonite Board of Missions and Charities (EMBMC) and the IMC worked hand in hand in ministry. Until today, EMM continues its connection, support, and prayers with the IMC. Mennonite Church Canada (MCC) has just officially established its partnership with IMC on April 2011 when they committed to work hand in hand and send missionaries that will start the Global City Church Planting vision of IMC.

Fellowship with other believers

In July 15, 2011, IMC was recognized as a member of the Philippine Council of Evangelical Churches (PCEC), which is the largest network of evangelical churches across the country. The membership of IMC in the PCEC was approved by the Board of Trustees to enhance fellowship with other believers, and to strengthen the Peace and Reconciliation ministry that is being supported by both the IMC and PCEC.

The local churches of IMC, on the other hand, also conduct fellowship with churches from different denominations and groups. Although there is a challenge in facing minor differences in the doctrine of other groups, the IMC churches choose to focus more on the similarities and how they can make an impact in the community as fellow believers and followers of Jesus Christ.

Other Mennonites in the Philippines (non-IMC members)

Conservative Mennonites

Aside from the IMC, a Conservative Mennonite group also exists in the country. As noted above, one of the IMC pastors, Eladio Mondez, served with the Conservative Mennonite group from 1984-1998. Mondez was ordained as pastor in the Conservative group, and he also served as a teacher in the Christian Day School. The conservative group does not allow their children to go to college. In 1998, Mondez and his wife decided to peacefully leave this group so they could provide their children with higher education. For two years, they independently held their worship service at home. In June 2000, Mondez re-united with the Lumban Mennonite Bible Church which is affiliated to IMC. The Conservative Mennonites, which is affiliated to the Nationwide Fellowship of Churches still exist in the country and are actively carrying the Gospel to different areas of the country, such as in the provinces of Cavite, Bulacan, and Pangasinan.

Church of God in Christ

The Church of God in Christ, duly registered in the Securities and Exchange Commission as a Mennonite Church, has no direct connection with IMC yet. However, it is recorded that they had 219 members in 2010, and they are also connected with the Mennonite World Conference.

Conclusion

The journey of the Mennonites in the Philippines has been both exciting and challenging. Indeed, God has been so faithful and gracious. Through many different obstacles, the Peace of Christ sustained our church and continually gives us hope and vision for a peaceful future.

As the Integrated Mennonite Church of the Philippines is being prompted to actively carry the message of peace throughout our land, we are taking on the task and are getting ready for more challenges. As the Body of Christ, we are committed to active nonviolence despite the violence happening around us: in our communities, society, and the nation as a whole. We envision a country that embraces peace and reconciliation. We dream of a younger generation that will work harder to sustain peace in our conflicted land. Looking back to our history helps us look forward to the long journey ahead of us. Together with the rest of the world, we sincerely pray for the Peace of Christ to reign throughout all His creation.

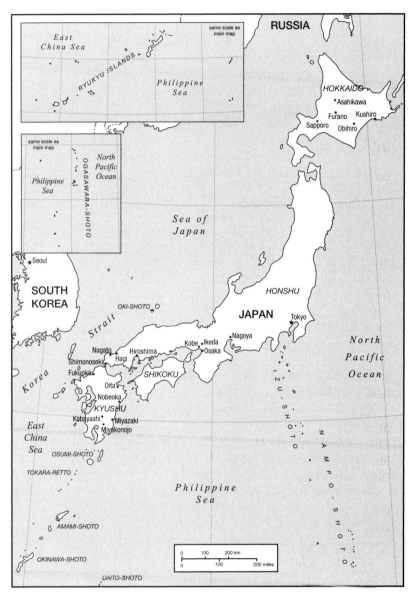

East
China Sea

RYUKYU ISLANDS

same scale as
main map

Philippine
Sea

RUSSIA

HOKKAIDO

•Asahikawa

Furano •Kushiro
Sapporo •Obihiro

same scale as
main map

North
Pacific
Ocean

Philippine
Sea

OGASAWARA-SHOTO

Sea of
Japan

★Seoul

SOUTH
KOREA

Strait

OKI-SHOTO

HONSHU

JAPAN Tokyo
★

Kobe •Ikeda •Nagoya
Nagato   Osaka
Shimonoseki• Hiroshima
Hagi
Fukuoka•

SHIKOKU

North
Pacific
Ocean

Korea

Oita•
Nobeoka•

KYUSHU

Kobayashi• Miyazaki
Miyakonojo

East
China
Sea

OSUMI-SHOTO

TOKARA-RETTO

AMAMI-SHOTO

OKINAWA-SHOTO

DAITO-SHOTO

IZU-SHOTO

NAMPO-SHOTO

Philippine
Sea

0   100   200 km
0   100   200 miles

Japan

The Anabaptist Mennonite Churches in Japan

by Masakazu Yamade

Introduction

Located at the eastern edge of Asia, Japan consists of four major islands – Honshu, Hokkaido, Kyushu, Shikoku – and many smaller islands. 127 million people live on these islands.

Blessed with a mild climate, the people of Japan took on a mild-mannered and industrious character as an agricultural people involved primarily in growing rice since ancient history. Between 500 and 600 CE, the teachings of Confucianism and Buddhism were introduced from the Asian continent along with literacy in the form of the Chinese writing (*kanji*) system. In 645 the Yamato dynasty established a foundation for centralized political power with the emperor at the center. Heijo-kyo (Nara), which became the capital, saw the construction of the Horyuji temple, now the world's oldest wooden building, along with Buddhist sculptures and other artwork such as the Great Buddha statue of the Todaiji temple.

After the subsequent establishment of the Heian capital in Kyoto in 794, a Japanese writing system was developed by modifying the Chinese writing system. Heian culture flourished in part through literature using this new system. The world's oldest novel, *The Tale of Genji* was written at this time.

After the establishment of the Kamakura Shogunate in 1192, the center of power moved to the Samurai class. The tea ceremony ritual and *ikebana* flower arranging enjoyed by Samurai were developed over the next few centuries. *Noh* drama was also popular during this time.

As overseas trade grew under Oda Nobunaga, who unified the country in 1567, Catholic Christian missions also became active. Culture flourished during the Azuchi Momoyama period of Nobunaga and his successor Toyotomi Hideyoshi. Architectural advances were applied to new castles such as the Osaka Castle, Samurai enjoyed *Noh* drama, and the tea ceremony ritual inspired developments in pottery for tea cups and craftwork for tools used in the ceremony. The tea ceremony valued a spirit of harmony (serenity and good relationship), subtle taste, and elegant simplicity. This spirit continues to influence the way Japanese live today.

After the death of Hideyoshi, the Tokugawa Shogunate set up in Edo (Tokyo) by Tokugawa Ieyasu codified the way of the Samurai in the Laws for the Warrior Households which taught Samurai to be loyal to their master and to maintain honor. The Tokugawa Shogunate suppressed Christianity and maintained Japan's isolation from the world for nearly 300 years. During this time Japan's distinctive art forms and cultural pursuits developed and gained popularity, including *kabuki* theater, *bunraku* puppet theater, and *ukiyo-e* woodblock prints.

In 1853, the arrival of Commodore Matthew C. Perry and the US Navy spurred Japan to break its policy of isolation. The Tokugawa Shogunate eventually collapsed, the social order of the Samurai warrior households came to an end, and the new Meiji government was established with the emperor at the center. To counter the influence of western powers, the new government adopted a "rich country, strong military" policy, strengthening the military and industrializing the nation. This led to Japan defeating China and Russia in successive wars, followed by Japan's colonization policy which eventually pushed the nation toward war and defeat in World War II.

Japanese society sets a high value on a person's educational background. This leads to excessive competition to get into the best schools, but the positive effect is that nearly 100% of school age children attend school, and the literacy rate is at the highest level in the world. Educational standards are high and the people are well educated. In some ways, though, this overemphasis on intellectual training is an obstacle to a receptive faith in the Gospel of Christ.

The religious environment in Japan, reflecting its historical background, accommodates faith in "eight million gods." Seeing no contradiction in mixing Shinto and Buddhist faith expressions, this pantheistic approach has trouble accepting the monotheistic concept of only one God.

The code of law set forth in 607 by Prince Shotoku extended beyond the realm of politics and challenged society with a close bond between political power and Buddhism. In 676 Emperor Temmu made Buddhism the state religion and promoted the building of Buddhist temples. Temmu also set in motion the creation of traditional State Shintoism and in 700 raised emperors to the level of divinity – a status that remained until 1945. This dual Shinto-Buddhist religious consciousness matured through medieval times, and as feudalism developed in the late medieval period, it was influenced by the Confucian culture of China's Ming dynasty. From that point on Confucianism was added as a third aspect of religious consciousness especially among the Samurai warrior class.

By contrast, Christianity has not been freely accepted into Japanese culture. It may seem contradictory on the surface, but this attitude pervades daily life in Japan. Though less overt in this modern information age, there have been instances as recently as in the latter half of the 20th century where people were ostracized by their communities when their behavior didn't conform to the community's norms.

Many Japanese still see themselves as being under the protection of the natural and ancestral deities of their village as espoused in their Shinto faith while at the same time observing Buddhist rituals as members of a local temple. This dual religious allegiance is a matter of custom that developed through history.

An illustration from a Christian pastor of the Japanese view of religion, passed on until today

I came home to a surprise one day in the early autumn after I took up my assignment in the city of Kanazawa. The leader of our neighborhood association, who happened to be a carpenter, was placing a Shinto symbol made with rope material (*shimenawa*) on the entrance of my church building. I counted as my friend this kind man who lived across the street from the church. When I asked him to take the *shimenawa* down, he didn't understand what the problem was, but he finally relented and removed it since I made such an issue of it. When there is a local Shinto shrine festival, all of the houses on the other side of the street are surrounded by one of these Shinto ropes. His perspective was that a festival celebrating local gods would naturally include the neighborhood church.

Unable to welcome my church members into a church building with a *shimenawa* on it, I of course refused it. As he took the *shimenawa* off, he said "What a pity. We were planning to collect offerings from members of our neighborhood association and bring them to you for Christmas, but that won't be possible any more."

Now this did not mean we were ostracized from the community. We continued to be on friendly terms with our neighbors. The daughter of the leader of our neighborhood association enrolled at *Hokuriku Gakuin* (a Christian school) and began attending our worship services. When I told her that it was nice that her father allowed her to attend worship, she replied, "Yes, my father said I'm in good hands listening to you. He tells me I should pay close attention to your sermons, but he also says I shouldn't get too involved." "Too involved" means getting baptized. The father was afraid that his daughter would have trouble marrying if she were baptized. This is a common Japanese response to Christianity.

What about Christianity, which bears allegiance to just one God? Many of the central figures involved in the formation of Protestant churches in the 19th century Meiji era were lower class Samurai who were committed to living lives of allegiance, so their loyalty to their new Lord Jesus was unwavering. As will be explained later, they left indelible marks in various avenues of society in addition to working earnestly to develop their churches.

In 1940, to rally support for World War II, the government unified religious denominations and forced them to cooperate with the war effort. Protection of religion was granted as long as the religious bodies upheld the emperor system and remained faithful to government policies. This was an attempt to force homogeneity through imperial ideology.

Because of this experience, when Japan lost the war the people lost hope in the wartime ideology of allegiance to a divine nation and its emperor. Gone was their loyalty to the state and the god linked to state power. In reaction to material deprivation and hunger brought on by the war, the Japanese now pursued materialism and turned their attention away from religion. Under the lifetime employment system in the latter half of the 20th century, employees were expected to be loyal to their company in exchange for having their livelihood guaranteed. This made it hard to accept Christianity because of its expectation of exclusive loyalty to the one God.

The freedom of religion granted after the war led to the formation of various new religions. Based mostly on Shinto or Buddhism, these new religions tended to attract converts by promising worldly benefits.

Enacted in November 1946 and put into effect the following May, Japan's postwar constitution clearly stipulates freedom of religion and the separation of church and state, but such separation is jeopardized by a common perception that certain customs and practices with religious roots are no longer religious in nature. This point is illustrated in the twelve-year battle arising out of a 1965 lawsuit claiming the unconstitutionality of a publicly-funded Shinto groundbreaking ceremony performed in Tsu City. While not denying that the ceremony appeared to be religious, the initial ruling considered it to be essentially a customary ritual rather than a religious activity that promotes Shinto, and therefore not in violation of the constitutional separation of church and state. The court made a clear distinction between religion and custom and concluded that customs aren't included in the realm of religion protected by the constitution.

The Supreme Court also acknowledged that the Shinto-style ground-breaking ceremony is a ritual unique to Shinto, but it did not consider it to be a religious activity prohibited in the constitution. While not denying that the ceremony has religious aspects, the court concluded that it is a secular ritual that follows common social customs.

When religion becomes deeply entrenched in people's lives in Japan, it appears that it is no longer considered religious. Even the judge admitted that the Japanese have a low level of religious consciousness which believes in Shinto gods and Buddha residing together and that the Japanese lack sensitivity in responding to the principles of "freedom of religion" and "separation of church and state."

In recent years secularization, aided in part by vulgar TV programs, has contributed to spiritual impoverishment as the attention of the Japanese people has shifted away from spiritual matters. With the bursting of Japan's economic bubble, loyalty to one's company is also starting to waver, and as has been repeated in the past, young people in particular have lost their spiritual footing and are looking instead to various forms of fortune-telling to guide them.

Christian Missions in Japan

Roman Catholic missions

In 1549 Oda Nobunaga became lord of the castle of Owari-Nagoya, strategically located in present-day Nagoya in central Honshu, and played a critical role in Japan's medieval civil war era as Japan began an historical shift toward the formation of a centralized feudalistic state. That same year Francis Xavier of the Roman Catholic Society of Jesus (Jesuits) arrived in Japan. Portuguese trade had made inroads into Asia since the early 16th century as Portugal set up settlements in Goa in India, Malacca in the Malay Peninsula, and Macao in China. Jesuit missions in Asia paralleled this expansion in trade. Francis Xavier became fascinated by a Japanese man he met in Macao and was inspired to initiate mission work in Japan. Other Jesuit missionaries followed and gained permission from local feudal lords to engage in mission work in Kyushu, Yamaguchi and Kyoto. Some feudal lords even accepted baptism, and their subjects followed suit.

At the height of this first Christian expansion there were over 200 churches, more than 100 clergy and 2 million believers out of a total population of 20 million. More than 20 medical clinics ("mercy shelters") were built as well. To his credit, Xavier established his mission policy based on a careful assessment of Japanese culture and its views about religion.

In 1584 the military ruler Toyotomi Hideyoshi, who had been friendly toward missionaries, decreed their expulsion and began a policy of suppression. Hideyoshi saw the changes in religiosity of Christian feudal lords' subjects, and he learned that Portuguese merchant ships were increasingly involved in the slave trade. He evidently feared revolutionary developments would threaten traditional rulers, and that it would become difficult to rule people who no longer shared the faith of their rulers. His decree to expel missionaries began with this declaration: "Japan is a nation of the (traditional Shinto) gods. The entry of the Christian heresy is therefore deplorable."

After Hideyoshi's death Tokugawa Ieyasu wrested control of the nation as shogun and developed economic ties with the Netherlands, a Protestant country that had defeated Spain. While deepening trade with the Netherlands, which he found was unencumbered by religious concerns, Ieyasu strengthened persecution against Catholics in 1611. In 1614 Ieyasu announced an edict forbidding Christianity and ordered the expulsion of all foreign missionaries, after which missionary activity died down. In 1637 about 40,000 Christians involved in uprisings in Shimabara and Amakusa were massacred in three days. The uprisings had occurred spontaneously among Christians who were enduring severe material and spiritual hardships in the face of the national policy to eradicate Christianity and in light of persecution by the local feudal lords. The national government reacted to this incident with an even stricter policy of isolation from the outside world. This brought to a complete close the first era of mission.

Protestant Missions

In 1859, after Japan abolished an isolation policy that had lasted 220 years, J. C. Hepburn and five other missionaries entered Japan. These missionaries served as instructors in the fields of agriculture and civil engineering to young people who were eager to absorb western knowledge and technology. Other US, Canadian and British missionaries followed them to help translate the Bible into Japanese, establish schools of western learning and open clinics to administer western medicine. Their work brought to faith young men who had lost their

Samurai status as the new Meiji era dawned. As followers of the way of the Samurai, these men considered loyalty to their master to be their purpose in life. Having lost their master, Jesus Christ in a sense filled the void as their new master requiring their loyalty. These men grew to be talented pioneers of modern Japanese culture and Christianity.

In January 1876 thirty-five young men formed the "Kumamoto Band" of Christians. The feudal lord of Kumamoto in western Kyushu had set about to regain Kumamoto's standing in Japan by starting a western-style school in 1871 to provide higher education. L. L. Janes, a US artillery captain stationed in San Francisco, was invited to direct the new school. Janes stressed training of character based on the style of education he had learned at West Point. In three years, he began teaching the Bible once a week at his home. Fifteen students attended the first meeting. The number grew to sixty a year later, and Sunday worship was added. By the 1875 winter holiday the number of believers reached forty. Nightly Bible study and prayer meetings led to a revival, and on January 30, 1876 thirty-five persons gathered at Mt. Hanaoka near Kumamoto to sign a pledge to dedicate their lives to Christian service. Thus they formed the "Kumamoto Band" of Christians and later formed the Congregational (Kumiai) Church denomination.

Also in 1876, the government established the Sapporo Agricultural College, inviting Dr. William S. Clark from the US to lead the effort. Under Clark's tutelage sixteen first-year students chose to be baptized as did seven second-year students. These students pursued active roles in society, among them Uchimura Kanzo, who influenced the development of the church in Japan, and Nitobe Inazo, who became under-secretary general of the League of Nations and acted as a bridge between Japan and the US.

In the 1880s Japan took a turn toward greater nationalism and absolutism. The Meiji Constitution of 1889 and the Imperial Rescript on Education of 1890 became definitive declarations of nationalism. Christian views of God and humanity were decisively rejected, Christians were viewed more and more as un-Japanese, and the church suffered a period of decline. During this time the emperor was worshiped as a god incarnate under state-sponsored Shinto, and citizens were expected to be absolutely loyal as the emperor's subjects.

In the twentieth century government policies pushed nationalism and Shinto ideology even more in an effort to further develop loyal citizens. As militarism grew in the 1930s, all Protestant churches were forced to merge into the United Church of Christ in Japan (*Nihon Kirisuto Kyodan*) which was established as part of the government's wartime policy. Some groups, especially the Holiness Church, suffered persecution and even martyrdom at this time.

Post-World War II

Soon after his arrival in 1945, Douglas MacArthur, commander of the occupation forces, repealed the restrictive Religious Bodies Law in November and took away the special status of Shinto as state religion in December. MacArthur put out a call for US churches to send missionaries, and many responded to that call.

Having lost the war and their spiritual base, the demoralized people of Japan grew interested in new religions. Young people especially set their hope in Christianity and took the initiative to visit churches. The years 1948 to 1955 were considered "a golden opportunity for evangelism," and mission activity was greatly blessed during those years.

The outbreak of the Korean War in 1950 brought rapid growth to the Japanese economy, especially in the mining and manufacturing industries. This fueled demand for consumer goods, diverting attention away from spiritual matters toward materialism. Until about 1970 there was heightened interest in socialism and religions that promised materialistic rewards in this life. In the 1990s forced conversions into fundamentalist religions became a social problem, resulting in suspicion against religion in general and also resistance to Christianity.

Anabaptist/Mennonite Churches in Japan

Anabaptist-related churches in Japan were founded by four different conferences: the Mennonite Brethren (MB), the Brethren in Christ (BIC), the Mennonite Church (MC), and the General Conference Mennonite Church (GC).

The Japan Mennonite Brethren Churches (MB) are found on Honshu Island. Fourteen churches are situated in and around Osaka, Japan's second largest metropolis, with one more in the neighboring Nara Prefecture. To the east there are six MB churches in and around Nagoya, Kuwana and Kawasaki. West of Osaka there are five churches in cities in the Hyogo Prefecture. In all there are 29 MB churches, located primarily in urban settings.

The Japan Brethren in Christ Church (BIC) began its mission in the Yamaguchi Prefecture, at the western edge of Honshu. There are five churches in key cities in the Yamaguchi Prefecture as well as churches in Nagoya and in Kodaira, a suburb of Tokyo. The Japan Mennonite Christian Church Conference (*Nihon Menonaito Kirisuto Kyokai Kyogikai*) (MC) has its twenty churches on the large island of Hokkaido, north of Honshu. Russia lies just beyond narrow straits to its north and east. Mission work in Hokkaido started on the east side of the mountain range that divides the island between east and west. The main mission field was the expansive agricultural region of the eastern plains. Five churches are in key cities scattered throughout the region, ten in nearby towns and villages that are declining in population, and five churches in Sapporo, Hokkaido's capital city of 1.88 million people.

The Japan Mennonite Christian Church Conference (*Nihon Menonaito Kirisuto Kyokai Kaigi*) (GC) has 15 churches in the Miyazaki, Oita and Fukuoka Prefectures on the island of Kyushu, south of the western tip of Honshu. The conference also has churches in Hiroshima and Kobe. Most of the churches are in urban settings.

Tokyo is home to the Honancho Church, which began in a missionary house to accommodate Mennonites from various conferences who had moved to the nation's capital. It is joined by two churches in neighboring Saitama Prefecture and one in the Ibaraki Prefecture to make up the Tokyo Area Fellowship of Mennonite Churches (TAFMC), established in 1964.

The mission field first chosen by the Brethren in Christ mission committee (Yamaguchi Prefecture on Honshu island) had a long local history and culture that was relatively closed to outsiders, making it difficult for Christian mission work to make inroads. By contrast, establishing churches was easier in Hokkaido because it was a newer culture with communities still in the process of being formed. Nevertheless rural eastern Hokkaido, chosen by the Mennonite Church's mission board, suddenly began to decline in population after 1960, just ten years after mission work began. The forestry and agriculture that had sustained the economy of the area suffered due to competition from imports from the United States and elsewhere. With the exception of some churches in key regional cities, this decline was felt in the churches as well.

Churches in regional cities also lost young people who left for big cities such as Sapporo and Tokyo to pursue opportunities in education and employment. This trend affected the development of GC churches in Kyushu and BIC churches in Yamaguchi as well.

In contrast to the Yamaguchi Prefecture, which was steeped in traditional Japanese culture, the metropolitan Osaka area chosen by the MB mission board was more open to foreign cultures and religions. In addition, young people who had left home to come to the city, especially for university studies, took an interest in American culture and approached North American missionaries, sometimes out of a desire to learn English. Many such young people were eventually baptized into the church. The urban area also had the advantage of having more people with higher education. These factors roughly influenced the formation of each church for the next fifty years.

Mennonite and BIC Churches in Japan

The Birth of Japan Mennonite Christian Church Conference (MC)

"We enter Japan, December 17, 1949." This was the declaration of the first missionaries sent by Mennonite Board of Missions and Charities (MBM) to Japan. The missionaries had earlier been inspired at the Fall Missionary Conference of 1948 at Goshen College. There they heard Dr. Takuo Matsumoto, principal of the Hiroshima Girls' School, tell of his experience of the atomic bombing, followed by an appeal to bring the Gospel of Jesus Christ to Japan. This left a great impression on the student body who then took up an offering to support a mission investigation in Japan.[1]

At its annual meeting held on June 11, 1949 in Hesston, Kansas, MBM passed a resolution to initiate mission work in Japan. It then appointed Ralph and Genevieve (Genny) Buckwalter and Carl and Esther Beck as its first missionaries to Japan. The two couples sailed into Yokohama by the end of that year. The Becks then went to Osaka and the Buckwalters to Tokyo to learn the Japanese language.

At the recommendation of MBM secretary J. D. Graber, Ralph and Carl toured ten potential mission sites in northeast Honshu and Hokkaido in August 1950. After consulting with MBM, the city of Obihiro was chosen for the Becks and the city of Kushiro for the Buckwalters.

Meanwhile in Osaka, Masakazu Yamade, a department store employee, became acquainted with the Becks and joined them in their move to Obihiro in June 1951 against the wishes and advice of his parents and friends. That November, Yamade joined nine others from Obihiro and two others from Kushiro in the first baptism which was held in the Obihiro missionary house. And so began the Mennonite church in Hokkaido.

Later Yamade would study in two seminaries in Tokyo and return to Hokkaido employed as a high school educator while serving the church in pastoral roles and as the conference's third executive chairperson as well as editor of publications. He also

The second group of baptized members of the Obihiro church (front row, sitting) with the first baptized members (back row, standing), 1952

served as chairperson of the Japan Mennonite Fellowship, a fraternal Mennonite/BIC organization.

At about the time Yamade went to Obihiro, Takio Tanase followed Ralph Buckwalter, whom he admired, from Tokyo to Kushiro. Tanase did seminary studies in Goshen and Elkhart, Indiana and served as pastor at Kushiro (Tsurugadai) Church. He also served as the conference's second executive chairperson and applied his gifts in the field of education. Ralph Buckwalter would later comment on what an amazing change had occurred in this man, whom he first met as a cynical young chain-smoker with slouching shoulders.

The Birth of Japan Mennonite Brethren Conference

Masaru Arita describes how MB Mission headquarters chose Osaka, Japan as a mission field. "At its 44th annual conference in August 1948, the North American Mennonite Brethren Church passed a resolution to provide Mennonite Brethren church personnel to MCC for relief work in Japan with the intent of eventually making a transition to evangelism. Henry G. and Lydia Thielman were then sent to Japan as MCC workers. Departing from Ontario in March 1949, the Thielmans arrived at the port of Yokohama, but were not given permission to land there, so they proceeded to Kobe where they landed on April 27. From there they went to Kyoto where they spent about two months in prayer. One day while on a fact-finding visit to Osaka, Genjiro Yoshida,

MB missionary Ruth Wiens describes MB beginnings in Japan

In August 1949 shortly before missionaries arrived, five workers sent by Mennonite Central Committee (MCC) began post-war relief work in Osaka. Before long MCCers in Japan requested the MB headquarters in the US to send missionaries to start churches. The headquarters asked me to go to Japan and look into Japanese language learning opportunities. When I arrived in Osaka on August 9, 1950, it was a hot day with a typhoon approaching. It was the time of the Obon festival. The smell of pickles and the sound of wooden geta sandals and festival dancing all contributed to the sense that I had arrived in the Orient.... After three weeks my belongings finally arrived from the US, but before I could even unpack, Typhoon Jane struck Osaka, suddenly sweeping the city with high tides. With no chance to flee, everything other than what I had on hand was hit by the flood and became unusable.

a disciple of Toyohiko Kagawa, approached the Thielmans near the Osaka train station and spoke to them in English. As they talked, the Thielmans began to feel the Lord leading them to serve in the city of Osaka. After much prayer and deliberation, they became convinced of the Lord's leading and acquired land in Kasugade, where they began relief work."[2]

Convinced of the need for evangelism in Osaka, Thielman requested MB headquarters to send missionaries. Because of the shortage of housing, Wiens and Thielman then bought a house with land in the Ishibashi Soen district of Ikeda, a city in Osaka Prefecture, to prepare for the arrival of missionaries. In March 1951, Harry Friesen and Harold Gaede arrived with their families, followed in July by others.

In April 1951 the missionaries chose the name *Eiwa* ("Glory and Peace") Church for the Mennonite Brethren Church in Japan and began Sunday worship service in a rented meeting place on May 13. The first baptism was held in July in the rushing waters of the Ina River. One of the three young people baptized that day was Masaru Arita, who later served as pastor of Ishibashi Church. Arita also served demanding leadership roles as chairperson both of the church conference and the seminary board. He eventually fell ill from overwork in 1986 and went to heaven in 1991.

Masaru Arita

According to his wife Teiko, Arita struggled through high school and university before graduating and becoming an English teacher at Momoyama Gakuin (St. Andrew's). While a university student, Arita became totally disillusioned with life and sought out the Christian church. In an autobiographical tract Arita later wrote, "As I listened to the words of Christ, a light shone on me from above. The soul of my eyes were then opened up to the eternal world, and the image of Jesus

Christ as the Son of God and Savior came into vision.... I then decided to believe in Christ and give my life to him."

Ruth Wiens, whom he had come to know through English conversation lessons, led Arita to the first Mennonite Brethren meetings and then on to baptism. After his baptism Arita continued to pray about his desire to dedicate his life to church ministry. Certain of his call, he then left his job in 1961 to pursue studies at Osaka Biblical Seminary. Before finishing his four years of study he took the pastorate of Ishibashi Church. He was a man of prayer who constantly sought Christ's love.

The Birth of Japan Mennonite Christian Church Conference (GC)

In 1950, William C. Voth, a missionary returning from China, visited Japan on behalf of the North American General Conference Mennonite Church to determine whether there was a need to establish missions. As a result of his findings, four families and two single women missionaries were sent to Japan in 1951. The mission board then approved the choice of the Miyazaki Prefecture in Kyushu as its mission field based on another survey by Voth and Verney Unruh.

William and Matilda Voth moved to Miyazaki City in January 1952, and by July, the first person came to faith. Later that year in October, Leonore G. Friesen and Esther Patkau joined the work in Miyazaki, and Verney and Belva Unruh began work in Miyakonojo.

While the first group of missionaries studied Japanese in Kobe, several young people who met them were baptized and formed the first fellowship. The missionaries, however, had no plan to start a church in Kobe. As they left for their assignments in Kyushu, the missionaries encouraged each of the believers to transfer to another church of their choice. The new group of believers was at a loss, but after discussion they formed their own fellowship group and received permission from the mission board to keep meeting in the garage. That is how this small flock came to be known as the Kobe Garage Group. Takashi Yamada was one of the key figures of that group.

About five years after World War II ended, Yamada was in his hometown of Kobe working for a major shipping company. He had enlisted in the navy during the war, and experienced first-hand the horrors of war. He then became secretly opposed to war while still in the military, and when he was told to join a suicide attack force, he refused. He was entirely alone in taking such an unusual stance for that time. Psychological pressure within his military unit was intense. Yamada attempted to escape the military but was caught. The fate of escaped soldiers in wartime was the worst imaginable. Just as he contemplated taking his own life, it was his good fortune that the war ended. By then most of his fellow soldiers had died in battle.

The end of the war brought with it a great sense of liberation, but soon he fell into a deep depressing state of nihilism. Having just turned twenty, he had no idea how to face the future, and there was no one to teach him how to live. Everyone was hungry and had to spend all their energy on survival.

Since he had to do something in order to eat, Yamada became a day laborer and later learned English while spending about two years working for the American occupation army. Using his English skills he then landed a job with a foreign trading company. There he immersed himself completely in his work to achieve social status and success, and to direct his thoughts away from his spiritual emptiness. Yamada managed to get another job at a prestigious shipping company. There too he fully immersed himself in a harsh, competitive environment, wearing himself down every day, desperately trying to get ahead in life. It was only a matter of time, though, before he felt spiritually exhausted and was unable to go on much longer.

For two years he had been attending an evening class at a foreign language school annexed to a church. The class was like an oasis in the desert for his high-stress life. There he met Mennonite missionaries who happened to come teach at the school. Yamada was forever grateful for this providential encounter. One day one of these missionaries, Peter Voran, invited him to his home. In a totally unexpected development, Takashi Yamada then decided to believe in Christ.

Yamada had attended worship at a church while he was attending English classes. Based on his wartime experience he sub-consciously disliked authoritarian Christianity, but the Mennonite missionaries he met made a very good impression on him. He asked Peter Voran to hold meetings. Fellow missionaries agreed and meetings began in the garage of the missionary house. And so began GC Mennonite mission work.

Takashi Yamada was invited in 1956 to move to Miyazaki Prefecture to become the first pastor of the conference at the Aburatsu Church in Nichinan. After going to Tokyo for theological training, fellow garage group members Masami Homma and Hiroshi Yanada also took up pastorates in Miyazaki Prefecture; Homma at Shinwa

Mennonite Church (now Oyodo Church) in 1958 and Yanada at Namiki Church in Miyakonojo in 1960. Several years later Masami Homma moved to Tokyo, and Takashi Yamada moved to Kobayashi Church where he continued unique church building efforts. Hiroshi Yanada transferred to the Oyodo Church after Homma left and served as pastor there until his retirement in 2001. Yanada also served several terms as chairperson of the conference.

The Birth of Japan Brethren in Christ Church (BIC)

Peter and Mary Willms arrived in Japan in July 1953 at the request of the BIC foreign missions committee. They began their work in Hagi in Yamaguchi Prefecture, one of the areas with the least number of churches in Japan. It was this former castle town of 30,000 inhabitants that saw the birth of the Japan Brethren in Christ church. The first baptism took place in 1953, the year the Willms began their mission work, and the Hagi Omotomachi Church was born.

Over time, the choice of this location affected the development of the church. Hagi, the first place chosen by the BIC mission board for evangelistic work, was a fishing and farming town. Formerly it had been a prosperous castle town in the feudal Choshu domain. Hagi had been home to Shoin Yoshida and his disciples, who contributed to the ideological underpinnings for the Meiji Restoration of Japan's national government in 1868. Hirobumi Ito, a student of Yoshida, and six others from this small region went on to become prime ministers of Japan.

Because of this background, Tojo notes that the Yamaguchi Prefecture has a tradition of people leaving for the big cities, especially Tokyo. Tojo writes, "By 1965, when Japan's economy was on the road to fast growth, over 60 Hagi Church members had left for Tokyo, but many of them were living lonely lives, unable even to go to church. Pastoral care for these people then became a major concern. Furthermore, the question was raised about possibly changing the location of the mission field if the continuing migration of church members could not be abated."[4]

The problem of rural or provincial churches in the context of the flight of young people to big cities and the decline in local populations has been a concern not just for BICs but for MC and GC conferences as well. Since the economy of the GC conference's Miyazaki Prefecture was based on agriculture, it was especially hard-hit by the nation's industrialization policies. Young people were supposed to be the focus of mission work and the driving force of church growth, yet they were leaving Miyazaki in droves.

When the Willms declared their intention to move from Hagi, their first location, to Yamaguchi City, and Doyle and Thelma Book moved their work from Nagato to Shimonoseki, turmoil ensued at the churches in the smaller cities that they left behind in June 1961.

One person who joined the BIC conference in its early years came from a Roman Catholic background. In September 1945 when World War II had just ended, Asao Nishimura narrowly escaped with his life by boat from Moppo, Korea and arrived eleven days later in the port of Hagi. He was fifteen at the time. When he entered high school the following year he joined the school's book club, since he liked reading.

During his first year in high school he found a Bible in the library and pored over the Gospel of Matthew. He could not afford a Bible since his repatriated family was poor, so he hand-copied the Gospel during summer break. Before he knew it the Word of God permeated the depth of his heart, and he was gradually changed by it. When he was in his second year a teacher told him he could find lots of Christian books at the Catholic church, so he visited the church right away. Attracted by the personality of the Spanish priest he went to church every week and was baptized a year later on January 1, 1948.

As time passed and he graduated from university, Nishimura became an elementary school teacher. Desiring to commune more deeply with God, he quit teaching after about two years and joined a Trappist monastery in Hokkaido. The life of silence, labor and study was ideal for satisfying his yearning for deeper communion with God. Yet he began to question whether it was enough just to satisfy himself, and that maybe he should communicate the Gospel to others who were struggling in their everyday lives. As he pondered these things Nishimura became stricken with uremia. Urged by his doctor he left the monastery to return home to Hagi. When he recovered he happened to meet an elementary school principal whom he knew and decided to return to teaching at his urging.

One Christmas he met American missionary Peter Willms in town and was invited to a Christmas celebration event. Working diligently in pioneer evangelism, the missionary couple accepted Nishimura warmly and made him feel at home. Nishimura then learned that this was the Brethren in Christ church. He then discussed with his Catholic priest about transferring membership, but the priest did not easily agree to a transfer to a Protestant church. Approval did eventually come, though, and he became a member of the Japan Brethren in Christ church. In 1965 he married a member of the Fukagawa congregation. Their daughter Nobue now serves as a missionary in Cambodia with Overseas Mission Fellowship. The Nishimuras moved to Nagato after they were married and assisted the mission work of Doyle and Thelma Book.

The Nishimura family, Nobue on far left

When the Books left for Shimonoseki, the Nishimuras moved their residence to the "house church" and continued the heavy responsibilities of evangelism and pastoral work. Nishimura also contributed to the formation of the Japan BIC Church as its first presiding officer.

The Birth of a church in the Tokyo Area

In the 1950s a large number of young people who had come to faith in the various conferences migrated to Tokyo to pursue higher education or employment. Since there was no Mennonite church in Tokyo, MBM decided that follow-up work was needed. In 1953 the board sent Don and Dorothy McCammon, who had earlier been forced out of China, to Japan. The McCammons purchased a missionary house in Honancho in Suginami Ward. Meetings began there and the Tokyo Church (now Honancho Church) was born. Three members were added to the church in 1956 at its first baptism. The McCammons were followed by Charles and Ruth Shenk who came to Tokyo in 1957 and supported the work of the con-

Bible class at the Honancho church, 1957

gregation while preparing for mission work in Hokkaido. They began special evangelistic meetings with the help of seminary students from Hokkaido and Kyushu who had come to Tokyo to study. Neighbors also began to attend church meetings at this time. After the Shenks left, Don and Barbara Reber served the Honancho Church for about ten years.

The Formation of the Churches from 1955 to 1970

From 1955 to 1970 the earliest churches were founded, church groups were organized, and various evangelistic activities and the training of Japanese leaders took place. Missionaries were still an important driving force for such church formation work during this period.

Japan Mennonite Brethren Conference Convention

By 1956 evangelistic activity was in full swing, with ongoing meetings in Amagasaki, Nagase, Minato, Tsurugaoka, Ishibashi and Kasugade. Many came to faith, churches were active, and men and women dedicated themselves to serve the church. In September 1956, there was a conference of representatives from the churches that had been established in those six areas. At that meeting a motion was made that a church conference organization be established with the aim of becoming self-sufficient. With the recommendation of the missionary organization, a council with seven Japanese believers was created the following March to function as a consulting body with the missionaries. The Japan Mennonite Brethren Conference Convention was then formed in 1958.

> The MB Mission in Japan held a conference at the Nosegawa campgrounds from August 30 to September 3, 1955 and passed resolutions to select the greater Osaka area as its mission field and to invite Kyoichi Kitano as its evangelist. Kitano had already served in Summer Bible Camps and in other ways and had gained the missionaries' trust.... Kitano expressed his heartfelt agreement and support for the Mennonite Brethren Confession of Faith.

New MB churches continued to be added to the conference in the following years in key cities in the Osaka and Hyogo Prefectures. Evangelistic work was also extended to the Nagoya area in June 1968 by Jonathan and Alice Bartel.

Japan Mennonite Christian Church Conference (Hokkaido)

In Hokkaido the first believers' conference was held in 1954 in Obihiro. Forty-three people from seven churches gathered for the sixth believer's conference in 1958 and formed the Japan Mennonite Church Conference, with Eiichiro Hatano as executive chairperson. In 1975 the name of the conference was changed to Japan Mennonite Christian Church Conference.

Summer Bible Camp at Atsunai Beach, Hokkaido, 1958

Church work extended beyond Obihiro and Kushiro during this period. Carl and Esther Beck sowed the seeds of evangelism far and wide in the towns and villages of the Tokachi area and began meetings in many of these places. Some of the follow-up missionaries assigned at this time were Don and Barbara Reber to Honbetsu and Ruth and Rhoda Ressler to Kamishihoro. Honbetsu Church was born in 1955, followed by Kamishihoro in 1956 and Ashoro and Taiki in 1957.

In the Kushiro area, Ralph and Genevieve Buckwalter also made inroads into surrounding towns and villages. Ralph was also involved in disaster relief work in Hamanaka in 1952. In 1953 Lee and Adella Kanagy started work in Nakashibetsu in the Nemuro area with the help of Takio Tanase and others. In June 1955, four were baptized and the Nakashibetsu Church was born. The Shibecha Church began worshiping in October 1959 soon after the arrival of Charles and Ruth Shenk. Five were baptized in January 1961 at the first baptism there.

Around 1960 believers who moved to the city of Sapporo began meetings at the Hokkaido Christian Center. At that time MBM revised its original mission policy in order to reflect the importance of evangelism in the cities. This brought Eugene and Luella Blosser from the Taiki Church to the city to aid in the founding of the Sapporo Church. Full-scale meetings in Sapporo continued from 1961, leading to the birth of Sapporo Christian Church (now Shiroishi Church).

Joe and Emma Richards came to Sapporo in 1963 to direct the work of Mennonite Hour; they held English classes in a rented room and began English worship services and home meetings. Kazuko Kanaya is a sister in the Lord who became a Mennonite and joined the Richards in the newly-formed Yuai Church. A friend whose husband had

died once asked her, "Why are you so strong and free of anxiety even though you were suddenly widowed yourself?" She then realized how much her Mennonite brothers and sisters in the Lord greatly comforted and supported her. Her important first meeting with Mennonites was when she studied English with Joe and Emma Richards. She herself grew up in a Christian home and was already a member

Kazuko Kanaya (far right) with Dr. Gan Sakakibara at an English Bible class

of the United Church of Christ in Japan, but she was attracted to Joe and Emma from the first time she met them, and ended up attending the fledgling Yuai Church.

Kanaya began learning about the history of Mennonites and their lifestyle by reading books such as *Contemporary Christian Communes*

Kazuko Kanaya's Testimony

I am pleased to be involved in "Menno Village," a community-building venture with a Mennonite farming focus. It is so heartwarming to fellowship with the many Japanese and international people who I meet here. Everyone has a heart for peace. I play with cute little children in the beautiful natural environment and cook for people working in the fields or building a new house. I have a lot of fun and my soul and body are strengthened. I am revived so much that I forget my age.

and 10 other books published by Professor Gan Sakakibara, an old acquaintance of hers. With more than an academic interest in anecdotal stories, she strives to live like the Anabaptist forebears, to practice peace and reconciliation and model the community life (*koinonia*) of the early church.

Kazuko Kanaya currently is involved in Menno Village, a project that is building koinonia centered on agriculture. She enjoys generously hosting and getting acquainted with visitors to Menno Village from elsewhere in Japan and from abroad. Kazuko Kanaya was also an active volunteer in the 1995 Hanshin-Awaji earthquake disaster relief work in the Kobe area as well as in the 2000 Mt. Usu volcano disaster relief efforts in Hokkaido. Her life

Kazuko Kanaya (second from left) at Menno Village

of service and her gentle, welcoming spirit continue as a witness to Christ.

One of the persons who has played a key role in the five Mennonite churches in Sapporo is Yorifumi Yaguchi. Yaguchi came to faith when he was assigned to teach high school in Kushiro and met the Buckwalters. After serving as interpreter in 1961 for Dr. Howard Charles, who came from Goshen Biblical Seminary to teach Bible, Yaguchi himself left Japan in 1962 to study at Goshen Biblical Seminary. When he returned three years later he took a teaching position at Hokusei Gakuen University in Sapporo.

Yaguchi preached and taught at Shiroishi Church and Yuai Church while teaching at his university. He later helped with the founding of the Shalom, Bethel and Grace Churches. His model of church is to have believers support each other's lives of faith through deepening fellowship and study. Feeling that a small church provides the best opportunity for all members to use their gifts, Yaguchi has encouraged the branching off of new groups as membership in one church grows beyond thirty. Indeed Kazuko Kanaya transferred her membership from the United Church of Christ in Japan to the Yuai Church not only because the Mennonite church is a pacifist church, but also because small house church groups have warm fellowship and support each other well.

As MBM's mission policy changed, church development spread also to key cities in other regions of Hokkaido. With the leadership of the Nakashibetsu Church left in the hands of a Japanese pastor, the Kanagys moved to the city of Furano to start meetings there in 1966. A Japanese pastor was called there the next year, and the Furano Nozomi Church was born. Located in an agricultural region, the church in Furano has grown steadily to this day. In 1967 the Shenks also left their church (Shibecha) in the hands of a Japanese pastor as they moved to Kushiro to start meetings in the Tottori district of the city in February 1968. Tottori Church was then established and the first three members were baptized in November 1969.

Japan Mennonite Christian Church Conference (Kyushu)

Meanwhile, the Mennonite Conference (GC) in Kyushu saw the birth of another three churches by 1960, bringing the total to six. These were the Kirishima Brotherhood in Kobayashi, Hyuga Church in Hyuga, and Atago Church in Nobeoka. The six churches met for fellowship every new year, and the Kyushu Mennonite Conference quite naturally came into being. In 1965 the GC Mennonite Mission and the churches in the Kyushu Mennonite Conference joined to establish the Kyushu Mennonite Church Conference.

In the 1960s Takajo Church in Takajo, Oita Church in Oita, and Kirishima Church in Miyazaki City were born, and in 1973 the Kobe Church that grew out of the Kobe Garage Group joined the conference. This was followed by a name change for the conference in 1975 to Japan Mennonite Christian Church Conference.

Japan Brethren in Christ Church Conference

After the founding of the Omotomachi Church in Hagi, the BIC proceeded to establish the Nagato Fukagawa Church, Takibe Preaching Place, Shin-shimonoseki Church and Shimoneseki Yamanota Church in Yamaguchi Prefecture. In 1963 John and Lucille Graybill moved to a Tokyo suburb to aid in the education of the children of missionaries. After starting English classes and cooking classes in their home, the Graybills began meetings in 1964 that led to the formation of the Nukui-minamimachi Church.

In 1971 the four BIC churches in the Yamaguchi Prefecture together formed a conference which they named the Brethren in Christ Church Conference in Yamaguchi Prefecture. This was superseded in 1983 by the founding of the Japan Brethren in Christ Church Conference, totaling seven churches including those in Nagoya and Tokyo. The conference values freedom in matters of faith as well as self-governance and self-determination. Some congregations have self-supporting evangelists while others have full-time pastors. The same is true for the Mennonite churches in Hokkaido.

Takanobu Tojo, who was the first conference chairperson and continues to exercise leadership to this day, came to faith in an unusual way. Tojo grew up in a Buddhist temple with a 1200-year history. Many of his relatives were priests, and his grandfather was the founder of his sect's university. By the time he was in high school, Tojo was reading Buddhist scriptures and taking part in the ascetic ritual of standing under a waterfall in the dead of winter. Even so, he became disillusioned by the infighting and jealousy that ruled his extended family.

When he left home for university in Tokyo, Tojo visited a church for Christmas. He then read the Bible, became convinced that Jesus Christ is the true God who saves people from their sins, and received baptism. He eventually became a college professor and returned to Shimonoseki to teach. There he met BIC missionaries, and by God's mysterious leading, became leader of his congregation when the missionaries left Japan for home. He then led many of his students to Christ and trained them to become pastors and lay evangelists. At the age of 43 Tojo himself enrolled in seminary, earned a doctorate in ministry and continues to exercise leadership today in the BIC church in Tokyo. He also serves as a leader of KGK, a fellowship of Christian students in universities throughout Japan.

The Takanobu Tojo family

Tokyo Area Fellowship of Mennonite Churches

In metropolitan Tokyo, Honancho Church was joined by Misato Church and Nukui-minamimachi Church to form the Tokyo Area Evangelism Cooperative Conference in 1964. This was then reorganized in 1980 as the Tokyo Area Fellowship of Mennonite Churches (TAFMC), taking as its members Mennonite-related churches in the Tokyo area.

Training of lay members and leaders

To train future Japanese church leaders, the MB conference opened the Mennonite Brethren Biblical Institute at the Kasugade Church in April 1957. Four men and two women enrolled the first year. In April 1961, the school was replaced by Osaka Biblical Seminary, a cooperative effort with the Baptist General Conference and North American Baptist General Mission organizations in Japan. At this time the location was moved to the Ishibashi Church where a seminary building and dormitory were eventually built. This arrangement continued until 1971, when the cooperative venture with the other groups was dissolved out of a need to unify doctrine and practice within the conference. The MB conference then started its own school again with the name of Evangelical Biblical Institute and renamed it Evangelical Biblical Seminary in 1976. This serves as a training center for MB leaders to this day.

The GC conference had no plan to open its own theological school. As a result, with the exception of Takashi Yamada, who studied on his own, the first generation of leaders mostly trained at Japan Christian College, later renamed Tokyo Christian College and superseded by the current Tokyo Christian University. A missionary, Robert Ramseyer, served part-time on the faculty of TCU for several years. Beginning in the 1950's and continuing to this day, the conference has had a representative on the TCU's Board of Trustees. The conference eventually chose not to recommend any one specific school in recognition of each church's varying needs and various levels of training needed. Students were thus trained at various schools, resulting in a broad spectrum of theological backgrounds among church leaders.

Among the BIC, Peter Willms initiated in 1961 a training school for Christian evangelism that met in Hagi for three hours on Friday

nights. Graduates Masaharu and Kikumi Okano became lay leaders in the Hagi Church, and Kimiko Nishimura became wife of the pastor of Nagato Church. Other graduates also contribute to the work of the churches in Yamaguchi Prefecture.

Bible class, Tsurugadai church, 1959

From the very early stages of its history, the Hokkaido conference, much like other conferences, held Summer Bible Camps and Winter Bible Schools to provide education and training for its members. In

addition to missionaries, evangelical church leaders were invited to teach. Basic systematic Anabaptist education was offered for the first time by Melvin Gingerich, visiting lecturer for the summer of 1957. Fall Spiritual Life Conferences begun in 1957 continue to the present.

Farewell for Melvin Gingerich, 1957

Hiroshi Kaneko, the first seminary student from the conference, enrolled in the interdenominational Tokyo Covenant Seminary in 1956. Another two followed him in 1957. Upon graduation, Kaneko continued his studies at Tokyo Christian College.

In 1965 Eastern Hokkaido Bible School (EHBS) was begun at the Kushiro (Tsurugadai) Church, with a branch school at Obihiro Church. And so the conference finally began its own formal leadership training with 7 credit-earning students and 15 auditing students.

This development arose in part at the Tsurugadai Church where Takio Tanase had been pastor ever since returning from his studies at Hesston College and Goshen College in 1957. With churches begun by missionaries and their co-workers now scattered throughout Hokkaido, there was a growing need for Japanese leadership in order to become self-reliant as a church. By this time the Tsurugadai Church had become a hub of young people who were enthusiastic in their faith. EHBS began here with the aim of providing leadership training from an Anabaptist perspective. Training in the faith and history of the Anabaptists especially emphasized discipleship, absolute pacifism, and the nature and work of the church as involving ministry shared by its members. Four of the students eventually became full-time pastors while two became self-supporting church leaders. All of them have played key leadership roles in the church conference.

In 1987 Mennonites in Sapporo formed a discipleship center to train leaders for home meetings and Bible studies in urban settings. Under the auspices of the conference, this venture was combined in 1989 with EHBS and became the Hokkaido Mennonite Education and Research Center. Guided by the notion that each congregation is to develop leaders, lecturers travel to churches to hold classes there.

Publication activity

The MB conference began publishing *Eiwa Geppo* (Glory and Peace Monthly) in 1956. It was renamed *Yokiotozure* (Good News) in 1960 and continues to this day. Hokkaido's conference publication was started in 1954 as *Menonaito*, renamed *Izumi*, and now continues as *Michi* (The Way). The Kyushu conference began *Izumi* (Kyushu edition) in the early 1960s, renamed it *Menonaito* and it continues today as *Mana* (Love). Guided by their editorial objectives, these periodicals have been used for lay education and for sharing information between congregations and organizations.

In November 1963, the MC, GC and BIC conferences formed the Japan Mennonite Literature Association (JMLA), and in 1966 published a translation of Harold Bender's *These are My People*. Since then,

JMLA has published over twenty titles in translation, most of which are Anabaptist-related.

Another significant source of literature has been the Anabaptist Study Series edited and authored by Gan Sakakibara. Formerly a member of the United Church of Christ in Japan (UCCJ), Sakakibara met GC missionary Ferdinand Ediger in 1953 and then became acquainted with Paul Peachey, who came to Japan in 1957 as an MCC Peace Section representative.

When Sakakibara traveled to the United States in 1959, he visited communities such as the Society of Brothers, Koinonia Farms, and Reba Place at the encouragement of Peachey. Sakakibara was greatly moved by what he found. Sakakibara began vigorous research on Anabaptism. He eventually transferred his membership to the Honancho Mennonite Church in 1976 even though some Mennonites urged him to remain in the UCCJ to continue spreading the truth about Anabaptism to the broader church.

Broadcast evangelism

Beginning in the 1950s, the GC conference sponsored a Christian radio broadcast produced by Pacific Broadcasting Association. In April 1961, the MB conference began a short, daily radio program. This led to successful monthly gatherings of music and messages for listeners at the Central auditorium in Osaka. The MC conference's radio broadcast evangelism work began in June 1959, accompanied by special meetings for listeners during the 1960s. In 1968 this activity was superseded by Hokkaido Radio Evangelism and Mass Communication (HOREMCO), a combined effort with other Christian broadcasters in Hokkaido.

Relief work

In November 1959, missionaries, seminarians and various lay people formed a disaster relief mission in Kuwana, a city devastated two months earlier by a typhoon in the Ise Bay area. The work continued for five weeks and eventually led to the planting of a church in Kuwana. This was the one instance

Inter-Mennonite relief work at home for the aged in Kuwana City, following a typhoon, 1959

when participants of all Mennonite groups in Japan did relief work together.

The Growth of the Churches, 1970 to the present

While the city of Osaka was busy playing host to Expo '70, the MBs held a three-day event at the large auditorium of the city's central public hall to commemorate its twentieth anniversary of mission. The conference had just performed its first ordination service the previous year, ordaining Jiro Takeda, who served as pastor of Osaka Central Grace Chapel for many years.

In October 1973 the MB conference adopted a ten-year plan with a goal of more than doubling its active membership from 600 to 1500. Church planting began in 1972 in Oji, Nara Prefecture, moving to Tawaramoto the next year. In 1975 new work began in Tokuyama, Yamaguchi Prefecture; Togo, Aichi Prefecture; and Senboku and Kawachinagano in Osaka Prefecture. Work also began in Hiroshima the following year.

Sending missionaries abroad

As the church expanded within Japan, the MB conference looked abroad as well for opportunities. Takashi and Kazue Manabe responded to their calling to serve in Papua New Guinea as the first MB missionaries from Japan. In 1988 Keiko Hamano was sent to serve in Pakistan.

Takashi Manabe came to faith when he was a student at Osaka University, feeling all alone in the busy metropolis. Through a group of Christian students at the university he was introduced to Ishibashi Church where he was baptized in his junior year. Each time he went home he fervently communicated the Gospel to his family until his mother and three sisters accepted the faith; they were followed later by his father. Takashi comments that his family was saved in a way reminiscent of Acts 16.

Rev. Manabe and his family in Papua New Guinea, 1985

After being appointed as a minister in 1975, Takashi and his wife Kazue went to Papua New Guinea in 1978 to translate the Bible into the Kwanga language. The work began by using the alphabet to put the sounds of the language into writing and teaching people how to read. It was very difficult to communicate the Gospel to a people who were practicing shamanism. After much struggle, and with

Rev. Manabe and the newly-published Bible in the Kwanga language

the translation nearly complete and publication arranged, the MB conference asked the Manabes in 1989 to return to serve in Japan. Takashi then concluded his missionary work and became senior pastor at Ishibashi Church.

The MC conference sent Hiroshi and Chieko Kaneko to Ecuador in 1969 as radio evangelists for Japanese language broadcasts at HCJB, a Christian short-wave radio station. Growing up in Tokyo during World War II, Hiroshi Kaneko and his family of ten lost all their possessions when an American bomber destroyed their home. They then fled the city to eastern Hokkaido with only the clothes on their backs. Life was extremely miserable. The hatred toward westerners that Hiroshi learned through militaristic schooling only deepened with this misery. One day Hiroshi set out to visit an American missionary, Carl Beck, to give him a piece of his mind. Carl could not yet carry on a complex conversation in Japanese, but he insisted that Hiroshi attend vespers and worship services. Attending his first meeting, he was shocked by the words that he heard: "Love your

Hiroshi and Chieko Kaneko

enemy." Captivated by the Mennonite way of life, Hiroshi repented of his own sin of hatred and became a disciple of Christ at Obihiro Church's second baptism service. With a desire to serve God and others, he went to seminary and became director of Mennonite Hour broadcasts upon graduation. Opening up their home, the Kanekos planted the Asahikawa Church, and after serving in Ecuador for four years, they moved to Nakashibetsu where Hiroshi served as pastor until his retirement in 1999.

In the GC conference, the Atago Church in Nobeoka organized a mission support group to send Chizuko Katakabe, one of its members, to work in England with a Japanese Christian Fellowship beginning in 1980. A daughter of an evangelist for Tenrikyo (a new Shinto-based religious movement), Chizuko was originally invited by missionary Raymond Reimer to attend Sunday worship when she was a middle school student. Chizuko respected her father who had died two years previous, and she was determined to follow his instructions to "become a person who pleases God and others." Struggling, though, with a sense of unworthiness, she found solace in the message of Christ's salvation that she heard on Sundays; she was baptized in 1964.

Chizuko Katakabe (center) at a home meeting in Kent, UK, 1984

After graduating from college and working for a publishing company, Chizuko served in Swaziland with MCC for three years as a high school teacher of English, mathematics and Bible. She then decided to enter seminary to learn even more about God. Feeling the Lord's leading, Chizuko enrolled in London Bible College. As an MCC worker she had no savings to draw on, but strangely enough, her needs were met for her to study for three years. After returning to Japan, Chizuko was called again to London where she worked for 13 years as an evangelist to the Japanese. She then left for home in 1993 to care for her bed-ridden mother. Back in Japan the Atago church welcomed her as associate pastor, then senior pastor upon the retirement of Takeomi Takarabe in 1997.

Other missionaries from the GC conference include Teruko Yano, a nurse from the Hyuga Church who served with MCC in Vietnam for three years, and Toshiko Oshita, a nurse from the Oita Church who served in Malawi, Sri Lanka and Ghana for many years. The Oita Church also gave regular support to one of their first members, Rick Derksen, who served with Africa Inter-Mennonite Mission in Zaire (Democratic Republic of Congo) from 1976 to 1998.

At the invitation of retired missionary Anna Dyck who had established a Japanese Mennonite church in the Vancouver area, Takahiko and Mari Yoshiyuki went to Canada in 1998. The Sadowara Church organized a support group to send them partly as a way to express gratitude to the North American Mennonite Church for sending many missionaries to Japan. The Yoshiyukis worked in pastoral and church planting roles with Mennonite Church British Columbia and served two Japanese Mennonite churches in the Vancouver area until 2008.

Facing a changing, diversifying society

The MB conference has continued to grow with Japanese leadership continuing the original work of the missionaries. In 1979, the conference sent Kiyotsugu Kurokawa to Inami, Hyogo Prefecture for pioneer evangelism. In 1985 church planting began in Yokohama. A total of 29 MB churches are now active from Yokohama in the east to Yamaguchi Prefecture in the west. Having followed through on the 10-year growth goals established in 1973, the MB conference numbered 1,900 members by the 1990s. Strong growth also occurred in offerings, exceeding 350 million yen (nearly $3 million US) in 1992. Today the MB conference is the largest Mennonite group in Japan.

In the MC conference new churches began in eastern Hokkaido as members moved to towns without churches. Hiroo began in 1974, Bekkai branched off from Nakashibetsu Church in 1978, and Shibetsu was established as a result of church planting by the Nakashibetsu Church in 1992. The Bekkai Church uses creative approaches such as music programs as it continues to appeal to young people. In 1988 a church began in Kitami among Mennonites who had moved there, bringing to fruition a long-held dream of the conference to have a church in that city. The church has had missionary support for thirteen years now, but with many members leaving the city for employment reasons, church development in Kitami has been a struggle. As of 2003 there were 20 churches in the MC conference.

An issue requiring urgent resolution in the MC conference is the question of how to deal with a broad spectrum of views on the nature of ministry and ordination. Some churches are led by pastoral leaders while others emphasize the sharing of ministerial roles among the laity, with congregational representatives chosen from among church members. The conference does not have a clear, unified policy for ministerial leadership. Half of the churches are led by lay leaders who have other employment. As society becomes more diverse it is important for the increasingly diverse church to consider again what it means to be Anabaptist today and to reach a proper understanding of discipleship and ministry.

Meanwhile, for the GC conference in the south numerical growth in the churches hit a plateau in the late 1960s, as the nation's industrialization policy drew young people away. To address this situation, the GC conference decided in its annual meeting in 1969 to move away from pastor-dependent congregational life to an emphasis on the priesthood of all believers. To that end, the conference decided to establish a school for its lay members, appointing a committee to design a curriculum and select teachers. The school, however, never got off the ground. Even if it had, it is questionable whether it would have attracted earnest students when young people were leaving the area anyway.

Coming out of these struggles, the GC conference began to set its sights on mission in larger cities, sending teams of North American missionaries and Japanese church

Tadayuki Ishiya (front, 2nd from right) is ordained pastor of the Hiroshima Mennonite Christian church

leaders to plant churches in Fukuoka in 1976, Beppu in 1978, and Hiroshima in 1979. The 1980s saw the births of Hiroshima, Beppu and Miyazaki Minami churches and the addition of Sadowara Church to the conference. With Hakata Church added to the conference in the 1990s, the conference numbered 15 congregations.

As Japan weathered two oil crises in the 1970s, companies worked frantically to survive. Surrounded by overworked and exhausted company employees, big city evangelism struggled to grow beyond small groups of believers. One unique venture in church development is the Kirishima Brotherhood in Kobayashi, Miyazaki Prefecture. Its pastor, Takashi Yamada, described the group's philosophy and practice. "In our brotherhood we are interested in examining our religion, faith, ideas and lives in light of the Bible and our religious tradition, namely the spiritual legacy of 16th century Anabaptists, and to carefully consider how our faith and practice can continue to take root and grow in the real world. We hope to share our own growth with others in the most natural ways through our everyday lives.... Meaningful encounters and ongoing association with others who seem to have similar interests and inclinations become very important."[5]

Many members of the Kirishima Christian Brotherhood's Kobayashi Church have moved away to other parts of Japan. This is especially true of young people when they graduate from high school. To encourage further development of faith and practice, Takashi Yamada sent copies of each week's sermon and other literature to far-flung members and travels himself to Fukuoka, Tokyo and other points in between to visit them.

As urbanization continues unabated, there is much to be learned from this approach of helping believers grow after they have moved to the big cities, encouraging the Gospel to spread like dandelion seeds wherever they go. Starting in 1982, Yamada also organized peace gatherings first named "Hiroshima Gatherings," and then "Cornerstone Peace Meetings."

Inter-conference cooperation: Japan Mennonite Fellowship

As mentioned earlier, the Japan Mennonite Literature Association was formed in 1958 as a cooperative venture. As MCC work in Japan drew to an end toward the end of 1960, hopes were expressed that the churches in Japan would continue that work. This led to discussions between the conferences and the eventual establishment of Japan Mennonite Fellowship (JMF) in May 1971 by the GC, MC and BIC conferences. The Fellowship's main objectives are to (1) study Anabaptism and apply it to the work of the church today, (2) promote fellowship between conferences, and (3) relate to Mennonite organizations overseas.

To achieve its objectives, JMF holds seminars, exchanges conference publications, participates in the Asia Mennonite Conference and promotes the International Visitor Exchange Program. In October, 2010, for example the 13th Anabaptist Seminar was held in Sapporo with 69 participants representing five Mennonite groups. JMF also raises funds for disaster relief for typhoons, earthquakes, etc. in Japan and abroad. It also raises funds for famine relief in Asia and Africa.

Conclusion: mission strategies, organization and education

Mission strategies adopted in the beginning greatly influence the way church development unfolds. First comes the selection of a geographical "mission field." Perhaps it was difficult to anticipate societal developments 10 or 20 years down the road, but it seems only natural that people would desire to move to ever-larger cities in the 20th century. There were times when people distanced themselves from Christianity due to extreme intolerance toward religious customs such as Shinto shrine festivals or Buddhist funerals. The cause of the Gospel would likely have been advanced in a different way if customs and beliefs had been addressed based on greater familiarity with the culture of the mission field.

Another concern was that those who came to faith in the early pioneer missionary period often were baptized without an adequate biblical understanding of the Christian faith. In other words, they were baptized without sufficient faith in the salvation and resurrection that comes from the cross of Jesus Christ.

Even after most mission agencies stopped sending missionaries to Japan, the Overseas Mission Fellowship (OMF) continues to send missionaries from many countries and is gaining converts through their work in urban settings. OMF uses multiple missionaries in one congregation and develops Japanese lay workers into leaders. The transition goes smoothly from missionary to Japanese leaders. There may be some lessons to be learned from OMF's organization-building and mission strategy.

Another initial task of mission is to find people who will form the core of the future church. Ideally these people will be adults with influence in their communities. Such people hold the key to building the church's foundation and for its ongoing development.

It is certainly easier to find many gifted people with various types of talents in large cities as compared to the rural areas. Many of the young people who dedicated themselves to become pastors early on in the MB church were university graduates. This was not true of the three groups who started their pioneer evangelism work mostly in rural areas. (This is not to deny that there have been gifted pastors from rural areas as well.)

A third task is to form an educational policy, especially for leadership education. Training in a theological school or seminary setting should be emphasized. As Anabaptists/Mennonites who hold to a unique faith perspective, we should not entrust the education of our future church leaders to seminaries of other denominations, even if they are inter-denominational. The value and benefit of having one's own school is evident from the experience of the MB seminary and of the MC conference's Eastern Hokkaido Bible School.

In English all of the church groups except the Tokyo group use the word conference in their names, but each of them functions in a different way. It is hard to say which group's style works better. What matters is that each must be able to unite together as a whole to advance the cause of the Gospel. This requires systems to be in place for resolving issues and moving forward together. Each group has a different agenda that it needs to address toward establishing a certain degree of common understanding. Prayer and unity in the Holy Spirit is the key to this end.

The faith development of baptized Christians is an ongoing need. The church must make good use of its new members, helping them fully grow and exercise their gifts as witnesses to the Gospel in today's world. Anabaptism must be fully rooted and the path of discipleship firmly followed and creatively passed along to the next generation. In spite of varied circumstances, each group has an ongoing need for spiritual growth, sanctification and unity through the Holy Spirit.

Each Mennonite and BIC group in Japan is now trying to find ways to help rejuvenate the church as members age. The training of successors to aging leaders is also an urgent concern today.

Korea

Anabaptism in Korea

by Kyong-Jung Kim

The Anabaptist witness in Korea began following the Korean War in 1953, when Mennonite Central Committee (MCC) initiated a relief ministry in and around the city of Daegu. In addition to offering food and clothing relief, MCC established a social welfare agency and the Mennonite Vocational School (MVS). MCC volunteers served as nurses, teachers, social workers and relief agents. As post war Korea's economic stability increased, MCC closed its programs in 1971. The quality MCC's workers and the positive impact of their programs, resulted in many calls for Mennonite mission boards to establish Mennonite churches in Korea. However, these requests were not acted on by mission boards since Korea already had many Christian churches. Perhaps the most significant influence of MCC's work was the ongoing enthusiasm for Mennonite life and practice carried into Korean society by MVS graduates.

A Presbyterian pastor who had served as a chaplain at MVS, and later studied at Eastern Mennonite College, shared his experience of Anabaptist theology and life with one of his associates, Lee Yoon Shik. Lee's desire for further Anabaptist education took him to Canadian Mennonite Bible College from 1992-1995. Upon his return to Korea, he moved to the northern city of Chun Cheon where he met a group of university professors who were disillusioned with the hierarchical and militaristic nature of the church in Korea and were eagerly seeking an alternative. As Lee and the others studied and prayed, their question was, "What is the nature of the New Testament Church and how can we bring that church into our lives?" Their studies brought them to the conclusion that the Anabaptist understanding of church was as close as they could get to the New Testament Church. In 1996 they left their traditional churches and founded Jesus Village Church, a self-identified Anabaptist congregation, the first Anabaptist church in Korea.

Jesus Village Church (JVC) has grown from a house church to a community of 50 to 60 people. In addition to developing an alternate

school (V School) for its children and starting an after school program for needy children, JVC has sought to share its Anabaptist identity by reaching out to the broader Anabaptist community. Four North American Mennonite couples have worked within JVC's ministries. In 2003, JVC hosted the executive committee of the Asia Mennonite Conference. Later that year, JVC

Bible study at the Jesus Village church

became an associate member of Mennonite World Conference.

Perhaps JVC's most significant outreach was when it joined with MC-Canada Witness and Mennonite Mission Network of MC-USA in founding the Korea Anabaptist Center (KAC) in Seoul in 2001. KAC was established as a resource center to offer information about Anabaptist theology and practice to those interested. An extensive library of Anabaptist materials offers students the opportunity to read and research. It also offers an opportunity to clarify Anabaptism to those in established churches who consider it a heresy.

KAC has grown into a multi-faceted ministry with an active peace program which teaches peace in Korea and throughout North East Asia. It offers conflict resolution workshops and practices victim-offender reconciliation. KAC also has a publishing arm (KAP) which translates and publishes Anabaptist books and writings for wider distribution. Connexus is an English language school associated with KAC which uses a faith-based, peace-oriented curriculum. KAC has significantly changed Korean attitudes toward Anabaptism by bringing in accomplished theologians such as Allan and Eleanor Kreider to teach and lecture in Korean churches and seminaries.

In order to support a new church plant in Seoul and to coordinate the growing Anabaptist network, MC-Canada Witness, MC-USA Mission Network, JVC and KAC formed Korea Anabaptist Mission Fellowship (KAMF), a forum for Anabaptist Christians involved in Korean ministries for fellowship, networking, resourcing, mutual account-

ability and coordinating ministries
with each other. With the support of
KAMF, Grace and Peace Mennonite
Church was established in Seoul in
2007 under the leadership of Pastor
Nam Guishik, a graduate of Associated Mennonite Biblical Seminary
(AMBS). Yellow Creek Mennonite
Church of Goshen Indiana also
offered significant early support to
this church plant.

KAMF gathering, 2010

Grace and Peace Mennonite Church in Seoul and Jesus Village
Church in Chun Cheon are currently the only clearly identified Anabaptist congregations in Korea. However, in reaction to the powerful,
politically motivated mega-churches, many individuals and groups
throughout Korea are looking for ways to make their churches communities of sharing, service and peace where each member's gifts are
valued and all are given opportunity to exercise their gifts. A group of
pastors in the city of Daejeon are meeting regularly to explore what
Anabaptist theology and practice means for them and their congregations The challenge to develop a healthy network through which
these emerging groups can meet, support and encourage each other
continues to be a top priority.

In November of 2009, a group of Korean Anabaptists flew to Los
Angeles, meeting with North American Anabaptists to explore ways of
strengthening their individual and congregational Anabaptist identities. The Los Angeles meeting was followed by further meetings in Cal-
gary in July of 2010. At these meetings, the name, Korea Anabaptist
Fellowship was approved for
this international gathering.
A third series of meetings
with wider representation
was held in Chun Cheon,
Korea in October of 2010.
A result of the Chun Cheon
gatherings was the forma-
tion of a formal structure
for the Korea Anabaptist Fellowship with representation

Prayer meeting, Jesus Village church

from Korea, Canada and the USA. A Korea Anabaptist Convention is planned for August of 2011 to bring together not only leaders but representatives from all congregations and agencies that identify themselves as Anabaptist.

Anabaptism in Korea had early ties to MCC and more recently to Mennonite Church Canada Witness and Mennonite Church USA Mission Network. However, the current widespread interest in Anabaptism and the formation of Korea Anabaptist Fellowship are driven by a deep desire within Korean Christians to find an alternative form of Christian expression that follows the New Testament model of the church and its head, Jesus Christ. The parallels between emerging Anabaptism in Korea and sixteenth century Anabaptism in Europe are striking and exciting.

Vietnam

CHAPTER IX

The Mennonite Church in Vietnam

by Luke Martin, Nguyen Quang Trung,
Nguyen Thanh Tam and Nguyen Thi Tam

Vietnam is a densely-populated nation, bordering the sea south of China, once identified with Laos and Cambodia as Indo-China. Catholic missionaries introduced the Gospel of Jesus Christ to Vietnam in the early 16th century and significant missionary work was done by Jesuits in the 17th century. Foremost among these missionaries was Alexandre De Rhodes, who not only evangelized, but prepared a catechism for new believers and set up a church hierarchy. The Latin script he used became the foundation of the national written Vietnamese language. The church was established first in central Vietnam, and then spread to the north and south. The Catholic Church developed throughout the next two centuries in spite of periodic repression and martyrdom. In the 19th century during the reign of the Nguyen emperors Minh Mang, Thieu Tri and Tu Duc (1820-1883) an estimated 100,000 Christians were killed. French colonial forces used this repression as a pretext for sending military forces into the country. Thus many people linked the Christian church to the long French colonial occupation. Even today some associate the Catholic faith with French colonialism.

Traditionally the Vietnamese people lived in a world populated by many malicious and auspicious spirits to be avoided, manipulated and controlled. Influenced by a thousand years of Chinese domination, Confucianism was embraced by the literate class while the majority of the people followed the Taoist understanding of life as taught by Lao Tzu and others. Mahayana Buddhism also came by way of China and was widely accepted. (Hinayana or Theravada Buddhism is dominant in neighboring Cambodia, Laos and Thailand). People had no trouble embracing elements of all three religious systems. Whatever the religious orientation of the people, ancestral veneration provided an order within Vietnamese society. The living continued their care for the departed, and the dead guided the living.

Evangelical Christianity was introduced into Vietnam in 1911 through the witness of the Christian and Missionary Alliance (CMA) in Tourane (Da Nang) in central Vietnam. The church developed rapidly there, and a Bible school was established in 1921. A Bible translation was published in 1926. Churches were also established in the cities of the north, but self-supporting congregations of the Evangelical Church in Vietnam (ECVN) developed more rapidly in the south.[1]

The French colonization of Vietnam naturally gave rise to strong resistance movements. The communist Viet Minh faction led by Ho Chi Minh would eventually succeed in driving out the French and later the American military forces. The defeat of the French garrison at Dien Bien Phu by the Viet Minh in 1954 and the Geneva Accords brought an end to the French era. With the partitioning of the country and population exchanges, large numbers of Catholic Christians and a much smaller group of Evangelicals in North Vietnam went south in 1954 and 1955.

Mennonites come to Vietnam

Mennonites from North America expressed interest in Vietnam in the mid-twentieth century. During the French Indochina War, the Mennonite Central Committee (MCC) considered a program of relief assistance to the Vietnamese people.[2] MCC continued following developments there, and in early 1954 executive secretary Orie O. Miller projected a program of relief assistance. When the Geneva Accords, ending French rule, were signed on July 21, 1954, Delbert Wiens, a Mennonite Brethren college graduate from California, came to Vietnam to direct a relief program. Wiens arrived in Saigon August 16. J. Lawrence Burkholder, a Mennonite who had worked in China for MCC, also came to Vietnam on a short assignment for Church World Service (CWS). Burkholder and Wiens together evaluated relief needs, and both CWS and MCC began relief programs there. MCC soon sent additional personnel.

The initial MCC relief to displaced persons was given in the Da Lat area, but MCC soon focused its work in the Buon Ma Thuot area of the central highlands where material aid assistance was given to displaced persons and to ethnic minorities. Dr. Willard Krabill came in 1955, and was invited to serve as director of the CMA leprosarium near Buon Ma Thuot, and expanded the medical services there. The last MCC person to work there, Daniel Gerber, was abducted on May 30, 1962 together with CMA missionaries Rev. Archie E. Mitchell and Dr. E. Ardel Vietti. They never returned.

In Saigon MCC personnel made friends with students, taught English classes, and assisted in the founding of a Vietnamese YMCA. MCC personnel developed a close relationship with the Evangelical Church leaders. For many years the Evangelical Church assisted MCC in distributing material aid to victims of floods in central Vietnam. In 1960 MCC developed a joint clinic and hospital with the Evangelical Church in the central Vietnam coastal city of Nha Trang; another joint medical program was opened in Plei Ku in 1966.

Hospital in Nha Trang, ca. 1965

Eastern Mennonite Missions (EMM), the mission agency of the Lancaster Mennonite Conference (Pennsylvania, USA), sent missionary personnel to Vietnam in 1957. Orie O. Miller also served as executive secretary of EMM, then called Eastern Mennonite Board of Missions and Charities. James and Arlene Stauffer arrived in Vietnam in May 1957, and Everett and Margaret Metzler came later that year to form the Vietnam Mennonite Mission (VMM). The main evangelical Christian presence in South Vietnam was the 30,000 member Evangelical Church; there was also a much smaller Seventh Day Adventist Church.

While learning the Vietnamese language, the new missionaries lived together in Gia Dinh, a provincial city adjacent to northeastern Saigon (now Binh Thanh District of Ho Chi Minh City). They regularly visited Evangelical Church (ECVN) congregations and developed close relationships with many pastors and lay leaders, and assisted the Alliance Mission in evangelistic ministries. They maintained close association

[The Mennonite Church] is similar to the Evangelical Church of Vietnam in many ways, yet consciously Mennonite. In defining the distinctions, the members refer to flexibility in worship and fellowship patterns, feet-washing, stronger social concern and a growing conviction regarding war. ... There is deep appreciation for the style of missionary service and the close identification of the missionaries with people and their suffering. The congregations feel a relationship to the larger world-wide Mennonite fellowship and also made a significant gesture in sending a verbal message of greeting to the Christians in North Vietnam via Doug Hostetter several months ago.

Paul Kraybill, EMM, reporting in 1971

with MCC personnel who encouraged them to work directly with ECVN rather than establish separate Mennonite congregations. However, ECVN leaders, who expressed appreciation for the Mennonite missionaries, said it would be best for them to work independently. Vietnam Mennonite Mission was granted official status by the government in 1964.

Phan Ba Phuoc, the first believer baptized (photo ca. 1965)

As the missionaries developed friendships, they began their own evangelistic ministries, including visitation, telling Bible stories in their homes to neighbor children, and teaching Bible classes in English and Vietnamese. The first believer, a young man, was baptized in 1961. Missionaries organized English language classes for high school and university students and adults throughout their years of service. Students were pleased to study English with native speakers. Some missionaries later taught English at the University of Saigon.

In 1960 the Mennonite Mission developed a student center located on a main street in Saigon across from the Binh Dan Hospital. The mission office was also here. This student center maintained a continual schedule of seven or eight English language classes with 200 students enrolled. Through the witness at this center, occasional persons embraced the Christian faith, were nurtured and baptized. By Easter 1963 four young men were part of the fellowship that met at the Saigon student center on Sunday mornings for worship services with singing, Bible reading, preaching, prayer and testimonies. Missionaries spent much time studying the Bible with these first believers, individually and in groups,

Mennonite Student Center

seeking to live out the Christian life with integrity in a country increasingly torn apart by war. Some of these new Christians became members of local Evangelical Church congregations. It was not until 1974 that a significant Christian community formed here at this Saigon center; the dynamic Christian youth group that blossomed here continued its witness throughout the revolutionary era of 1975.

With additional missionary personnel, the Mission in late 1964 began a witness and service program in Gia Dinh (now the Binh Thanh district of Ho Chi Minh City). The property was on the edge of Dong Ong Co, a public cemetery that became a slum as people fleeing the war in the countryside squatted among the tombstones. The community had both stable families and marginal people. There were many one-parent families. Some women had lost their husbands

Huynh Thi Dung teaching day care children at Mennonite Community Center, ca. 1965

in the war, and others had been abandoned. There was much sickness; tuberculosis was endemic. The area was also a hideout for draft resisters and army deserters.

The community center opened with a day care nursery. In 1966 this evolved into the *Rang Dong* (Sunrise) primary school (Grades K-5) under an experienced principal. By 1970 there were around 600 students enrolled in half-day classes; an MCC educational assistance sponsorship program provided tuition for 150 children. MCC also supported a family child assistance program which enabled dozens of young people from poor families to learn trades. A small business loan program helped families. Later a clinic served students and community people.

Phan Thi Tuyet Nga, principal of *Rang Dong* (Sunrise) primary school, with first grade class, ca. 1966

English language classes were also offered here; many of the students were teachers and government workers. From the beginning missionaries organized Sunday afternoon evangelistic meetings with Bible study, preaching – often by pastors from the Evangelical Church – and occasionally question and answer sessions or gospel films. Within a few months a congregation was established here when several adults and youth confessed faith in Jesus and were baptized. The small group of Christians from the Saigon center became part of the group here in Binh Thanh district. With the growth of the church at the community center, a five-member Representative Committee was elected by the church in 1965. Three members were Vietnamese, one woman and two men.

The Church Grows

Missionaries early sensed the limitations of giving pastoral leadership to Christians of a different culture. In 1965 Mr. Tran Xuan Quang[3] was

Pastor Tran Xuan Quang, his wife
Nguyen Thi Tam and their children
(l to r): Hong, Huong, Hang, Dat

invited to teach a Sunday afternoon Bible class. Quang was a graduate of the ECVN Bible Institute and directed a Navigators Bible correspondence course. The fathers of both Quang and his wife, Nguyen Thi Tam, were well-loved pastors in the Evangelical Church. The congregation eventually called him to pastor the church, and he was ordained on March 16, 1969.

One of the young men from the Binh Thanh congregation in 1965 enrolled in the Evangelical Church's Bible Institute in Nha Trang. After two years Nguyen Huu Lam became one of the assistants to Pastor Quang in charge of the children's Sunday school. Mr. Nguyen Quang Trung, a staff member in the student reading room since 1965, also assisted Pastor Quang.

A Bible school to train members of the congregation was begun in May 1969. The program included Old and New Testament introduction, evangelism, Christian education, doctrines of God, man, and the church, church history, and book studies on Matthew, John and Genesis. Ten courses were completed by mid-1971. Twenty students studied in this program; one took all ten courses. Later in 1974 MCC staff member James Klassen taught a course on evangelism with thirty persons enrolled.

The Vietnam Mennonite Church was birthed amid war and revolution. When national elections were not held in 1956, the National Liberation Front forces in the south, later called Viet Cong, began launching military attacks against the Saigon government. As attacks increased, the United States began bombing North Vietnam in August 1964 and introduced combat troops into South Vietnam in March 1965 while the Saigon government expanded its armed forces. Three members of the Evangelical Church who worked in the Mennonite centers were arrested and forcefully inducted into the armed forces that year.

The military draft was an obstacle to leadership training in the church. The two assistants to Pastor Quang were deferred in late 1965, and Pastor Quang and another man were deferred later. One youth leader managed to dodge the draft for the duration of the war. Two young men who hoped to avoid the draft by working as interpreters for government agencies were later inducted into the armed forces.

The area nearby the Binh Thanh community center was devastated by allied bombing following the 1968 Tet (New Year) and May military offensives by Viet Cong forces. The center property remained intact, but hundreds of nearby houses were destroyed in the bombings. Vietnam Christian Service (VNCS), formed in1966 as a union of MCC with Church World Service and Lutheran World Relief, provided resources which were used to feed and clothe many displaced people. At personal risk, missionaries hauled water into the area even before security was restored. The center distributed emergency relief: rice, flour, corn meal, canned meat and other foods, vegetable oil, clothing, blankets and cloth. Later VNCS provided materials to assist more than one hundred families in this area to rebuild their homes.

Mennonite congregation, Binh Thanh district, ca. 1972

Most of the MCC personnel within Vietnam Christian Service came from Canada and the United States, but MCC tried to internationalize the staff. Among the volunteers were Yoshihiro Ichikawa from the Japan Mennonite Christian Church Conference in Hokkaido (*Nihon Menonaito Kiristo Kyokai Hokkaido Kyogika*) and Devadoss Maddimadugu from the Conference of Mennonite Brethren Churches in India. Though both had assignments in central Vietnam, they had opportunities to fellowship with the new Christians in the Binh Thanh congregation.

Many community adults came into the Binh Thanh congregation after the 1968 fighting. Sixty-three persons were baptized in 1968 to 1970. While many of these had received relief assistance, others were attracted to the Gospel message after seeing the way the center and the congregation served the people. Not all of these persons stayed, but others were zealous in their new-found Christian faith, brought others into the church, and later assumed leadership within the congregation.

The Mennonite missionaries, all from the United States, were greatly troubled by the invasive American political and military involvement in Vietnam which at one time reached 500,000 soldiers. Many people consciously associated Protestant Christianity with the United States in much the way they associated Catholic Christianity with French colonialism. For this reason missionaries limited their association with American military and diplomatic personnel. Beginning in 1965, they released several public statements in the United States, calling for peace and a change in American policy in Vietnam. They also posted notices in the two centers disassociating themselves from American government policies.

There were thirty-six persons employed in the two Mennonite centers in 1971, though that number dropped a year later. The Rang Dong School at the Binh Thanh center employed the largest number. Some of the teachers who were not Christians also chose to follow Christ and became active members of the church. When some Christian staff from the Evangelical Church (ECVN) asked to become members of the Mennonite congregation, this was encouraged by the ECVN district superintendent. The 107 members of the Mennonite Church in 1970 included eighteen persons who had transferred from the ECVN. The Binh Thanh center programs were turned over to the local congregation in 1971. Pastor Quang, who worked part time with the VNCS material aid program for a few years, became director of the community center in March 1972. New facilities built the same year included a pastor's residence, worship area, enlarged facilities for the Rang Dong School, a clinic, sewing room, and office space.

The Binh Thanh congregation had a full schedule of activities. On Sunday mornings at 8:00 Nguyen Huu Lam and Nguyen Quang Trung led the children's Bible class. The men and women met at 9:30 for Sunday school classes. The main worship hour was 11:00 to 12:00 with more than one hundred persons attending. Services consisted of singing hymns to piano accompaniment from the Evangelical Church

(ECVN) hymnbook, mostly hymns and gospel songs which Christians had translated from the missionaries' hymn books, Bible readings, prayer, testimonies and preaching. The first Sunday of the month the Lord's Supper was commemorated, a pattern practiced by the ECVN. There were baptismal services every few months after several months of catechetical instruction. Both adults and young people were being received into the church. Baptism was usually by pouring; in ECVN congregations it was by immersion in a baptismal pool.

Pastor Tran Xuan Quang baptizing, assisted by Nguyen Quang Trung, ca. 1968

The youth group met Sunday afternoons. There was a Tuesday afternoon women's home Bible study, a very significant nurture ministry that involved as many as eighteen people. There were Thursday evening prayer meetings at the church led by various lay members. Thirty-

Women's witnessing group led by Mrs. Cu Trac (on right)

five adults plus children would gather to talk about the Christian life and to pray for each other with various lay men and women leading the Bible discussions. On Saturday evenings there were home Bible study and prayer gatherings.

With the school and social service ministries, the center was always a buzz of activities. There was a monthly program including Gospel preaching for the young people studying trades. At Christmas time the congregation and center prepared three programs: for the youth studying trades, for the Rang Dong School, and for the congregation. Some years a summer Bible school was held; in June 1972 there were 250 children enrolled in morning classes.

Wishing to see vibrant congregations formed in other areas, church and mission leaders in 1970 established another center in the Mekong delta at Can Tho, a city 170 kilometers south-west of Saigon. Here a reading room was opened, and missionaries taught English, both at the center and in the university. There were weekly Bible classes, and a girls' homemaking class. The mission also worked with Christian Youth for Social Service (CYSS), a fledgling organization of ECVN Christian university graduates and professional people who were inspired by MCC and other international Christian agencies to carry out service ministries. A CYSS male student hostel was opened here. In early 1975 the Mennonite Mission purchased an apartment building for the hostel and student center, but this program never developed fully due to the dramatic events of April 1975. The church learned about Mennonite churches in other countries through visits of church leaders from Japan, India, Indonesia, Taiwan and the United States. Pastor Quang and Mr. Nguyen Van Ninh, a long-time staff member of MCC and VNCS, attended the first Asian Mennonite Conference in India in October 1971. The following year the Vietnam church hosted the Mennonite-sponsored Eighth International Reconciliation Work Camp with a work project at the Evangelical hospital in Nha Trang. Participants came from Japan, Hong Kong, Taiwan and the Philippines.

Representatives at First Asia Mennonite Conference, Dhamtari, India, 1971 (l to r): *Tran Xuan Quang*, Vietnam; *Soehadiweko Djojodihardjo*, Indonesia; *Pyarelal Joel Malagar*, India; *Everett G. Metzler*, Hong Kong missionary; *Takashi Yamada*, Japan; *Paul Lin* (*Lin Ching-he*), Taiwan

Church growth led to the formation of a seven-member Joint Administrative Council in August 1971 consisting of three missionaries and four local persons. The church became autonomous in 1973 as the *Hoi Thanh Tin Lanh, he phai Mennonite* (Evangelical Church, Mennonite). A five-member Church Administrative Committee was selected to give overall direction to church development. Missionaries expressed readiness to work under an all-Vietnamese committee, but local leaders requested that two missionaries serve on this committee. There was also a larger Advisory Council, which included the deacons, that met quarterly to share concerns and ideas. These meetings were opportunities for very frank conversations between missionaries and local church leaders.

Church leaders drew up a preliminary statement of faith, and began preparing a constitution. In August 1974 the Church Administrative Committee called a meeting of twenty-five church leaders and missionaries where the local authority of the church was affirmed, an emphasis of critical importance in light of the military and political revolution of April 30, 1975. Total membership in the Mennonite Church on the eve of the revolution was 152.

Although the Mennonite Church came into being during a turbulent war period, there was hardly any way the church could anticipate the chaos that characterized March and April 1975 as the revolutionary military forces closed in on Saigon. In early March Pastor Quang went to North America to attend the annual EMM missionary conference. By late March South Vietnam's President Nguyen Van Thieu ordered his troops to leave the highlands after the army from the North attacked. Still no one realized how quickly things would change. On Easter Sunday, March 30, there were not enough seats for the 200 people who gathered to worship at the Binh Thanh congregation. By the next Sunday, several missionary families due for a summer furlough had left the country. The remaining missionary went to Bangkok late April on business. When the People's Revolutionary Army rolled into Saigon and to victory on April 30, 1975, the missionaries were all gone, though four MCC men remained.

The Revolutionary Period

On Sunday morning, May 4, 1975, both congregations in Saigon and in Binh Thanh district met for worship, but hardly "as usual." Everyone was aware that the former political order was gone. A battle for Saigon had been averted, and all thanked God that the military conflicts spanning three decades were ended. The war was over.

Fear of living under a communist government, fear of reprisals, and fear of an unknown future had caused unimaginable panic among much of the urban population in preceding weeks. The rapid rout

---

We will stay!

On April 22, 1975 just a week before the victorious army occupied Saigon, Nguyen Dinh Tin, an MCC staff person who was youth leader of the Binh Thanh congregation, composed a statement which he and other members of the Mennonite Church signed, entitled *"A Declaration of Mennonites Willing to Remain in Vietnam."*

We, Vietnamese Mennonites, ... declare:

We will not emigrate to a foreign country, regardless of the events which take place in Vietnam.

We are ready to serve people in any situation.

We Mennonites believe that God is above all else, even government. We are willing to accept any suffering.

We Vietnamese believe that Vietnamese must live and die in Vietnam. In difficult situations, we must be even more prepared to serve the people.

We Mennonites call on all Vietnamese who remain in the country to remain calm and take part in rebuilding the ruins, and work to ease the sufferings of our brothers and sisters.

We use love as a basis for reconciliation among all people.

We believe in God's power to change difficult situations.

Mennonites must live a life of peace and joy, regardless of the environment.

We Vietnamese Mennonites believe that "to live for God is to serve the people," and "to die is to die for God and thus live with him."

of the Saigon armies by the swift movement of the revolutionary military forces, the flight of the civilians from many cities in central Vietnam, and frightful rumors had combined to propel many people to leave the country. But most of the church members stayed.

The next days and weeks saw many changes affecting all religious groups within South Vietnam.[4] The entire leadership team of the Binh Thanh Mennonite congregation was intact except for Pastor Quang. The congregation elected Nguyen Quang Trung to administer the church and the community center, and assigned some pastoral ministries to Nguyen Huu Lam. The Rang Dong School closed, but the social programs and the clinic continued for a time. Some of the church members who had fled the countryside during the war now returned to their fields. One of these farmers was killed when his hoe detonated unexploded ordnance in his field. But two-thirds of the congregation remained in the city.

The local government revolutionary committee confiscated the Binh Thanh church center on May 23, although the church auditorium and parsonage were returned two days later. But there was more trouble to come. Lam, living alone at the church center, invited a local government official to move in, and by September it was difficult for the church to meet there due to armed guards. At this point the congregation was approached by Mr. Nguyen Thanh Long, an Evangelical Church layman and member of the National Liberation Front presidium of Ho Chi Minh City, who was working to unite all the evangelical churches into a United Evangelical Church. Believing he could assist them in evicting the governmental official and his armed guards, the congregation joined this united church.

In early October the congregation signed an agreement with the Department of Education for the classrooms to be used as a public school since private schools were no longer permitted to operate. Most of the previous teachers were retained, and the school – which kept the Rang Dong name – reopened with around 700 students in two levels (grades 1-5, 6-12). The church was permitted to use the auditorium for congregational meetings. The crowd attending the traditional Christmas Eve service included some who had already moved back to the countryside and returned for this special occasion. By this time the local district People's Committee and the Fatherland Front required all churches and pagodas to register their religious activities and special holiday celebrations with the local authorities.

James Klassen, one of the MCC men who had stayed, assisted the congregation at the Saigon center after the government change, often teaching in the Sunday morning worship service, and leading the class for new believers on Thursday evenings. Several young adults were baptized into the church in June and others in December. Choirs from the Binh Thanh Mennonite congregation participated in the Christmas service Sunday afternoon, December 21. Soon after the revolution it became clear that the new government would not permit the four MCC men to engage in any meaningful social services, so they made plans to leave. The last of the men left in October 1976.

Uncertain Years

The Binh Thanh congregation continued to meet until 10 June 1978 when the People's Committee of Ho Chi Minh City confiscated the church properties. Many other church and pagoda properties throughout the country were also confiscated. The Saigon youth center property was eventually used by the Binh Dan Hospital located across the street.

In the first years after the revolution some religious leaders – Buddhist bonzes, Catholic priests and Evangelical Church pastors – were imprisoned and many worship centers closed. Some of the leaders of the Binh Thanh congregation were denounced by local authorities and detained for a short time. There was pressure exerted on those without employment to move out into New Economic Zones, a government program to depopulate the city and to exploit untilled land, often in areas with poor soil and little rainfall. Trung encouraged believers of the Mennonite church remaining in the area to attend the Grace Baptist congregation or other Evangelical Church congregations in Ho Chi Minh City that still remained open.

This next decade was a difficult time in Vietnam. Though the country was now united, outside aid ended and trade was restricted; life became extremely difficult for most people. Many people fled the country by boat. Tens of thousands of military officers and some civilian leaders associated with the former government were imprisoned in re-education camps. Even though many religious leaders were imprisoned, courageous Christian pastors continued their ministry. When a few Evangelical Christian leaders who espoused the expression of charismatic gifts were no longer welcomed within the Evangelical Church, they began meeting in homes, starting what became a most significant house church movement throughout the whole country. In Ho Chi

Minh City two ECVN pastors of rapidly-growing congregations were imprisoned for several years and eventually exiled from the country. During these years MCC continued a ministry in Vietnam. When the war ended in 1975, MCC proposed and was able to implement a large medical and educational aid program and later gave agricultural assistance. Since the government did not permit resident personnel, MCC administered these ongoing programs from a Bangkok base. By 1990 MCC was able to open an office in Hanoi. MCC in 2004 celebrated a half-century of service in Vietnam.

New Hope

In 1986 the government began to implement a market economy which slowly led to improved economic and social freedom for the whole society. Already in 1983 Nguyen Quang Trung, now functioning as pastoral leader of the Mennonite church in Vietnam, invited believers to meet to worship the Lord in his home in Binh Thanh district. Sometimes only a few people gathered; as many as seventy came to a Christmas celebration. Permission had to be requested from the local authorities for each meeting. The church experienced much harassment; often consent was not granted before the time of the announced meetings and, even with permission, security police sometimes dismissed the meetings.

Pastor Trung, who supported his family by teaching English, reported in 1988 that there were thirty families totaling 200 persons related to the Mennonite church, most of them living in Binh Thanh district of Ho Chi Minh City. Some of these had recently come to faith. A new church council was formed, and the congregation made plans to resume regular meetings for Bible study, fellowship, and worship. Trung contacted local and city representatives of the People's Committee and the office of religious affairs, requesting that the church properties be returned to the church. As of this writing, the government has not yet done so.

In 1995 a representative of Eastern Mennonite Mission visited Vietnam to consider renewed ministry, and conferred with government officials and visited persons in the Mennonite Church. The Mennonite Church in Canada had translated into Vietnamese a draft of the *Confession of Faith in a Mennonite Perspective* which was prepared by two North American Mennonite bodies, the Mennonite Church and the General Conference Mennonite Church. Pastor Trung was given a copy of this statement of faith as a resource. He copied this document and sent it to local and national government officials as an expression of Mennonite faith and life, reminding them that the Mennonite Church was committed to both worshipping God and serving the people. This international expression of the Mennonite faith also reinforced the Vietnam Mennonite Church's argument that it was not a local cult.

Gerry and Donna Keener came to Vietnam in 1997 as representatives of Eastern Mennonite Mission. They studied the Vietnamese language in the University of Ho Chi Minh City, and eventually became involved with an international school in the city. As he was able, Keener attended special meetings organized by the Binh Thanh congregation. He also accompanied church members on some of their relief teams to distribute food, clothing and blankets to flood victims in central Vietnam and in the Mekong delta. These projects were coordinated with the local Red Cross chapters or local government agencies. Mrs. Ngo Thi Bich, Pastor Trung's wife, who had many years of social work experience at the Binh Thanh community center, also arranged for teams of doctors and medical students to provide relief and medical assistance. In addition to flood relief assistance, since 1998 the Vietnam Mennonite Church has organized other relief projects, like a medical team to perform eye cataract surgery in central Vietnam. Church members also organized "love classes" to teach poor and neglected children to read and write in Ho Chi Minh City's Binh Thanh district.

Community women preparing clothing to donate to flood victims in central Vietnam

In the late 1990s local authorities still would not give permission for the congregation to regularly meet for worship, and even threatened to confiscate Trung's home if meetings were held there. Church members tried to meet monthly in homes. On occasion the congregation would meet on Sunday afternoons in the facilities of an Evangelical Church congregation nearby. Pastor Trung became more active in teaching and instructing for baptism, and rented vans to take new Christians to nearby lakes for baptism. Over a period of

Pastor Nguyen Quang Trung

a few years Trung baptized 150 believers into the Binh Thanh congregation, and nearly 300 believers in Quang Ngai province of central Vietnam. During this difficult period church leaders committed their lives to deal with all kinds of needs, motivated by the Lord's call to carry out the Great Commission entrusted to them. It was not until 2003 that the Binh Thanh congregation again began meeting for worship regularly on Sunday afternoons in a rented property on a main street. When this was closed after eight months at the request of authorities, the congregation soon rented a smaller place in a back street.

After the government in 1976 closed the Bible Institute of the Evangelical Church at Nha Trang, leaders of the Evangelical Church and other independent churches developed many different training programs; some of these were lay training programs used in the churches before 1975. During the late 1980s and into the 90s visiting pastors from the Philippines, Singapore, Korea and other Asian countries came to provide teaching seminars, and later teachers came from North America. Trung and other Mennonite Church persons enrolled in some of these training programs.

New Developments

Following the flight of many Vietnamese from their country at the time of the 1975 revolution and the later exodus of the "boat people," several Vietnamese Mennonite congregations were founded in Canada and the United States. Pastor Tran Xuan Quang with his family settled in Philadelphia where he became the founding pastor of a Vietnamese Mennonite congregation. In the early 1990s he and his wife visited his mother in Vietnam and were able to fellowship with and encourage members of the Mennonite church in Binh Thanh district of Ho Chi Minh City.

These Vietnamese Mennonite churches formed the North American Vietnamese Mennonite Fellowship (NAVMF) with a stated vision of encouraging evangelism and church development both in North America and in Vietnam. Early in 1998 Pastor Pham Huu Nhien, president of NAVMF, traveled to Vietnam and met with leaders of independent house churches, inviting them to work with the NAVMF in evangelism and church planting. The *Mennonite Confession of Faith* was accepted by an association of house churches with around 300 members and seven workers and this group received a certificate of recognition by NAVMF and Mennonite Church, Canada. The following year Pastor Nhien participated in the establishment of a provisional Vietnam Mennonite Church with Pastor Nguyen Hong Quang as chairman.

Nguyen Hong Quang came from Quang Ngai province in central Vietnam and was active in evangelism for two decades in his native area as well as in the central highlands among ethnic minorities. Frequently imprisoned for short periods by the authorities for his evangelistic work, he eventually came to Ho Chi Minh City where he gave leadership to a growing house church. Here he also studied law. With his legal training he was invited to provide legal counsel to an association of house churches. Frequently challenging the restrictive policies of local authorities, Quang built a large meeting room at the rear of his home in the city's District 2 where his congregation met. An effective mentor who has trained many young leaders, he also developed creative ministries like a Christian scouting organization.

There were other unplanned developments. In early 1999 a former missionary had a serendipitous encounter with Nguyen Minh Sang, pastor of several independent house congregations at Hoi An, an old city south of Da Nang. When Sang requested guidance on several theological issues, he was sent a copy of the Mennonite *Confession of Faith*. A few months later he and other leaders requested a relationship with the Mennonite Church.

Nguyen Minh Sang, General Secretary of VMC, baptizing a new believer at Hoi An, central Vietnam, 2010

Although many congregations of the Evangelical Church continued to meet after 1975, even with restrictions, it was granted legal status only in early 2001 as the Evangelical Church of Vietnam, South. This brought greater freedom for religious activities to most congregations related to this church body. In the central highlands, however, many ethnic minority congregations historically related to the Evangelical Church were not permitted membership and were even denied permission to meet.

The total number of baptized Protestant Christians in Vietnam at this time was around one million, or 1.2 percent of the country's population. More than half of these Christians came from some of the more than fifty ethnic minority groups who make up more than ten per cent of the country's population. These dedicated Christians insisted on meeting for worship and fellowship even though some leaders were imprisoned, and some pastors even killed. Unable to associate with the Evangelical Church (South), many associated with other denominations or independent groups. When leaders related to the District 2 Mennonite church group offered spiritual support, a few of these ethnic Christian communities affiliated with the Mennonite church. In early 2003 a pastor in Kon Tum province related to the District 2 Mennonite administration reported the formation of a Mennonite conference in the highland area with several thousand members.

Given the restrictive government religious policy at that time, these leaders of Mennonite-related groups in different parts of the country had no opportunity to meet one another, and in many cases were not even aware of the other groups. However, by early 2003 Pastor Nguyen Quang Trung (Binh Thanh district church) and Pastor Nguyen Hong Quang (District 2 church) met and called for the convening of a general conference of the Mennonite Church in Vietnam. When the Conference convened on July 27-29, 2003, twenty-some official delegates came from churches in several provinces, as well as from Ho Chi Minh City. While most of the delegates were from the majority Kinh (Vietnamese) ethnicity, there also were delegates from the Stieng (Binh Phuoc province) and Jarai (Kon Tum province) ethnic groups. The planners also invited several international representatives: pastors Dang Hong Chau and Chau Van Hoa from the NAVMF, and EMM representatives Luke Martin and Gerry Keener, who was living in Ho Chi Minh City.

The conference officially adopted the *Confession of Faith* they had been using. After declaring the formation of the Vietnam Mennonite Church, the conference affirmed a provisional church leadership group: Pastor Nguyen Quang Trung was chosen president, and Pastor Nguyen Hong Quang vice-president and general secretary. Recalling the Mennonite Church established in Binh Thanh district four decades earlier and to the more recently-formed groups, Trung declared, "There is now neither a pre-1975 church nor a post-1975 Mennonite Church. There is one united Mennonite Church."

Following the conference, the executive committee arranged the various congregations of the Mennonite Church into five geographic districts. With the successful registration in 2001 of the Evangelical Church of Vietnam (South), Pastor Trung, now president of the Vietnam Mennonite Church, saw the registration of the church as a primary task. Together with pastors from the Adventist Church and the Grace Baptist Church in Ho Chi Minh City, Trung met with representatives of the government office of religious affairs to learn what procedural steps to take.

Pastor Nguyen Hong Quang and the other leaders from the District 2 center gave greater priority to evangelism and church planting than to church registration. Insisting that the national Constitution already guaranteed the freedom of religion, Quang and others maintained that it was not necessary to register. Among the many independent Evangelical house churches, and even within the now-registered Evangelical Church in Vietnam (South), there was not a clear consensus among church leaders about whether national registration was advantageous. Many house churches only sought permission to meet from local authorities.

In March 2004 there was an incident in District 2 that led to the arrest of several persons. When District 2 leaders reported to the local ward officials that secret agents were harassing visiting church leaders from the highlands, these secret agents fled. Pastor Quang insisted that local authorities investigate this incident. Instead, four of their young leaders were arrested and beaten. A few months later Pastor Quang himself and a young Bible teacher, Ms. Le Thi Hong Lien, were also arrested. In November all six were convicted of "preventing officials from carrying out their duties" and Quang was convicted of inciting persons to resist arrest. All were given prison terms. These "Mennonite Six" became an international issue with many people and

Pastor Nguyen Hong Quang with police officer in 2006, after his release from prison

organizations advocating for their release. Though sentenced to three years imprisonment, Pastor Quang was granted amnesty after sixteen months imprisonment.

A few months after this incident, Nguyen Quang Trung from the Binh Thanh church visited the United States. Before he returned home, he was ordained a minister by Lancaster Mennonite Conference at a ceremony in Philadelphia on July 18, 2004. Nguyen Hong Quang – then in prison – was also ordained in absentia.

Shortly after Pastor Trung's return to Vietnam, officials from the government's Committee of Religious Affairs in Hanoi came to Trung's home to give filing instructions for legal status. As president of the Vietnam Mennonite Church, Trung met on July 26 with the Church's Leadership Board together with the leaders and assistant leaders from each of the Church's districts to explain the legal registration process. The young leaders associated with the District 2 center were strongly opposed to Trung's plan to register, claiming that the Vietnam Mennonite Church already had legal status based on the September 1964 authorization granted to the Vietnam Mennonite Mission. Furthermore, they insisted that Pastor Nguyen Hong Quang must be released from prison before they would consider registration.

After waiting many years for this authorization to register, Trung could not agree with the position of the District 2 leaders. When they convened their own meeting and voted to remove him as president of the Church, Trung did not recognize the action. He called other district leaders together who elected a new leadership team for the Church. Although Trung contacted the District 2 leaders several times, they declined to register. After Pastor Quang was released from prison, the District 2 cluster of churches asked about joining the registration process. Aware that Nguyen Hong Quang's frequent challenges to government policies was delaying official recognition, Trung declined the late offer, and promised that the matter would be reconsidered only after the Vietnam Mennonite Church received official status.

Official Registration

After a very restrictive period after the 1975 revolution, the Communist Party leaders in Vietnam gradually came to recognize the positive contributions religious communities made to the nation. In March, 2004 the National Assembly passed an *Ordinance on Religion and Belief* which relaxed government oversight on religion to some extent, while still stipulating that religious denominations must be officially recognized or registered.

With greater freedom and the government urging registration, many independent house fellowships looked for a welcoming denominational group to join. Pastor Trung and his team adopted specific criteria for accepting these groups. First was the requirement that they accept the *Confession of Faith in a Mennonite Perspective*. In addition, their sole purpose for joining the Mennonite Church would be to "expand the realm of the kingdom of God." If a group already belonged to an evangelical denomination, they needed to bring a letter of introduction from that body. Groups and their leaders would have to join the Mennonite Church with no preconditions; pastors would be considered apprentice pastors for one year before being accepted as pastors for possible ordination.

In 2007, after several years of effort, Pastor Trung's efforts to register the Vietnam Mennonite Church bore fruit. The national Religious Affairs Committee issued a certificate granting permission for the *Hoi Thanh Mennonite Viet Nam* (Vietnam Mennonite Church) to engage in religious activities throughout the entire country. In addition, this Committee authorized the Church to hold an organizing assembly to complete the legal registration process and to elect a church leadership board.

This assembly was held in Binh Thanh district of Ho Chi Minh City November 15-17, 2008. In business meetings the constitution was ratified and officers were elected for four-year terms. Pastor Nguyen Quang Trung was elected president. Among the seventeen-member Leadership Committee were persons designated to work in the areas of building affairs, medical and social work, Christian education, evangelism, minorities, women's ministries, and youth and children.

A mixed choir sings at the VMC conference, 2008

In September 2008 the Vietnam Mennonite Church had a total of 6,123 members in 24 cities and provinces nationwide within 90 congregations. Most churches met in homes; only four had separate houses of worship. There were 138 pastors, apprentice pastors and evangelists.

With full legal status, the church could now hold corporate title to real estate property, establish a formal Bible institute for training pastors and leaders, officially ordain leaders, publish materials, forge relationships with other denominations to sponsor joint projects, serve as an official partner with MCC and other international agencies for relief and community development work, and extend and accept invitations to attend international conferences. In February

2009 the leadership team of the Church was invited to a ceremony in Ha Noi at the office of the national Committee for Religious Affairs. Mr. Nguyen The Doanh, Chairman of the National Committee for Religion, presented the official registration certificate for the Vietnam Mennonite Church. In July 2009 the Vietnam Mennonite Church was received as a member of the Mennonite World Conference at Assembly 15 in Paraguay.

Beginning in 2005 the Mennonite Church instituted leadership training programs with the help of North American teachers. In March, 2010 Pastor Trung was able to ordain 26 pastors. Nguyen Minh Sang, general secretary of the VMC, reported that as of 2010, the VMC has 90 local churches and about 8,500 members with 140 pastors and evangelists.

Also in March, 2010, the Vietnam Mennonite Institute in Theology and Renewal opened with fourteen students enrolled in a BTh program. The school follows a pattern of four week-long courses a month, followed by two months of study, research and work in home congregations over a four- to five-year period.

The unregistered cluster of Mennonite churches related to the District 2 administrative center has also continued to develop. Less willing to accommodate to the government's structures, they have suffered more harassment. However, local authorities recognize many of their 78 congregations with 6,700 members centered in five areas. The congregations are organized in a cell group structure with strong cohesion and accountability. Pastor Nguyen Hong Quang coordinates an extensive training and mentoring program for young leaders, and the church has a strong core of experienced evangelists and pastoral leaders. Quang's wife, Pastor Mrs. Le Thi Phu Dung, serves as church president, and Pastor Nguyen Thanh Tam is general secretary. There is some informal association between the two Mennonite groups.

Christians within the Mennonite churches in Vietnam continue to witness daily to the Gospel of their Lord and Savior Jesus Christ. Following Jesus Christ as Lord in Vietnam calls for an uncommon commitment.

Conclusion: Asian Mission as *Missio Dei*

by *Takanobu Tojo*

History and Missions

What does Missio Dei mean for the Asian world? In *Transforming Mission*, David J. Bosch noted that there were several paradigm shifts in mission from the early church until today.[1] From the perspective of the history of God's mission, how shall we view the mission to the Asian world?

For the purposes of this writing, Asia includes India, Sri Lanka, Nepal, Bhutan, Bangladesh, Myanmar, Laos, Thailand, Cambodia, Vietnam, Malaysia, Indonesia, Brunei, Philippines, People's Republic of China, Taiwan, Mongolia, North and South Korea, and Japan.

As already noted, Christianity had reached India already by the early third century. There were churches in India linked to the name of the Apostle Thomas, introduced by way of Arabia and Persia. By the seventh century the message of Christianity had reached China by way of the Silk Road overland trade routes. In the twelfth century, however, as Islam spread throughout the Asian world, the door to Christianity was closed and Christian missions became impossible.

Islamic religion transformed Arab tribal religion into a monotheistic world religion. Influenced by the Bible through contact with Jews, the shapers of Islam placed Muhammad as the successor to Abraham, Moses and Jesus Christ. Islam was formed as a community based on everyone being equal in the sight of their God Allah. Islam began building a global religious empire encompassing a vast area including Arabia, Persia and parts of Africa and Asia. Before that, Brahmanism, representing a Caste-based religion for Indo-Aryans, became the Hindu religion and ruled the Indian subcontinent. Brahmanism then spawned Buddhism through religious reform and spread to Indochina, China, Korea and Japan, but Islam spread into this

337

region as well. The expansion of the Islamic world came to an end in the sixteenth century when Spain and Portugal counterattacked the Islamic world and the two Catholic Iberian countries expanded their colonies globally.

The Mission of Christianity to the Asian World

Christian missions to the Asian world moved ahead as modern European countries fought over colonial lands in the wake of the age of great voyages of the sixteenth century. The Christian message was defined by the assumptions of the Imperial Christianity of the fourth-century Roman Empire, revived in the West by the emperor Charlemagne in the ninth century. The union of Christianity with imperial or royal power (called Constantinianism by some) defined medieval Catholic religion as well as the Protestant denominations which became the national religions of modern European countries.

Missionaries from the Catholic Church, bearing the tradition of Constantinian Christianity, began mission work in Asia, and the message of Christianity even reached Japan by way of Francis Xavier in the 16 century. Non-Catholic Christianity from Holland and England was preached in Sri Lanka, along the Malay straits and in Taiwan in the seventeenth century as Protestant denominations began mission work in the Asian world.

The Asian world soon suffered from the discrepancy between the Christianity described in the Bible as God's word, including the Gospel of Jesus Christ's crucifixion, and the imperialistic Christianity that they faced in real life. Catholics and Protestants were equally imperialistic. European Christianity, transformed by a spirit of Constantinianism and Roman imperialism totally foreign to the message of the apostolic age, rushed into the Asian world. Contrary to the Hebraic spirit of shalom, the prevailing spirit had become an ideology formed by the warrior values of empire. Asian missions were carried out by modern sovereign states deemed to be earthly kingdoms based on the "divine right of kings." These states aimed to rebuild modern Europe in the spirit of ancient Greece. They utilized modern scientific doctrine deemed to be the theology of these earthly kingdoms, by bureaucratic State Christianity built on the ideology of the Enlightenment, and by the Protestantism of the theological faculties of universities which served as educational institutions to support those who ruled over modern society. India, Myanmar, Cambodia,

Vietnam, Indonesia, and the Philippines came under the colonial rule of European nations.

The Beginnings of Anabaptist missions in Asia

Mennonite missions were caught up in the broader context of missions. Mennonite missions began in the seventeenth century on the west coast of Australia, and in 1851 missionary Pieter Janz arrived in what is now Jakarta. The first Mennonite missionary to China went there in the 1890s under a non-Mennonite mission agency. In 1920 an Anabaptist fellowship began in Indonesia.

Anabaptism, which had been persecuted in Europe, began missions in Asia together with other Protestant denominations. After World War II, MCC work began in Asia by North American mission organizations. MCC workers went to the Philippines (1946), Japan (1950), Vietnam (1954) and Hong Kong (1960s). In 1971 the first Asia Mennonite Conference was held in India.

Toward a Theological Foundation for Asian Missions

From the perspective of *Missio Dei* today, there needs to be a missiological reassessment of the significance of the fact that Nestorianism, drawing from the Greek Orthodox tradition, bore the first message of Christianity from Persia to India and China and took hold in China. For the sake of the Christian mission in Asia, a thoroughgoing comparison of Greek Orthodoxy and Catholic theology is necessary. Protestantism is less well-equipped for this task, inasmuch as the European Reformation was born out of conflict with the Catholic Church, and did not fundamentally overcome Catholic characteristics.

Protestantism, which began with Luther, was critical of Thomism (the doctrines of Thomas Aquinas) but did not overcome Augustinianism. What is important for Asian mission is the reassessment of European Christianity in general. It is our duty to reappraise, in the light of the Bible as the word of God, the nature of European Christianity which lost the true spirit of Christianity as it provided a religious foundation for modern sovereign nationalism and accomodated itself to the Enlightenment, modem imperialism and colonialism.

The Reformation that took place in sixteenth century Europe failed to overcome Constantinianism, the medieval doctrine of *Corpus Christianum* and the crusading spirit.

Perhaps only the Anabaptists, persecuted by Catholics and Protestants, both originators of the theology of modern imperialism, are
qualified to do a critical self-examination of European Christianity.
The center point for reappraising Constantinianism from an Anabaptist perspective is the ideology of *pax romana*. European Christianity after the Reformation cannot overcome its imperialistic nature
because peace, expressed as central to the Gospel as the way of *shalom*
that leads to the way of the cross of the Son of God, has been changed
into a military/political peace reminiscent of the Roman Empire's *pax
romana*.

To inquire into the relationship between *shalom* and *jihad* (Islamism)
as well, we need to shed light on relationships with Islam formed in
the seventh century under the influence of Judaism and Christianity. We must also shed light on relationships with Hinduism and
Buddhism. Missions today have the characteristics of missions that
began in the Age of Great Voyages as part of the European nations'
drive to colonize Asia. Resistance movements against imperialism and
colonialism began in Asia as Asian religions and Asian nationalism
grew in strength. Christianity was subjected to intensified criticism
and it became more difficult to pursue Christian missions. All along
Christianity has failed to seriously dialogue with Islam, Hinduism,
Buddhism or Confucianism in Asian nations. Rather than pursuing
jihad, Asian missions must pursue the spirit of *shalom* as the way of
the cross of Jesus Christ. This *shalom* is the spirit of forgiveness and
love toward the enemy.

Foundations of Anabaptist missiology

Given the history of missions, the Anabaptist church which was persecuted by European Christians is gifted to be involved in missions
as *missio dei* inasmuch as it was not involved in modern European
imperialism and colonialism. The "divine right of kings" and the new
crusade doctrine which resulted in European Christianity's theological
support of modern nationalism and imperialism have crumbled. It is
decisively important to Asian mission that the Anabaptist movement
has borne witness to the gospel of peace as it practiced its religious
conscience in the form of conscientious objection to military service
and has practiced peace and justice.

Harold Bender's assertion that the basic spirit of the Anabaptist
movement is found in discipleship, brotherhood and the peace witness

is foundational to Asian missions. The foundation of 1 Corinthians 3:11 as stressed by Menno Simons, and the doctrine of Michael Sattler, who objected to war with Turkey and was executed as a heretic, are absolutely critical even today. Their doctrines are essential in correcting the current understanding of the Gospel in Christian churches which have fallen into a new crusade mentality since September 11.

It is questionable whether Anabaptist missions from the United States of America are able to carry on the Anabaptist agenda, although missions from North America are decisively important for Mennonite missions in Asia today. Anabaptism has the potential to convert Christianity into a *shalom* mission of the cross. Certainly missionary agencies from the old continent, such as the London Missionary Society, pursued mission work in nineteenth-century China, but such efforts faced difficulties as Christianity was criticized for being a cultural weapon for the sake of the invasion of European imperialism. In the early twentieth century, four Mennonite conferences established themselves in different regions as did other Protestant denominations. However, it does not appear that Mennonite missions set forth mission principles that were clearly different from the mission principles of the Catholic and Protestant churches. An emphasis on discipleship as the bearer of the *shalom* mission of the cross is needed to overcome imperialistic theology, even for the purpose of starting missions in the People's Republic of China, which began as an atheistic state after World War II in reaction against modern European imperialism, colonialism and modern capitalism.

Missions in China as Missio Dei

The most important field of action for *missio dei* in Asia from now on is China, which has the longest-running tradition among the world's cultures. It has its own tradition of Confucianism, which the socialist state attempted to destroy, especially during the Cultural Revolution of the 1960s. State dogma constructed by Marxism-Leninism deemed religion to be an opiate of the people. Christianity was considered a weapon used for invasion by European imperialism and is still considered to be an enemy of the Communist Party. Nevertheless, the Confucian tradition forms the very depth of the psyche of the people of China. How should Christianity relate to China's cultural and religious traditions?

Is mission in China possible? Since China has no future but to advance as a modern nation, it will proceed in the direction of accepting freedom of ideology and creed. If this takes place, China will have to tolerate Christian missions. Since research findings on the great contribution of Christianity to education in China have now been publicized, the road to Christian missions is opening. The mistake that must be avoided is the mistake that American fundamentalists are making with their imperialistic tendency of pursuing American national interests. Each missionary and mission agency must be tested with the question of whether they have been given the courage by God to potentially stand with China against their own country, if the US and China come into a state of conflict.

Korea and Japan as a test case for mission

The cases of Japan and Korea are useful case studies when thinking about Asian missions. Korea's traditional religious values crumbled as a result of Japan's takeover, although this actually worked to the advantage of Christian missions. During Japan's colonial rule of Korea (1910-1945), when Japan's State Shinto religion perpetrated a crime of historic dimensions by mandating Shinto Shrine worship as a means to reinforce the rule of the emperor, the Korean church revived the tradition of resisting emperor worship of the early pre-Constantinian church. In this way Korean Christians acted as living witnesses in history for Christian mission. Christianity also provided a moral basis for opposing the atheistic socialist regime of North Korea (Democratic People's Republic of Korea) after World War II. However, the nationalistic character of the Korean Christian church makes it very difficult for Korean Christians to take a stance of Anabaptist pacifism, oppose militaristic nationalism and take up conscientious objection to military service.

Unlike Korea, the religious traditions of Shinto and Buddhism spanning more than a thousand years have made it difficult for Christian mission to take root in Japan. Japan developed an emperor system with a hierarchical ruling structure and value system based on a cultural emphasis on group harmony which mirrors the European imperial spirit. This could be called "Japanism" in a religious sense. Japan played the role of the Roman Empire for Asian nations, and State Shinto, which supported the emperor system, played the role of the Roman emperor Nero for Asia. After the nineteenth century Meiji

Restoration of Japan, State Shinto built the Meiji Shrine as Japan's version of European Catholicism's Vatican palace in an attempt to establish state rule based on the emperor system. Japan deified its emperor just as Europe attempted to build modern sovereign nation-states using the notion of the divine right of kings.

Facing this situation, Christian mission developed its approach to Christian mission in the post-Meiji era with European imperialism and colonialism intact. The United Church of Christ in Japan that was formed by the Japanese state to support World War II functioned as an organization subservient to Japan's State Shinto, and after World War II Christianity was used as a base for anticommunist religious policies of the US occupying regime led by General MacArthur. Christianity in Japan had meaning only as the basis for American-style utilitarian doctrine of prosperity, with fundamentalist churches in Japan acting as bases for American utilitarian Christianity. After September 11, Christianity in Japan is facing a serious situation of having to choose how to relate to the new crusade mentality of American fundamentalism.

The Agenda of Peace Theology

This is where the agenda of historical theology begins. After losing in World War II, Japan gained the ninth article of the Constitution, also known as the Peace Constitution. As an ideological expression of unconditional surrender the constitution rejects war and chooses peace. For the first time in human history the state rejected military force and placed the realization of peace as its greatest goal. After pursuing a policy of "Rich country, Strong military" after the Meiji era, when Japan lost the war it established a constitution which, for the first time in human history, rejected imperialism and colonialism in favor of pacifism.

However, Japan's peace constitution faces contradictions. Using the peace constitution as leverage, all physical, technological and mental energies were employed to gain economic prosperity through scientific, industrial economic growth. Through pacifism Japan finally succeeded in the national goal of the Meiji era to make itself prosperous and powerful ("Rich country, Strong military"). It was discovered that peace is the best strategy for national prosperity. Japan achieved a level of economic prosperity that amazed the world. The peace constitution brought forth mammonism.

It was also discovered that the development of globalism made just wars between modern sovereign nation-states impossible. Instead of applying the efforts of the labor force for military purposes, the labor force was mobilized for corporate needs as part of the economic war to create economic prosperity and prepare the way to win the competition of the global market.

Missio dei does not exist outside the peace of the cross. And yet the pacifism of Japan's ninth article of the constitution seeks subjection to global mammonism, and is a pacifism is based on nationalism. It is not founded on the same foundation as the peace of the kingdom of God. It is theologically difficult to find a way for the pacifism of the kingdom of God, which is at the base of the. Anabaptist understanding of the Gospel, to penetrate the pacifism of the modern sovereign nation-state.

Anabaptist versions of missions in Japan

Mennonite and Brethren in Christ (BIC) missions in Japan began after World War II. Following the same path as other Protestant mission agencies, they redirected their efforts to Japan after their missions had suffered setbacks in China. This meant that no preparations were made specifically for doing missions in Japan. Neither was there any understanding about Japan, outside of a sense of missions as MacArthur's tool for ruling Japan.

As a nation with a "peace" constitution, Japan was interested in the Mennonite church as a "peace church." But there was no research done to learn how the peace of the nation's constitution differed from peace as a basic expression of the Gospel of Christ. Not enough basic understanding was reached on Bender's "discipleship," and how it relates to Luther's "justification by faith" which functioned as a basic doctrine of the Reformation, and how the church should be formed as a brotherhood.

Post-war Mennonite and BIC conferences in Japan struggled to clarify their understandings of the Gospel. Calvinistic denominations were the most serious about theological education. As a result, Japanese theology is basically Calvinistic. Ethically it is puritan. Aside from their veils of discipleship and pacifism at their foundations, Mennonite and BIC missions in Japan have puritanical fundamentalism at their core. The theological orientation of most pastors and missionaries is Calvinistic.

Mennonite and BIC missions took theological education lightly and focused primarily on pioneer evangelism. As a result, there was no theology to determine what kind of understanding of the Gospel to apply in church formation. Theologically the churches became Calvinistic. It is difficult to overcome both the hierarchical authoritarian structures arising out of Confucian Calvinism and the authoritarianism of the Japanese emperor system. The ideology of group harmony that feeds Japanese vertical organizational structures, identical in nature with European models, became foundational to Mennonite and BIC missions. Anabaptist mission as the *shalom* way of the cross has only just begun.

Asian missions in the future

How should Asian missions proceed from now on? Missions in Japan, the Chinese speaking world, the Philippines, Indonesia, India, Mongolia, and so on represent missions in areas with divergent cultures. Each situation requires a separate missiology.

The biggest issue for missions will be to determine the mission of Christ in the midst of the economic applications of science and technology, the vast tide of industrialization and the advance of information technology in the world. From the twenty-first century on, the Asian world will be building nation-states based on industrialization, science and technology. It will be the region with the fastest economic growth in the world, surpassing growth in the European and American continents. Any attraction to Christianity as a European religion will probably fade. The pursuit of happiness through science and technology will take away interest in religion itself

Speaking in broadest terms, the Protestant era in Asia has ended. Only post-Vatican II Catholicism will survive in Asia. Only Mother Theresa's type of evangelism will speak to the hearts of Asians. For Mennonites and BIC, only MCC-inspired missions and the practice of the gospel of peace will make Asian missions possible.

Until now Protestant religion has tried to determine how church and state should relate to each other. In the sixteenth century it was Luther's two-kingdom theology and Calvin's doctrine of the autonomy of the church. In the twentieth century it was Karl Barth's Confessing Church movement and Dietrich Bonhoeffer's *Nachfolge Christi* during World War II, and after World War II it was Catholic liberation theology. Through J. H. Yoder's *Discipleship as Political Responsibility* a way beyond the Reformation and beyond Christianity's Constantinian order has been found.[2] It is a direct return to the way of Jesus – the relationship between Jesus and politics. While Luther went back to Augustine and Karl Barth went back to Anselm, Bonhoeffer and Yoder went back to Jesus Christ.

The theological discovery of contemporary Anabaptism is that it is not enough to return to the theology of the Reformation. The only choice is to return directly to Jesus Christ. Likewise the only choice for Asian missions is Jesus' way of discipleship. From this faith perspective Asian missions must face the faith question of how to live in the contemporary scientific age.

Modern theology, and especially Protestant theology, has not succeeded in answering questions posed by capitalism, market economics and industrial society. Much of American Christianity has simply criticized socialism as a demonic system without noticing the danger of its own mammon-god of capitalism and market economics. The American Christian church has fundamentally adopted a utilitarian corporate business model because it has not theologically clarified its relationship with capitalism and market economics. The church growth doctrine (church inflation doctrine) that spread throughout Christian missions after World War II is nothing other than a religious version of the corporate business model. American missions will likely be exported together with American global market economics. Opposition to American global market economics was evident in the September 11, 2001 destruction of the World Trade Center buildings in New York. The American churches have only understood this event as an act of terrorism. At the core of the American Christian church is *pax americana* – an extension of *pax romana* – and church corporatism.

The important thing for Asian missions from now on is overcoming global market economics originating in the US and going about the work of *shalom*, the kingdom of God and the development of the family of God as the way of the cross. It is time to return the Christianity of two-thousand years of European culture back to God's world and living in the grace of receiving the *evangelion* from God through Jesus Christ. This is how Asian missions will find meaning as *missio dei* in Asia.

Translated by Ken J. Shenk

Abbreviations

ADS   *Algemene Doopsgezinde Sociëteit* (General Mennonite Conference, Netherlands)
AKWW   Wiyata Wacana Christian Academy (*Akademi Kristen Wiyata Wacana*)
AMB   American Mennonite Brethren
AMBS   Associated Mennonite Biblical Seminary, USA
AMC   Asia Mennonite Conference
BCC   British Church of Christ
BGCMC   *Bharatiya General Conference Mennonite Kalisiya*
BIC   Brethren in Christ
BICDS   Brethren in Christ Development Society
BJCPM   Bharatiya Jukta Christo Prachar Mandli church ("The Indian United Christ Evangelistic Church": United Missionary Church)
BMM   *Bihar Mennonite Mandali*
BMS   *Baptist Missionary Society*
BOMAS   Board of Mission and Services, North America
CASA   Committee on Social Action of the National Christian Council
CCA   The Christian Conference of Asia
CCC   China Christian Council
CCGA   Christian Church Gospel Association, China
CCMSM   Cross Culture Mission Service
CEE   China Educational Exchange
CIM   Commission on International Mission
CMA   Christian and Missionary Alliance
CMBCI   Conference of the Mennonite Brethren Church in India
CMCHK   Conference of Mennonite Churches in Hong Kong Limited
CMS   Church Missionary Society
COM   Commission on Overseas Mission, USA
CPCRS   Center for Peace and Conflict Resolution Studies, India
CSI   Church of South India
CWS   Church World Service
CYSS   Christian Youth for Social Service
DGI   Council of Churches in Indonesia (*Dewan Gereja-Gereja di Indonesia*)
DZV   *Doopsgezinde Zendings Vereniging* (Mennonite Missionary Society)
DZR   Dutch Mennonite Mission
ECVN   Evangelical Church in Vietnam
EFI   Evangelical Fellowship of India
EHA   The Emmanuel Hospital Association, India
EHBS   Eastern Hokkaido Bible School
EMBMC   Eastern Mennonite Board of Missions and Charities
EMEK   European Mennonite Evangelism Committee
EMM   Eastern Mennonite Mission, USA
EMU   Eastern Mennonite University, USA
ETANI   Evangelical Trust Association of North India
FOMCIT   Fellowship of Mennonite Churches in Taiwan
GC   General Conference Mennonite Church, US

GITJ   *Gereja Injili di Tanah Jawa* – (Javanese Evangelical Church)
GKI   Reformed church, Indonesia
GKJ   Central Java Christian Church
GKMI   *Gereja Kristen Muria Indonesia* – GKMI (Muria Christian Church of
          Indonesia)
GKJW   East Java Christian Church
GKJ   The Central Java Christian Church
GMT   Gilgal Mission Trust, India
GPS   Goals, Priorities and Strategies
HMI   Henry Martyn Institute for Interfaith Relations and Reconciliation
HOREMCO   Hokkaido Radio Evangelism and Mass Communication
III   *Institut Injili Indonesia* (Evangelical Institute of Indonesia)
IMBC   Indian Mennonite Brethren Church
IMC   Integrated Mennonite Churches, Inc., Philippines
JKI   *Jemaat Kristen Indonesia* (Christian Congregation in Indonesia)
JMF   Japan Mennonite Fellowship
JMLA   Japan Mennonite Literature Association
JVC   Jesus Village Church, Korea
KAC   Korea Anabaptist Center
KAMF   Korea Anabaptist Mission Fellowship
KKEM   Joint Economic Commission, Indonesia
KKR   Spiritual Revival Meeting (*Kebaktian Kebangunan Rohani*)
KMT   China Nationalist Party (Kuomintang)
MB   Mennonite Brethren
MBBI   Mennonite Brethren Bible Institute, India
MBCBC   Mennonite Brethren Centenary Bible College
MBDO   Mennonite Brethren Development Organization
MBM   Mennonite Board of Missions, US
MC   Mennonite Church ("Old" Mennonite), US
MCI   Mennonite Church in India
MCC   Mennonite Central Committee
MCES   Menno Christian Education Society, India
MCH   Mennonite Christian Hospital, Taiwan
MCSFI   Mennonite Christian Service Fellowship of India
MEDA   Mennonite Economic Development Associates
MNI   Missions Now, Inc. , Philippines
MSA   Mennonite Service Agency
MVS   Mennonite Vocational School, Korea
MWC   Mennonite World Conference
NAVMF   North American Vietnamese Mennonite Fellowship
NCCI   National Christian Council of India
NCF   Churches Fellowship of Nepal
NZG   *Nederlandsche Zendeling Genootschap*
OMF   Overseas Missionary Fellowship
PBCI   Peacebuilders Community, Inc.
PCEC   Philippine Council of Evangelical Churches

PGI   Community of Churches in Indonesia (*Persekutuan Gereja-Gereja di Indonesia*)
PIPKA   *Pekabaran Injil dan Pelayanan Kasih* (Foundation for Missions and Charities)
PMBI   Philippine Mennonite Biblical Institute
PMY   Philippine Menno Youth
REACH   Rural Economic Development and Community Health program, India
SDI   *Sarekat Dagang Islam* (Union of Islamic Merchants, Indonesia)
SIBS   South Indian Bible Seminary
SMP BOPKRI   Organization for Promoting Christian Education (*Badan Oesaha Pendidikan Kristen*)
SPCK   Society for Promoting Christian Knowledge
SPG   Society for the Propagation of the Gospel in Foreign Parts
STT   The Higher Theological School (*Sekolah Tinggi Theologia*)
TAFTEE   Association for Theological Education by Extension
TAFMC   Tokyo Area Fellowship of Mennonite Churches
TCU   Tokyo Christian University
THHK   *Tiong Hoa Hwe Koan* (Chinese organization carrying out religious and educational activities, Indonesia)
UBS   Union Biblical Seminary, India
UCCJ   United Church of Christ in Japan
UKDW   Duta Wacana Christian University, Indonesia
UMC   United Missionary Church. See BJCPM
UMN   United Mission to Nepal
UMS   United Missionary Society, also known as *Bharatiya Jukto Christian Prachar Mandali*
VEP   Visitors Exchange Programme
VMC   Vietnam Mennonite Church
VMM   Vietnam Mennonite Mission
VNCS   Vietnam Christian Service
VOC   *Vereenigde Oostindische Compagnie* (East India Trading Company)
YAKEM   The Muria Cooperative Development Foundation

End Notes

Chapter 1: Asia: A Brief Introduction
Literature used:

Howard M. Federspiel, *Sultans, Shamans, and Saints. Islam and Muslims in Southeast Asia* (Honolulu: University of Hawai'i Press, 2007).

Andre Gunder Frank, *The Centrality of Central Asia* (Amsterdam: VU University press, 1992).

Claude Guillot, Denys Lombard and Roderich Ptak (eds), *From the Mediterranean to the Chinese Sea* (Wiesbaden: Harrassowitz Verlag, 1998).

Kishore Mahbubani, *The New Asian Hemisphere. The Irresistible Shift of Global Power to the East* (New York: Public Affairs, 2008).

Anthony Reid, "An 'Age of Commerce' in Southeast Asian History," in *Modern Asian Studies* (1990), 1-30.

Anthony Reid, "The Seventeenth-Century Crisis in Southeast Asia" in *Modern Asian Studies* (1990), 639-659.

Anthony Reid (ed), *Sojourners and Settlers. Histories of Southeast Asia and the Chinese* (St. Leonards NSW: Allen & Unwin, 1995).

Nicholas Tarling (ed), *The Cambridge History of Southeast Asia, Volume Three, From c. 1800 to the 1930s* (Cambridge: Cambridge University Press, 1999).

Chapter 2: Christianity in Asia

For further reading:

Fred Richard Belk, *The Great Trek of the Russian Mennonites to Central Asia 1880-1884* (Scottdale, PA: Herald Press, 1976).

De schipbreuk van de Batavia 1629, ingeleid door V. D. Roeper, (serie Linschoten Vereniging XCII) (Zutphen: Walburg Pers, 1993).

John C. England, *The Hidden History of Christianity in Asia. The Churches of the East Before 1500* (Delhi/Hong Kong: ISPCK & CCA, 1998).

Adrian Hastings (ed), *A World History of Christianity* (London, England: Cassell, 1999).

Anske Hielke Kuipers, *In de Indische wateren* (serie Linschoten Vereniging XCVIII), (Zutphen, Netherlands: Walburg Pers,1999), edited by Marietje E. Kuipers.

Dik van der Meulen, Multatuli. Leven en werk, van Eduard Douwes Dekker (Amsterdam: Uitgeverij SUN, 2002), especially 31-53.

Samuel H. Moffett, *A History of Christianity in Asia, Vol. I: Beginnings to 1500* (San Francisco: Harper Collins 1992; New York: Orbis, 1998, second revised and corrected edition).

Samuel H. Moffett, *A History of Christianity in Asia, Vol. II: 1500-1900* (New York: Orbis, 2003).

Stephen Neill, *A History of Christian Missions. The Pelican History of the Church: 6* (Hammondsworth, Middlesex, England: Penguin Books, 1966).

Mennonite Encyclopedia, Volumes I-V.

Bob Whyte, *Unfinished Encounter. China and Christianity* (Harrisburg PA: Moorehouse Publishing, 1988).

Chapter 3: The Mennonite Churches of Indonesia

[1] Denys Lombard, *Nusa Jawa: Silang Budaya* [The Island of Java: Intersecting Cultures], Volume 1 (Jakarta: Gramedia Pustaka Utama, 1996), 1.

[2] Setiono, Benny S., *Tionghoa Dalan Pusaran Politik* [Chinese in the Political Vortex] (Jakarta: Elkasa, 2003), 17.

[3] Ibid., 18.

[4] Denys Lombard, *op. cit.*, Volume 2, 84-124.

[5] Handoyomarno, *Benih Yang Tumbuh VII: Gereja Kristen Jawi Wetan* [The Growing Seed VII: Christian Church of East Java] (Flores: Arnoldus, 1976), 27.

[6] Mount Muria is only 1600 meters high, one small mountain surrounded by small towns, an area of thirty-five square miles with about 6 million inhabitants.

[7] In a Javanese manuscript of the 1970's written by Sumardi Raharjo, it says that Tunggul Wulung, named Raden Mas Tondo, was originally from Surakarta. This opinion is supported by an official genealogy from the Surakarta Palace.

[8] Alle Hoekema, *Dutch Mennonite Mission in Indonesia. Historical Essays* (Elkhart, IN: Institute of Mennonite Studies, 2001), 37.

[9] Thomas K. Kartomo, "*Teologi Mistik Toenggoel Woeloeng dan Runtuhnya Utopia Kerajaan Toenggoel Woeloeng Ratu Adil Bondo: Sejarah Pergulatan Ratu Adil dalam Mistik Kejawen* ["The Mystical Theology of Tunggul Wulung and the Collapse of the Utopia of Tunggul Wulung's Just King Kingdom of Bondo" : A History of the Struggle of the Just King in Kejawen Mysticism"] Yogyakarta: Master's Thesis, Duta Wacana Christian University, 2003, 57-60.

[10] *Mancapat* or *mancalima* is a system of numerology that focuses on the four directions of the wind and one central position. This system is characteristic of the social structure of the traditional Javanese village in which the numbers 4 and 5 are sacred numbers.

[11] Martati Ins. Kumaat, *Benih Yang Tumbuh V: Suatu Survey Mengenai Gereja Injili di Tanah Jawa* [The Growing Seed V: A Survey of the Javanese Evangelical Church] (Salatiga: Satya Wacana Christian University Press, 1974), 12.

[12] Ibid.

[13] Archives Dutch Mennonite Mission, in Stadsarchief Amsterdam, PA 305: 619-620.

[14] Brief report of the southern district (*Klasis Selatan*) June 6, 1949, by the secretariat.

[15] Lawrence Yoder, "The Life, Ministry and Leadership of Soehadiweko Djojodihardjo," unpublished article, February 9, 2004.

[16] Lawrence Yoder, unpublished draft of a history of GITJ, chapter 29, p. 415.

[17] KKEM announcement, Kudus, August, 1969.

[18] Lawrence Yoder, unpublished draft of a history of GITJ, p. 350.

[19] Samuel Edy Rabini, "*Perpecahan dan Rekonsiliasi di Tubuh GITJ: Suatu Tinjauan Teologis Terhadap Pola Kepemimpinan*" ["Dissension and Reconciliation in the Body of GITJ: A Theological View of Models of Leadership"], Thesis, Theology Faculty of Universitas Kristen Duta Wacana, 2001, p. 68.

[20] In 1930 there were only 1,030 doctors in all of Indonesia, and of those only 667 lived in Java. This means that there was only one doctor for every 62,500 people.

[21] Benny S. Setiono, *Tionghoa dalam Pusaran Politik*, 376.

[22] The Salatiga Mission was initiated by Mrs. E. J. le Jolle- de Wildt, who preached the Gospel to the laborers of the plantation Simo near Salatiga in 1853. Later they were ministered to by a pupil of missionary Jellesma (East Java), Paulus Sadoyo. After Mrs. Le Jolle had to return to the Netherlands due to her husband's death, the responsibilities were taken over by a committee from independent

churches in Germany and the Netherlands. From its beginnings there had been warm personal relations with Dutch Mennonite missionaries, and one of the Salatiga missionaries became Pieter Jansz's son-in-law.

[23] Lawrence M. Yoder, *The Muria Story. A History of the Chinese Mennonite Churches of Indonesia*, (Kitchener ON: Pandora Press, 2006), 70.

[24] Lawrence M. Yoder, *The Muria Story*, 89.

[25] Jochanan Herlianto, "*Sedjarah GKMI Pati: 2 Djuni 1941 – 2 Djuni 1971*" ["History of GKMI Pati: June 2, 1941 – June 2, 1971], printed for the 30th anniversary of GKMI Pati, 6.

[26] List of Donations (Bestuur and Kerkraad from the Chinese Christian Organization Kie Tok Kauw Hwee, Pati, October 15, 1940). See also Yoder, *The Muria Story*, 112.

[27] Tee Yan Poen was ordained as assistant pastor by Tee Siem Tat on January 30, 1940.

[28] Herman Tan, *Karya Indah* [A Beautiful Work], written to clarify the Lawrence Yoder's earlier, Indonesian version of the history of GKMI, *Tunas Kecil* [Small Bud], 1995, 14.

[29] Herman Tan, *Karya Indah*, 43.

[30] Herman Tan, *Karya Indah*, 44.

[31] A young woman was present at the conference; as the congregation prayed, she suddenly screamed. She was possessed by an evil spirit. She spoke fluently in a Jakarta dialect, although she had never sojourned in Jakarta. Several members prayed, and the Lord God showed the same vision to some of them. They saw a *kris* (a curved dagger) under the young woman's chair. Adi Sutanto and other youths immediately went to the house of her parents to tell them about the young woman's condition. At first the parents denied that they kept a satanic object; Adi and others prayed again, and the Lord God showed them the exact location of *kris*: the lowest shelf of a cupboard in the house. At last the parents surrendered the object and it was burned in the yard. A grotesque thing happened; the fire from *kris* twirled, the young woman screamed out loud and the demon was cast out. The young woman fainted. From that moment on a great fear overwhelmed inhabitants of Bangsri, and many families surrendered their satanic objects to be burned.

[32] The for this paragraph is Th.E. Jensma, *Doopsgezinde Zending in Indonesië*, ('s-Gravenhage: Boekencentrum, 1968), chapter VII, 114-125.

[33] Th.E. Jensma, *Doopsgezinde Zending in Indonesië*, 145-147.

[34] *Responding to Worldwide Needs. The Mennonite Central Committee Story Volume 2*, (Scottdale: Herald Press, 1980), 95-98.

[35] Lawrence Yoder, "Christmas Eve on a bus in Sumatra," in Shirlee Kohler Yoder, *Savoring the Times. Stories on MCC Indonesia's 50th anniversary 1998*, (n.p., n.d.), 47.

[36] See for this part: Jensma, *Doopsgezinde Zending*, chapter IX, 153-175 and Hoekema, *Dutch Mennonite Mission*, 134-140.

[37] See for brief reports Shirlee Kohler Yoder, *Savoring the Times. Stories on MCC Indonesia's 50th anniversary 1998*.

[38] See for information, among other sources, the commemorative booklet *PIPKA 1965-1995* (Jakarta 1995).

Chapter 4: The Mennonite and Brethren in Christ Churches of India

[1] J. H. Hutton, *Caste in India: Its Nature, Function, and Origins*, 3rd ed. (London: Oxford University Press, 1961), 47. The caste system was introduced into India by Aryans about two thousand years before Christ. Steadily this gave rise to a new social order. Later Manu, the supreme lawgiver, gave justification and detailed regulations. The Portuguese first used the word "caste" in 1567.

[2] *Varna* refers more to the four class divisions and *jati* to its numerous divisions and sub-divisions.

[3] M. N.Srinivas, *Caste in Modern India* (Bombay: Allied Publications, 1966), 3.

[4] They were known as untouchables, *Chandalas, Panchama, Avarna, Dasya* and outcastes for centuries. These degrading terms were changed by the British administration into "Depressed Classes" in 1919. M. K. Gandhi called them *Harijans* (children of the god Hari), his favored term to be used in the place of untouchable, but Ambedkar did not accept Gandhi's term. In 1935, the British government defined them as the "Scheduled Castes." See James Massey, *Indigenous People: Dalits* (ISPCK, 1994), 6-9, and James Massey, *Roots: A Concise History of Dalits* (ISPCK, 1991), 9-10.

[5] B. R. Ambedkar, *Writings and Speeches Vol.2* (1282), 492. G. K. Gokhale stated that "we may touch a cat, we may touch a dog, we may touch any other animal, but the touch of these human beings (Dalits) is pollution." Cited in M. R. Arulraj, *Jesus the Dalit; Liberation Theology by Victims of Untouchability, an Indian Version of Apartheid* (Hyderabad: Published by the author, 1996), 1.

[6] A. P. Nirmal, "Towards A Christian Dalit Theology," paper presented to UTC, Bangalore, (n.d.), 6.

[7] See Irfan Habib, *Essays in Indian History: Towards a Marxist Perception* (New Delhi: Tulika, 2000), 176-177.

[8] Monica Datta, *Forming an Identity: A Social History of the Jats* (New Delhi: Oxford University Press, 1999), 4; M. N.Srinivas, *Caste in Modern India*, 41.

[9] By 1917 British government had prepared a list that included twenty-one "untouchable Hindu and Animist castes or tribes." In the Census of 1921 a fresh list was made of the "depressed classes." In 1931, at the suggestion of the Census Superintendent of Assam, the term "depressed classes" was abandoned as a census category because of the stigma attached to it. Castes that suffered from some amount of social disability were to be classified as "exterior" castes, while the rest were classed as "interior" Hindus. From then on they were classified into the Hindu fold. This social division was sanctified in the Scheduled Caste Order of 1936.

[10] See Eleanor Zelliot, "The Dalit Movement," *Dalit International Newsletter* (February, 1996), 1; also V. T. Rajshaker, *Why Dalits Hate Hinduism*, 4; Shrirama, "Untouchablity and Stratification in Indian Civilisation," in Michel, *Dalits in Modern India*, 9; 39.

[11] See Nirmal Minz, "A Theological Interpretation of the Tribal Reality in India," *Frontiers in Asian Christian Theology: Emerging Trends*, ed. by R. S. Sugirtharajah (Maryknoll: Orbis Books, 1994), 71ff.

[12] Wati Longchar, a prominent Tribal theologian writes, "though the tribals are not Hindu and do not come under Hindu caste structure, they are always treated as low caste people who are poor, illiterate, simple people and impure. Therefore, in a caste ridden society they suffer the stigma of being untouchable." A.Wati Longchar, *In Search of Identity and Tribal Theology* (Assam: Eastern Theological College, 2001), 45.

[13] Peter Haokip's expression, cited in Wati Longchar, *In Search of Identity*, 44. Bishop Nirmal Minz, another Tribal theologian, writes "the tribal person is a strange animal to many in our country even today." Ibid. See also James Massey, "Dalits-Tribals at the Crossroads: Faced with a New Form of Violence," *Dalit International Newsletter* (October, 2000), 1; 4.

[14] With colonization and the spread of Christianity, the term "tribe" was used to denote a group of people speaking a common language, observing uniform rules of social organization and working together for some common purposes such as trade, agriculture and warfare. In India, tribal people prefer to be identified by the name of their respective communities, such as Naga, Mizo, Oraoan, Munda, Santal, etc. The constitution of India says simply that a "tribe" must be a homogenous community, belonging neither to the Hindu or the Muslim communities, and that the group must be economically poor and socially marginalized. Those who are officially recognized as 'tribal' are entitled to receive benefits and opportunities granted by the Indian government. See Wati Longchar, *An Emerging Asian Tribal Theology*, 2-3.

[15] Wati Longchar, *An Emerging Asian Tribal Theology*, 3.

[16] See Pachuau, *Ethnic Identity and Christianity* (Germany: Peter Lang, 1998), 34; 39.

[17] V. K. Nuh, *Struggle for Identity in North-East India* (Guwahati: Spectrum Publications, 2001), 11-14.

[18] Kancha Iilaiah, 'Dalitism vs. Brahmanism: The Epistemological Conflict in History", *Dalit Identity and Politics*, ed. By, Ghanshyam Shah, (New Delhi: Saga Publications, 2001), 115;119-20. Hereafter, Iilaiah, *Dalitism.*

[19] N. M. Srivnivas, *The Changing Position of Indian Women* (Delhi: Oxford University Press, 1978), 18.

[20] The *Manusmrti*, the Brahminical legal code, decreed that women should be subject to their fathers in childhood, in youth to their husbands, and when the husband dies, to her sons. A woman must never be an independent. The whole duty of wives is to obey their husbands even if husbands are unworthy; the husband must be constantly worshiped as a god by a faithful wife.

[21] Nanda, *Indian Women*, xv.

[22] S. Ram, *Women's Socio-Economic Problems* (New Delhi: Common wealth Publishers, 2004), 323.

[23] Dick Kooiman, *Conversion and Social Equality in India* (New Delhi: Manohar Publications, 1989), 1. O. L. Snaitang, *Christianity and Social Change in North East India* (Shillong: Vendrame Institute, 1993), 28.

[24] North-east India is a region made up of seven states with a rich cultural diversity and many religious beliefs and practices distributed among more than 200 tribal groups.

[25] See Puthenpurakal, ed. *The Impact of Christianity on North East India* (Shillong: Vendrame Institute Publications, 1996), 198.

[26] Downs, *History of Christianity*, 29.

[27] See F. S. Downs, "Administrators, Missionaries and a World Turned Upside Down: Christianity as a Tribal Response to Change in North East India," *Indian Church History Review* (October 1980).

[28] Downs, *History of Christianity*, 43.

[29] See O. L. Snaitang, "Churches of Indigenous Origins in North East India," in *Churches of Indigenous Origins in North East India* (New Delhi: ISPCK, 2000), 177; also *idem.*, *Christianity and Social Change*, 181; 183.

[30] The word Dalit is not a new word. Jotiba Phule (1827-1890), a Marathi social reformer, used this term to describe the outcasts and "untouchables." In the modern period Dr. B. R. Ambedker used the word Dalit to indicate the Scheduled Castes.

[31] Ghasi Das (1756-1836) provided leadership for the protest movement of a group called Satnami. Ghasi Das preached the unity of God and the equality of all human beings. This was another direct challenge to Brahmanism in north India. See. Saurab Dube, *Untouchable Past: Religion, Identity, and Power among a Central Indian Community, 1780-1950* (New York: 1998).

[32] See Abe Dueck, ed., *The Mennonite Brethren Church Around the World: Celebrating 150 Years* (Kitchener: Pandora Press, 2010), 376.

[33] "Transforming lives in Mission, Karuna Shri Joel Preaching extract," *MBMSI Witness* (Spring 2010), 4.

[34] P. B. Arnold, "Objects of Mission to Agents of Mission," Inaugural Address, 150th Anniversary of Mennonite Brethren Church," January 17, 2010, 1.

[35] James Hough, *The History of Christianity in India from the Commencement of the Christian Era, Vol. III* (London: Church Missionary House, 1845), 379-380.

[36] See J. W. Pickett, *Christian Mass Movements* (New York: The Abingdon Press, 1933). John E. Clough, *Social Christianity in the Orient* (New York: The Macmillan Company, 1914), 96-97.

[37] John E. Clough, *Social Christianity in the Orient*, 52. See also Stephen Fuchs, *Rebellious Prophets:A Study of Messianic Movements in Indian Religions* (Bombay, Asia Publishing house, 1965); M. E. Prabhakar "Caste-Class and status in Andhra Churches. Implications for mission today," *Religion and Society* (September 1981); Emma Rouschenbusch-Clough, *While Sewing Sandals or Tales of a Telugu Perriah tribe* (London Butler and Tanner, 1899), 119.

[38] Clough, *Social Christianity*, v.

[39] R. Joseph, *A History of the Telugu Baptist Churches: American Baptist Telugu Mission (Telugu)* (Hyderabad, A.C.T.C., 2003), 33.

[40] Fuchs, *Rebellious Prophets*, 264.

[41] As quoted by Peter Penner, *Russians, North Americans and Telugus: The Mennonite Brethren Mission in India 1885-1975* (Hillsboro: Kindred Publications, 1997), 141.

[42] Peter Penner, *Russians, North Americans and Telugus*, 4.

[43] See Peter Penner, "Baptist in All But Name," *Mennonite Life* (March, 1991) 17-24.

[44] *Our Mission Among the Telugus* (Kansas: the Board of Foreign Mission of the Mennonite Brethren Church of North America, 1939).

[45] Peter Penner., *Russians, North Americans and Telugus*, 4.

[46] During this time the American Mennonite Brethren established four stations in the Mahabubnager district: Nagarkurnool, Wanaparthy, Kalvakurthy and Janampet. The Baptists had two stations at Mahabubnagar and Gadwal.

[47] See the profile of the Rev. Jonnalagadda John, IMB Historical Commission & B.
     A. George, *The History of Mennonite Brethren Church*, Published by the Governing
     Council of the Conference of the M.B. Church of India, 1990, 109.

[48] A. R. Jaipal, "Telugu Village Mission," *El-Shaddai* (Sep.-Oct.,1989) 4-10.

[49] James C Juhnke, *A People of Mission: A History of General Conference Mennnonite
     Overseas Missions* (Kansas: Faith and Life Press, 1979), 27.

[50] Viola B. Wiebe and Marilyn Wiebe Dodge, *Sepia Prints: Memories of a Missionary
     in India* (Winnipeg: Kindred Press, 1990), 59.

[51] Peter Penner, *Russians, North Americans and Telugus*, 75.

[52] A. E. Janzen, *Survey of Five of the Mission Fields of the Conference of the Mennonite
     Brethren Church of North America located in India, Africa, Brizil, Paraguay and
     Colombia* (Hillsboro, Kansas: Board of Foreign Missions, 1950), 25.

[53] Peter Penner, *Russians, North Americans and Telugus*, 72.

[54] N. P. James, "The Bible Teaching Programme in our Conference," *Indian M .B.
     Church at the Cross Roads: A Souvenir*, Published by the Governing Council of the
     Conference of the M.B. Church of India (1972), 41.

[55] V. K. Rufus, "Response," *Theological Education on Five Continents: Anabaptist Perspec-
     tives*, ed. by N. R. Heisey and D. Schipani (Strasburg, France: MWC: 1997), 121.

[56] Interview with M. B. John , 12 April 1997.

[57] P. B. Arnold , Inaugural address, *A Festival of 100 years, Souvenir*, 1990, 4.

[58] A. E. Janzen, *The Andra Mennonite Brethren Church in India, 1904-1954* (Hillsboro,
     Kan.: Board of Foreign Missions, 1955), 12.

[59] P. B. Arnold, "Objects of Mission to Agents of Mission," Inaugural Address, in the
     150th Birth Anniversary Celebrations of the MBChurch, Jadcherla, 2010, 9.

[60] Rajendra Prasad, *The Law of Social Status* (Pune: Hind Law Publications, 1998), 8.

[61] K. C. Das, *Indian Dalits*, 85. See also *Dalit Voice* (March, 2005), 1-15.

[62] *Dalit Voice*, (March, 2005), 1-15.

[63] See Peniel Rajkumar, *Dalit Theology and Dalit Liberation; Problems, Paradigms and
     Possibilities* (Farnham, England: Ashgate Publishing Limited, 2010), 25-37.

[64] George Oommen, "The Emerging Dalit Theology: A Historical Appraisal," *Indian
     Church History Review* (June, 2000), 19.

[65] Sathianathan Clark and Yoginder Sikand, "Dalit Theology," *Counter Currents*
     (October, 2007). See also K. C. Abraham, "Emerging Concerns in Third World
     Theology," *Bangalore Theological Forum* (September-December, 1994); Aravind
     P. Nirmal, "A Dialogue with Dalit Literature," in *Towards a Dalit Theology*, ed. by
     M. E. Prabhakar (New Delhi: ISPCK, 1988); and James Massey, "A Review of Dalit
     Theology," in *Dalit and Minjung Theologies: A Dialogue*, ed. by S. Prabhakar and
     J. Kwon (Bangalore: BRESSC/SATHRI, 2006).

[66] See Arvind P. Nirmal (ed.), *A Reader in Dalit Theology* (Madras: Gurukul, n.d.);
     Arvind P. Nirmal, ed., *Towards a Common Dalit Ideology* (Madras: Gurukul, n.d.);
     Bhagwan Das and James Massey, eds., *Dalit Solidarity* (Delhi: ISPCK, 1995); James
     Massey, *Dalits in India: Religion as a Source of Bondage or Liberation with special
     Reference to Christians* (Delhi: Manohar, 1995); Sathiananthan Clarke, A. M.
     Abraham Ayrookuzhiel, "Essays on Dalits, Religion and Liberation," (Bangalore:
     CISRS, 2006).

[67] Frederick S. Downs writes, "the historical experience of Dalit Christians provides a significant basis for the construction of a Dalit theology." Fredrick S. Downs, "Preface," in Franklyn J. Balasundaram, *Dalits and Christian Mission in Tamil Country* (Bangalore: Asian Trading Corporation, 1997), ix.

[68] George Oommen, *The Emerging Dalit Theology*, 30.

[69] See Abe Dueck ed., *The Mennonite Brethren Church Around the World*, 376.

[70] John A. Lapp, *The Mennonite Church in India* (Scottdale, PA: Herald Press, 1972), 31.

[71] See Saurab Dube, *Untouchable Past: Religion, Identity, and Power Among a Central Indian Community, 1780-1950* (New York: 1998).

[72] J. A. Lapp, *The Mennonite Church in India*, 41.

[73] See J. A. Lapp, *The Mennonite Church in India*, 91-3.

[74] Some of the data for this section is taken from Sushanth Rajnat Nand, "Bharathya General Conference Mennonite Church in Chhattisgarh from 1980-2005," unpublished B D Thesis, Union Biblical Seminary, Pune, 2008.

[75] See P. A. Penner, *Twenty five years with God in India* (Bern, IN: Mennonite Book Concern, 1925), 67.

[76] Ruth Unrau, *A Time to Bind and a Time to Loose: a history of General Conference Mennonite Church Mission Involvement from 1900-1995* (Newton, KS: Mennonite Press, 1996), 198.

[77] Bharatiay General Conference Mennonite Church, Annual Conference, Minutes, 1987-1988.

[78] Jai Prakesh Masih, "Leadership In Bharatiya General Conference Mennonite Church In India," Elkhart, Indiana, 2002, 37-38.

[79] Ibid.

[80] Bharatiya General Conference Mennonite Church Conference Minutes, 2002-2003.

[81] Ibid.

[82] Sivaji Koyl, "A critique of the Missionary Movement in Chotanagpur," *Indian Church History Review* (1988), 140.

[83] J. W. Pickett, *Christian Mass Movements in India: A Study with Recommendations* (New York: Abingdon Press, 1933).

[84] J. W. Pickett, D. A. McGavran, G. H. Singh, *Christian Missions in Mid-India* (Jubbulpore: The Mission Press, 1938), 2, cited in J. A. Lapp, *The Mennonite Church in India*, 214.

[85] Cited in J. A. Lapp, *The Mennonite Church in India*, 218.

[86] Statement of Policy in the Minutes of the MBMC, May 16-17, 1944.

[87] Albart Vasanthraj (ed), *Bihar, Church and People Groups* (Madras: Church Growth Association of India, 1992).

[88] For the detailed history of the beginnings of the BIC church, see Shamlal Hembrom, "Brethren in Christ Church Missionary Approach: With Special Reference to the Santal Communities in Northeast Bihar and Southeast Nepal," M.Th. thesis, South Asia Institute of Advanced Christian Studies, Bangalore, 1995, 25-95.

[89] Kishore Khosla, *Orissa Church and People Groups* (Madras: CGAI, n.d.), 32-33.

[90] Interview with MCC Director David Graber, January, 2000, Kolkatha.

[91] P. J. Malagar, *The Mennonite Church in India* (Nagpur: The National Council of Churches in India, 1981), 33; J. A. Lapp, *The Mennonite Church in India*, 74-75.

[92] P. J. Malagar, *The Mennonite Church in India*, 41.

[93] More research needs to be done on the reasons behind this rapid transition. The Indian government's refusal to renew missionary visas was certainly the primary reason but there also appears to have been declining support for such mission efforts among Mennonites in North America.

[94] Archival Records from 1963_03EX (MCC Archives, Akron, PA).

[95] Memorandum of Association of Mennonite Christian Service Fellowship of India, Certificate of Registration No. S/ 8816 of 67-68 Government of West Bengal (MCC India MCSFI files, Kolkata, India).

[96] Ibid.

[97] P. J. Malagar, "Reminiscences, Observations and Comments," n.p., n.d., 3-4.

[98] Ibid., 4-5.

[99] Ibid., 7.

[100] Emmanuel Minj, "A Brief History of MCSFI" (MCC India MCSFI files, Kolkata, India).

[101] Letter from David Gerber, MCC Director, to MCSFI Executive Committee Members, May 15, 1999 (MCC India MCSFI files, Kolkata, India). A year earlier MCC India director David Gerber had written a confidential three page memo in which he expressed serious doubts about the continuing viability of MCSFI as an organization. See "MCSFI and the Future," April 20, 1998 (MCC India MCSFI files, Kolkata, India).

[102] Report of the MCSFI Self Study held on May 2nd, 1975 at the Lee Memorial Centre, Kolkata (MCC India MCSFI files, Kolkata, India).

[103] Emmanuel Minj, "A Brief History of MCSFI" (MCC India MCSFI files, Kolkata, India).

[104] One of the most critical observations I found in my research reads, "MCSFI was set up by MCC in the 60s and continues to be dependent on MCC funding however limited. Is it any wonder that it be so? It was not created because the grass roots felt a need for it, and they still don't see its importance. It is MCC's baby whether we like it or not. Whether the churches want the responsibility of adopting a lazy spoiled baby is not yet clear. Neither is it clear if the baby will mature into adulthood with no support from underneath and a parent ashamed to claim him." See Fred Kauffman, "Reflections on Korba Meeting MCC/MCSFI," Oct. 20. 1980 (MCC India MCSFI files, Kolkata, India).

[105] A. C. Lobe, "MCC India – History, Program and Method of Operation," paper presented to the May 5, 1978 MCSFI Annual General Meeting (MCC India MCSFI files, Kolkata, India).

[106] Neil Janzen, "Mennonite Central Committee Management Trip to Ranchi, Jharkhand," July 17-18, 2007 (MCC India MCSFI files, Kolkata, India).

[107] Emmanuel Minj, "A Brief History of MCSFI" (MCC India MCSFI files, Kolkata, India).

[108] "MCSFI – Looking Ahead Policy Statement," adopted at the Joint Consultation on Mission and Service at Ranchi, Jharkhand on March 4, 2009.

Chapter 5: The Mennonite Churches in Chinese-speaking Areas

[1] Leung, Ka-lun, *Blessing Upon China—Ten Talks on the Contemporary Church History of China* (Hong Kong: Tian Dao Press, 19880, 13.

[2] Moffett, Samuel Hugh, *A Introduction of Christianity in Asia*, Volume I (Maryknoll, New York: Orbis Books, 1998), 313.

[3] Leung, 24. also Moffett, 454.

[4] Küng, Hans and Julia Ching, *Christianity and Chinese Religions*, Chinese translation, (Taipei, Taiwan: Lian Jing Press, 1989), 203.

[5] Leung, 30.

[6] Lam, Wing-hung, *A Half Century of Chinese Theology 1900-1949*, (Hong Kong: China Graduate School of Theology, 1989), 6-7.

[7] Ibid. 15.

[8] Lu, Shi-Chiang, *The Reasons Why Chinese Officials and Gentries Opposed Christianity*, (Taipei: Sino Academic Assistance Committee, 1973), 198-200.

[9] Lutz, Jessie G., "China and Protestantism: Historical Perspectives, 1807-1949" in Uhalley, Stephen, and Xiaoxin Wu, eds. *China and Christianity: Burdened Past, Hopeful Future*, (Armonk, NY: M. E. Sharpe, 2001), 189.

[10] H. C. Bartel, *A Short Review of the First Mennonite Mission in China with a Testimony of the Workers*, published by the Author, 1913, 53-55.

[11] The China Mennonite Mission Society, *Field Report 1924* (Hillsboro, Kansas: Home Committee of the China Mennonite Mission Society, 1924), 2.

[12] China Mennonite Mission Society, *Word of Testimony*, Vol. IV, No. 3. Tsao Hsien, Shantung, China, April 1932. However, under the "Three-Fix Policy," Christians in China were not allowed to preach in the public, and "tent-work" was no longer possible.

[13] *Mennonites in China*, 19.

[14] *Mennonites in China*, 21, 29.

[15] Ibid. 24.

[16] China Mennonite Mission Society, *Word of Testimony*, Vol. IV, No. 3. Tsao Hsien, Shantung, China, April 1932.

[17] Lam, Wing-hung, *A Half Century of Chinese Theology 1900-1949*, Hong Kong: China Graduate School of Theology, 1989. 349

[18] Ying, Fuk-tsang, *Christianity's Failure in China? Essays on the History of Chinese Communist Movement and Christianity*. Hong Kong: Institute of Sino-Christian Studies Ltd, 2008. 78.

[19] Chao, Jonathan, and Rosanna Chong. *A History of Christianity in Socialist China, 1949-1997* (Taipei, CMI Publishing , 1997), 115.

[20] Robert and Alice P. Ramseyer, *Mennonites in China*, 76.

[21] Chao and Chong, *A History of Christianity in Socialist China, 1949-1997*, 193-194.

[22] While Christianity was legalized and emerged again after the Cultural Revolution, congregations who choose to register to the Chinese government have to be institutionally integrated into the China Christian Council, or the so-called Three-Self Church. These congregations are able to freely, according to Chinese state laws, worship in church buildings and in Christians' houses registered as the "meeting points" as well, and to request the church property confiscated during the chaostic political campaigns in the 1950s and 60s. Those who rejected registration had to go underground, and became the so-called house churches. House churches are illegal and, sometimes and in some places, under severe state persecution. As the author can tell, the churches in the former Mennonite mission fields in northern China now are all registered churches.

[23] Oral report by elder Wen-Ming Lee in Tsao Hsien (Caoxian), August 8, 2000.

[24] Huang, Zhang-Yung, ed., *Christianity in Sichuan Province* (Chengdu: Ba-Shu Bookstore, 1992), 151.

[25] Cf. *Daming County Religious Gazetter*, 62.

[26] Latourette, Kenneth Scott, *A History of Christian Missions in China*, (New York: The Macmillan Company, 1929), 691.

[27] Lutz, Jessie G., *China and Protestantism: Historical Perspective: 1807-1949*, 188-189.

[28] Lutz, Jessie G., ed. *Christian Missions in China: Evangelists of What*, (Boston: D. C. Heath And Company, 1965), 61.

[29] *Mennonites in China*, 33.

[30] Pannabecker, S. F., *Open Doors: A History of the General Conference Mennonite Church*, (Newton,KS: Faith and Life Press, 1975), 324.

[31] James C. Juhnke, *A People of Mission*, 56; *Mennonites in China*, 32.

[32] *Mennonites in China*, 31.

[33] James Juhnke mentions that Pastor Brown lost two children due to bad hygienic condition in China. Pastor Kaufman and Pastor Voth both lost children. Pastor Kaufman himself almost died of smallpox. Cf. *A People of Mission*, 53. One of Pastor Bartel's sons died young in 1910. His eldest daughter and he himself also suffered from typhoid. Many missionaries and their children died of infectious diseases in Tsao Hsien. Cf. *The Mountain is Mine*, 78-79;106.

[34] Pannabecker S. F., *Open Doors: A History of the General Conference Mennonite Church*, 323-324.

[35] Juhnke, *A People of Mission*, 55.

[36] Ibid., 60.

[37] Ibid., 59.

[38] Ibid., 61.

[39] Roland P. Brown recounted his experience: the Japanese army was kind to the Americans in China before the Pearl Harbor Attack in 1941. He said that one day he bought clothes for the Chinese who had no winter coats and passed the Japanese's sentry post. The Japanese soldiers were kind to him. Cf. Oral record of R. P. Brown, Newton, KS, June 14, 2001.

[40] Lutz, *China and Protestantism: Historical Perspective: 1807-1949*, 192.

[41] Cf. Oral record of Ms Liu and Mr. Xing, in Puyang, August 7, 2001. Ms Liu was 72 years old; Mr. Xing was 84.

[42] Interview with the leaders of Daming, March, 1998.

[43] Huang, Zhang-Yung, ed., *Christianity in Si-Chuan Province*, 152-154.

[44] Cf. *Mennonites in China*, 51.

[45] Mrs. H. T. Esau, *First Sixty Years of M. B. Missions*, (Hillsboro, KS: Mennonite Brethen Publishing House, 1954), 273.

[46] *Mennonites in China*, 52.

[47] Ibid., 54-55.

[48] Ibid., 55.

[49] Ibid., 59-60.

[50] Ibid., 81.

[51] Ibid., 63-64.

[52] Wiens, A. K. and Gertrude, *Shadowed by the Great Wall*, (Hillsboro, KS: Board of Christian Literature of the General Conference of Mennonite Brethren Churches, 1979), 31.

[53] Peters, G. W., *Foundations of Mennonite Brethren Missions*, (Hillsboro, KS: Kindred Press, 1984), 153.Ibid., 72.

[54] *Mennonites in China*, 63.

[55] Ibid., 66.

[56] *Mennonites in China*, 67, 72.

[57] Wiens, *Shadowed by the Great Wall*, 9.

[58] *Mennonites in China*, 66-67.

[59] Wiens, *Shadowed by the Great Wall*, 9.

[60] *Mennonites in China*, 83.

[61] *Mennonites in China*, 93.

[62] Huang, Zhang-Yung, ed., *Christianity in Sichuan Province*, 182.

[63] *Mennonites in China*, 94.

[64] Ibid., 20.

[65] Ibid., 36-37.

[66] Ibid., 52.

[67] Ibid., 55.

[68] Ibid., 21.

[69] *Mennonites in China*, 36-37.

[70] Robert Kreider ed. *Christians True in China*, 45.

[71] *Christians True in China*, 82-86.

[72] *Mennonites in China*, 51.

[73] Ibid., 56-58.

[74] Latourette, Kenneth Scott, *A History of Christian Missions in China*, 828.

[75] *Mennonites in China*, 20,29.

[76] Ibid., 38.

[77] *Mennonites in China*, 38.

[78] Ibid., 44; Huang, Zhang-Yung, ed., *Christianity in Sichuan Province*, 152-153.

[79] *Mennonites in China*, 39.

[80] Mrs. H. T. Esau, *First Sixty Years of M. B. Missions*, 287.

[81] *The Mountain Is Mine*, 188, 201. (Chinese version)

[82] *Mennonites in China*, 85.

[83] Ibid., 87.

[84] Lutz, *China and Protestantism: Historical Perspective: 1807-1949*, 192.

[85] According to the general regulation of *Puyang General Conference Mennonite in China*, issued on 1 January 1938, the regulation about weddings and funerals are more moderate. There are eight articles on weddings and funerals, respectively, by which the church could take a middle way toward these two customs.

[86] Küng, Hans and Julia Ching, *Christianity and Chinese Religions,* Chinese translation, 224.

[87] Lutz, *Christian Missions in China: Evangelists of What?* Viii.

[88] Oral record Mr. Xin, Puyang, Aug. 2001.

[89] This was the very problem that James Juhnke raised in 1979. Cf. *A People of Mission*, 63.

[90] Wang, Peter Chen-Main, "Christianity in Modern Taiwan—Struggling Over the Path of Contextualization" in Uhalley, Stephen, and Xiaoxin Wu, eds. *China and Christianity: Burdened Past, Hopeful Future.* (Armonk, NY: M. E. Sharpe, 2001), 322.

[91] A conflict between agents of the Alcohol and Tobacco Monopoly Bureau and a cigarette vendor on the evening of Feb. 28, 1947 soon became an island-wide riot in which Taiwanese people appealed for political reformation. Finally, about 20,000 Taiwanese many of them medical doctors, lawyers, teachers, and pastors were slaughtered by Kuomintang soldiers. After that, the so-called "White Terror" followed with martial law which silenced Taiwanese for decades.

[92] Corcuff 2002a, xiv

[93] Ibid., 323.

[94] Ibid., 331.

[95] Pannabecker, S. F., *Open Doors: A History of the General Conference Mennonite Church,* (Newton, KS: Faith and Life Press, 1975), 327.

[96] Sawatzky, Sheldon V., *The Gateway of Promise: A Study of the Taiwan Mennonite Church and the Factors Affecting Its Growth,* (unpublished MA thesis, Fuller Theological Seminary, 1970,) 126.

[97] *The Mennonite Church in Taiwan: 1954-1964,* 11.

[98] *Commemorative Album of 40th Anniversary of FOMCIT,* 39. Cf. James C. Juhnke, *A People of Mission,* 134.

[99] *The Mennonite Church in Taiwan: 1954-1964,* 12.

[100] Ibid., 26.

[101] *Commemorative Album of 40th Anniversary of FOMCIT,* 10.

[102] Wang, Peter Chen-Main, 323.

[103] Ibid.

[104] Ibid., 325.

[105] The chart of benefit-loss ratio shows the great dependence of FOMCIT on COM. According to the 1976 chart, the total annual income of FOMCIT was NT$3,064,027.66, but NT$2,438,141 was from COM. Cf. the 19th annual booklet of FOMCIT, 14-15.

[106] Sawatzky, Sheldon V., *The Gateway of Promise,* 90. He thinks that the building-to-convert approach is wrong and inefficient.

[107] Juhnke, James, *A People of Mission,* 136.

[108] According to a leading anthropologist Y. Y. Lee, the nature of the ceremony of pilgrimage around the village among Taiwanese temples is a compatriot territorial cult. Cf. Ying, Fuk-tsang, 309.

[109] Lin, Ji-Ming, *The History of the Mennonite Churches and Mission in Taiwan,* 111.

[110] Ibid., p. 112.

[111] Sawatzky, Sheldon, *The Gateway of Promise,* 195.

[112] *Commemorative Album of 40th Anniversary of FOMCIT,* 13.

[113] Qu Haiyuan provides a statistic about the growth of Christianity in Taiwan: 298% from 1950 through 1964, but only 29% from 1964 through 1979. Cf. *A Socio-Political Analysis of the Change of the Religions in Taiwan,* 267.

[114] Lin, Ji-Ming, *The History of the Mennonite Churches and Mission in Taiwan,* 113-114.

[115] No proper program overseer has long been a problem of FOMCIT. Lin, Ji-Ming also mentioned this problem. Cf. ibid., 117.

[116] James Juhnke quotes the words of Wung Tien-Min saying, "Becoming a Christian causes a revolution in the family--like the revolution of Sun Yat-Sen." Cf. *A People of Mission,* 135.

[117] Paul Lin, "A Thought Picture" in *Taiwan Home Bond,* Vol. 7 No. 3, (Annual Missionary Field Conference) Fall 1961

[118] James Juhnke, 144.

[119] This term came from James C. Juhnke. cf. *A People of Mission,* 132.

[120] Howard H. Loewen, "Mennonite Theology" in *New Dictionary of Theology,* (Downers Grove, IL: Inter Varsity Press, 1988), 420.

[121] *Confession of Faith From Mennonite Perspective,* (Scottdale, PA: Herald Press, 1995), 39.

[122] Lee, Zhi-Gang, "Early Study on the History of Christianity in Hong Kong" in Lin Zhi-ping, ed., *From A Risk to the Dominion: Essays of studies of church history of China, Hong Kong, and Taiwan.* (Taipei: Cosmic Light, 2001), 252.

[123] Ying, Fuk-tsang, "Present Studies of the History of Christianity in Hong Kong" in Lin Zhi-ping, ed., *From A Risk to the Dominion: Essays of studies of church history of China, Hong Kong, and Taiwan.* (Taipei: Cosmic Light, 2001), 284.

[124] Ibid., 280.

[125] Ibid., 281.

[126] *Manna,* No. 286, (Taipei: FOMCIT, July 31, 1983), 1.

[127] EMM news available at http://emm.org/index.php?option=com_content&view=art icle&id=114:hong-kong-mennonites-honor-founders-and-look-ahead&catid=104: news-and-stories-asia-and-australia&Itemid=120, accessed Jan. 4, 2011.

[128] Kurtz, Ira A. and Hugh D. Sprunger, *Hong Kong Church Conference Long-term Plan and Request for Financial Assistance,* dated February 1, 1989 in Mennonite archives, North Newton, Kansas. Box 22 Folder 502.

[129] Interview Ms. Faena Tjung, Hong Kong, July 2001.

[130] Interview Ms. Faena Tjung, Hong Kong, July 2001.

[131] Yeung, Arnold, *Crisis and Challenge Facing Church in 1990s,* (Hong Kong: Tien Dao Publishing House, 1989), 52.

[132] Ibid., 80.

[133] Leung, Ka-lun, *The Urgent Theological and Social Issues in the Churches of Hong Kong in the 1980s,* 6.

[134] Young, Arnold, 116.

[135] At Grace Mennonite Church, 18 people left in a year. Their leaving discouraged others members who chose to stay. Interview Daniel Ngai, July 2001.

[136] Shenk, David W., "Hong Kong Trip Report and Recommendations" to Executive committee of Eastern Mennonite Board of Missions and Charities, date: November 7, 1989.

[137] Mennonite Mission Network online news available at http://www.mennonitemis sion.net/Stories/News/Pages/LocalTreasureassumesMacauMennonitehelm.aspx, accessed Jan 4, 2011.

[138] Hugh Sprunger, "Taiwan: Challenge of Change", *Mission Today,* Aug. 1966. (Newton, Kansas: Board of Missions General Conference Mennonite Church.)

Chapter 6: The Mennonite Church in the Philippines

Printed sources:

G. D. Balucas, "The Mennonite church in the Philippines," unpublished manuscript, 2004.

S. Bulfa, "Philippines," in Paul N. Kraybill, ed., *Mennonite World Handbook* (Wichita: Mennonite World Conference 10th Assembly, 1978), 178-182.

Circling the Globe. A young people's guide to countries and cultures of the world (Richmond Hill, ON, Canada: D. S. Max International under License from Larousse Kingfisher Chambers, 1996).

C. J. Dyck, ed., *An introduction to Mennonite history* (Scottdale, PA: Herald Press, 1981).

Online sources:

Bangued Christian Hospital (2010). In Wikipedia the free encyclopedia. Retrieved 21 July 2011 from http://en.wikipedia.org/wiki/Bangued_Christian_Hospital

Dyck, D. (2006, January 20). From Maoist revolutionary to Mennonite peace worker. Mennonite Church Canda News Releases. Retrieved 12 August 2011 from http://www.mennonitechurch.ca/news/releases/2006/01/Release08.htm

eTravel Pilipinas (undated). Religion in the Philipines. Retrieved 07 July 2011 from http://www.etravelpilipinas.com/about_philippines/philippine_religion.htm

Important Events in Philippine History (2009). In Camperspoint. Philippine travel and adventure. Retrieved 07 July 2011 from http://www.camperspoint.com/spip.php?article259

Metzler, James E and Richard D. Thiessen. (October 2010). Philippines. Global Anabaptist Mennonite Encyclopedia Online. Retrieved 04 July 2011, from http://www.gameo.org/encyclopedia/contents/P515.html.

Miller, J. (1982). Religion in the philippines. Asia Society's Focus on Asian Studies, Vol. II, No. 1, Asian Religions, pp. 26-27. Copyright AskAsia, 1996. Retrieved 07 July 2011 from http://filipinokastila.tripod.com/religion.html

Philippines (2011). In Infoplease. All the knowledge you need. Retrieved 07 July 2011 from http://www.infoplease.com/ipa/A0107887.html

Showalter, J. (2006, October 17). Philippine Mennonite churches host Holy Spirit in Mission Conference & International Missions Association. Mennonite World Conference News Releases. Retrieved 12 August 2011 from http://www.mwc-cmm.org/News/MWC/061017rls2.html

The Philippines (2011). In Countries and their cultures. Advameg, Inc. Retrieved 07 July 2011 from http://www.everyculture.com/No-Sa/The-Philippines.html

The Philippines (2002). In Pinas. Your gateway to Philippine information. Retrieved 07 July 2011 from http://pinas.dlsu.edu.ph/history/history.html

Chapter 7: The Anabaptist Mennonite Churches in Japan

[1] J. D. Graber, *We Enter Japan* (Mennonite Board of Missions and Charities, n.d.), 10.

[2] Masaru Arita, *MB Kyokai Shoki Nihon Senkyo Shoshi (A Short History of MB Church Mission Beginnings in Japan)*, (Japan Mennonite Brethren Church Conference, n.d.), 2-3.

[3] Masaru Arita, *Inochino Mizuwo Motomete (In Search of the Water of Life)* Self-testimony Tract, (MB Ishibashi Church, n.d.)

[4] Takanobu Tojo, *Nihon no Senkyo ni okeru 'Chiho' no Mondai (The Problem of Provincial Regions in Japanese Missions)* (Kansai Mission Research Center, 1995), 25-26.

5 Takashi Yamada, *Kirishima Kyodaidan no Nettowaaku (The Kirishima Brotherhood Network)*, Kirishima Christian Church Document I.

Chapter 9: The Mennonite Church in Vietnam

1 An excellent summary of Vietnamese Christianity is found under "Vietnam" by Peter C. Phan and Violet James in *A Dictionary of Asian Christianity*, (Grand Rapids and Cambridge: Wm. B. Eerdmans Publishing Company, 2001), 876ff.

2 This section draws heavily from material in *An Evaluation of a Generation of Mennonite Mission, Service and Peacemaking in Vietnam, 1954-1976*, an unpublished report prepared by Luke S. Martin for the Vietnam Study Project, July 1977.

3 Vietnamese names follow the local pattern with the family name first and the given name last.

4 Much of this material is documented by James R. Klassen in *Jimshoes in Vietnam*. (Scottdale, PA: Herald Press, 1986).

For further reading:
Beechy, Atlee. *Seeking Peace: My Journey*, (Goshen, IN: Pinchpenny Press, 2001).
Ediger, Max. *A Vietnamese Pilgrimage*. (Newton, KS: Faith and Life Press, 1978).
Martin, Earl S. *Reaching the Other Side*, (New York: Crown Publishers, Inc., 1978).
Metzler, James E. From *Saigon to Shalom*, (Scottdale, PA: Herald Press, 1985).

Chapter 10: Conclusion

1 David J. Bosch, *Transforming Mission: Paradigm Shifts in Theology of Mission* (Maryknoll, NY: Orbis Books, 1992).

2 John H. Yoder, *Nachfolge Christi als Gestalt politischer Verantwortung* (Basel: Agape Verlag, 1964); in English translation *Discipleship as Political Responsibility*, trans. by Timothy J. Geddert (Scottdale,. Pennsylvania: Herald Press, 2003).

Sidebar Credits

Page	Chapter 3
33	Unattributed
34	*Pieter Jansz, Diary, Sunday April 16, 1854*
41	Lawrence M. Yoder, The Introduction and Expression of Islam and Christianity in the Cultural Context of North Central Java, 1987 (diss. Fuller Theological Seminary), 339, slightly edited.
45	*Brieven aan mevrouw R.M. Abendanon-Mandri en haar echtgenoot* (Dordrecht: Foris Publications 1987), 324.
52	C. J. Dyck, *Twelve Becoming. Biographies of Mennonite Disciples from the Sixteenth to the Twentieth Century* (Newton, KS: Faith and Life Press, 1973), 122-123.
55	Shirlee Kohler Yoder, *Savoring the Times. Stories on MCC Indonesia's 50th anniversary 1998*, 11.

Index

I. P. Asheervadam, *India.* Principal and Professor of Church History, Mennonite Brethren Centenary Bible College, Shamshabad.

Adhi Dharma , *Indonesia.* Pastor of the GKMI Gloria Patri church, Semarang, and General Secretary of the GKMI Synod.

Alle Hoekema , *Netherlands.* Former missionary in Indonesia (1969-1977), now pastor in Alkmaar and Haarlem and Associate Professor, missiology, Vrije universiteit Amsterdam.

Kyong-Jung Kim, *Korea.* Director of the Korea Anabaptist Center, and member of Jesus Village Church, Chuncheon, Korea.

John A. Lapp, *USA.* Executive Secretary Emeritus, MCC, former Professor and Dean, Goshen College, coordinator Global Mennonite History Project, MWC.

Luke Martin, *USA.* Former missionary in Vietnam (1962-75), now retired pastor, Allentown, Pennsylvania.

Regina Lyn Mondez, *Philippines.* Church Resourcing Coordinator, Peacebuilders Community Inc., Luzon, and National Coordinator of Communications, IMC.

Chiou-Lang (Paulus) Pan, *Taiwan.* Adjunct Professor, theology and missions, Chung Yuan Christian University and Research Fellow, Hakka Christian Seminary.

C. Arnold Snyder, *Canada.* Retired Professor of History, Conrad Grebel University College, editor, Global Mennonite History Project, MWC.

Nguyen Thanh Tam, *Vietnam.* Pastor and General Secretary of the unregistered Mennonite church, Ho Chi Minh City, Vietnam.

Nguyen Thi Tam, *USA.* Retired congregational leader, Vietnamese Mennonite Church, Philadelphia, Pennsylvania.

Takanobu Tojo, *Japan.* Professor, Waseda University and pastor of BIC church in Tokyo.

Nguyen Quang Trung, *Vietnam.* Pastor and President of the registered Mennonite church, Ho Chi Minh City, Vietnam.

Masakazu Yamade, *Japan.* Retired High School Teacher and Principal, former Mennonite pastor and Chairman, Japan Mennonite Fellowship.

Earl Zimmerman, *USA.* Former Professor, Eastern Mennonite University and MCC peace representative, Kolkata.